George Rogers Clark's Fort Jefferson 1780-1781

Kentucky's Outpost on the Western Frontier

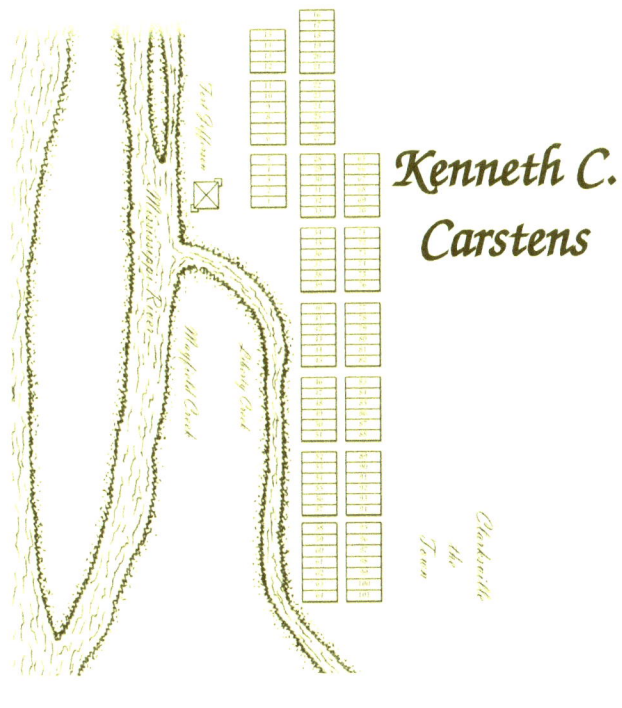

Kenneth C. Carstens

HERITAGE BOOKS
2009

HERITAGE BOOKS
AN IMPRINT OF HERITAGE BOOKS, INC.

Books, CDs, and more—Worldwide

For our listing of thousands of titles see our website
at
www.HeritageBooks.com

Published 2009 by
HERITAGE BOOKS, INC.
Publishing Division
100 Railroad Ave. #104
Westminster, Maryland 21157

Copyright © 2005 Kenneth C. Carstens

Other books by the Author:

The Personnel of George Rogers Clark's Fort Jefferson and the Civilian Community of Clarksville (Kentucky), 1780-1781

The Calendar and Quartermaster Books of General George Rogers Clark's Fort Jefferson, Kentucky, 1780-1781

All rights reserved. No part of this book may be reproduced or transmitted in any form or by any means, electronic or mechanical, including photocopying, recording or by any information storage and retrieval system without written permission from the author, except for the inclusion of brief quotations in a review.

International Standard Book Numbers
Paperbound: 978-0-7884-3322-1
Clothbound: 978-0-7884-8071-3

"There is no future without remembering the past."

Jacques Chirac
French President
June 6, 2004
60th Anniversary of D-Day Celebration

Arromanches, France

Dedication

This book is dedicated to my parents,
Cal and Dotty Carstens of Pinconning, Michigan,
for instilling my sense and appreciation of history at an early age.

ACKNOWLEDGEMENTS

The Fort Jefferson research program began in 1980. Since then, it has touched the lives of my many students, fellow faculty members, friends and family, institutions, and organizations. How do I thank appropriately the hundreds of persons who have contributed in so many different ways to the Fort Jefferson research project? I cannot list them all, but among those who have helped with the project, financed the project, or given their permission to conduct the project are the following:

Friends and family: the late Dr. Robert R. Rea, Hollifield Professor of Southern History at Auburn University, Robert J. Holden from Indianapolis; Jameson Carstens; Bill Black, Jr., William P. Young, and the late George Crounse, friends and financiers from Paducah, Kentucky. A special thank you to Greg Holm.

MSU Students: Bobby Bell, Cathy Biby, William Potter, Ted Belue, Chris Canty-Girard, Tony Girard, Linda Horner, Andy Lucy, Buddy Dowdy, Pamela Dawes, Carrie Griffin, Dana Kilby, G. Speidel, Deana Landwerth, T. and J. Templeton, Bob Bradley, Michael Adams, Keith Sensing, R. Jones, R. Watkins, C. Williams, S. Durbin, (Charles) Dwayne Sims, Cindy Lawson, Marteze Hammonds, January Futrell, Steve Ross, Jacob Stone, Lawrence Buck, Megan Dorgan-Carpenter, and many, many more. A special thank you is extended to Cathy Biby and Marteze Hammonds. For four years Cathy inputed Fort Jefferson data and maintained our massive word processing files for the Fort Jefferson project. More recently, Marteze Hammonds typed the entire text for all of the Fort Jefferson letters that appear in Chapter 4, no small task when you consider that typing those documents with their original spelling (and misspellings!), poor grammar, and poor punctuation took great amounts of concentration. To all of these students and the many more that worked on this project, I express my sincere gratitude for your assistance with the Fort Jefferson study.

Faculty and Staff: Drs. Kit Wesler, Tom Kind, Frank Elwell, Robin Zhang, Mr. Andy Kellie, Louis Boldt, Chris Hildebrand, and Ms. Pamela Schenian, Carruth Kitrell, MSU; Jim Foradas, Paul Curran, Ohio State University; R. Berle Clay, Cultural Resource Analysts; Ms. Nancy O'Malley, University of Kentucky; Dr. Julie Stein, University of Washington-Seattle; and Dr. Patty Jo Watson, Washington University-St. Louis. To the MSU Departments of Sociology, Anthropology, and Social Work, and Geosciences, I owe a debt of gratitude for the work space and financial support they have given to the Fort Jefferson project.

Murray State University's Committee on Institutional Science and Research (CISR) Program (principally, Dr. Peter Whaley and his committee members between 1980-2004).

MSU's Sabbatical Program, authorized by the MSU Board of Regents.

MSU's College of Humanities and Fine Arts, and College of Science, Engineering and Technology (Deans Ken Harrell, Joe Cartwright, Ken Wolf, Sandra Jordan, and Neil Weber).

MSU Provosts Jim Booth and Gary Brockway.

MSU Presidents Deno Curris, Kayla Stroup, Ronald J. Kurth, Kern Alexander, and King Alexander.

MSU's Pogue Library directors Drs. Keith Heim and Ernie Bailey; John Griffin and the staff of Waterfield Library's Inter-Library Loan Department.

Archives Division, Virginia State Library, Richmond: Jane Pairo, Conley Edwards III, Alan Golden, and Tom Crew.

Westvaco and the Mead-Westvaco Corporation, Wickliffe, Kentucky: Sandra Jones Wilson, Pat Elliot, and Richard K. Boyd.

Kentucky Office of the Secretary of State: Kandi Adtkinson.

The Kentucky Historical Society, Frankfort.

The Kentucky Genealogical Society, Frankfort.

The Filson Historical Society (principally Jim Holmberg, Pen Bogert, Rebecca S. Rice, and Dr. Mark Wetherington).

The George Rogers Clark National Historical Park: Bob Holden (retired), Frank Doughman, Pamela Nolan, Dennis Latta, and Dale Phillips.

James Alexander Thom, writer and special friend, who has brought Clark to life.

Sal Mayolo, Mayor, Wickliffe, Kentucky.

Locust Grove Historic Home: former director Julia C. Parke and her staff.

Lastly, this book has benefited greatly from the careful copy-edit eye of my friend, Dr. Ted Brown, MSU English Department, and the fine staff at Heritage/Willow books.

    To these persons and more, I owe a debt of gratitude for believing in a project that at times was tenuous and trying, and for giving me your support, expertise, ideas, and labors so that the persons who lived and died at Fort Jefferson would never be forgotten.

Thank you.

Ken Carstens, Department of Geosciences, Murray State University, Murray, Ky.

George Rogers Clark's Fort Jefferson, 1780-1781:
Kentucky's Outpost on the Western Frontier

Acknowledgements		vii
Table of Contents		ix
List of Figures		xi
List of Tables		xii
Preface:	Bob Holden	xv
Permissions		xviii
Chapter 1:	Introduction	1
Chapter 2:	Locating the Fort: A Study in Maps (Kellie, Kellie, Carstens)	3
Chapter 3:	Fort Jefferson, 1780-1781: A Summary of Its History	27
Chapter 4:	Letters To, From, and About Fort Jefferson	37
Chapter 5:	Structural Composition	90
Chapter 6:	Issues at Fort Jefferson	108
Chapter 7:	Munition Supplies at George Rogers Clark's Fort Jefferson	118
Chapter 8:	Subsistence	126
Chapter 9:	Gender Roles at Fort Jefferson	142
Chapter 10:	Legal Matters	148
Chapter 11:	Medical Concerns (Lucy and Carstens)	163
Chapter 12:	Frivolity at Fort Jefferson	171
Chapter 13:	Friends and Family, Death and Dying	178
Chapter 14:	Inventory of Military Companies	183
Chapter 15:	What the Military Companies Wore: Clothing	193
Chapter 16:	Archaeological Studies Performed	200
Chapter 17:	Forts, Famine, and Failure?	210
Chapter 18:	A Fort Jefferson Resource Bibliography	214
Index		241

List of Figures

Figure 2.1	Fort Jefferson and the civilian community of Clarksville, 1780	13
Figure 2.1	William Clark map of Fort Jefferson, 1795	14
Figure 2.3	A portion of "A Map of the State of Kentucky" by Luke Munsell, Published at Frankfort, Kentucky, 1818	15
Figure 2.4	A portion of "A Map of that Part of the State of Kentucky Lying West of the Tennessee River Surveyed Agreeably to the Act of the Legislature Passed on the 15 of February 1820" by William Henderson	16
Figure 2.5	Deed Compilation of Virginia Military Surveys in the Vicinity of Fort Jefferson, Kentucky	17
Figure 2.6	Todd Survey by Deputy Surveyor Samuel McKee, 1821	18
Figure 2.7	Myers (Meyers) Treasury Survey, 1784	19
Figure 2.8	Portion of the Forsythe Map, 1855	20
Figure 2.9	Depoyster Map by Fleet C. Mercer, 1878	21
Figure 2.10	Stovall Map showing Fort Jefferson at Foot of Bluff and East of the Railroad	22
Figure 2.11	Depoyster Map in Draper Collection	23
Figure 2.12	Mobile and Ohio Railroad at Fort Jefferson	24
Figure 2.13	Deed compilation registered on Delorme 3D quad for Kentucky Showing both Virginia Military and Treasury Surveys in Vicinity of Fort Jefferson as Registered to Ground	25
Figure 2.14	Enlargement of Deed Compilation Showing Todd, Nelson, and Merewether Military Surveys	26
Figure 5.1	Cross-section of Fort Jefferson Physiography	106
Figure 5.2	Illustration of Fort Jefferson Raised Bastion	107
Figure 6.1	The Western Department, 1780-1781	116
Figure 6.2	Distribution Diagram of Food, Dry Goods, and Other Supplies throughout the Western Department	117
Figure 8.1	Five-Kilometer Site Catchment Area around Fort Jefferson	141
Figure 12.1	A Portion of a Musical Score from Fort Jefferson, Dated March 23, 1781	176
Figure 12.2	A Hand-written Request for 12 Pounds Sugar "for a festival"	177
Figure 16.1	Research Regions in the Fort Jefferson Study Area	207
Figure 16.2	Photograph of Four Possible 18th Century Artifacts from the Fort Jefferson Research Area	208
Figure 16.3	NASA Low Altitude Color Infra-red Photograph of Fort Jefferson Anomaly	209

List of Tables

Table 5.1	General Characteristics of Selected Kentucky Forts	102
Table 5.2	Dimensions of Fort Jefferson and Clarksville Community Based on Measurements of the 1780 William Clark Map	103
Table 5.3	Structures Built at Clark's Fort Jefferson and Clarksville Community	104
Table 7.1	Pounds of Gunpowder and Lead Received, Issued, and Distributed at Fort Jefferson, 1780-1781	124
Table 7.2	Armament and Munitions Received and Issued at Fort Jefferson, 1780-1781	125
Table 8.1	Estimate of Annual Biomass for Selected 18th Century Animal Species within a Five-Kilometer Area of Fort Jefferson	136
Table 8.2	Recorded Consumption of Meat at Fort Jefferson, 1780-1781	137
Table 8.3	Beverages Issued at Fort Jefferson, 1780-1781	138
Table 8.4	Schedule of Disbursement for Meat, Corn, and Drink at Fort Jefferson, 1780-1781	139
Table 8.5	Projected Theoretical Disbursements per Person per Day Based on a Population Estimate of 150 Persons for 416 Days at Fort Jefferson, 1780-1781	140
Table 9.1	Activities of Men and Women at Fort Jefferson, 1780-1781	147
Table 11.1	An Excerpt from Dr. Connard's Medical Ledger, June 24, 1779-May 30, 1780	170
Table 13.1	A List of Known Fort Jefferson/Clarksville Families	178-9
Table 13.2	A Listing of Known Deceased Individuals at Fort Jefferson, 1780-1781	180-2

Permissions to republish or reproduce the following materials in this book are gratefully acknowledged by the author and Heritage Books, Inc.:

The Kentucky Heritage Council, for chapters 2, 8, 9, and 11.
Greenwood Publishing Group, Inc., Westport, Connecticut, chapter 5.
The National Park Service, George Rogers Clark National Park, chapters 3, 6, and 7.
Vincennes University, chapters 3, 6, and 7.
The American Historical Association, a portion of chapter 4, letters edited by Kinnaird.
The State Historical Society of Wisconsin, for various letters in the Draper Collection, and in particular, figures 2.1, 2.10, and 2.11, and for allowing us to use the 1780 William Clark Map for the cover art of this book.
The Virginia State Library, Archives Division, for the Unpublished George Rogers Clark Papers.
The Ballard County Courthouse, Ms. Lynn Lane, for permission to reproduce figures 2.9 and 2.12.
To the Library of Congress, for permission to reproduce figures 2.2 and 2.8.
Murray State University's Pogue Library, Dr. Ernie Bailey, for permission to reproduce figure 2.3, the Luke Munsell Map; and to the Mid-America Remote Sensing Center for permission to reproduce the 1983 NASA-flown color IR imagery, figure 16.3.
To the William T. Young Library at the University of Kentucky for permission to reproduce figure 2.4, the William T. Henderson Map.
To Kandi Atkinson of the Kentucky Secretary of State's Land Office for permission to reproduce figures 2.5-2.7, 2.13-14.
To the DeLorme Company of Maine to allow us to use a portion of the Wickliffe quadrangle as the base map for figure 2.13.
Last, but not least, to DeWayne Sims, of the Department of Geosciences at Murray State University for allowing the reproduction of figure 16.3 from his master's thesis, work in progress.

Preface
Robert J. Holden[1]

George Rogers Clark's Fort Jefferson, 1780-1781: Kentucky's Outpost on the Western Frontier is the third in a series of publications about Fort Jefferson by Dr. Kenneth C. Carstens. By his painstaking work in compiling, editing, and writing, Dr. Carstens has transformed Fort Jefferson from an essentially unstudied fortification to one of the most thoroughly documented frontier forts. Whether read separately or together, these volumes vividly recreate life at this isolated Revolutionary War outpost on the Mississippi River. The author has used a vast amount of untapped primary source material to clearly illuminate the daily routine and events on this farthest fringe of the early frontier. In addition, the book gives the reader a real understanding of what existence must have been like at countless other fortifications during the long westward course of colonial and national expansion.

Fortifications of one sort or another go far back in prehistory and may have been used for protection against wild animals as well as humans. The earliest attempts to provide a barrier against danger undoubtedly included the use of brush, branches, tree trunks, rocks, and other natural materials readily at hand. Among nomadic people, there never was any significant advance from these simple efforts at defense. For those who settled down in one place with the beginnings of agriculture, however, there was more to protect as well as more time and resources to develop this protection. By 3,000 B.C. substantial fortifications secured towns and cities along the Tigris, Euphrates, and Nile rivers.

When agricultural civilizations spread to Europe, the Greek and Roman empires further developed the technical aspects of fortifications. By this time, such works fell into the following categories: 1) walled settlements or cities; 2) strongholds for refuge in time of danger; 3) forts protecting strategic points; and, 4) fortifications combining elements of all these types. Most forts were for the purpose of defense. Others could serve an offensive role if they were built in a no man's land or in enemy territory.

After the collapse of the Roman Empire and the beginning of the Dark Ages, the art of fortification declined for a period as feudal warlords regressed to constructing simple strongholds. These structures were first made of timber and then of stone, and eventually evolved into the imposing castles of the Middle Ages. The main threats to these elaborate structures were catapults, battering rams, and moveable towers. With the advent and improvement of gunpowder and cannons that coincided with the age of colonization, radically new designs for fortifications (that could withstand bombardment) were required.

The basic idea of fortification that had played such a major role in the Old World quickly became a part of the European settlement of North America. Forts figured prominently in the colonial competition among Spain, France, England, Sweden, and the Netherlands, but they also served as protection against the sometimes hostile native inhabitants. For that reason, barriers against potential enemies ranged from those elaborately designed by military engineers to withstand shot and shell to those built

---

[1] Robert J. Holden is a retired Chief Park Ranger from George Rogers Clark National Historical Park in Vincennes, Indiana. He holds an M.A. degree in history from Northwestern University and has written numerous articles about pioneer America. He and his wife, Donna, wrote *The Hunting Pioneers, 1720-1840: Ultimate Backwoodsmen on the Early American Frontier*, published by Heritage Books in 2000.

primarily to stop arrows or small arms fire. Forts located along the coasts and inland rivers of North America were always potentially vulnerable because of the ease with which an opposing force's cannon could be transported by water. Conversely, when the enemy had to move such heavy and bulky weapons through deep forests the difficulties involved greatly reduced their threat.

From early colonial days, the simplified fortifications utilized on the frontier to protect against Indian attacks were broken down into two basic categories: civilian and military. Private forts often were no more than fortified homes, the garrison house of New England being one example. Log blockhouses with the upper story projecting out over the lower also were common. Some private forts consisted of a group of dwellings utilizing a log stockade barrier, and in some instances could even include blockhouses or bastions on two or more corners to allow enfilading fire. A stout, barred gate was an important feature. Military forts on the frontier, also of log construction, usually were larger and more elaborate than private forts. Around both types of forts trees and brush were usually cleared to remove any cover for an enemy and to provide defenders with an unobstructed field of fire. At some frontier forts, settlers' cabins were not only built within the walls, but outside of them as well. Preferably these exterior cabins were located close enough for quick and easy access to safety in the event of an impending attack, yet not so close that they would provide cover for the foe. Even if a siege were unsuccessful, as most were, the attacking force would routinely destroy these dwellings before they withdrew.

During the French and Indian War and the subsequent Pontiac's Rebellion, a large number of both civilian and military forts were built on the frontiers of the English colonies. In the Revolutionary War, fortifications again became of primary importance. Nowhere was this more true than west of the Appalachians. From their fort at Detroit, the British spread their influence over the tribes north of the Ohio River and set them in motion against the frontier settlements. The Americans made an effort to control the upper Ohio River from Fort Pitt, as well as from the smaller forts Henry, Randolph, McIntosh, and Laurens.

In Kentucky, the great majority of the fortifications, frequently called stations, were civilian. Although the term "fort" and "station" were often used interchangeably, generally a station was smaller than a fort. Some forts and stations were surrounded by a log palisade. In other cases, the tall windowless backs of cabins with sharply inward slanting roofs were linked together by short stretches of wall to form a barrier. Bastions or blockhouses could be part of the gated perimeter.

Forts in Kentucky, as elsewhere on the frontier, were not pleasant places to live. When Indian dangers were great, people (particularly women and children) were restricted to their environs. Overcrowding, polluted water, poor sanitation, and widespread disease were major problems. During Indian raids, crops and cattle were destroyed, and horses were often taken. Needed salt was difficult to obtain. The very survival of forts often depended on men who hunted in the surrounding woods, where they ran a great risk of becoming the hunted themselves. Such isolated and threatened communities were subject to virtually every possible psychological and sociological stress. It is difficult to imagine anywhere that the dangers, problems, and pressures could have been greater than at Fort Jefferson.

George Rogers Clark's Fort Jefferson, 1780-1781: Kentucky's Outpost on the Western Frontier is an extremely well-written and organized account of a way of life in America that has long since disappeared. These pages provide vivid reminders of what it really was like to risk one's life on the cutting edge of civilization more than two centuries ago. This book and the two that preceded it truly give readers an insider's view. Dr. Carstens is to be commended for the meticulous research that has gone into these excellent and welcome additions to the frontier and Revolutionary War bookshelf. Forts have played a central and crucial role in the march of civilizations across the world, and at no time was this more true than during the westward expansion of our nation.

CHAPTER 1: INTRODUCTION

Fort Jefferson. George Rogers Clark's fort at the mouth of the Ohio River. Fort at the Iron Banks. Clark's Town. Clarksville. These names and others describe the fort and civilian community of Fort Jefferson and Clarksville built by George Rogers Clark and the Illinois Battalion beginning on April 19, 1780, but abandoned by June 8, 1781, only 416 days later. The site had been commissioned by the State of Virginia and sanctioned first by Governor Patrick Henry, then Thomas Jefferson, the fort's namesake. Was the fort a government idea (Henry), or an idea conceived first by Clark and transmitted to Henry during their meeting in 1777? We may never know. But shortly thereafter, Governor Henry wrote the Spanish governor in Louisiana to seek an obligatory political blessing. . .after all, Henry did not want the building of an American (Virginian) fort across the Mississippi River from Spanish territory to be viewed as a threat to Spain, a potential ally for the American cause during the American Revolution.

History records that Fort Jefferson had several purposes. I would categorize those purposes as being either "overt" or "covert." The overt reasons for building the fort included furthering the cause of the American Revolution in the West by reducing arms and munitions traveling from the British-held north (out of Detroit) to southern Indian allies (primarily Chickasaws); reducing the numbers of deserters traveling down the Ohio River to New Orleans (or at least returning the deserters to service), and having a physical presence in support of the newly captured, formerly British-controlled French communities at Kaskaskia, Cahokia, and Vincennes.

A more covert reason allowed Virginia physically to lay claim to the east bank of the Mississippi river, invoking the claim of the 1665 Carolina Charter, a charter that until 1780 had been hollow and invited unwanted land speculation. And, of course, there were the Virginia land claims, most by Virginia's gentry of which Clark, Henry, Jefferson, Mason, and others were a part. The strongest idea was the interest in land claims that would accompany the settlements of the West and the establishment of a military presence on the banks of the Mississippi River.

In this book, I try to describe various aspects of the day-to-day existence of the people who lived on the western frontier as exemplified by Fort Jefferson and Clarksville. Prior to 1983, Fort Jefferson was believed to have been an out-of-the-way frontier station consisting of little more than a few dozen hardy souls and having no consequence in the American Revolution or impact on the settlement of the West. But new information, available only after 1983, has shed new light on the role of Clark's fort at the mouth of the Ohio. As it turns out, Fort Jefferson during 1780-1781 was Clark's economic supply depot for forts Clark, Bowman, and Patrick Henry. Fort Jefferson was Clark's military stronghold at which, or from which, six different military forays would occur, including saving Cahokia from the British-led Indian assault in May 1780 or supplying more than 20% of Clark's 1,000-man military army when he attacked the Shawnee villages in August of 1780. Too, Fort Jefferson would come under attack by the Chickasaw Indians, and twice Kaskaskia Indian–led forays against the Chickasaw would be initiated from Fort Jefferson. But the elements of mother nature, the sheer distances from supplies (Fort Jefferson was "beyond" the frontier), and depredations to the settlers' livestock and agricultural crops proved too much for the nascent fort to handle. Half of the Clarksville civilians (more than 20 families) evacuated Fort Jefferson following the third and final assault by the Chickasaw in August 1780. According to Captain Robert George, the fort commandant in Clark's absence, "numbers were daily dying." More than 49 persons gave their lives in the 416 days Fort Jefferson was garrisoned (an average of one death every eight days!). The remaining civilians and officers of the fort pleaded for Clark's return and guidance. But corruption within the quartermaster corps, jealousies, racial slurs, overindulgence of liquor, and bickerings affected everyone from command on down. Good-natured teasing gave way to harassment and abuse. One soldier, David Allen, received 50 lashes on his bare back "well laid on." In an attempted coup, Lt. Col. John Montgomery from Fort Clark in Kaskaskia tried to replace Captain Robert George with Major John Williams, but George, Clark's distant cousin, refused to relinquish command without proper authorization from General Clark. And so the plot thickened. By late fall or early winter, comments appear in the Fort Jefferson letters indicating that the newly established garrison and community might break up. Often cited as the cause was the absence of Clark's powerful leadership and command style, as well as Captain George's own ineptness and drunkenness. By the spring of 1781, courts of inquiry became common place, as was an overindulgence of rum throughout the entire month of March in celebration of St. Patrick's Day. The Irish officer contingent did nothing to hide their cultural traditions, maybe even at the risk of delivering a final death blow to the command at Fort Jefferson. By May 30, 1781, Lt. Col. John Montgomery, in the absence of Clark, and in the absence of any prospect of procuring food for the Fort Jefferson community, pulled rank over Captain George and began the organization of the evacuation of Fort Jefferson, which transpired on June 8, 1781.

In this book I examine the 416 days that Fort Jefferson was occupied. Chapters examine the location of Fort Jefferson, summarize what is known about its history on a month-to-month basis, provide copies of all Fort Jefferson and Clarksville correspondence from published and unpublished sources, detail the structured landscape of the outpost and civilian community, discuss the role of the fort quartermaster corps, examine munitions present at the fort and the food consumed by the inhabitants, gender/work-roles of men and women at the fort, legal matters, medical concerns, and frivolity. The book provides a listing of military companies assigned to Fort Jefferson, a description of what those companies wore for clothing, and an overview of the archaeological studies that have been accomplished to date in an attempt to locate the fort and place it in a broader context (was the fort a success or a failure?). The book concludes with a research bibliography for persons interested in studying frontier history and frontier archeology in the Ohio and Mississippi river valleys relevant to Fort Jefferson. It is the purpose of this book to shed new light on a little-known, and poorly understood, aspect of frontier history, a story that belongs to Kentucky and Virginia but which is a child of the American Revolution and the cry for freedom from British rule. Most important of all, it is a true story, written about the lives of men, women, and children who gave the ultimate sacrifice on Kentucky's western frontier.

CHAPTER 2: LOCATING THE FORT: A STUDY IN MAPS

Andrew C. Kellie, Kenneth Carstens, Brandon J. Kellie[1]

The research in this chapter involved the review and examination of records and physical evidence of land ownership pertaining to the location of Fort Jefferson, a Revolutionary War fortification situated in Ballard County, Kentucky. Records used included maps within the Draper Manuscripts, Virginia Military Surveys, a Virginia Treasury Survey, the rectangular survey of the Jackson Purchase, and field notes, plats, and deeds of record in Ballard and Carlisle counties, as well as documents within the National Archives. Additionally, physical lines as marked on the ground or as they appear on aerial photos and U.S. Geological Survey topographic quadrangle maps were used to define the land settlement pattern in the area of interest.

Introduction

Based solely on record evidence, the general location of Fort Jefferson is east of the Mississippi River at the mouth of Mayfield Creek in Ballard County, Kentucky. Recovery of physical evidence on the ground has enabled a deed compilation registered to existing USGS topographic maps. This shows the fort to be located south of the south line of the Meyers Treasury Survey, within the Todd Military Survey, and south of the north line of Section 3, Township 5 North, Range 4 West of the Kentucky Meridian. The fort was adjacent to (and probably east of) the former Mobile & Ohio railroad grade at the point of tangency of the curve immediately south of the Meyers line, possibly in the squarish light-toned area (aerial anomaly) visible on an historic aerial infra-red photograph taken by NASA in 1983. With this phase of the research complete, preliminary archaeological surveys can be planned to narrow still further the location of the fort.

Background

The land system of a region constitutes the patents, deeds, and surveys that define the location of real property. Indeed, current property boundaries are based on the original surveys that first marked the lines on the ground. Evidence of boundary location includes not only the physical marks left by past owners and surveyors, but the written records of ownership, maps, and plats. In the Jackson Purchase area of western Kentucky (that part of Kentucky west of the Tennessee River), the land system is a composite of parcels based on both the metes and bounds and rectangular survey systems. Thus, it reflects both the townships and ranges established by the original survey of the Purchase and surveys based on Virginia military and treasury warrants that pre-date the rectangular survey. Both types of surveys reflect the history of the Jackson Purchase area.

---

[1] Andy Kellie is in the Department of Engineering Technology, Murray State University; his son, Brandon Kellie, is a student at the University of Louisville. A version of this paper titled, "Warrants, Surveys and Patents" was published in *Current Archaeological Research in Kentucky*, Vol. 7, edited by Charles Hockensmith and Kenneth Carstens, Kentucky Heritage Council, Frankfort, Kentucky. A revised version of that paper is published here with the permission of the Kentucky Heritage Council.

The earliest boundary surveys in the Jackson Purchase are associated with the construction of Fort Jefferson. In 1780, Virginia forces under the command of George Rogers Clark constructed this fort south of the confluence of the Ohio and Mississippi Rivers in what is now Ballard County, Kentucky. The purpose of Fort Jefferson was to assert Virginia's sovereignty to land extending to the east bank of the Mississippi River and to bolster United States claims to the Northwest Territory. Fort Jefferson also was to provide protection for an adjacent civilian community, named Clarksville, which was intended to adjoin the fort. The fort and the adjoining community are shown in Figure 2.1.

As early as 1777, Virginia Governor Patrick Henry proposed to Spanish Governor Bernardo Galvez that the Virginians be allowed to construct a fort and settlement near the confluence of the Ohio and Mississippi Rivers to justify Virginia's chartered claim to that land, but also to thwart any possible movement by the British against either Spanish or American interests in that area (Henry 1777). It would not be until January 29, 1780, that Virginia Governor Thomas Jefferson selected George Rogers Clark to enact the proposal first made by Henry (Jefferson 1780). On April 19, 1780, the first soldiers and civilian inhabitants arrived at the confluence and selected an area north of Mayfield Creek (then called Liberty Creek) on the east side of the Mississippi River in which to construct the fort and settlement. This area was approximately five miles below the confluence of the Ohio and Mississippi Rivers. In all, more than 550 persons would, for the next 13 months and 20 days, live at Fort Jefferson and the civilian community, Clarksville.[2] Unfortunately, with the destruction of corn crops and livestock at the hands of the Chickasaw Indians in July and August, 1780, and the lack of incoming food supplies from outside sources, Fort Jefferson would be short-lived, being abandoned at the request of Lt. Col. John Montgomery on June 8, 1781.[3] In spite of the short duration, Fort Jefferson was a significant outpost for the Virginians. Soldiers from it helped thwart the British-led Indian assault on St. Louis and Cahokia in May, 1780, and in August, 1780, many of its soldiers participated in Clark's attack on the Ohio Shawnee villages at Old Picqua and Chillicothe. Moreover, Fort Jefferson was the only fortification built in Kentucky expressly at the request and support of the Virginia government. Today, locating the exact position of the site of Fort Jefferson is important because it has the potential of being one of the few remaining American Revolutionary War period sites in the Midwest left intact by the Virginians. Fort Clark at Kaskaskia Island was washed away by the Mississippi River, Fort Bowman was destroyed by urban development in Cahokia, Fort Patrick Henry in Vincennes was destroyed by the Rotunda built to honor the memory of George Rogers Clark and the men and women who fought with him, Fort Nelson in Louisville was destroyed by urban expansion, and Fort Harrodsburg has been covered over by an asphalt church parking lot. Should the archaeological site of Fort Jefferson be discovered, its research significance will be multiplied significantly when added to the plethora of published documentation about the fort and community.[4]

---

[2] Kenneth C. Carstens, *The Personnel of George Rogers Clark's Fort Jefferson and Civilian Community of Clarksville [Kentucky], 1780-1781*. Heritage Books, Bowie, Maryland, 1999. Kenneth C. Carstens, *The Calendar and Quartermaster Books of George Rogers Clark's Fort Jefferson, 1780-1781*, Heritage books, Bowie, Maryland, 2000.

[3] Lt. Col. John Montgomery letter to Governor Thomas Nelson, Aug. 10, 1781. James Alton James, editor, *George Rogers Clark Papers*, I:585-586, AMS Press, New York. Carstens, 1999, 2000.

[4] Kenneth C. Carstens, "The Structural Landscape of George Rogers Clark's Fort Jefferson, 1780-1781," this volume; Carstens, 1999, 2000.

The exact location of Fort Jefferson is uncertain today, but the general location of the fort is evidenced by the land system. It is the intent of this research to investigate early land ownership patterns in the area of the fort. Specifically, the work has the following objectives:
1) Review records of early surveys in the western part of the Jackson Purchase;
2) Identify the lines of the rectangular survey system (if any) in the Fort Jefferson area;
3) Compile Virginia military and treasury surveys that relate to the location of Fort Jefferson;
4) Relate the lines of the above surveys to the ground based on existing U.S. Geological Survey topographic maps.

Early Surveys in Western Kentucky

Perhaps the earliest survey involving the confluence of the Ohio and Mississippi Rivers was an observation for latitude performed during the French expedition by Marquette and Joliet in 1673.[5] Marquette's journal gives the latitude at that location as 36 degrees. However, by the time of the Revolutionary War, a precise determination of the latitude of the confluence was of material interest to Virginia, which claimed the east bank of the Mississippi River by virtue of the Carolina Charter of 1665. This charter placed the southern boundary of Virginia at 36 degrees 30 minutes north latitude.[6] Consequently, in January, 1780 Virginia Governor Thomas Jefferson requested Dr. Thomas Walker and Daniel Smith to determine this location on the ground.[7] In his journal for May, 1780, Smith notes the following:

> Wednesday 10 th. Observed. Thursday 11th. Agreed with Yesterdays observ. We were 3'19" in Virginia—from this point of the Island we ran east to the main land where I marked a buck eye elm & Sugar tree then South 3 m. 265 po. Then west 106 po. To riv. 96 po. of which we mark'd. new land is forming here, nothing to mark but cotton trees.[8]

The observations by Walker and Smith were instrumental in ensuring that fortifications erected by George Rogers Clark at Fort Jefferson indeed were within the charter boundaries of Virginia and are the first precise surveying observation made in what is now western Kentucky. The only map drawn of Fort Jefferson while the fort was occupied was made in 1780 by William Clark[9] (this William is the cousin of George Rogers Clark, son of Benjamin Clark, and not George's younger brother by the same name). The first map of Fort Jefferson drawn after the fort was abandoned was made in 1795 by William Clark, George's younger brother.[10] This map

---

[5] Reuben G. Thwaites, *The Jesuit Relations and Allied Documents*, Vol. 59, University Microfilms, Inc., Ann Arbor, 1966.
[6] Francis N. Thorpe, *Federal and State Constitutions, Colonial Charters, and Other Organic Acts*, Vol. V, pp. 2743-53. Government Printing Office, Washington, D.C., 1909
[7] James, ed., I: 392, Jefferson to Walker, January 29, 1780.
[8] Daniel Smith, Journal of General Daniel Smith, One of the Commissioners to Extend the Boundary Line between the Commonwealths of Virginia and North Carolina, August, 1779 to July, 1780. *Tennessee Historical Magazine*, No. 1, March 1915.
[9] Kenneth C. Carstens, The 1780 William Clark Map of Fort Jefferson. *The Filson Club History Quarterly*, 67(1):23-43 (1993). Draper Manuscripts, 1 M 8, The Wisconsin Historical Society, Madison.
[10] The William Clark 1795 Map, Geography and Map Division, Library of Congress, Washington, D.C.

shows the fort as being on the north bank of a creek on the east side of the Mississippi at the first island south of the confluence of the Ohio and Mississippi. A portion of the 1795 Clark map is shown in Figure 2.2.

Following the Revolutionary War, the United States recognized title to land between the Tennessee and Mississippi Rivers in western Kentucky as being in the Chickasaw Nation. This land was purchased for the United States in 1818 by a delegation headed by Andrew Jackson and Isaac Shelby, and it was subsequently conveyed to Kentucky and Tennessee. The Kentucky portion of the Jackson Purchase is shown on a map published in 1818 by Luke Munsell. This shows the Jackson Purchase as "Land to which the Indian Title is (lately) Extinguished but has not yet been Surveyed." Interestingly, it also shows within the Jackson Purchase two grants: a grant labeled "G.R. Clarke's 37,000 Acres" and "Mayo's 17,000 acres." A portion of the Munsell map is shown in Figure 2.3.

Rectangular Survey

In 1819, the Act of February 8th authorized the governor of Kentucky to appoint two commissioners to survey the Kentucky-Tennessee boundary west of the Tennessee River.[11] Commissioners appointed were Robert Alexander and Luke Munsell. These men subsequently ran the line between Kentucky and Tennessee at 36 degrees 30 minutes north latitude.

By the Act of February 14, 1820, the Kentucky General Assembly provided for the surveying of the lands within the Jackson Purchase. A sectionalized land system was to be used that employed townships six miles "square," each containing 36 sections. William T. Henderson was the surveyor appointed to oversee this work. Henderson used the Kentucky-Tennessee boundary as surveyed by Munsell and Alexander as his baseline. He established a meridian six miles east of the Tennessee River, and conducted the subdivision based on these lines.[12]

Military claims within the Jackson Purchase were addressed by the Act of December 26, 1820. This act required the surveyor appointed for these claims to survey all entries made prior to May 1792 and to show where these claims "interfere with the townships and sections of the land as laid off by William T. Henderson."

Henderson returned field notes and a plat showing both the sectionalized land system and treasury warrant claims and military claims within the Purchase. Two things from Henderson's work are of particular interest. First, Henderson shows grants along the Ohio River and along the Mississippi River southerly to the vicinity of Mayfield Creek. Second, Henderson shows the location of Fort Jefferson by a symbol located in the north one-half of section 3, township 5, range 4 west. Section 3 is shown on the Henderson map as a fractional section located to the east of what appears to be Island No. 1. Further, the symbol representing Fort Jefferson is shown to the south of a dashed line which, according to the legend on the Henderson map, indicates the location of a survey based on a (Virginia) treasury warrant. The map also shows Mayfield Creek

---

[11] Acts of Kentucky, February 8, 1819, Frankfort, Kentucky.
[12] William T. Henderson, *A Map Showing Part of the State of Kentucky Lying West of the Tennessee River Surveyed Agreeably to an Act of the Legislature Passed on the 14th of February 1820.* University Kentucky Library, Lexington, Kentucky, 1820.

running southeast to northwest across the south half of section 3. This section of the Henderson map is shown in Figure 2.4.

During the survey of Township 5, Range 4 West, Henderson's survey crew meandered the bank of the Mississippi River. The field notes for this part of the work as returned by Henderson read:

> T5 R4W. Beginning at S.E. corner at a white oak. West 4 miles 278 poles to 2 cottonwoods and 5 maples on Mississippi. Up the River N4W 228 P. N 41E 120 P. N48E 225 P. N 48 E 97 P. N37E 240P. N22E 246 P. N24E 225 P. N12E 200 P. N 1609 P. N3E 129 P. N7W 157 P. N17W 104 P to mouth of Mayfield Creek. N 45W 93 P. to 4 cottonwoods between T5 & 6 R 4W.[13]

These notes are important because the meander lines and the call for Mayfield Creek enable the north line of Township 5 to be located with reference to other lines that also cite the mouth of Mayfield Creek.

Virginia Military and Treasury Surveys

Land grants from Virginia for land in the Fort Jefferson area were based on both military and treasury warrants. Below are detailed surveys for Robert Todd, William Clark, John Nelson, and James Merewether that were based on Virginia military warrants. In addition, the Jacob Meyers (Myers) survey—also in the Fort Jefferson area—was based on a Virginia treasury warrant. Warrant, entry, and survey documentation given below refers to the Kentucky Office of the Secretary of State. A deed compilation showing the relative location of these parcels as well is provided in Figure 2.5.

Todd. Robert Todd received Virginia Military Warrant No. 2580 on February 21, 1784 for 4,000 acres of land for his service of three years as captain in the Virginia State Line. His entry is dated August 2, 1784. The survey was recorded on May 5, 1821, and the grant to Todd was made on December 3, 1824. The entry described land to be surveyed as:

> Beginning at the mouth of Mayfield Creek on the lower side and running up the said creek with the meanders thereof 640 poles when reduced to a straight line, thence at right angles from the end of said reduced line and up the Mississippi River for quantity *including Fort Jefferson and the village*[14] (italics added).

The survey by Deputy Surveyor Samuel McKee is shown in Figure 2.6. This figure illustrates the parcel to be bounded on the west by the meanders of Mayfield Creek, on the south by the William Clark survey of 666 2/3 acres, and on the east and north by bearing and distances only. The southwest corner of Todd is described as being "three ash trees and a walnut corner to William Clarks survey of 666 2/3 acres," and the south line of Todd is described as running with

---

[13] *Ibid.*
[14] West of the Tennessee River Military Survey (WTRMS) No. 30, Book 1, Page 28, May 5, 1821, Frankfort, Kentucky.

Clark's line. The southwest corner of Todd is the same corner called for in the William Clark survey and the same trees are identified. Interestingly, no mention is made of either Fort Jefferson or "the village" in the survey description to Todd. The grant to Todd contains 1,000 acres of the 4,000 acres authorized under Virginia Military Warrant No. 2530.[15]

Clark. The William Clark (coursin of GRC) survey adjoins the Todd survey on the south. William Clark received Virginia Military Warrant No. 2681 for 2,666 2/3 acres on March 3, 1784 for his service of three years as a lieutenant in the Virginia State Line. His entry is dated August 3, 1784. The survey was recorded on May 3, 1821, and the grant to Clark was made on May 6, 1825. The survey describes his parcel as:

> Beginning at three ash trees and a walnut on the west bank of Mayfield Creek Robert Todd's upper corner running thence with Robert Todd's upper line...[16]

This description of the corner agrees with that in Todd's survey. The call for Todd's line is interesting, however, because the Todd survey is dated two days later than that of Clark. Surveyor McKee was apparently being very careful to ensure that persons referring to the Clark and Todd surveys understood that the two had a common line. This is important to this research because plotting the Todd Survey on a U.S.G.S. topographic quadrangle is based on the location of the Clark survey. Examination of the survey shows that the parcel described in Book 1 Page 70 contains 666 2/3 acres of the 2,666 2/3 acres authorized under Military Warrant 2681.

Merewether (also Meriweather). The James Merewether survey adjoins Todd on the north and east. James Merewether obtained Virginia Military Warrant No. 2468 for 2,666 2/3 acres on February 11, 1784 for his service of three years as lieutenant in the Virginia State Line. His entry is dated August 26, 1784. The survey was recorded on May 5, 1821, and the grant to Merewether was made on January 15, 1824. The survey describes the south line of the Merewether survey as:

> Beginning at the upper line of Robert Todd survey which *includes Fort Jefferson and the village at the edge of the lands overflowed by the Mississippi* a cottonwood, beech, and ash on a bank...[17]

This point of beginning is not the northwest corner of Todd (two cottonwood trees and a willow) as described in his survey, nor does McKee call for the northwest corner of Todd. Rather, it appears that McKee is simply describing the point of beginning of the Merewether survey as being on the "upper line" of Todd.

The southeast corner of the Merewether survey is described as a "red oak, hickory, and gum on Robert Todd's backline." The west line of Merewether then runs "with his [Todd's] line N 21° West 382 poles to a poplar, red oak, and gum said Todd's corner." This description agrees with that in the Todd survey except that in Todd the trees are more specifically described as being on a ridge. The south line of Merewether is then described as running "thence with his

---

[15] *Ibid.*
[16] *Ibid.*, Survey No. 72, Bk 1, Pg. 70.
[17] *Ibid.*, Survey 21, Bk 1, Pg. 12.

[Todd's] upper line S 69° West 140 poles to the beginning." From this description, it is apparent that Merewether and Todd share common boundaries and corners. Further examination of the grant to Merewether shows it to contain 1,000 acres of the 2,666 2/3 acres authorized by Virginia Military Warrant No. 2468.

Nelson. The Nelson survey adjoins Todd on the east. John Nelson received Virginia Military Warrant No. 1790 for 5,333 2/3 acres on September 25, 1783 for his service of three years as a major in the Virginia State Cavalry. His entry is dated August 12, 1784. The survey of this tract was recorded on May 6, 1821, and the grant to Nelson is dated March 2, 1825. Nelson's survey describes the land conveyed as:

> Beginning at a red oak, hickory, and gum James Merewethers corner on Robert Todd's upper line of his survey *including Fort Jefferson*, thence with Todds line South 21° East 480 poles to four hickories and an ash, with oak and black oak on the west bank of Mayfield Creek corner to said Robert Todd and William Clark line...[18]

Hence, the southwest corner of Nelson is the same as the southeast corner of Merewether. The south line of Nelson follows the east line of Todd, and the southeast corner of Nelson is located at the southeast corner of Todd on the north line of Clark. The grant to Nelson is for 1,000 acres of the 5,333 2/3 acres authorized by Virginia Military Warrant No. 1790.

Meyers. The south line of Jacob Meyers survey overlaps the north portions of the Todd, Nelson, and Merewether surveys. Meyers obtained Virginia Treasury Warrant No. 7069 on October 10, 1781 for 10,000 acres for a payment of £16,000. His entry is dated November 20, 1781. The survey was dated June 12, 1784, and the grant to Meyers was made on December 2, 1796.[19] The survey described the land involved as:

> Beginning at the mouth of a creek at the head of the first island in the Mississippi below the mouth of the Ohio, thence up the meanders of the river at high water mark 800 poles, thence to run back parallel with Brigadier General Clarkes (sic) entry made on behalf of the State of Virginia of 101,920 acres for quantity.[20]

As shown in Figure 2.7, the map accompanying the survey shows the south line of Meyers' grant to be located to the north of the symbol labeled "Fort Jefferson." Further, the grant to Meyers describes the point of beginning of the survey as:

> Beginning at a willow and two cotton trees...on the bank of the Mississippi at the mouth of the creek emptying into the Mississippi at the head of the first island below the mouth of the Ohio and about 200 poles above Fort Jefferson...[21]

---

[18] Ibid, Survey 106, Bk 1, Pg. 44.
[19] Old Kentucky Surveys, No. 8935, Grant Books 2, Pg. 18, Secretary of State's Land Records, Frankfort, Kentucky.
[20] Lincoln County Entries, Book 1, Page 173, Secretary of State's Land Records, Frankfort, Kentucky.
[21] *Op. cit.*

Examination of the maps and grants above make it apparent that there is overlap between the military and treasury surveys, and that Fort Jefferson is located between the Todd and Meyers surveys. Both are overlapped by the rectangular survey of Henderson.

Surveys Subsequent to the Virginia Military Surveys

Young, Poussin, and Tuttle Map, 1821.[22] This map is Mississippi River chart No. 10. It was prepared as part of a reconnaissance of the Ohio and Mississippi Rivers in 1821 by the U.S. Army Corps of Topographic Engineers. This shows Fort Jefferson to be south of Moffield (sic) River (Mayfield Creek).

Terrill Map, 1830.[23] The Chiles Terrill Map (July 2, 1830) appears to be a compilation of land grants and surveys in extreme western Kentucky. Terrill shows Fort Jefferson by symbol to be located north of Mayfield Creek and south of the Myers (later Benjamin Logan) line.

Forsythe Map, 1855.[24] A portion of this map, which was prepared by William Forsythe, is shown in Figure 2.8. Apparently, the location of the Myers survey was the subject of litigation before the Ballard Circuit Court in 1844. Forsythe shows the south boundary of Meyers to overlap the Todd survey. Neither the Merewether nor the Nelson surveys (which would also be overlapped by the Meyers line) are shown on the plat. Forsythe's bearings show the north and south lines of Meyers to bear S 82 degrees E and the east line to bear N 8 degrees E.

Dupoyster Map, No. 1.[25] This map dated 1868, was prepared by Fleet C. Mercer. A portion of this map is shown in Figure 2.9. It is labeled as "Exhibit A to indenture between Elizabeth B. McComb and others and William Butler Duncan dated May 31, 1883" and "Exhibit A to deed from Joseph C. Dupoyster & his wife Rebecca S. to Henry S. McComb dated May 4th, 1875." The land involved appears to be all or part of the Todd Survey. The north line of Dupoyster (labeled S 83 degrees E) appears to be the south line of Meyers. The east line (labeled N 21 degrees W) appears to be the east line of Todd. The south line, which is shown in dispute, bears N 69 degrees E and corners at the intersection of Black Slough with Mayfield Creek.

The location of the "L.& C.R.R." also is shown on the Depoyster map. The railroad bears N 44 degrees 45 minutes W from its intersection with the east line of Depoyster to the point of tangency of a horizontal curve north of the depot and hotel. West of the horizontal curve, the map is labeled "Deep Overflow."

Dupoyster Map, No. 2.[26] This map, Figure 2.10, was sent to Lyman C. Draper on October 21st, 1886 along with a series of questions regarding the location of fort Jefferson posited by Draper to which Joseph C. Dupoyster responded. Dupoyster's map is significant for several reasons: it illustrates that Fort Jefferson is located just north of the Illinois Central Railroad and that it is situated on ground that "is above overflow," as opposed to lower-lying ground that is subject to seasonal flooding. It also correctly illustrates Mayfield Creek flowing into a chute of the Mississippi that separates the middle of Island No. 1 from the shore. Lastly,

---

[22] U.S. Army Corps of Engineers, Memphis District.
[23] Original located in Deed Book A, McCracken County Court House, Paducah, Kentucky.
[24] Ballard County Court House, Deeds and Plats, Wickliffe, Kentucky.
[25] Ballard County Courthouse, Wickliffe, Kentucky.
[26] Draper Manuscripts, 27J1, Wisconsin Historical Society, Madison, Wisconsin.

it locates "where the cannons was found" along the north edge of Mayfield Creek south of the Fort Jefferson location.

Stovall Map.[27] This map is illustrated in Figure 2.11. The map shows Fort Jefferson to be located north of Mayfield Creek, east of the chute of Island No. 1, and at the point of tangency of the horizontal curve on the railroad. It is the most detailed of all the fort Jefferson maps, and includes the location of "old graves" and "new graves," the stockade, the bluff, the fort, lands that were farmed, the location of springs, and the location of two rail lines south of the fort. As with Dupoyster, B. Hardy Stovall also answers a series of interrogatories about the location of Fort Jefferson posited by Lyman Draper.

Mobile & Ohio R.R. Co. Map.[28] This map, dated August, 1922, was issued by the Office of the Chief Engineer of the Mobile & Ohio R.R. Co. and was accepted for record in the Ballard County courthouse on May 2, 1923. The map shows the point of tangency of the horizontal curve, the "Old Depot," and additional buildings. A portion of this map is shown in Figure 2.12.

Existing Land Occupation Patterns

Land occupation patterns represent the attempt by land owners to use and mark the boundaries of their land. Such patterns are most evident when the land is viewed from the air. The patterns also are visible on topographic maps as roads, fence lines, and changes in land use. Collectively, such lines are termed "lines of occupation."

When the lines of occupation are plotted on a map, a pattern often becomes evident. In this research, lines of occupation shown on the Wickliffe and Blandville (1983 and 1977 editions, respectively) U.S. Geological Survey 7.5-minute-quadrangles were digitized together with principal roads and drainages. This work disclosed two distinct patterns. In the eastern half of the Blandville quadrangle, lines of occupation trend north-south, east-west in a marked grid system. This apparently reflects the rectangular Henderson survey. This north-south, east-west pattern is missing on the western part of the quad. There is, however, an apparent trend--S 80 degrees E/ N 10 degrees E—to the lines of occupation. This orientation matches closely the lines of the Meyers survey as shown on the Forsythe plat described above.

Because finding the location of Fort Jefferson involves historical data, earlier government surveys showing Fort Jefferson area also were examined. Corps of Engineers maps dated 1882 and 1890 show Port [sic] Jefferson north of Mayfield Creek. The railroad grade is shown extending northward from that point along the west side of the bluff to Wycliffe [sic, Wickliffe]. In 1945, the Army Map Service mapped the east bank of the Mississippi as it existed in 1765. This shows the bank to have been coincident with the chute for Island No.1 and places the mouth of Mayfield Creek at approximately its present position. The 1951 Wickliffe U.S.G.S. quadrangle shows M&O Railroad to have been abandoned and shows the grade to terminate south of the bluff. In summary, none of the government maps consulted showed a definitive location for the missing fort.

In order to correctly place the Virginia military and treasury grants on the Wickliffe 7.5-minute topographical quadrangle map, it was necessary to relate the grants to ground features shown on the quad sheet. In this research, attempts to relate current and past ownerships of the

---

[27] Draper Manuscripts, 27J17-22, Wisconsin Historical Society, Madison, Wisconsin.
[28] Ballard County Courthouse, Wickliffe, Kentucky.

land surrounding Fort Jefferson were hampered by destruction of land records in a courthouse fire in Ballard County in the late 1800's. However, deed research at the Carlisle County, Kentucky courthouse showed the Winford County Road in Carlisle County to be the east line of the William Clark grant. A road intersection fixed as well the southeast corner of the grant. The site was visited on the ground and could be identified on the Wickliffe quadrangle. Consequently, a plot of the Todd and adjoining grants was rotated to match existing lines of the Clark survey. (See Rowland to Compton, Book 114, Page 128; Watson to Rowland, Book 65, Page 458; Hatley to Watson, Book 63, Page 447; and Botkin to Sampson, Book 13, Page 327.) The results of this work are shown in Figures 2.13 and 2.14.

In addition to the topographic quads, existing aerial photography was examined in an attempt to reconcile the various record evidence listed above. Included was photography taken by various agencies in 1937, 1943, 1950, 1959, 1964, 1972, and 1981. While this photography showed land use changes, the only indications of the possible location of Fort Jefferson were discolored soils to the east of the M&O Railroad grade that might possibly indicate previous disturbance.

Conclusion

The surveys, land records, and physical lines of occupation when taken together provide a general location for Fort Jefferson. Based on the Todd entry, the Meyers survey, the Henderson survey, and the Forsythe survey, Fort Jefferson is located south of the south line of Meyers. Based on the both Depoyster maps, the Stovall map, and on the right-of-way plat of the Mobile and Ohio Railroad, Fort Jefferson is located in the vicinity of the former M&O railroad grade at the point of tangency of the curve immediately south of the Myers line. Based on the topographic description contained in the Merewether survey, Fort Jefferson must be south of the bluff at the south line of section 5 T5N R4W of the Henderson survey and the south line of Meyers. The east-west location of the fort is less certain, but must be east of the "edge of the overflowed lands" as described in Merewether and Depoyster. The edge of the overflow as of the 1780 is difficult to determine, but must be close to the location of the M&O Railroad grade. This is because railroad grade location would have maximized the flat grades adjacent to the river, but been located far enough to the east to prevent repeated inundation. Finally, photographic evidence shows a light-toned area east of the former railroad grade at the base of the bluff. Whether this results from recent disturbance or from compaction of the land incidental to construction and use of a fort is uncertain without excavation.

Further work is suggested by this research. First, additional deed research of current land ownerships and surveys of record should be undertaken to enable location on the ground of the south line of Meyers. Second, field investigation to locate the former M&O Railroad grade is indicated. Third, archaeological reconnaissance should be undertaken to locate artifacts and other physical evidence bearing on the location of Fort Jefferson.

Figure 2.1: Fort Jefferson and the civilian community of Clarksville, 1780 (Draper Manuscript, 1M8-11, Wisconsin Historical Society, Madison).

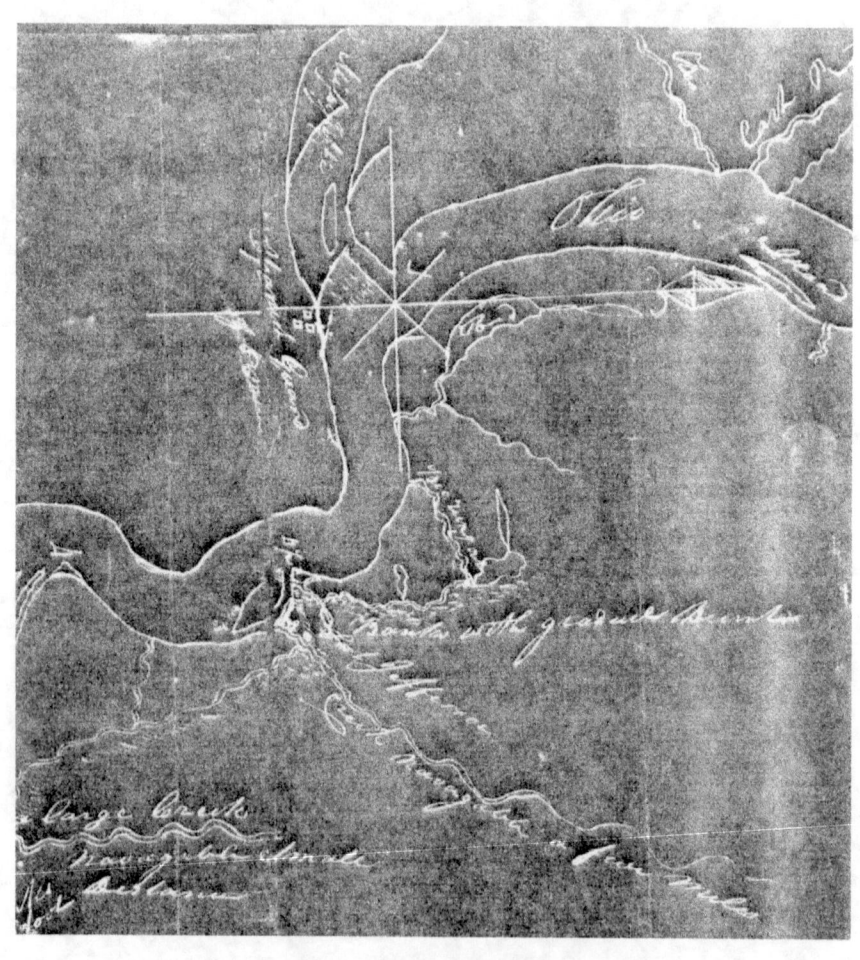

Figure 2.2: William Clark map of Fort Jefferson, 1795
(Library of Congress, Lewis & Clark Collection "b").

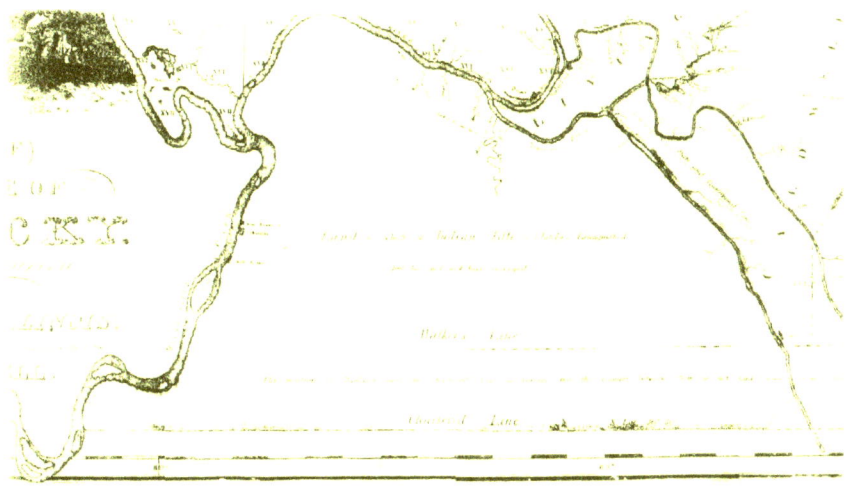

Figure 2.3: A portion of "A Map of the State of Kentucky" by
Luke Munsell published at Frankfort, Kentucky, 1818
(Murray State University Map Collection).

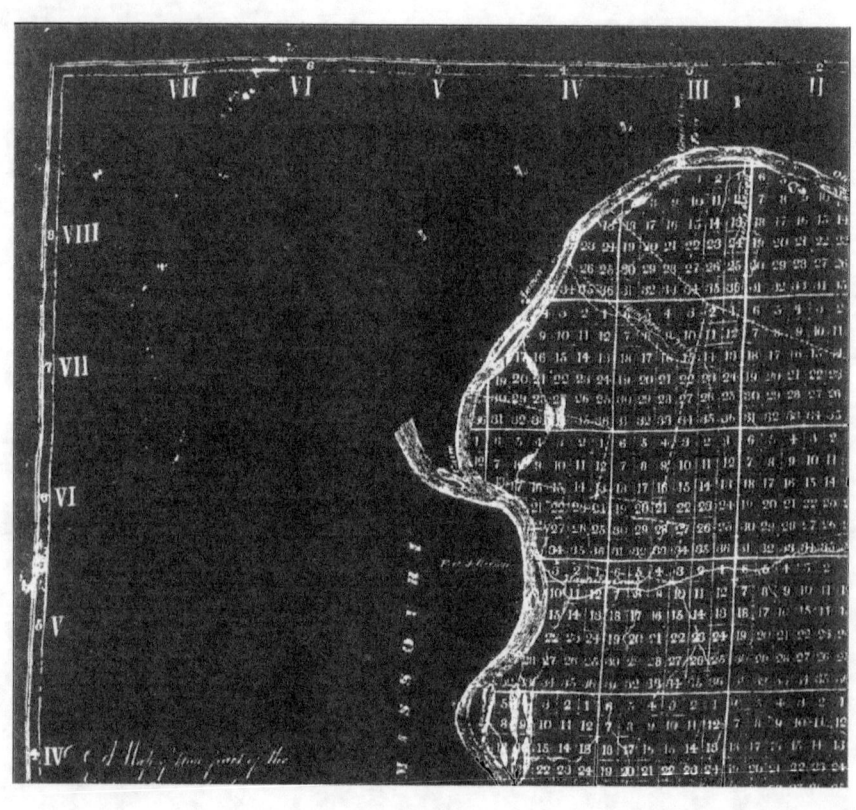

Figure 2.4: A portion of "A Map of that Part of the State of Kentucky lying west of the Tennessee River surveyed agreeably to the act of the Legislature passed on the 15 of February 1820" by William Henderson (University of Kentucky Map Collection).

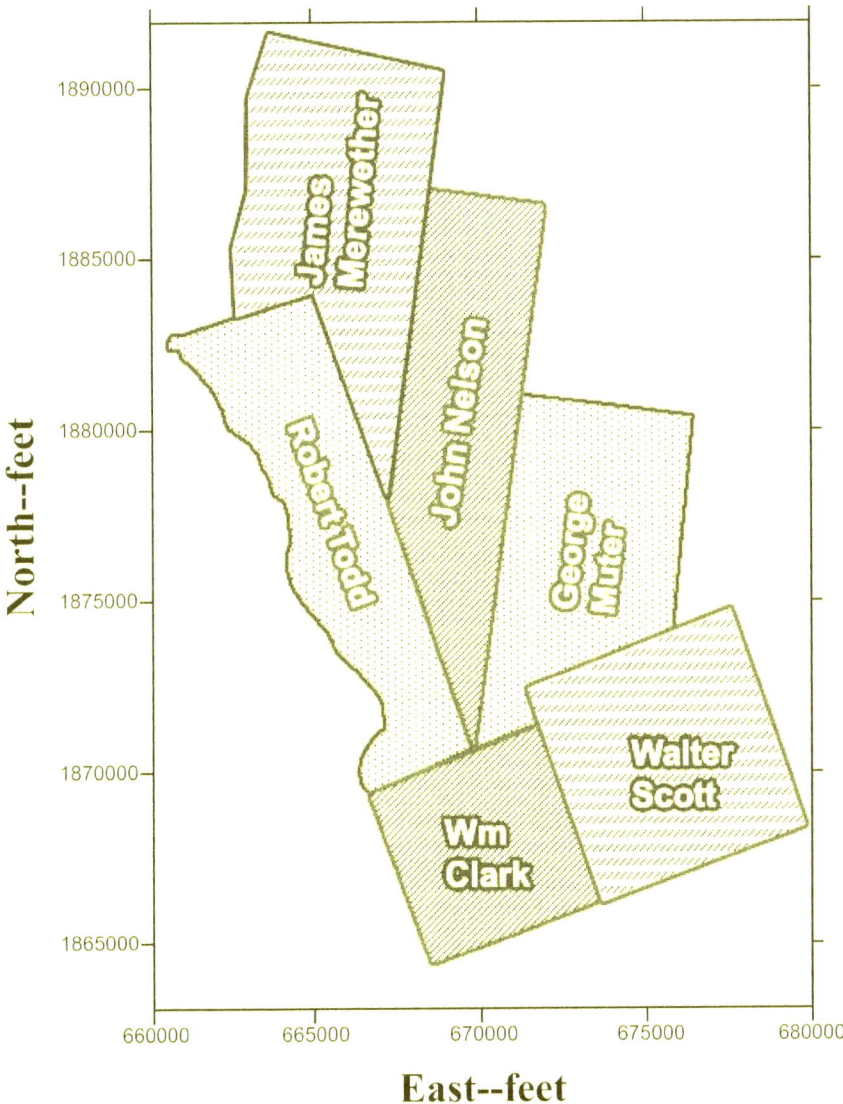

Figure 2.5: Deed compilation of Virginia Military Surveys in the vicinity of Fort Jefferson, Kentucky.

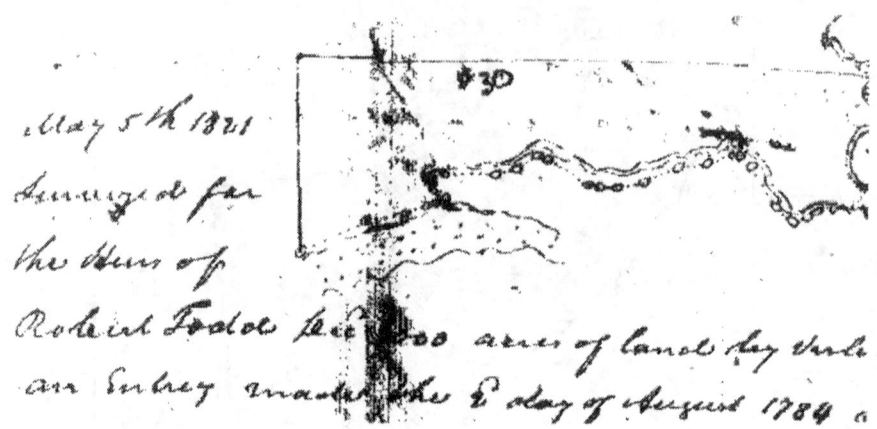

Figure 6. Todd Survey by Deputy Surveyor Samuel McKee, 1821 (WTR Mil. Surv. #30 Bk 1 Pg 28).

Figure 2.7: Myers (Meyers) Treasury Survey, 1784 (Old Kentucky #8935, Grant Book 2, Pg 18).

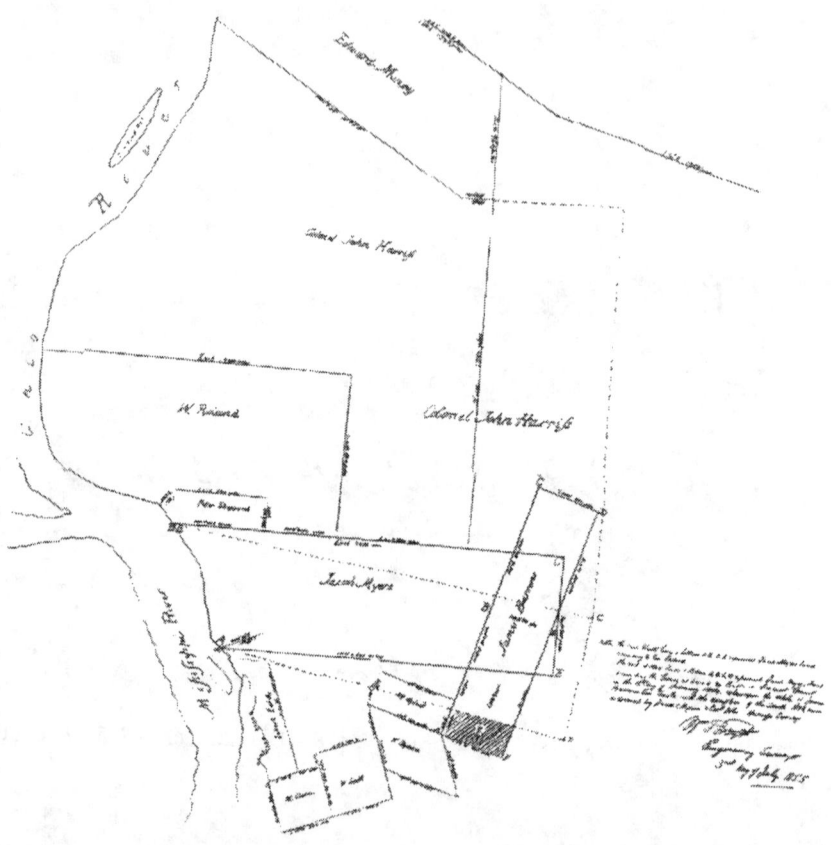

Figure 2.8: Portion of the Forsythe Map, 1855. Apparently the result of litigation, this maps appears to explain the trend of metes and bounds property lines in the vicinity of Fort Jefferson. Note the overlap between the survey for Jacob Myers and that for Robert Todd (Library of Congress, Map Division, Nov. 25, 1912).

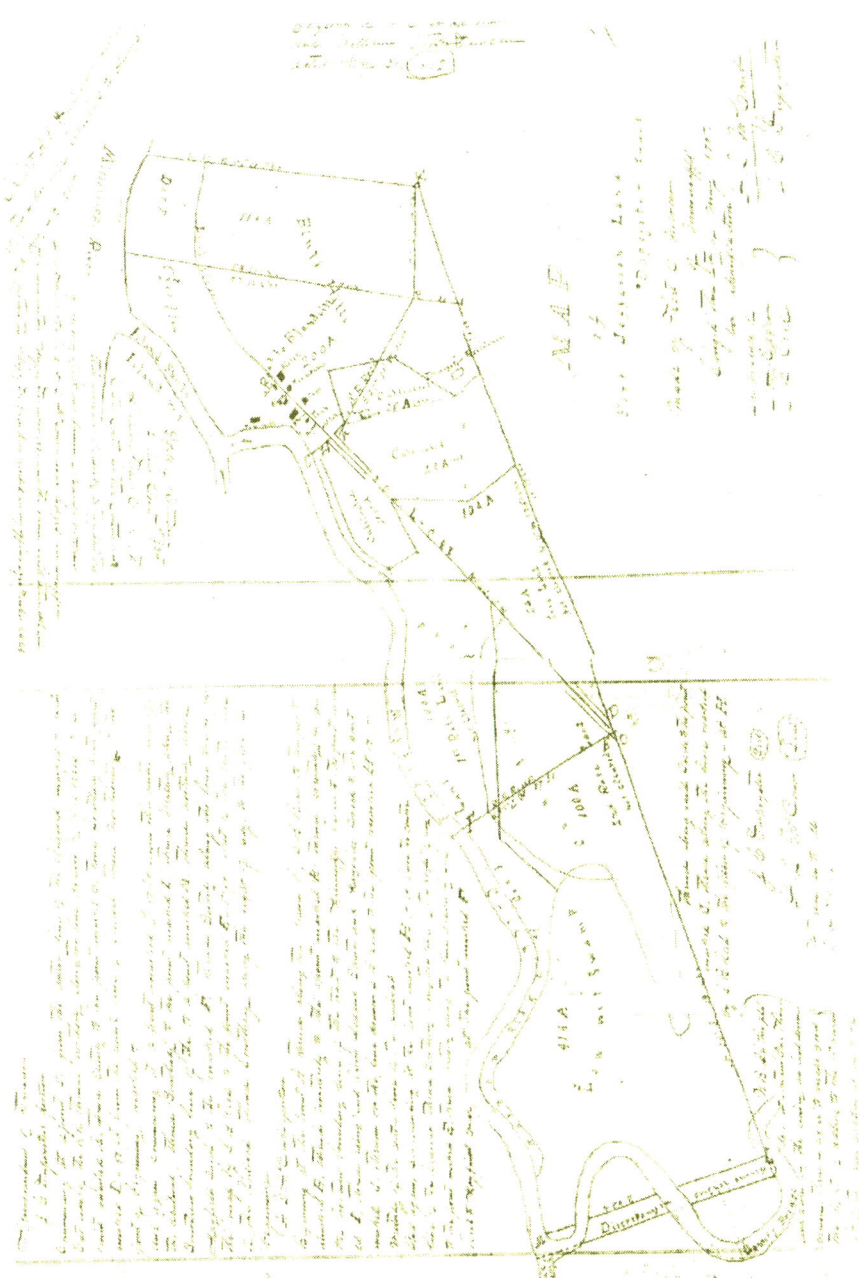

Figure 2.9: Depoyster Map by Fleet C. Mercer, 1878. Land shown appears to be part of the Todd Military Survey. Note location of railroad.

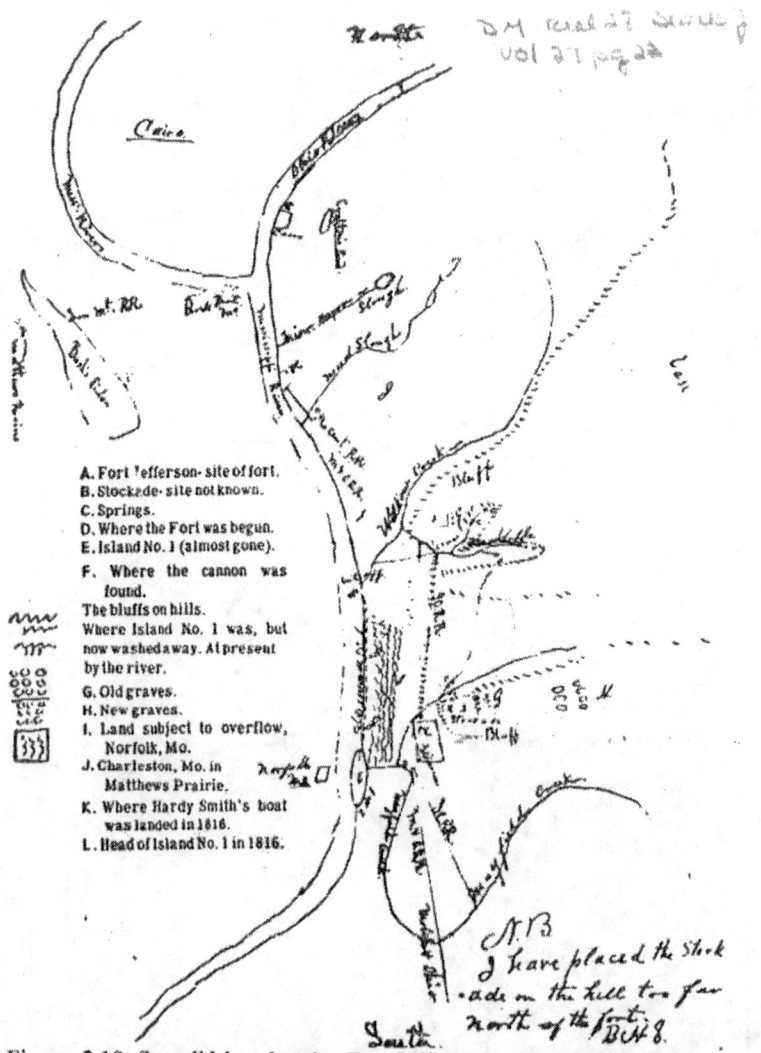

Figure 2.10: Stovall Map showing Fort Jefferson at foot of bluff and east of the railroad (Draper Manuscripts Reel 28, series J, volume 24, p 91; see also volume 27, p 22.).

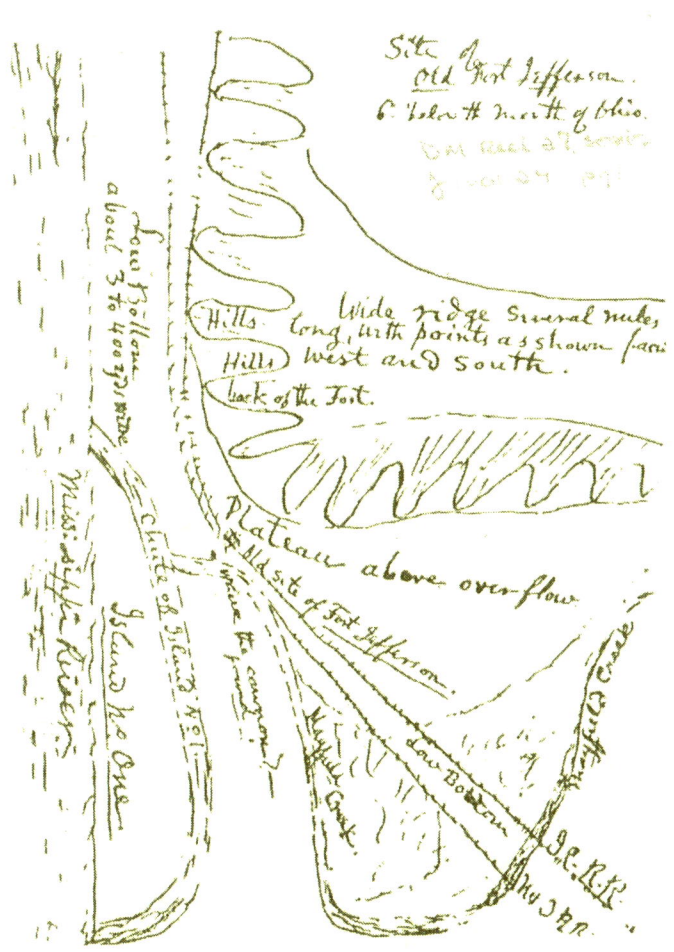

Figure 2.11: Depoyster/Draper map (Draper Manuscripts Reel 28, series J, volume 24, p 91; see also volume 27, p 22.).

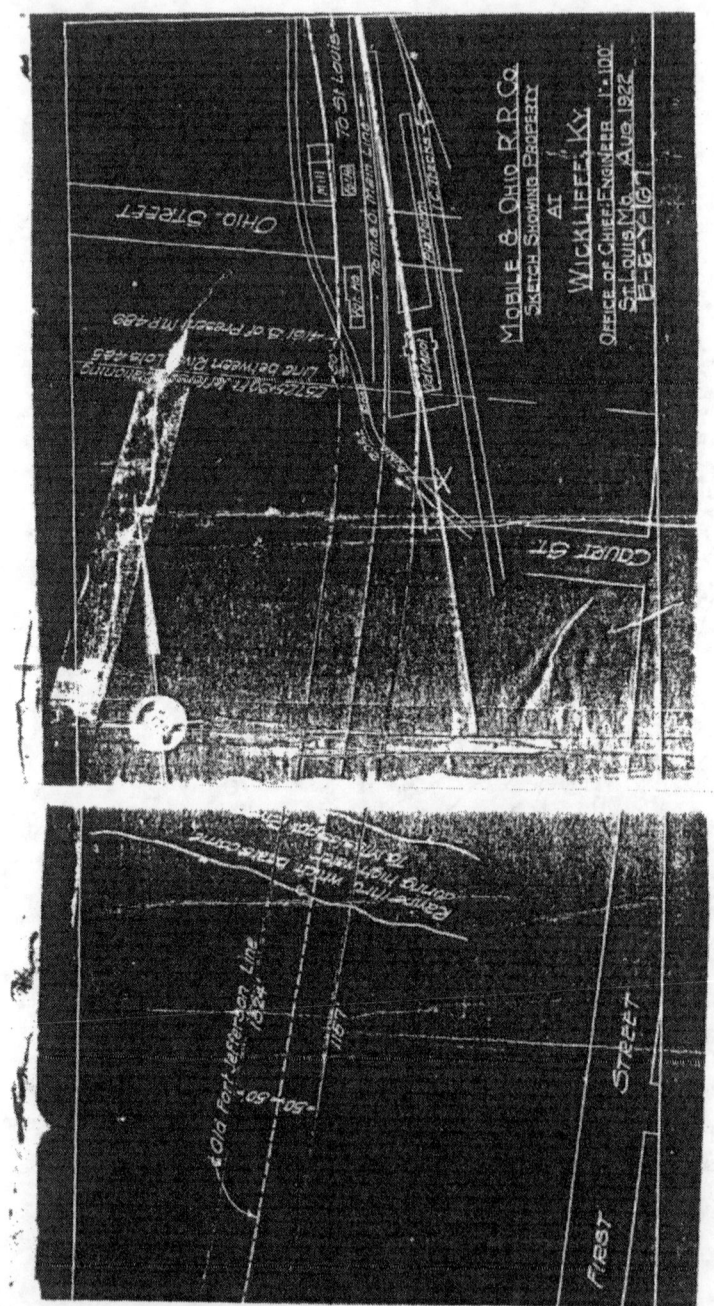

Figure 2.12: Mobile and Ohio Railroad at Fort Jefferson, 1922 (Ballard County, KY).

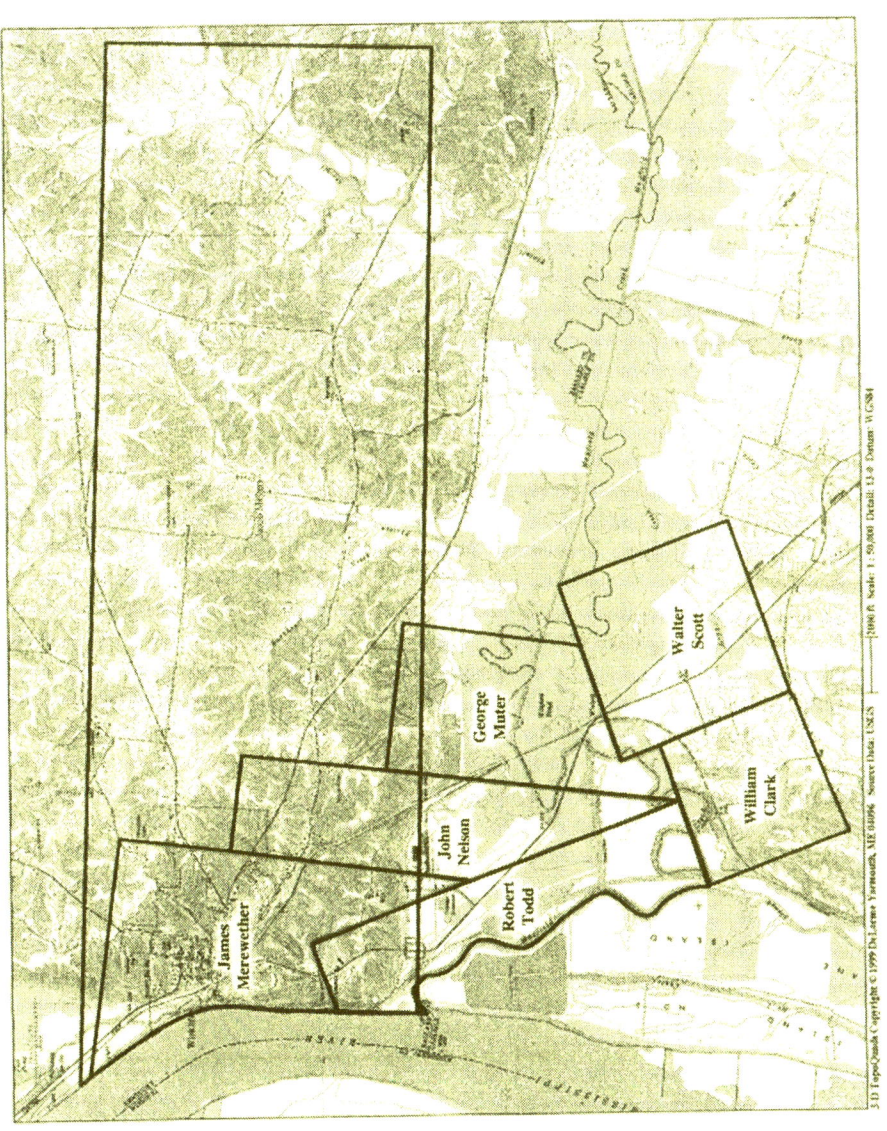

Figure 2.13: Deed compilation registered on Delorme 3D quad for Kentucky showing both Virginia Military and Treasury Surveys in vicinity of Fort Jefferson as registered to ground.

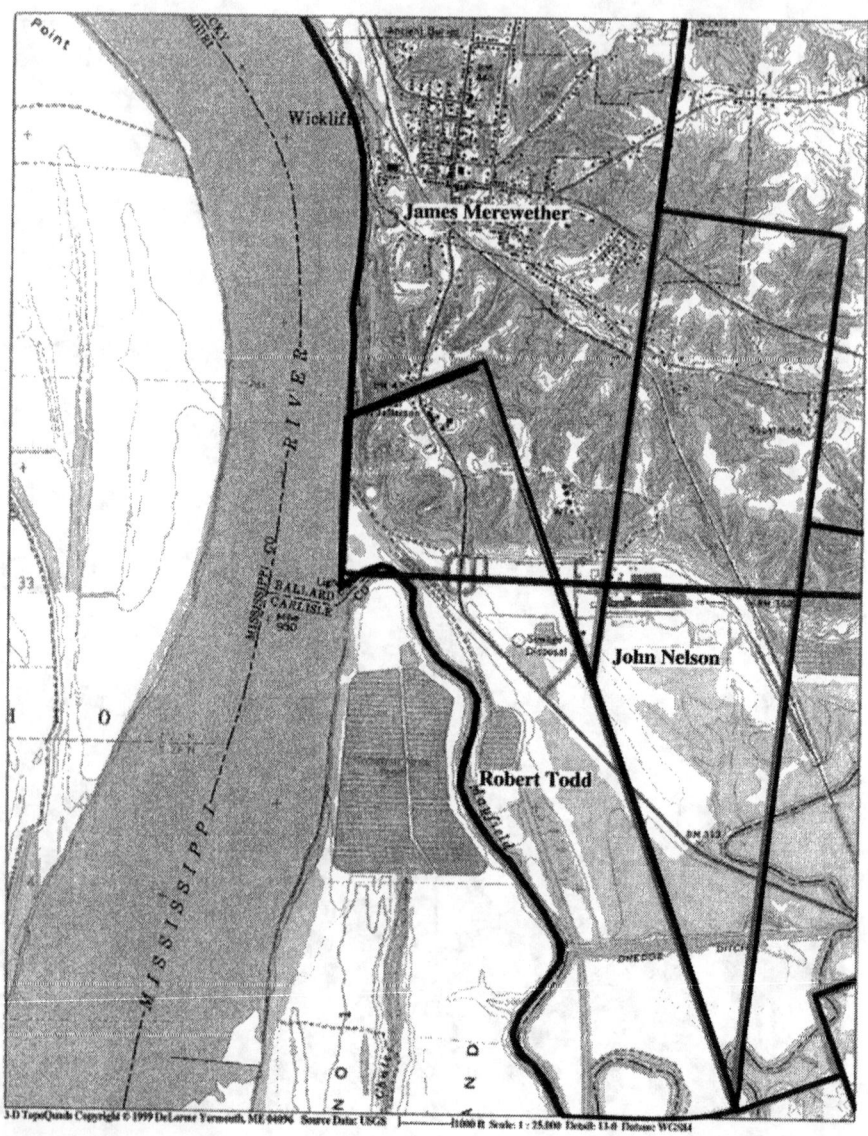

Figure 2.14: Enlargement of deed compilation showing Todd, Nelson, and Merewether Military Surveys.

CHAPTER 3: FORT JEFFERSON, 1780-1781: A SUMMARY OF ITS HISTORY[1]

In 1777, Virginia Governor Patrick Henry, in consultation with George Rogers Clark, conceived the idea of physically laying claim to Virginia's western border by building a chain of forts along the Mississippi. No doubt, both Henry and Clark were driven to do so militarily, but also for individual profit through the acquisition of large tracts of land. Clark's subsequent capture of Kaskaskia, commanding Fort Clark, and Cahokia, commanding Fort Bowman, were the first forts in the Mississippi River chain that physically delineated Virginia's state claims. In April of 1780, Clark built Fort Jefferson at the Mouth of the Ohio River, a strategic location, which, however, proved to be located too far from sources of supplies to make the settlement practical. Due to a lack of supplies, Indian depredations, and a re-thinking of military strategies, the fort was abandoned on June 8, 1781, just 13 months and 20 days after it was settled. This chapter looks briefly at the history of that military and civilian occupation on the western frontier.

Introduction

The origin of George Rogers Clark's Fort Jefferson dates from the summer of 1777, when Clark first developed plans to capture the British posts of Kaskaskia, Cahokia, and Vincennes in the Illinois country in conjunction with Virginia Governor Patrick Henry.[2] By June of that year, Clark had received word from his spies that the Illinois country could be taken easily. Clark formulated plans that included constructing a fort near the mouth of the Ohio River to facilitate trade with the Spanish and French settlements. A fort located at the mouth of the Ohio also would support, through possession, Virginia's revised (1763) "paper claim" to her western boundary. By January, 1778, Clark received permission from Virginia Governor Patrick Henry to proceed with his secret operation.[3]

Without firing a shot, Clark captured Kaskaskia, the first of the British-controlled posts, on July 4, 1778. Even more remarkable was his success in approaching that community completely undetected. Clark and his small force, approximately 175 members of the Illinois Battalion, had traversed the entirety of the Ohio River from Fort Pitt to the mouth of the Tennessee River and overland from the Tennessee River to Kaskaskia on the Mississippi River, undetected.[4]

---

[1] This chapter is based on a publication by the same name: Kenneth C. Carstens "Fort Jefferson, 1780-1781: A Summary of Its History" in *the Selected Papers from the Ninth and Tenth George Rogers Clark Trans-Appalachian Frontier History Conference*, edited by Robert J. Holden (1994:42-58) and published by the Eastern National Park & Monument Association and Vincennes University. The paper has been revised and republished here with the permission of Vincennes University, the National Park Service, and the Eastern National Park & Monument Association. Funding support came from the Eastern National Park & Monument Association.
[2] Patrick Henry letter to Governor Bernardo de Galvez. Archivo General de Indias Seville, Estante 87, Cajon 1, Legajo 6, Spain.
[3] James Alton James, ed. *George Rogers Clark Papers, 1771-1784*, Vols. 1 & 2. reprinted 1972 by AMS Press, New York.
[4] Katherine Wagner Seineke, *The George Rogers Clark Adventure in the Illinois and Selected Documents of the American Revolution at the Frontier Posts*, 1981, Polyanthos Press, New Orleans.

To counter Clark's ambitious move westward, British Lieutenant Governor Henry Hamilton brought his forces south from Detroit to take control of the garrison called Fort Sackville in Vincennes. Arriving at Fort Sackville late in the year of 1778, Hamilton decided to wait out the winter along the Wabash River before attacking Clark at Kaskaskia. Clark, however, seized the initiative.[5]

Clark and his followers, accompanied by newly allied Frenchmen, left Kaskaskia during February, 1779 and headed northeasterly toward Vincennes. This move by Clark was planned to surprise the British garrison at Vincennes by bringing the fight to them, as well as to catch the British off guard and without their usual complement of Indian allies who had gone home for the winter.[6]

Clark's strategy worked. Hamilton and his British soldiers and French militia surrendered Fort Sackville after two days of half-hearted defense. The Americans, jubilant with their victory, renamed the Vincennes garrison Fort Patrick Henry to pay homage to the Virginia governor who had backed the enterprise of wrestling the West from British control.[7]

Everybody loves a winner, and George Rogers Clark was a winner. Between March and November, 1779, Clark's Illinois Battalion grew steadily as word of his undertaking reached the frontier settlements. Recruitment for the Illinois Battalion improved as a result of Clark's battlefield successes.

In November, 1779, Clark called a Council of War with his junior officers to discuss the final part of his enterprising campaign–the building of a fort and a civilian community near the Mouth of the Ohio River, thereby forming a chain of defense to Virginia's western border, but also visibly marking Virginia's claim of land stretching from the Atlantic Ocean in the east to the Mississippi in the west.[8]

During January, 1780, the new governor of Virginia, Thomas Jefferson, wrote letters to Joseph Martin, Indian agent; Daniel Smith, surveyor for Virginia; Thomas Walker, surveyor for Virginia; and George Rogers Clark.[9] He directed Martin to contact the Cherokee Indians from whom Martin was to purchase land for the new fort. Jefferson did not know at the time, that rather than the Cherokee, it was the Chickasaw Indians–allies of the British–who claimed the area upon which the fort would be constructed. This error would prove costly for the American cause.

Jefferson further instructed Daniel Smith and Thomas Walker to meet Clark at the site and to determine precisely the exact location, or latitude, of Clark's new fort, making sure it fell within Virginian territory and not within state rival North Carolina's land. In his communication to Clark, Jefferson gave permission to build the fort and an adjacent civilian community. The latter, Jefferson wrote, could be used to support the fort by growing food supplies Virginia could not afford to send. A civilian community also would attract young men whom Clark could actively recruit. Jefferson's words to Clark in the former instance proved prophetic. Virginia would not send food.

---

[5] John D. Barnhart, editor, *Henry Hamilton and George Rogers Clark in the American Revolution with The Unpublished Journal of Lieut. Gov. Henry Hamilton.* 1951, R.E. Banta, Crawfordsville, Indiana.
[6] James, ed., 1972.
[7] Barnhart, ed., 1951.
[8] James, ed., 1972.
[9] *Ibid.*

Clark and Robert Todd, the brother of John Todd and acting paymaster of the Illinois country, discussed the feasibility of reducing the garrisons in the Illinois country and concentrating the populations at the new fort at the Mouth of the Ohio. Some resettlement occurred, and Kentucky County, the westernmost Virginian county in 1780, saw its single largest influx of settlers, more than 10,000 during a single year. More than 500 would venture to Fort Jefferson. By midyear, reshuffling of the Illinois population no longer seemed necessary.

To obtain settlers for the community and additional soldiers for his army, Virginia authorized Clark to grant 300 land warrants, each worth 560 acres, to every new soldier. By April, 1780, only a few additional supplies were needed before Clark could leave the Falls of the Ohio (present-day Louisville) for the new post. So promising were the prospects of the new settlement and garrison that William Shannon, Clark's commissary at the Falls, requested six months' provisions for 1,000 men, an optimistic action to say the least.[10]

Clark, about 175 soldiers, and an untold number of civilians arrived April 19, 1780, at the spot selected for the new settlement.[11] In honor of the presiding Virginia Governor, Thomas Jefferson, Clark called the new post Fort Jefferson. The adjacent civilian community became known as Clarksville, or Clark's Town, also called Iron Banks because of the yellowish color to the eroded hills fronting the Mississippi River. The fort and community were on a slightly elevated floodplain between Mayfield Creek, also then called Liberty Creek,[12] and a series of eroded bluffs located to the north. The main stream of the Mississippi River was then about one-half mile west of the fort (Figure 3.1). Clark's men and the settlers set to the task at hand: clearing the woods and constructing the outpost and town. Approximately 17 acres of ground would be cleared on Island No. 1 in the Mississippi River adjacent to the fort, and 30 acres of ground in the "outlands" outside, but adjacent to the civilian community of Clarksville. A small picketed fort, approximately 100 feet square with several buildings built within, including two floored bastions, at least three storehouses, a barracks, and a powder magazine. Outside the fort were houses, a saw pit, and several other structures spread throughout a 101-in-lot area immediately east of the fort, between the fort and newly cleared and planted corn fields.[13] Clark, however, would have little further time to invest with the fort or settlement.

Jefferson, writing from Williamsburg, suggested Clark lead a force into the Shawnee country to counter Indian attacks on the central Kentucky settlements. Jefferson did not realize that a more pressing issue was developing near Clark's new post. Word arrived at Fort Jefferson that a strong force of Indians and British soldiers was expected to attack both St. Louis (also referred to as Pancore) and Cahokia. Taking all but 18 regulars from Fort Jefferson, and leaving Captain Robert George in charge of the new post, Clark proceeded north to Cahokia, arriving May 24, two days before the Battle of

---

[10] James, ed., 1972.
[11] Kenneth C. Carstens, *The Calendar and Quartermaster Books of George Rogers Clark's Fort Jefferson, 1780-1781*. Heritage Books, Bowie, Maryland, 2000.
[12] By no co-incidence, Clark and his soldiers arrived at the selected location of Fort Jefferson on the fifth anniversary of the Battles of Lexington and Concord. It is not any wonder, then, that they named Mayfield Creek "Liberty Creek," possibly in remembrance of the former military action outside of Boston five years earlier.
[13] Draper Manuscripts, Wisconsin Historical Society, Madison, 1M8-11.

St. Louis. Clark and the united forces of French, Spanish, and American soldiers promptly defeated the British and Indian raiders, although casualties on the Spanish side of the river were high. Clark and his soldiers successfully defended Cahokia.[14]

Meanwhile, word reached Fort Jefferson from O'Post (Fort Patrick Henry in Vincennes) that British attacks on the central Kentucky settlements were expected any day. News also was received that the Spanish planned to attack the British strongholds at Mobile and Pensacola, actions which would help free trade on the Mississippi and further strengthen the economic vitality of Fort Jefferson. A free Mississippi River meant free access to world markets *vis-a-vis* New Orleans.

By June 1, Clark's triumphant Illinois Battalion relocated at Fort Jefferson. On June 4, 1780, Captain Robert George, Fort Jefferson's commandant, advised Clark that the construction of the new post was nearing completion. Captain George hoped to have the garrison enclosed with pickets by the end of that week and the settlers, George wrote, were nearly finished with planting their crops (corn and turnips).[15]

The fort was enclosed none too soon. By June 7, marauding Chickasaw Indians began killing members of the Clarksville militia who were surprised on the outskirts of town. Although it had not been a full-scale attack, the Indians' presence was a considerable menace to the fort and settlement.[16]

By June 10, Clark had returned to Fort Jefferson with his soldiers, and the Indian problem faded into the background. A more demanding obstacle redirected Clark's attention.

An express messenger from the Falls of the Ohio brought word of an increased number of hostile Indian attacks in the central Kentucky area. Colonel Daniel Brodhead at Fort Pitt preferred not to deal with the problem, recommending, instead, that Clark attack the Shawnee "from his quarter."[17]

On June 10, 1780, Clark and two other men left Fort Jefferson for the Falls of the Ohio. Between June 10 and 14, considerable issues of goods and clothing were made at Fort Jefferson to outfit Clark's army for the impending Shawnee campaign.[18] By mid-June, half of the Fort Jefferson troops traveled to meet Clark at the Mouth of the Licking River (across from present-day Cincinnati) to launch the expedition against the Shawnee. Clark had begun recruiting for the operation as soon as he had reached the Falls, hoping to use more than 1,000 soldiers against the Shawnee.

The civilian community at Fort Jefferson continued to grow and to prosper. On June 13, several Clarksville trustees (James Piggott, Ezekiel Johnson, Henry Smith, Joseph Hunter, and Mark Iles) wrote to the Virginia government to have Clarksville and its surrounding area recognized as a new Virginia county, which, if approved, would give the county a vote in the Virginia legislature. Their petition was sent along with the troops leaving Fort Jefferson June 14, 1780 on their way to join Clark's Shawnee expedition.[19]

---

[14] John Francis McDermott, "The Battle of St. Louis, 26 May 1780." *Bulletin of the Missouri Historical Society*, St. Louis.
[15] Unpublished George Rogers Clark Papers, Virginia State Library, Richmond. Also, James, ed., 1972.
[16] Margery Heberling Harding, *George Rogers Clark and His Men: Military Records, 1778-1784*. The Kentucky Historical Society, Frankfort.
[17] James, ed., 1972.
[18] Carstens, 2000.
[19] James, ed., 1972.

For the next two weeks, all went well at the post on the Mississippi. Numerous issues of cloth were made into soldiers' clothing for officers and enlistee alike. The fort's bartering system was well established, as witnessed by the type and kind of payments received by the tailors and seamstresses who made clothing for the soldiers. A company of Virginia light dragoons (cavalry) commanded by Captain John Rogers, a maternal cousin of George Rogers Clark, was newly outfitted with clothing and was provisioned at Fort Jefferson with everything, including saddles--only there were no horses.[20] On July 14, 1780, the company departed by foot for Cahokia, and Lieutenant Colonel John Montgomery left for Fort Clark at Kaskaskia.

At daybreak, three days later, the Chickasaw Indians again attacked the Clarksville community, killing two of the militia and wounding several others. The fight, however, was brief and led to relatively little destruction. The shooting was primarily a test by the Chickasaw to determine the military strength of both the fort and community. After obtaining the information they needed, the Indians withdrew.[21]

On July 20, 1780, Laurence Keenan and Joshua Archer were sent as expresses to Fort Clark, where they sought the assistance of Lieutenant Colonel Montgomery. Sixty-five Kaskaskia Indians and 10 members of Captain Richard McCarty's company arrived from Fort Clark to assist Fort Jefferson on July 31, 1780. The Indian allies were employed primarily by Captain George to hunt for the garrison, the garrison being too fearful of venturing beyond the confines of the fort's walls to fend for themselves. Also arriving from Fort Clark was William Clark, paternal cousin to George Rogers Clark, not George's young brother. John Bailey and William Clark brought with them 1,400 pounds of flour, 50 bushels of corn and 28 men from Bailey's company of infantry to help shore up the defenses of Fort Jefferson.[22]

Members of the fort and community entered August pleased that they successfully had thwarted two attacks by the Chickasaw Indians. Undoubtedly they also were proud that they had helped defeat the combined Anglo-Indian assault on St. Louis and Cahokia the preceding May. Recent arrivals at Fort Jefferson, Captain Richard McCarty and his French military company from Kaskaskia, along with Timothe B. Monbreun, added to the feeling of security at the post. But it now was understood that an attack by the Chickasaw might occur at any time and might come from any quarter. Therefore, a higher status of alert was ordered and arms and munitions were issued to the troops to maintain a "prepared" normalcy.

On the morning of August 27, 1780, the civilians and soldiers of Fort Jefferson once again were tested by the Chickasaw.[23] This time, however, a larger band of Chickasaw attacked the community and its garrison, first firing upon African slaves who had gone into the corn fields early in the morning, then upon the blockhouses, fort, and community. Estimates of the attackers' number varied. The most conservative figure came from Captain George, who suggested that 150 Chickasaw had assailed the post. In this encounter, the Chickasaw were led by Lieutenant William Whitehead, a member of

---

[20] Kenneth C. Carstens, "Issues at Fort Jefferson, 1780-1781," this volume.
[21] James, ed., 1972.
[22] Kenneth C. Carstens, *The Personnel of George Rogers Clark's Fort Jefferson and Civilian Community of Clarksville [Kentucky], 1780-1781*. Heritage Books, Bowie, Maryland, 1999.
[23] Seineke, 1981.

the British Southern Indian Department, and by James Colbert, a Chickasaw half-breed "Big Man."

Halfway through the battle, Colbert appeared with a flag of truce and demanded the surrender of the post to prevent additional bloodshed. Captain Leonard Helm, Captain George's second-in-command, told Colbert the Americans would not surrender. Wheeling to walk away from the parley, Colbert was shot in the back by a Kaskaskia Indian. Fighting recommenced later that evening. At the end of the fourth day of battle, August 30, the Chickasaw retreated, but not before they had destroyed much of the corn crop and had killed many of the settlers' cattle and sheep. In addition to these losses, several African American slaves had been shot by the Chickasaw, and a number of the militia were wounded severely or killed during the battle. Captain John Bailey's company had been ambushed by the Chickasaw while on a hunting party. Four members of his troop were killed and a fifth had been taken prisoner. Nevertheless, the state of preparedness during early August probably saved many more lives at the post and thwarted another attempt by the Chickasaw. But the damage was done, not in persons killed, but in crops that had been burned and destroyed the only guaranteed sustenance the fort and community had.[24]

September was a depressing time for the inhabitants and soldiers of Fort Jefferson. With much of the corn crop destroyed, there was little, if any, hope for food during the forthcoming months. The few bushels of corn garnered from the devastated fields barely fed the garrison, let alone the town's men, women, and children. Fearful of spending a winter with little or no food, 24 of the town's 40 families moved between September 12 and 14, electing to go down the Mississippi River to New Orleans, up the Mississippi to Kaskaskia, or up the Ohio River to the Falls area.[25] To make matters worse, there were many desertions from Clark's Illinois Battalion.[26] Although there were then fewer mouths to feed at Fort Jefferson, there also were fewer inhabitants and soldiers to defend the post or to assist with the continued construction of the new town.

September marked the beginning of the "sickly" season, as Captain George called it.[27] An examination of the September vouchers vividly illustrates that many persons, soldiers and civilians alike, became sick with the ague (flu) or began suffering from the effects of malaria.[28] As a result, the garrison and town had fewer people than before and those who remained generally were too ill to move or deserted their posts.

Not all was gloomy, however. On September 6, a load of supplies arrived by boat from New Orleans; part of the cargo included 1,200 pounds of gunpowder.[29] On September 10, a party of Kaskaskia Indian allies was granted permission by Captain George to seek revenge against the Chickasaw for the recent hostilities. George must have felt confident to let so many from his post abandon their post to carry the fight to the Chickasaw.

---

[24] Kenneth C. Carstens, "George Rogers Clark's Fort Jefferson, 1780-1781." *The Filson Club History Quarterly*, 1997 (71):259-284.
[25] James, ed. 1972.
[26] Harding, 1981.
[27] James, ed. 1972.
[28] Carstens 1997, 1999, 2000.
[29] Carstens, Munition Supplies at George Rogers Clark's Fort Jefferson, this volume.

October was not much of an improvement from September. Between the fourth and fifth, four more persons were killed by ambush near the fort.[30] Although additional ammunition was issued to the inhabitants of the post and town, the Indians never fully showed themselves, keeping just outside the community where they could harass the settlers and soldiers. Sickness continued to prevail, as did further desertions.

Physical problems now were accompanied by political intrigue. Lieutenant Colonel John Montgomery arrived with Captain John Williams from Kaskaskia on October 22. Lieutenant Colonel Montgomery wanted Captain George to relinquish his command to Captain Williams. George refused, subsequently writing to Colonel Clark to explain that he would not forego his command unless ordered to do so by Clark. Williams, obviously caught in an awkward situation, also wrote to Clark, stating that he would not take command until he received orders from Clark.[31] Although Montgomery and George did not get along, Montgomery assisted George in his efforts to save the post. By October 28, Montgomery left Fort Jefferson for New Orleans to procure additional supplies for the garrison and community. Writing later that day, Captain George observed that Fort Jefferson had been reduced severely by famine, desertion, and death. Now, during near-drought conditions, low water in the Mississippi hampered efforts to get supplies to the fort.

Montgomery's assistance in New Orleans paid off when a shipment of new supplies arrived in November. Even so, soldiers and civilians spent most of their time, when not too ill, making nets to seine for fish in the shallows of the Mississippi River. The American frontiersmen experienced a relatively better month during December, 1780. In his letter to George Rogers Clark during the first few days of December, John Donne, the Fort's deputy commissary, reported that militia Major Silas Harlan and other hunters had been successful in bringing more than 8,000 pounds of buffalo, bear, and deer meat to the fort. Unfortunately, there still were more than 150 persons in the garrison, 20 civilian families who had to be fed, and the expectation that several new military companies might arrive any day.[32] Food, although now available, was still in short supply.

On the 12th of December, and again on the 15th, cargo supplies arrived from New Orleans and from the Falls of the Ohio. Both shipments included primarily munitions and dry goods. No food. While these loads contained new shoes, which were welcomed, the newly arrived dry goods would have to be used as barter for food in Kaskaskia and other Illinois towns. In spite of a bleak outlook, Christmas was greeted by Captain George's company of artillery by expending 60 pounds of gunpowder in salutes fired from Fort Jefferson's five swivels and two cannon.[33]

Within a few days following Christmas another shipment from New Orleans arrived and was delivered by Captain Philip Barbour on behalf of Oliver Pollock, American agent in New Orleans. Barbour, seeing the depressed condition of the fort and civilian community, negotiated the sale of $25,000 worth of cargo for $237,320 hard specie. Not wanting to lose the supplies, Captain George conferred with his fellow

---

[30] Carstens, 2000.
[31] James, ed. 1972.
[32] Unpublished Clark Papers.
[33] *Ibid.*

officers and agreed to meet Captain Barbour's outrageous demand.[34] The cargo, consisting primarily of dry goods and tafia (watered-down rum), immediately was put to use. In subsequent years, Captain George would be called on the carpet for agreeing to Barbour's piracy.[35]

In high spirits from the tafia, the community and soldiers raised their cups to what appeared to be a bright and shiny new year. Supplies were unloaded, repacked, and sent to Kaskaskia and to the Falls to procure foodstuffs for the garrison and civilian community.

Another part of Barbour's shipment included munitions. Nearly every member of the garrison, including militia and Indians, received a new sword, and Clark's Illinois Battalion officers obtained their new clothing allotments for the year. In addition, the Kaskaskia Indians were granted permission, again, to attack the Chickasaw to the south. Dodge's quartermaster stores issued many scalping knives for use by the American allies.

January revealed the growing dislike shared by the fort's officers and civilians for Captain John Dodge, Indian agent and quartermaster of the Illinois Department. Although Dodge would have but a few months left at Fort Jefferson (he spent the first part of the spring at Kaskaskia, then left to settle his books at Richmond, taking Clark's records with him), several of the inhabitants felt cheated by his dealings, and he proved to be a constant source of friction with the officers.[36]

On January 23, 1781, another boatload of supplies was received at Fort Jefferson. A tafia ration (one gill each) for January 30 showed that 110 men remained in the garrison. Captain John Bailey and his company of infantry had departed for O'Post (Vincennes) earlier that month.

February and March of the new year witnessed several activities that would dominate post functions for the next several months. Fort Jefferson became the hub for the distribution of arms, munitions, dry goods, and liquor as military companies arrived from other Illinois outposts and companies from Fort Jefferson delivered supplies to them. Fort Jefferson finally was becoming Clark's economic center and military stronghold along the Mississippi as he and the two governors of Virginia had hoped. Except there was little to eat.

Fort Jefferson's prosperity began to erode, however, as quickly as it had been achieved. Although the post then had more dry goods, munitions, and rum (and whiskey) than it possibly could use, its larder still was quite empty in spite of daily hunting parties comprised of soldiers and Indians. No matter how much tafia was consumed (and incredible amounts were), daily meals consisted of little solid food. Grumbling and discontent with the post's conditions were made evident and settled only through courts of inquiry.[37]

During March, courts of inquiry were convened to examine the conduct and character of two of the fort's newly arrived officers, Captains Edward Worthington and Richard McCarty.[38] Worthington, who had postponed for months his trip from the Falls

---

[34] James, ed. 1972.
[35] *Ibid.*, Vol. II.
[36] James, ed. 1972; Draper Manuscripts, various.
[37] Draper Manuscripts, 56J18, 56J22, 56J25, 56J27, 56J29, 56J40, 56J45; see Fort Jefferson Legal Matters, this volume..
[38] *Ibid.*

to Fort Jefferson, was accused of retailing liquor, gambling with the soldiery, and frequently disobeying orders. McCarty, on the other hand, was charged with threatening to leave the service (as well as Virginia) and with insulting a fellow officer. The outcome of Worthington's court of inquiry is unknown. McCarty was found guilty, and a general court-martial was recommended. His chief accuser was John Dodge. McCarty would not suffer the embarrassment of a court-martial, however. Two months later, while en route to the Falls, he was killed by Indians.[39]

Near the end of March, a third court of inquiry was scheduled in the public store at Fort Jefferson. The session examined the conduct of Captain John Rogers, who had been in command at Fort Clark in Kaskaskia. These charges had been brought by Dodge again, but this time the court found the charges to be without substance and acquitted Rogers.[40]

March was a "happy" month for the majority of the Irish-American officers and soldiers. Their consumption of large quantities of tafia and whiskey truly was amazing, as were their excuses for imbibing the libations. Whether drinking to Saint Patrick's health or death, or maybe even toasting Saint Patrick's wife, Shealy, the Fort Jefferson community members properly celebrated their ethnic customs.[41]

On the other side of the coin, however, there existed discontent and boredom. Lieutenant John Girault, for example, pleaded in a letter to George Rogers Clark that he might be sent on an expedition or otherwise employed usefully somewhere, implying that nothing of consequence was occurring at Fort Jefferson. As tensions relaxed so did discipline. James Taylor and David Allen were court-martialed on charges of speaking disrespectfully to an officer, beating an officer's servants, and robbing an officer's kitchen. Taylor was acquitted, but Allen was found guilty and received 50 lashes on his bare back.[42]

April brought heavy rains, which, in turn, raised water levels dangerously high in nearby Mayfield Creek and the Mississippi River. As a result, by April 25, 1781, many items in the public store had to be removed to higher ground by the fort's soldiers.

Several letters were received in April from General George Rogers Clark. (Clark's promotion from colonel to general had occurred during January, 1781). The content of those letters is unknown, but as Clark had received permission to plan an assault against Fort Detroit from George Washington,[43] it is possible that these letters focused on Detroit and that Clark suggested to his officers that they begin preparing for the evacuation of Fort Jefferson.

By the 10th of May, Lieutenant Colonel Montgomery returned to Fort Jefferson. Shortly after his arrival, increased unhappiness at the post led one of the militia men to attempt a break-in at the fort's public store, forcing Captain George to call for the inspection of the town.[44]

---

[39] Carl R. Baldwin, *Captains of the Wilderness: The American Revolution on the Western Frontiers*. Tiger Rose Publishing Company, Belleville, IL, 1986.
[40] "Legal Matters," this volume.
[41] Unpublished Clark Papers.
[42] "Legal Matters," this volume.
[43] James, ed. 1972; "Letters," this volume.
[44] Carstens, Calendar, 2000.

Evidence of decline was all too apparent. By the first of May the number of men remaining in the garrison was down to 58.[45] It is evident that the decision to evacuate Fort Jefferson was made prior to June 5, 1781. On that date Captain Abraham Keller's company left the fort for the Falls area.[46] The remaining soldiers and civilians departed June 8, 1781, the official date of evacuation.[47] The order for evacuation came quickly and was carried out even more quickly. Numerous goods, far too cumbersome to remove, were left at the old fort, many of the items being tossed into the fort's well (e.g., a spiked iron cannon, 50 stand of old muskets, the pointed or "beak" end to the blacksmith's anvil, and an old wagon), and the earthly remains of at least 38 men, women, and children who were buried in coffins in the post's cemetery.[48]

The fort, occupied for only 416 days, had served its function. The fort's presence, though short-lived, on Virginia's western boundary (as well as the Virginian military occupations of Kaskaskia and of Vincennes) provided the physical evidence the state needed to justify its claim to its chartered boundaries. On July 12, 1781, tired and exhausted, the Fort Jefferson survivors arrived at General Clark's new stronghold, Fort Nelson, at the Falls of the Ohio.[49] Thus ended the saga of George Rogers Clark's Fort Jefferson.

---

[45] Unpublished Clark Papers.
[46] *Ibid.*
[47] Lt. Col. John Montgomery to Governor Thomas Nelson, August 10, 1781 gives the specific evacuation date of Fort Jefferson, in James, ed. 1972.
[48] Unpublished Clark Papers.
[49] Carstens, 2000.

CHAPTER 4: CORRESPONDENCE TO, FROM, AND ABOUT FORT JEFFERSON, 1777-1802

This chapter consists of a chronological listing of letters sent to, sent from, or written about Fort Jefferson between 1777 and 1802. This collection of letters is by no means complete. The letters themselves refer to other letters written from Fort Jefferson that have yet to be found. Yet for the first time, collected in one location, is the correspondence of Clark's Fort Jefferson. No attempt has been made to correct the often phonetic spellings used by the writers of these letters (some more than others) or add punctuation that frequently was not included--especially by George Rogers Clark or John Montgomery. Nor was capitalization (upper or lower case) corrected--even though in many instances correction was warranted. Where possible, the original source for each letter is cited as a footnote; when a letter has been copied from a previously published source, that source is also given. The following letters tell the story of Fort Jefferson in the words of the people who were there, or who were contemporary with the Fort Jefferson venture.

GOVERNOR PATRICK HENRY TO THE GOVERNOR OF LOUISIANA (Don Bernardo De Galvez)[1]

October 20, 1777   Williamsburg

Sir: I humbly conceive that it is an object worthy the attention of Your Excellency and of the Ministers of Spain, although the grandeur of your nation does not depend on Commerce, to secure the Trade at least of the Southern States of America, and thereby deprive their ancient and natural enemy the English of all those vast supplies of naval Stores, and many other Articles which have enabled them to become so powerful on the Seas; Immense Quantitys of Hemp, Flax, Skins, Furrs, Beef, Pork, Flower, Staves, Shingles &^{c}. the produce of our back country might be easily carried down the Mississippi to New Orleans, which place if it were made a free Port, would be resorted to by the French, and Dutch, who might take off the Tobacco and other Articles, which Spain would not want for her own consumption. Indeed if you were once more in possession of the two Floridas, you might enjoy a great part of the Trade of our Northern States. If your Excellency should think it would be worthy the attention of your Court to cultivate a correspondence with these States through the Mississippi, we would establish a post at the mouth of the Ohio, to facilitate the necessary intercourse between us. I have ordered our agent at St. Domingo to apply for some of the Stores, which by your kind assistance we understand are lodged at New Orleans for our use. We have not received your Excellency's letter on this subject, but are informed by the President of the Congress that such Letter has been delivered to the Committee of Congress. I shall also order a Boat down the Mississippi, for the remainder of the Stores at News Orleans, by which I shall do myself the honor to write more fully to your Excellency.

I have the honor to be with great respect.

---

[1] Lawrence Kinnaird (editor), Spain in the Mississippi Valley, 1765-1794. *Annual Report of the American Historical Association for the Year 1945, Vol. II*, 241-242, Washington, D.C.

Your Excellency's most obed^ت. Humble Servant.

Patrick Henry, Governor of Virginia

PATRICK HENRY TO THE GOVENOR OF LOUISIANA, January 14, 1778[2]

Sir: I have taken the Liberty to trouble your Excellency with several Letters lately which went by Sea And considering how Liable our Vessels are to be taken by the British Cruizers, and that the intercourse with New Orleans was precarious in that Rout, I informed your Excellency that I should send a Messenger to wait on you by way of the Mississippi. Colonel David Rogers will have the honour to wait on you with this, & to receive such Commands as your Excellency may please to have on that River, which by opening an easy and safe communication with the Gulph of Mexico invites to that Intercourse & correspondence between the Subjects of his Catholic Majesty & the good people of this Commonwealth which I flatter myself may be managed to the Advantage of both. An Infant State engaged in a formidable War, procuring with difficulty many Articles necessary for maintaining it with vigor, must feel considerable Distresses. These Virginia feels; but thanks to Heaven they are not greater than her Courage to encounter them. Her own internal Resources, aided by perseverance have removed some of them, while others have been alleviated by the friendly Interposition of the Spanish & French Nations, and signal Successes have in many Instances crowned the American Arms.

Sensible of the Value of that Friendship which your nation hath tendered to Virginia & of the Favours received from you, I am anxious to make the best Returns in my power—

1. I beg your Excellency to consider whether the annexing West Florida to the American Confederation will not greatly distress the English West India Settlements & hinder the progress of their Rivalship to Spain. I'm told they get supplies of Lumber & some provisions & other things from Mississippi. These the Americans can easily stop if it would be acceptable t your Nation.

2. I have thought it necessary, for securing the Intercourse with New Orleans, to build a Fort some where near the Mouth of Ohio (but that shall depend upon what your Excellency shall please to write me on the Subject.) The inland navigation of Mississippi & Ohio, althou at present subject to many Inconveniences, has this great Advantage that British Cruizers cannot infest it. Our trade by Sea is very much distressed by them, which occasions the want of Woollens, particularly Blankets, Linens, & Military Stores. In order to supply these, Colonel Rogers will receive from your Excellency such goods as you may please to send by him & which in your Letters to congress were said to be lodged at New Orleans for this State.

The Operations of the War with England have been carried on to great Extent, in so much that the expenses of it are become heavy. This induces me to ask of your Excellency whether it would be possible for you to furnish this State with a Sum of Money or Loan, suppose One hundred & fifty thousand Pistoles or what other Sum?

---

[2] Ibid., 248-250.

Whether this Sum would be most conveniently advanced at New Orleans, the Havanah, Cadiz, or what other place?

3. Your Excellency will naturally enquire what I have to give in Exchange for these Advances? I answer the Gratitude of this Free & Independent Country, the Trade in any, or all of its valuable productions , & the Friendship of its warlike Inhabitants (at present I know not upon which of these things you set the greatest value. But they are tendered to you & you will have a Right to chuse that which is most acceptable to your Excellency & the Spanish Nation.)

I beg leave to refer you to Colonel Rogers for the explanation of any matters you may wish to know concerning this Commonwealth & the progress of the War. He is a Gentleman in whom your Excellency may place Confidence. He will be able to give satisfaction in many particulars which cannot fall within the Compass of a Letter.

I must entreat your Excellency's peculiar Favor & protection to this Gentleman, and that in this progress Homewards he may meet with every assistance which his situation & circumstances may require.

Six hundred thousand people of all Ages are Subjects of this Commonwealth, very small proportion of our Country is, as yet, Cultivated, & we have more land than can be settled for many Ages to come. Our Manufacturers are yet in their Infancy, but Agriculture has flourished to great Extent & enables us to spare Commodities of great Value and Variety.

For an Inumeration of these Commoditys I must refer to my former Letters. I wish that such of them may be selected by your Excellency in Return for the goods & the Money I ask on Loan , as may best suit with your Occasions, & that I may have the earliest Information on the Subject. With Sentiments of the most perfect Esteem & Regards, I have the Honor to be Sir

Your Excellency most obedient & very humble Servant

P. Henry

I desire it may be remembered that I directed this Letter to be translated into French & have signed it & Col^o. Rogers will deliver it to his Excellency the Spanish Governor. But inasmuch as the French Language is not accurately understood by many persons here, the said Translation is imperfect, & particularly in the parts marked No. 1, No. 2, & No. 3, where the Sense is omitted in the French letter. But this Letter written in the English Language on this paper, I send as authentic, & that on which I rely, & will consider as containing the sense & meaning of the Executive Power of Virginia.

Done at Williamsburg aforesaid

P.Henry

THOMAS JEFFERSON TO GOVERNOR GALVEZ[3]

November 8, 1779   WILLIAMSBURG

Sir/ By M^r. Lindsay who was sent from our County of Illinois on the Mississippi, to New Orleans and lately arrived here on his return by the way of Havannah, we hear that Colo. Rogers had left new Orleans and proceeded up the Mississippi. We are anxiously expecting by him your Excellency's answer to the Letters of 14th January 1778 by Colo. Rogers and January 26th 17778 by Capt. Young from Governor Henry to whom I have had the honour of Succeeding on his resignation. the accession of his most Catholic Majesty since the date of these Letters to the hostilities carrying on by the confederated powers of France and North America, against Great Britain, thereby adding to their Efforts the weight of your powerful & wealthy empire, has given us all the certainty of a happy issue to the present contest of which human events will admit.—Our vicinity to the State over which you immediately preside, the direct Channel of commerce by the river Mississippi, the nature of those Commodities with which we can reciprocally furnish each other, point out the advantages which may result from a close connection and correspondence, for which on our part the best foundations are laid by a grateful sense of the favours we have received at your hands. Notwithstanding the pressure of the present War on our people they are lately beginning to extended their Settlements rapidly on the waters of the Mississippi and we have reason to believe that on this particularly and the branches immediately communicating with it there will in the course of another year be such as number of Settlers as to render their Commerce an object worth your notice fro New Orleans alone can they be tolerably supplied with necessaries of European manufacture, and thither they will send in exchange, Staves & peltry immediately & flour, pork, and Beef as soon as they shall have somewhat opened their Lands. For their protection from the Indians we are obliged to send and Station among them a considerable armed force, the providing of which with Clothing & the friendly Indians with necessaries, becomes a matter of great difficulty with us for the smaller forces have hitherto kept up at Kaskaskia on the Mississippi, we have contracted a considerable Debt at New Orleans with M^r. Pollock, besides what is due to your State for the supplies they have generously furnished, and a number of bills from Col^o. Clarke now lying under protest in New Orleans. We learn by Mr. Lindsay that Mr. Pollock is likely to be greatly distressed if we do not immediately make him remittances. The most unfavourable harvest every known since the settlement of this Country has put it out of our power to send flour obliging us for our own Subsistence to purchase it from the neighboring States of Maryland and Pennsylvania, to whom we have ever 'til this year furnished large quantities. The want of Salt disables us from preparing Beef and Pork for your market. In this situation of things we cannot but contemplate the distress of that Gentleman brought on him by services rendered us, with the utmost concern. We are endeavouring by remittances of Tobacco to establish a fund in France to which we may apply to a certain extent; but the Casualties to which those Tobaccoes and liable in their transportation render this dependence less certain than we could wish for M^r. Pollock's

---

[3] Ibid., 362-364.

relief and besides that we have very extensive occasion for them—Young as we are in trade and manufactures, and engaged in war with a Nation whose power on the Sea has been such as to intercept a great proportion of the Supplies we have attempted to import from Europe, you will not wonder to hear that we find great difficulties in procuring either money or commodities to answer the calls for our Armies and therefore that it would be a circumstance of great relief to us if we could leave our deposits in France for the Calls of that part of our State which lies on the Atlantic & procure a suspension of the demands from your quarter for supplies to our Western forces one two or three years or such longer time as could be obtained. With this view governor Henry in his letters of January 14 & 26, 1778 solicited from your Nation a Loan of Money, which your Excellency was so kind as to undertake to communicate to your Court. The success of this application we expect to learn by Col^o Rogers, and should not, til then, have troubled you on the same subject had we not heard of M^r. Pollocks distress, as we flatter ourselves that that application through the intervention of your Excellency may have been successful and that you may be authorized to advance for us some loans in money. I have taken the liberty of soliciting you in such case to advance for us to M^r. Pollock 65,814 5/8 Dollars. Encompassed as we are with difficulties we may fail in doing as much as our gratitude would prompt us to in speedily replacing these aids, but most assuredly nothing in that way within our power will be left undone. Our particular prospects for doing it, and the time it may take to accomplish the whole shall be the subject of another Letter as soon as I shall have the honor to learn from you whether we can be supplied and to what extent, By Col^o. Rogers I hope also to learn your Excellency's Sentiments on the other proposition in the same letters for the establishment of corresponding posts on your side and ours of the Mississippi near the mouth of the Ohio for the promotion of commerce between us.

After returning our most cordial thank to your Excellency for the friendly disposition you have personally shown to us, and assuring you of our profound respect and esteem beg leave to subscribe myself

Your Excellency's Most Obed^t. & Very h^{ble} Servant

Th. Jefferson
(Duplicate)

THOMAS JEFFERSON TO JOSEPH MARTIN, JANUARY 24, 1780[4]

W^{m}SBURG Jany 24, 1780

SIR We are very desirous of having a fort at the mouth of Ohio which together with other posts meant to be established on the Ohio may form a chain of defense for our Western frontier and at ye same time protect our Trade with New Orleans.[5] but the

---

[4] Original document, Draper Manuscripts, 46J57, Wisconsin Historical Society, Madison, Wisconsin, hereafter DMs Volume, Series, Page Number). Republished in James Alton James, ed., *George Rogers Clark Papers, 1771-1781*, Collections of the Illinois State Historical Library, Vol. VIII, Virginia Series, Volume III, Springfield, 1912. Republished by AMS Press, 1972: 385-386 (hereafter, *Clark Papers*).

[5] Major Joseph Martin was at the time Indian agent.

ground at the Mouth of Ohio on the South side belonging to the Cherokees we would not meddle with it without their leave. We wish you therefore to treat with them for as much as will do for this purpose and for a few settlements round it for the support of ye post. indeed if they should show a disposition to part with it you may treat for all their lands between the Mississippi, Ohio, Tanissee & Carolina boundary the whole being of but small extent. I think not exceeding 20 miles square if reduced to that form. If they do not discover a willingness to part with the whole, get ground for a fort & as much as you can round about it to make corn, furnish wood &c Obtain them on as good terms as possible to be paid for in goods, which we will have provided for them the whole when sold at our Land Office price will not bring in more than three thousand pounds Sterling. I think the goods must be got from New Orleans. I am in hopes they will not insist on our not beginning the fort till the delivery of ye goods, but if they do we must submit to it. Make your bargain, if you can, subject to our approbation or disapprobation, because this matter having never been proposed to the Assembly we should wish to have it in our power to decline it if they should so advise. Communicate without delay what you do to Colo Geo Rogers Clarke at Kaskaskias or the falls of Ohio & also to Sir

Your very hble Servant
TH JEFFERSON

MAJ^r MARTIN

THOMAS JEFFERSON'S INSTRUCTIONS TO CLARKE, JANUARY, 29, 1780[6]

WMSBURG Jan 29th 1780

SIR.

Your letters of October 26th and 28th and Nov^{br} 6th came safely to hand & lastly that of August 24th. I am glad the proposition of establishing a post at or near the Mouth of Ohio is likely to answer as well in practice as to us to us who judged on theory only, it seemed likely to do. I have therefore written to Messrs Walker & Smith as you will see by the enclosed copy of my letter to them, to stake observations of the Latitudes thereabouts that we may proceed on the surest grounds. You will please to furnish assistants, Guards, & all necessaries. I expect the description of the cliffs &c will be so minute as that when you see them you will know them in the plat & of course know their Latitude, the choice of the ground for your Fort must be left to yourself. It should be as near the Mouth of Ohio as can be found fit for fortification & within our own lines. Some attention would be proper also to the circumjacent grounds as it will probably become a town of importance. The nature of the defensive works & their extent you will accommodate to your Force. I would recommend your attention to the wood of which you make your stockades, that it be of the most lasting kind. from the best information I have had I take for granted that our line will pass below the Mouth of Ohio. Our purchases of the Cherokees hitherto have not extended Southward or westward of the Tennessee. of course the little Tract of country between the Mississippi Ohio Tennessee

---

[6] DMs 50J7; *Clark Papers*, 386-391.

& Carolina line (in which your Fort will be) still to be purchased from them before you can begin your works. To effect this I have written to Maj. Martin our Cherokee Agent of which letter I enclose you a copy.

If the new Fort should fall within this teritory & it can be purchased we may grant lands to Settlers who will fix round about the fort provided the Assembly should approve of it, as from its reasonableness I think they will. The manner in which the Lots of Land are laid off about the French Villages I have thought very wise & worthy of imitation perhaps besides guarding your promises of Lands to Settlers with the conditions above mentioned it would be well to add also the mode of laying them off. I send you recruiting instructions for having your Battalion filled up with men to be enlisted for the War as I wish to avoid receiving any on any other terms. Your instructions for recruiting which were communicated to us by some of your officers in the fall we took in and gave them such as are now sent you, instead of County money I send you three Hundred Land Warrants, for Five Hundred & Sixty acres of Land each which at Forty pounds the Hundred being the Treasury price amounts to the Bounty allowed by Law. these we think more likely to induce men to enlist than the money itself. I also send you twenty four blank Commissions which will be necessary to Officer eight companies the present plan of the Continental army having that number in a Battalion and a Captain Lieutenant & Ensign only to each company. The officers of your Battalion when commissioned will stand on a footing with the Officers of the other State Batt^{ns} The State of the Public Finances obliged the late Assembly to reduce very much their session in May. they discontinued raising both the additional Eastern Batt^{ns} & one of the Western. So there will be one Battalion only to send to you to which is to be annexed Major Slaughters Hundred men who have already marched as I expect for the falls of the Ohio. I wish that one Battalion may be raised in time to join you in the Spring, very few returns having been made to me I cannot say what number is raised probably not more than half. However, whatsoever number may be raised by that time shall march as soon as the season will admit. By them we will send such stores as to us occur to be necessary, such as Powder, Lead, Flints, Hoes, Axes, Saws, Gimblets, Nails, Hammers, Augurs, drawing Knives, Froes & Camp Kettles. If there be any other articles necessary I must get you to write to me on the Subject also to settle the best route of sending those articles hereafter there being no Guards to be had but Militia for conveying them form the Frontiers & no dependence on collecting Militia. Cannot you point out to us some place on the Frontiers where they may be safely lodged from time to time & from whence you can send for them with a proper escort? I would wish you also to inform me to what post I shall order the Battalion which is to join you. We received letters from Mr. Battalion which is to join you. We received letters from Mr. Pollock in the fall informing us of our debts at New Orleans & his distresses. We had just taken measures by shipping Tobacco to France to procure necessaries for our army having no other means of relieving Mr Pollock we were obliged to give him draughts on France which took the whole of that Fund & has distressed us exceedingly. The demands of Col Legras & Capt Lintot coming on us now & it being impossible to raise hard money to discharge them we are utterly at a loss what to do with them, indeed we shall not be able to determine them absolutely as to the sum we shall pay them till we know from you what proportion of the Dollars for which they have draughts were expended at the depreciated prices or in other words til we know from you what sum in hard money would reimburse their advances for which your draughts on us were made which we should be glad you would inform us by the first opportunity and send a duplicate by some second conveyance the difficulty of answering demands of hard money renders it necessary for us to contract no debts where our paper is not current it throws on us the tedious & perplexing operations of investing paper money in Tobacco, finding transportation for the Tobacco to France repeating this as often as the dangers of capture renders it necessary to insure the safe arrival of some part & negotiating Bills besides the expensive Train of Agents to do all this & the delay it occasions to the creditor. We must therefore recommend to you to purchase nothing beyond the Ohio which you can do without or which may be obtained from the East side where our paper is current. I am exceedingly glad you are making such a timely provision of your next years subsistence. A Commissary for the Western Deptmt: was appointed in the fall with orders to purchase provisions on the Frontier for one Battalion his instructions shall be enlarged & a notification sent him to comply with your requisitions besides this we leave to yourself to Commission Mr Shannon to act as Commisary of purchases Issues Stores, Quarter Master or what-ever else you may find him useful in. I suppose you will employ him principally about the Posts while the one acting in the Frontiers will be providing thereabouts. We shall use all our endeavours to furnish you men with necessary clothing but long experience renders it proper to warn you that our Supplies will be precarious You cannot therefore be too attentive to the providing them in your own Quarter as far as Skins will enable you to do it in short I must confide in you to take such care of the men under you as an economical householder would of his own family doing everything within himself as far as he can & calling for as few supplies as possible, the less you depend for supplies from this Quarter the less will you be disappointed by those impediments distance & a precarious foreign Commerce throw in the way for these reasons it will be eligible to withdraw as many of your men as you can form the West side of the Ohio leaving only so many as may be necessary for keeping the Illinois Settlements in Spirits & for their real defence. We must faithfully attend to their protection but we must accommodate our measures for doing this to our means perhaps this idea may render doubtful the expediency of employing your men in building a fort at Kaskaskia such Fort might perhaps be necessary for the Settlers to withdraw into in time of danger but might it not also render a surprise the more dangerous by giving the enemy a means of holding a Settlement which otherwise they could only distress by a sudden visit & be obliged to abandon Of this you must be ultimately the judge We approve much of a mild conduct towards the inhabitants of the French Villages It would be well to be introducing our Laws to their knowledge and to impress them strongly with the advantages of a Free Government the Training their Militia & getting it into subordination to proper Officers should be particularly attended to We wish them to consider us as Brothers & to participate with us the benefits of our rights & Laws We would have you cultivate peace & cordial friendship with the several tribes of Indians (the Shawanese expected) endeavor that those who are in friendship with us live in peace also with one another against those who are our Enemies let those the friendly Tribes The Kickapoos should be encouraged against the hostile Tribes of the Chickasaws and Choctaws and the others against the Shawnese with the latter be cautious of the terms of peace you admit an evacuation of their Country & removal utterly out of interference with us would be the most satisfactory. Amunition should be furnished gratis to those Warriors who go actually on expeditions against the Hostile Tribes As to the English notwithstanding their base example we wish not to expose them to the inhumanities of a savage enemy. Let this reproach remain on them, but for ourselves we would not have our national character tarnished with such a practice. If indeed they strike the Indians these will have a natural right to punish the aggressors and we note to hinder them it will then be no act of ours but to invite them to a participation of the [war] is what we would avoid by all possible means If the English would admit them to trade & by that means get those wants supplied which we cannot supply I should think it right provided they require from them no terms of departing form their neutrality, if they will not permit this I think the Indians might be urged to break off all correspondence with them to forbid their emissaries from coming among them & to send them to you if they disregarded the prohibitions, it would be well to communicate honestly to them our present want of those articles necessary for them & our inability to get them to encourage them to struggle with the difficulties as we do til peace when they may be confidently assured we will spare nothing to put their Trade on a comfortable and just footing in the mean time we must endeavor to furnish them with ammunition to provide Skins to clothe themselves, with a disposition to do them every friendly office & to gain their Love we would yet wish to avoid their visits except those who come with Capt Lintot We have found them very hard to please expensive & troublesome and they are moreover exposed to danger in passing our western counties it will be well therefore (especially during the War) to waive their visits in as inoffensive a way as possible.

In a letter to you of the 1st inst: I supposed you would in the ensuing Summer engage in either the Shawanee war or against Detroit leaving the choice of these & all other objects to yourself I must also refer to you whether it will be best to build the Fort at the Mouth of Ohio before you begin your campaign or after you shall have ended it, perhaps indeed the delays of obtaining leave from the Cherokees or of making a purchase from they may oblige you to postpone til the fall.

I have rec^d letter from Captains Shelby & Wortherington the former acquainting me he had rec^d your instructions to raise a Troop of Horse the latter that he had raised one form the date of your letter to Shelby I knew you could not have been apprised that the Assembly had authorized us to raise a Troop for you & that we had given a commission to Rogers by whom you sent us information of the capture of St. Vincennes, Rogers accordingly raised his men got all accoutrements & marched to join you in the fall. As to Capt Wotherington who sais he has raised his men you must state to us the necessity for your raising tow Troops, that we may ay it before the Assembly who alone have a power of giving sanction to the measure the distress of the Public Treasury will be a great obstacle so that it will be well for you to take measures for reserving to yourself the benefit of Capt Wotherington's men in some other capacity if they should be disapproved of as Horsemen.

I am Sir Your every humble Sev^t

TH JEFFERSON

THOMAS JEFFERSON TO THOMAS WALKER, January 29, 1780[7]

W^{MS}BURG Jany 29th 1780

SIR—

As we propose this spring to take possession of the fortify some post as near the mouth of Ohio as the ground will admit, it becomes very important for us to know the exact latitude thereabouts. I take it for granted that your present Line will be stopped before you get there by unpurchased Lands. We therefore wish extremely that one of you would take a trip to the mouth of Ohio with your instruments immediately upon finishing your present work. I Suppose it will be best for you to go to the falls of Ohio where Col^9 Clarke has orders to furnish you with Assistants, an escort and all necessaries. You will first find the point at which our Line strikes the Mississippi or Ohio, and fix it by some lasting immovable natural mark if there happen to be any on the spot, or if not, then by its course as corrected from the errors of variation, and the distance reduced to horizontal measure. the reason of requiring this accuracy in fixing the point where our Line strikes is, that in future, with common instruments is will be easy to find it which may perhaps be of importance. When you have found this point if it be on the Mississippi run from thence along up the river to the mouth of Ohio, and by protraction fix the point of the forks, or if it be on the Ohio, run up that river to where good Clifts for fortification shall make in and as you go along note the high grounds points or Clifts on the river which appear to you capable of Works of defence and at the same time to command a view of the river. This done I would ask the favor of you to return one plat of your work to Col^9 Clarke and another to me. Col^9 Clarke has in his eye a particular Cliff on the Mississippi which he expects is the nearest good ground for fortification. This he will describe to you, and you will please to note it particularly. I am in hopes that it will suit one of you to undertake this business. We think to have the fort begun, which cannot be till we are assured that the ground we should pitch on is within our own Country. The disappointment will therefore be of the greatest moment should you decline the Service.

I am Gent^l with the greatest respect Your most obed^t Hmble Servt

MESSRS THOMAS WALKER & DANIEL SMITH

GRANT OF LAND TO CLARK, January 29, 1780[8]

We the Publick auditors of the Commonwealth of Virginia do certify that George Rodgers Clark hath delivered to us the Treasurers receipt for Sixty-seven thousand two hundred pounds paid into the Treasury of Virginia—and that he the said George Rogers Clark, his heirs or assigns, are entitled to one hundred and Sixty eight thousand acres of

---

[7] DMs 50J6; *Clark Papers*, 392-393.
[8] DMS 46J22; *Clark Papers*, 393.

waste or unappropriated lands within this Commonwealth pursuant to an act entitled "an act for establishing a Land office, and ascertaining the terms and manner of granting waste and unappropriated lands." Given under our hands this twenty ninth day of January, 1780

THOS EVERARD
JAMES COCKER
EDWARD ARCHER

REGISTRATION OF GRANT OF LAND TO CLARK, January 29, 1780[9]

VIRG^A LAND OFFICE.
RICHMOND   25th Jan'y 1820

On the Register, No. 1, of Land Office Treasury Warrants issued at this Office, there are registered three hundred warrants, of five hundred and sixty acres each, numbered from 2087 to 2386, both inclusive, issued on the 29th day of January 1780, in favour of George Rogers Clark. At the foot of the registry of said 300 Warrants is a note in these words, viz:- "The above foregoing "three warrants, five hundred & sixty acres each, were "issued to Colo. George R. Clark for the purpose of recruiting his "Battallions, in lieu of the bounty of seven hundred and fifty "dollars." The document filed in this office as a voucher for said warrants is in the following words, viz:--"We the Publick Audi"tors of the Commonwealth of Virginia, do certify that George "Rogers Clarke hath delivered to us the Treasurer's receipt for "sixty seven thousand two hundred Pounds paid into the Treasury " of Virginia, & that he the said George Rogers Clarke, his heirs "or assigns are entitled to one hundred & sixty-eight thousand "acres of waste and unappropriated lands within this common"wealth pursuant to an act entitled, "an Act for establishing a "Land Office, and ascertaining the terms & manner of granting "waste and unappropriated lands." Given under our hands this "twenty-ninth day of January 1780.

THOS. EVERARD
JAMES COCKE
EDWARD ARCHER

Which document remains on file in this Office
Wm. G. Pendleton, Reg^r

---

[9] Unpublished Clark Papers, Archives Division, Virginia State Library, Richmond, hereafter, Unpublished Clark Papers; *Clark Papers*, 393.

CLARK TO JOHN TODD, JR.[10]

LOUISVILLE March 1780

D^R COL   By the Act^s from Every Post in the Illinois So nearly Corresponding I make no doubt of the English Regaining the Interest of Many Tribes of Indians and their designs ag^st the Illinois (Perhaps on Govr Hamiltons plan) and without some speady Check may prove Fatal to Kentucky and the Total loss of the West^n Countrey on the Mississippi I am not Clear but the Spaniards would fondly Suffer their Settlements in the Illinois to fall with ours for the sake of having the opertunity of Retaking Both I doubt they are too fond Territory to think of Restoring it again. Although there is but few British Troops on the Lakes defitiency is fully Replaced by the Immence Qualities of goods they have the effects of which among the Savages you well know not being apprehensive of a Visit I make no doubt of their having planed Some Expedition of Importance against our Posts which if they gain may be attended with the greatest Consequences than I have Hinted at they have greater opertunities of knowing our Cituation than we have of theirs which you know they Could not deprive us of, you well know the difficulties we have laboured under with our Joint Efforts to Maintain our Ground and Support our Interest among the Savages in that Dept and the reasons why wish is now greater than Ever as the bad Crops and the Severity of the winter hath Rendered it Impossible for the Towns in the Illinois to make any further Suppley untill next Harvest the Troops being Intituled to a discharge in a few weaks, Except those that have Reenlisted when Joined by Cap^tm Rogers when armed will not amount to more than one hundred and fifty which is too few under our present Circumstances to think of Deffending the different post we now Occupy. Letters from his Excellency and a promising Act from our Recruiting officers may perhaps soon alter our Apparent circumstances but as yet Receiving no advice from Either already meeting with many disadvantage of the Dep^t a few weaks Hesitation may be productive of long future disadvantage. I think it best to act as though we had no Expectation of being assisted Either with men or provitions. Your Councell not only necessary but which you know I prize is what I want. If we ware Tolerably formadable at any one post that we could Subsist at it might have a great and good Effect as I Hinted to lay aside all Expectation of a Reinforcement I see but the one probable Method of Maintan^g our Authority in the Illinois which is this by Amediatley Evacuating our present posts and let our whole force Center at or near the Mouth of Ohio which will be too Contemtable to answer the good effect proposed without fall upon some Method to draw of a Considerable Reinforce from Kentuck of Militia Families would be of the greatest Service as they are always followed by two or three times their number of young men they would with their Store provitions be able to Victual great part of our Troops in porportion to their numbers which if only one Hundred by the Ensuing fall would be able to Victual a Redgment besides Establishing a post that his Excellency is very Anctious for (the Reason I amigine we are boat Acq^td with) and the Interest of all the western Cuntrey Call for one Hund^d Families their followers the Troops we have already Ingaged, those whose time of Service is or Shortly will Expire that would Remain at the place when Joind would be Considerable the Report of which by the time it Reach our Enemies would be

---

[10] *Ibid, Clark Papers*, 404-406.

Augmented perhaps to Treble our numbers as such Intelligence is always agravated by the Indians and I don't doubt but that it would put a stop for some to their proceedings as I know it would greatly Confuse the Indians they are like to win form us as our force with the French Militia probably Counting the Spaniards would be too Considerable for them to Temper with our only Chance at present to save that Cuntrey is by Incourageing the Families but I am sensible nothing but land will do it I should be Exceedingly Cautious in doing anything that would displease government but their present Interest in Many Respects obvious to us boath, Call so loud for it that I think S^r that you Might even Venture to give a Deed for Forty or fifty Thousand Acres of Land at Said place at the price that government may dem^d for it it Interfears with no Claim of our friendly Indians the greatest Barriour to the Inhabitants of the Illinois against the Southern Indians Security of the Genl Commerce and perhaps the Saving of the Cuntrey to the State and probably in a few Months inable us to act again on the Offensive. I should be against Suffering families to settle promis^{ly} in any part of the Illinois at present but the Establishment of the said post is so necessary and as it cannot be Compleat without the Families I think it your duty to give the afforesaid Incouragement and such Instructions as would confine the people to a fort for sometime before you could Consult Government it might be too late Sustenance for some time will be procured with difficulty but I cannot think of the Consequence of losing possession of the Cuntrey without a more determined Resolution to Risque every point Rather than suffer it (for they the English Cannot execute any Matter of very great to be Eaqual to mine if you Concur with me in Sentiment let me know Amediatley or Such Amendment as you might think more advantageous

I am S^r with Real Esteem your very Humble Servt

G R CLARK

DANIEL BRODHEAD TO CLARK[11]

FORT PITT April 4th, 1780.

DEAR SIR I am honored with your oblidging Letter of the 22^d December last—The intelligence you have form Detroit is interesting and your proposals very pleasing.

I have wrote to his Excellency the Commander in chief to inform him of the Contents but have not yet received his answer, when I do shall take the earlist opp'y to communicate to you such parts as from our local situation & circumstances may be adviseable. I think it is probable that before next Winter I shall have the pleasures of taking you by the Hand somewhere upon the Waters of Lake Erie.

The Delawares at present continue their professions of Freindship towards us, but I am convinced there are many Villains in that Nation. If I am enabled as I expect to carry on an Expedition against the Shawnese the Delawares may afterwards be ordered as I may find most conducive to the public good.

---

[11] DMs, 50J24; *Clark Papers*, 408-409.

From the Newspapers it appears that the Spaniards are in possesion of the Natchez & Manchack if this report is true you will have very little to do upon the Missisippi further than establishing a small post or two to hold our possession on this side.

I have given Captn Rogers an order to take into his possession all Water Craft belonging to the United States below Wheeling which may perhaps prove serviceable to you, but I must entreat You to have the best care taken of them that circumstances will admit and send as many to this Place as you can find convenient safe opportunities to forward by.

I am amazed at the return made by Captn George of the men belonging to the Continental Service which were sent down the River under the Command of Captn Willing it difers much from the return I received from Captn Mc Intire—He alledges that some of those Mens terms are expired & that they do not incline to return to their respective Corps, but admitting their Terms were really expired (which is denied) they ought to have proper Discharges from the Command^g officers of their Corps and must be considered as Deserters untill they obtain them I wish you to inculcate this principle and order those men under some proper officer up to this place that Justice may be done them & the public. Mr Bentley (who has lately made his escape from Canada) accompanies Captain Rogers and intends to bring up some Goods & peltry to Fort Pitt and he I dare say will give the Company a clever compensation for bringing them under Convoy for him—Should it prove inconvenient to spare an officer from your Corps and the Men could be collected at the Falls, I would send an officer & party to bring them form thence.

Captain Rogers is so oblidging as to take down the names & Description of many Deserters and I hope you will afford him your Countenance & the necessary assistance for apprehending them—Such as return to their Duty voluntarily will be pardoned by authority from the Commander in chief.

I sincerely wish you great success & shall be glad to hear from you by every safe Conveyance I have the Honor to be with great regard Dear Sir

your most Obed^t Servt

DANIEL BRODHEAD
COL^o command^g W D

LAND GRANTS TO SOLDIERS, April 11, 1780[12]

Rec^d of Col: Ge^o R^s Clark this 11th day of Apr^l 1780 Six land Warrants Containing five Hundred & Sixty Acres of Land Each for which Warrants I promise to Deliver Col. Clark one Able Bodeyed Soldier for Each Warrant, p^r m^r

JN^o THRUTON

---

[12] Unpublished Clark Papers, 412.

SHANNON TO BAKER APRIL 12, 1780[13]

Rec^d of Col: Ge^O R Clark 12th day of Alprile 1780 four land warrants cont^g five Hundred & sixty Acres Each for which I promis to Recruit four Able Bodeyeded Soldiers Durring the war to serve in Col Clarks Reg^t

BU^D Worthington

WILLIAM SHANNON TO EVAN BAKER[14]

FALLS OF OHIO April 12, 1780.

SIR,
Agreeable to orders of this day to me given by the Commander in Chief of the Western Illinois Department I am directed to draw on you for Six Months provisions for one thousand men, to be at the Mouth of Ohio or near that place by the first of next June—at which place there will be a Store fixed, & proper Persons appointed to receive the same, and receipts properly given either by myself or some of my Deputies. I need not caution you that the provisions ought to be sound and wholsom and of good Quality. We shall probably have occasion to draw on you in August or Septr next for a large Quantity for which 'twould be well to prepare, & as I expect the Quarter Masters Store will be put under your Direction I beg you to forward them with all possible expedition, as they are much wanted as well as the Provisions.

I expect that proper necessaries of all kinds will be provided and sent for the use of the Officers, such as Liquors, Coffee, Tea, Sugar &ca. as no supplies of the same kind can be had in this Department, & if you have not already been furnished with Instructions for that purpose I beg you will not fail to apply to Government. I am Sir respectfully

Your mo. Obed^t hum^l Servt
WILL: SHANNON
Cond^r Genl W. Depart. Illinois

MR EVAN BAKER
Be pleased to Forward a letter of Col. Clark's to Govern^t as it will fall into your Hands
[Addressed:[To Mr Evan Baker Commissary of Washington County Virginia.

THOMAS JEFFERSON TO CLARKE[15]

RICHMOND April 19, 1780

SIR,

---

[13] *Ibid.,* 413.
[14] DMs, 50J30; *Clark Papers,* 413-414.
[15] DMs, 50J31; *Clark Papers,* 414-416.

Your Letter from Louisville of February 22'd—80 came safely to Hand. In answer to your Observations on the Spot proper to take Post on at the Mouth of Ohio we can only give our cordial Sentiments leaving the ultimate Determination to your Prudence on view of the Ground, as we can neither make the particular spot we would elect to be what we should wish nor recommend to you to take Post on it if Nature has rendered it unfit.

The Point of Land at the Mouth of the Ohio on the south side is the precise spot which would have been preferred had nature formed it capable of Fortification but this we were apprised was subject to inundation. How deep the Waters, may occasionally be there, we are quite uniformed and therefore are unable to decide on your Proposition for banking them out as at New Orleans. In general, undertakings of that nature are expensive, and not without great Danger that Floods of unexpected Magnitude may overwhelm the Works and Garrison, or that an enterprising Enemy may find Means to let in the water. Yet if those Lands lie so high as to be very little under Water, those objections become small in proportion, and may perhaps be less than that of taking the Post at a situation less favorable for vigilance over the Trade of the two rivers. Of this you will judge when you see the Lands and know the height of Inundation they are subject to. If this Place should be rejected, and we were to decide between two Posts one of which should be on the Ohio, the other on the Mississipi below the Mouth of Ohio equally near the Mouth, and equally proper in every other respect, we should prefer the one on the Missisipi because it would command a greater Part of the Trade than the other; for I take for granted more trade will go down the two Rivers to Orleans than down one river to the Mouth and up the other. If the question is between tow Situations on the north and south side of the Ohio, equal in other respects, the one on the south side would be greatly preferred. Indeed this circumstance would weigh against a good Degree of other superiority for Reasons which cannot be trusted to a Letter; Yet it would not so far weigh as to prefer a Post which cannot be made tenable to one which can. You describe a high Ground on the north side of the Ohio three or four miles above its mouth, yet the Missisipi, so near in that Part as that a Town might reach from the one to the other and a small river mouthing at the same place and forming a commodious Harbor for Vessels. This indeed is tempting, as in such a case the navigation of both rivers would be under you Eye as effectually as at the Mouth of Ohio, and holds out such advantages as may get the better of the objections to its being on the north side. However you must finally decide on view of the whole. As to the kind of Fortification I imagine you proposed in the first Place to build a Stockade for temporary Purpose. The Post is so important really as to merit Works of the best kind, but on this it would necessary to consult the Legislature who would be to provide for Expence. In the mean Time I imagine you will think it well first to plan & lay off the good works you would propose, and then build your temporary Fort so as to encourage them and protect those who would be working on them, or, if this would be too large to be manned by your Force, the temporary Work might be built within the Lines laid off for the good. When you shall have determined on your spot we should be glad to receive a minute description of it with a plan of the good Works you would propose to erect not meaning however thereby to suspend the temporary Works.

I am Sir Your very humble serv^t

TH. JEFFERSON

THOMAS JEFFERSON TO CLARKE[16]

RICHMOND April 19, 1780.

SIR, I have received information of many Murders recently committed by the Indians in Washington, Montgomery, Green Brian, Kentucky and the neighborhood of Fort Pitt, tho the Nations by whom com[mmi]tted are not specified in the Information, the extent of the mischief [MS. torn] extensive combination. In certain whether you were near enough at Hand to afford relief, and indeed rather expecting from your last Letter received that you are now at the mouth of the Ohio, satisfied at the same time that any Plan of enterprise determined and minutely directed here would prove abortive from want of Information and unforeseen Difficulties and Events, I have directed the Lieutenants of the Counties of Washington, Montgomery, Botctourt, Rockbridge and Green-Briar to assemble and concer, and immediately with a Portion of their Militia carry an Expedition into the Indian Country. To communicate their determinations to the Lieuten^{ts} of the Counties Northward of them between the Blue-ridge and Allegany who are also to assemble, concert, and execute similar offensive Measures with their Militia either by concurring in the same, or undertaking a separate Expedition; and those again to call for aids from the Counties West of the Allegany. They are to give Notice of their Plans to yourself, and should the combination of the Enemy appear still formidable for their Force I have desired them to ask such Assistance as you can give them, and in such way as you shall Think most effectual. Since the Conduct of the Indians has precipitated our meditated Chastisement of them, it seems to have determined on which of the Objects formerly submitted to you're the first Efforts of the Campaign are to be directed. Nothing is more desirable than the total suppression of Savage Insolence and Cruelties, and should your Affairs be in a condition to admit your going in Person, and taking command of the whole expedition—The object is of sufficient Importance to require it, yet unacquainted as I am, with the present State of your forces, where they are, and how employed, I am afraid that your distance from the scene of action, or other unknown circumstances might produce a greater Measure of Injury to the Public by interrupting your present operations than they might derive of good from your co-operation. I therefore leave to your Discretion and Zeal for the good of your Country to determine whether, and in what manner to concur in this Expedition, still considering it as so important as to [recommend it] to you, if very great Injury to the public may not attend the cutting you off on that Business. I also write to Major Slaughter (as he is probably so distant form you) to lend his Aid if called on in the Manner I have mentioned to him. I have it not in my Power to give you precise Information of the numbers recruited for Col. Crockett, or time of their March, I experience Mortification on every enquiry by [finding] that every Inquiry lessons my Hope both as to Numbers and dispatch. Nothing shall be left undone to forward them, and I do not Despair all together of their participating in the projected Expedition.

I am Sir Your Very humble serv^t
TH. JEFFERSON

P S inclosed is an answer to your's of Feb. 22

---

[16] DMs, 50J32; *Clark Papers*, 416-417.

CLARK TO JOHN DODGE[17]

MOUTH OF OHIO, April 20, 1780

I yesterday arrived at this place, & wish you immediately to convey all your stores to this post; I hope you have got what little furniture I wanted; I have not any, nor a seed for my garden: Pray, procure them and convey them in a few days. If you cd. procure me a few of those beans the French plant to make shades with, I shd. prize them much. Capt. Bently will give you the news.

I am, dr. Captn. yours
G. R. CLARK

BATISST TO CLARK[18]

FORT CLARK Aprile 29th, 1780.

SIR
I am Glad to here of your Safe arivel at The Mouth of the River & take this opertunity To Express My Zele for you informing you that I always have kept your Counsel and intends TO Com and See you as soon as Col° Montgomery is Redey to Com & Wish all the happiness your Station Can afford & am Sir you dutifull son untill deth.

BATISST THE KING[19]

COLONEL MONTGOMERY TO CLARK[20]

Fort Clark, Kaskaskia, May 7, 1780
Dear Colo
This Will Be handed you By your Brother to inform You that the perade we was about to Make is Fellen threw By the Rason the in habetents Refused to furnish Me with Flower and Corn to Supply My gtrupes for the Spase of two Months I cCalled a counsel of officers Both of the Sevel as well as the Milletery who were Unanimously of Opinion that if we Could be fited of for two Months Voige it mite Gave the inhabentents a grate dale of ase I then Requested of them to Furnish Me with Eigh thousand lb of Flower &

---

[17] DMs, 60J335; *Clark Papers*, 417-418.
[18] DMs, 50J33; *Clark Papers*, 418.
[19] Batisst was chief of the Kaskaskia tribe. The handwriting is that of John Montgomery.
[20] Kathrine Wagner Seneike, ed., *The George Rogers Clark Adventure in the Illinois and Selected Documents of the American Revolution at the Frontier Posts*. Polyanthos Press, New Orleans, 431-432 (hereafter, Seineke).

one Hundred bushels of Corn and nothing Else the upon that Asembled the in habetents to know if that it was out of Thire power to do aney thing Except I Could aprevale on some Gentle man to pay the peltrey amediateily the answer I Maide them that if the would not advance it on the Credit of the State for thire own profite & not for Mine I Should Geve My Self no farder Trowble about it I then Requested how Maney men the Wanted For to Remain as a Gard for them the Saide the wanted us all but Was note Able to Furnish More thin thirty Which if you would be Good anuf to leve with them the would Se that the Should not want for provision Mr. gillaspey start in two days from this date with a partey of men that thire times is out the 29 instant So I Geve him permitioni to ingagge as artificers ho will Bring you part of the arliterry Som salt 2000 lb of led the Ballince I Will Bring My Self as I hope you will soon Call for Me As I Want Much to See you and have the pleasure to Converse With you the Savagages is dealey Comikng in to hold Talks But the Misfortine that we have nothing to Geve Them Semes to be Much a Ganst us at present as the hav ben long promised to be supplied and finds that nothing is Com the Seem to be Quite out of patience & sais that poverty Srecks them so Hard that the don't know what do as you well no when poverty Coms in at the dore love Creps out of the window—But I get the promis to keepe the advise that is Geven Them to Remain Quiet I Send you a Spech I receved from one of the Sack Chiefs Colled the Lemone and the answer I Geve him as Capt Doge was absent I have not Spoke To aney others since his arrivel pray Sir inregard of the Number of Men you think proper to leve here let Me know by The Express on Whither aney or not as this place Sems toBe in the Center and not Much Exposed & I don't think That aney Bodey is a Gethering a ganst at present I Refar you for perticulers to your Brother and am Sir

Your Humble Sarvt

John Montgomery

CLARK TO OLIVER POLLOCK[21]

CAMP JEFFERSON MOUTH OF OHIO MAY 11th, 1780

D^R SIR

A few days past I arrived at this place to Execute the orders of my Superiors for the Establishment of a Post, for the Conveniency of Trade and other purposes, I have but little knews worth relating to you we have heard the Spanish forces have taken Pensicola and am Impatient for a Confirmation of it, the Illenois Settlement are much threatned by the British Gentlemen at Detroit they Count St Lewis their Seat of Government probably they will meet with the fate they have Once Experienced if they attempt it I must confess I am not a Sufficient Statesman to Comprehend the Policy of the Spanish Gentlemen, Protecting the Deserters of a People so fond to serve them as we are at a time when both Nations are at Warr against the same Enemy it cannot be good Policy at this time for nothing saves both Spanish & American Illenois from the hands of the English but the

---

[21] Unpublished Clark Papers; *Clark Papers*, 418-419; note, this letter and the next, which are very similar, have several differences, possibly because of different published translations, cf., Seineke, 432-433..

Troops we have and would keep in that Country if it was not for the aforsesaid Protection as we have fallen on the Method of Drawing our supplies from the States thro' the Channell of the [blank in MS.] the Deserters by no means add to the strength of the People they fly too but rather to the Contrary for reasons I dare say you are sensible of. I have to request of you Sir to make intercession with his Excellency the Governor Galvez to suffer Lieutenant Roberston whom I expect is at Orleans other ways some person whom you wil be pleased to Commission to take the Arms & Cloathing (the Property of the States) from the Deserters at Natches and other settlements in your Quarters a list of them I inclose Print [?] and Party on board of Brashears who has also run off with considerable property of other persons) is exceedingly well cloathed except Shirting I have nothing more to add but remain with esteem.

Sir Your very Humb^l Servt

Signed G R Clark

G. R. CLARK TO OLIVER POLLOCK[22]

Camp Jefferson, 11 May 1780

Dr Sir

A few days past I arrived at this place to Execute the orders of my Superiors for the Establishment of a Post, for the Conveniency of Trade and other purposes, I have but little knews worth relating to you we have heard the Spanish forces have taken Pensicola and am Impatient for a Confirmation of it, the Illenois Settlement are much threatned by the British Gentlemen at Detroit they Count St Lewis their Seat of Government probably they will metn with the fate they have once Experienced if they attempt it I must confess I am not a Sufficient Statesman to Comprehend the Policy of the Spanish Gentlemen, Protecting the Deserters of a People so fond to serve them as we are at a time when both Nations are at Warr against the same Enemy it cannot be good Policy at this time for nothing saves both Spanish & American Illenois from the hands of the English but the Troops we have and would keep in that Country if it was not for the aforesaid Protection as we have fallen on the Method of Drawing our supplies from the States thro' the Channell of the [blank] the Deserters by no means add to the strength of the People they fly too but rather to the Contrary for reason I dare say you are sensible of. I have to request of you Sir to make intercession with his Excellency the Governor Galvez to suffer Lieutenant Roberston whom I expect is at Orleans other ways some person whom you will be pleased to Commission to take the Arms & Cloathing (the Property of the States) from the Deserters at Natches and other settlements in your Quarters a list of them I inclose Print [?] and Party on board of Brashears who has also run off with considerable property of other persons) is exceedingly well cloathed except shirting I have nothing more to add but remain with esteem

Sir Your...G R Clark

---

[22] Seineke, 432-433; Unpublished Clark Papers.

DANIEL BRODHEAD TO CLARK[23]

HEAD QU^{RS} FORT PITT, May 20, 1780

DEAR SIR I have for some time past had in contemplation an Expedition against the Shawnese Towns but I find it is quite impracticable for want of resources. It is some time past since I was honored with a Line form his Excell^y the Commander in chief, but I have no reason to expect a reinforcement from him.

I don't know how far it may be in your Power to make an attack upon the Shawnese & their allies but if it can be done with a probability of success I hope you will attempt it, because I am persuaded that they are the most hostile of any Savage Tribe and could they receive a severe chastisement it would probably put an end to the Indian war. The people who pass this way towards the new Settlements will doubtless give you all the assistance in their Power, they are numerous and well supplied with provisions.

Major Slaughter will do me the Honor to forward this Letter to you. his detachment consists of about one hundred Men which I am persuaded he will join to aid you upon any attempt you may think proper to make against his troublesome Neighbours, the Shawnese.

I will endeavour to write you again after I receive his Excellencies answer to the proposed junction of our Forces and shall be happy to hear from you by every safe conveyance.

I have the honor to be with much respect Dr Sir Your most obed^t Servt

DANIEL BRODHEAD
Col^o command^g W D

JOHN TODD, Jr., TO THOMAS JEFFERSON[24]

MAY IT PLEASE YOU EXCELLENCY   June 2, 1780

On Consulting with Col^o Clark we found it impracticable to maintain so many petty posts in the Ilinois with so few men & concluded it better to draw them all to one post The Land at the Junction of the Ohio & Missisipipi was judged best Situated for the prupose as it would command the Trade of an extensive Country on both sides of each River & might serve as a Check to any Incroachments from our present Allies the Spaniards whose growing power might justly put us upon our guard & whose fondness for engrossing Territory might other wise urge them higher up the River upon our side than we would wish. The Expences in erecting this new post & victualing the men would have been Obstacles unsurmountable without a Settlem^t Contiguous to the Garrison to support it whose adventurers would assist the Soldiers in the heavy Work of Building their fortifications I therefore granted to a certain Number of Families four Hundred

---

[23] DMs, 50J39; *Clark Papers*, 419-420.
[24] Unpublished Clark Papers; *Clark Papers*, 422-423.

Acres to each family at a price to be Settled by the General Assembly with Commissions for civil & militia—offices & the Necessary Instructions. Copies of the principal of which I herewith send you The Others being agreeable to the printed forms heretofore delivered me by the Governor & Council Lest the withdrawing our troops form St Vincenne might raise suspicions among the Citizens to our disadvantage: I have sent to Maj^r Bosseron the then district Commandant blank Commissions with powers to raise one Company & put them in possession of the Garrison with assurance that pay & rations sh^d be allowed them by the Governm^t

  I inclose you also a Return of the Cloths &c. which I sent down by Mr Clark to Capt. Dodge who I appointed Agent agreeably to your Excellencys Letter as Mr. Lindsay desired to be discontinued. When Col. Clark left the falls his Officers & Men to the Amount perhaps of 120 were well Cloathed except in the article of Linens Mr Lindsay had not arrived the 8th of May last from Illinois & I have not heard whether the Goods From Orleans were yet arriven. Capt Dodge was also to receive them from Linday

  Mr Isaac Bowman with 7 or 8 men & one family set off from Kaskaskia the 15th Novr. last in a Batteau attended by another Batteau with 12 Men & 3 or 4 families in it bound to the falls of Ohio. I judged it safer to send to the Falls many Articles belonging to the Commonwealth by Bowman than to bring them myself by Land Bowmans Batteau fell into the Hands of the Chickasaw Indians & the other arrived in March or April at the French Lick on Cumberland with the Account that Bowman and all the men except one Riddle were killed & taken I inclose your Excellency a List of such Articles as belonged to the State as well as I can make out from me Detached Memorandums. My Books & many necessary papers being also lost.

  Many necessary articles of Intelligence yet remain unmentioned. I will enjoy no Leisure untill I shall have fully acquainted you Excellency with the Situation of Ilinois.

  I have the Honor to be with the greatest Respect Your Excellency Most Obedient & humble Servant

                                            JN^o TODD J^R

RICHM^D 2nd June 1780

CAPTAIN ROBERT GEORGE TO G. R. CLARK[25]

Sir   Camp Jefferson June 4th, 1780

  I had the pleasure of writing you by Captn. Shannon a little after your departure from this, since when nothing material has occurr'd except the arrival of Expresses from the Falls & St. Vincents, which I dispetch'd off immediately after you. This will be handed you by Colo. LeGras, accompanied by Mr. DeJean from Williamsburg, to which Gentn. I beg leave to refer you for the News of that Quarter & to the Letters which they carry with them. As to our situation here, we are endeavouring to make it as strong as possible, I have got the Trenches for the Pickets ready & the inhabitants are hurrying the Pickets to me as fast as their Circumstances do well admit. They are not yet done with

---

[25] Seineke, 441.

planting, nevertheless I hope to have the Fort enclosed within this week. Our Provisions I am as sparing of as possible, issuing but single Rations of Corn, in order to make it hold out the Longer, & tho' we hear frequent accounts of Provisions being inteded down the Tenessee, yet the prospect of their Timely arrival is very uncertain. Mr. Don[illeg.] has done all in his Power to procure us meat, but without success – the best hunters that go out generally return empty handed, & our present store of Corn amounts to little more than one hundred Bushels. Fortunately for us Capt. Worthington has sent down but four of his recruits to augment our Numbers, /two of which go with Mr. LeGras/ nor have we reason to expect himself or any more of them, as I understand he don't intend coming 'till you return to the Falls. Colo. LeGras can inform you more particularly.

What few Troops are here are really in a naken Condition. I conceive that did you permit me to issue but one Shirt each to them, it would be of much service.

From what Major Harlan has informed us we have great reason to expect something decisive has been done ere this; if so, or when it shall happen I earnestly hope it may be attended with all the Success to our Cause that the Justice of it deserves, and flatter myself with seeing you returned again in a little time crown'd with Victory. Be pleased to make my Compts. acceptable to the Gentn. with you, and assure yourself that I am Dear Colonel with sincere good wishes for your success and Welfare

Your mo: Obedt…

Robt George

PETITION OF TRUSTEES AT FORT JEFFERSON FOR NEW COUNTY[26]

Clarksville 13th: June 1780

SIR

We the Trustees elected for the Borough of Clarksville, convinced of your unbound friendship & good will towards our young Settlement, beg leave to communicate to you some circumstances, which thro' your Interest we would wish you have laid before Government. Viz.—

That Our present Settlement being form'd by your permission only, causes an anxiety in the Minds of the People lest Governm^t should not give it necessary Sanction.

That Gov^t is at present unacquainted with our Situation, Circumstances and Necessities, which 'tis requisite should be made known to them.

That for Want Proper authority, the regulations made by the Trustees, have not their due weight with the People.

That we conceive it necessary our Settlement should be erected into a Corporation, or Separate County distinct from Kentucky, & proper Magistrates and other Officers Commissioned for executing the Laws, which would be a means of preventing that Confusion likely to take place for want of such authority.

---

[26] DMs, 50J44; *Clark Papers*, 425-426.

Finally, we beg leave to refer you to Col⁰ Walker whom we have personally made acquainted with our Wishes & wants & whose Friendship we cannot too much commend. He has promised us all the assistance in his power, & as we make no doubt you will think it advisable to consult him respecting our Affairs, we could wish you to make application for us by that Gentleman. We submit all our wants to you, satisfied that you are as well acquainted with them as ourselves, & request you will lay them before Government in their proper light. We sincerely wish you success in your present as well as every other undertaking, and a Speedy return to our little Settlement of which you are the Patron. & beg leave to Subscribe ourselves with the utmost Respect—Sir

Your most obed and very hum^l Serv^{ts}:
JAMES PIGOT
EZEKIEL JOHNSON
HENRY SMITH
JOSEPH HUNTER
MARK ILES

TO COLu GEORGE ROGERS CLARK &ca

We farther request that in Case Government should be pleased to erect our Settlement into a Corporation or County, you would recommend the Officers already elected among us, and Such other persons for such officers as you may think necessary, in order for their being duly Commissioned.

THOMAS JEFFERSON TO THE SPEAKER OF THE HOUSE OF DELEGATES[27]

IN COUNCIL June 14th, 1780

SIR,
In a Letter, which I had the Honor of addressing you on the meeting of the present General Assembly, I informed you of the necessities which had led the Executive to withdraw our western troops to the Ohio. since the date of that Letter I have received the inclosed of the second instant from Colo Todd communicating the measures he had adopted in Conjunction with colo Clarke to procure such a Settlement contiguous to the post which shall be taken as may not only strengthen the garrison occasionally, but be able to raise provisions for them. as the confirmation of these measures is beyond the powers of the executive, it is my duty to refer them to the General Assembly, it may be proper to observe that the grant of Lands by colo Todd was made on a supposition that the post would be taken on the north side of the Ohio wheras I think it more probable it will be on the south side in the Lands lying between the Tanissee Ohio Missisippi Indians, who from intelligence which we think may be relied on, have entered into war with us.

---

[27] Unpublished Clark Papers; *Clark Papers*, 427-428.

The expenditures of the Ilinois, have been deemed from some expressions in the act establishing that county not subject to the examination of the board of Auditors As the auditing these accounts is very foreign to the ordinary office of the Council of State, would employ much of that time and attention which at at present [blank in MS.] called to objects [blank in MS.] general importance and as their powers would not enable them to take into consideration the justice and expediency of indemnifying Colo Todd for his Losses and services as desired as desired in the inclosed Letter from Him of the thirteenth instant they beg leave to submit the whole to the consideration of the General Assembly.

I have the honor to be with great respect & esteem Sir Your most obedient & most humble ser^t

TH: JEFFERSON

LETTER OF CAPTAIN GEORGE TO G. R. CLARK [28]

Fort Jefferson, 31 July 1780

Sir

On Monday morning the 17th, Inst. a little before daybreak, we were Allarm'd with the firing of a Gun in the lower end of the Town which proved to be done by an Indian, apparently with Intention to decoy us out into an Ambuscade, laid by a large party of Savages, who lay concealed in the woods around the Town; they killed one Man who lay concealed in the woods around the Town; they killed one Man who lay at a fire opposite his ~~Camp~~ Cabin & in their flight Tomahawked another, who is like to do well: Immediately at the upper end of the Town, the Militia Centinal, who was posted there was fired on by three other Savages, & Dangerously wounded (who is since Dead of his Wound) and in a little time a General Attack took place in that Quarter- The Savages appear'd to be very numerous and kept up a Constant & brisk fire on a House at the upper end of the Street adjacent to the ~~Block-House~~ Woods, & also on the Block-House; from both of which they received several very Galling Shot-

At length the Attack on the Village became General, & the few men that Occupied the Block-House and the other House behaved gallantly the firing continued about two Hours one half hour of which 'twas kept up very hot without any Intermission; Finding they could make no Impression, & having several of their Men killed & Wounded, which we are assured of they thought proper to Retreat, after killing an maiming most of the Stock- During the Engagement, one of the Soldiers (of which I had five ~~it~~ in the Block-House, besides about as many of the Militia) received a Wound through his Shoulders- The Swivel was of great Service, & I was well prepared to receive them in the Fort had they thought proper to Shift their object- Various are the opinions of People with regard to the number of Savages, but the most moderate Calculate them at one hundred & fifty, of some even to five hundred; the Tracks every where being numerous & deep; and the Yells which accompanied the Firing seem'd to re-echo from every Quarter- The Swivel I am assured kept off numbers from coming into Actual Engagement, & though it was very Ill Manned did execution The Inhabitants are in high Spirits and determined Almost to a Man to Stand their Ground, but Numbers of

---

[28] Seineke, 448-449.

them are becoming daily Sick, & to add to that, Misfortune are almost all Quite out of provision- As I am aware of the great Value Government sets on this Settlement, I am constrain'd to divide the mouthful of provision I have with them Well knowing should they evacuate this place I cannot maintain my post with the Handful of sick Men I have in Garrison, Besides the few Inhabitants that are able to go out to hunt dare not ~~dare not~~, as we ~~have just~~ [illeg.] are not certain that the Enemy are intirely gone off, having been seen lately, Sculking about since the attack, & tracks discovered but a few days ago-.

The Troops are victualed with Bread to the 2nd. of August inclusive, only two days, and not one Bushel of Corn in Store—Between 50 & 60 of the Inhabitants drew the last week, but have not one Mouthful of at present to give them- Their dependance is altogether on their Gardens which is really a poor Shift- They have lost almost all their Stock, & every Horse fit for use-

I Just received a few lines from Colo. Montgomery- he promises me a Small Supply of provision, but it must be paid for out of this Store, I was also forced to purchace on the same fund about Twenty eight Barrels of Corn, which is Quite Exhausted, as the vast Number of Women & Children of our own & the great many Destitute Inhabitants have Drained me Considerably.

Colo. Montgomery sent me down a part of the Kaskaskias Indians- they are here, about 3 days. tomorrow or next day, go out to hunt for us- He promises to send us a Company of Men for our Defence which we Expect daily, with what provision can be Collected- We have given over all hopes of Colo. Crockets Arrival.

Colo. Montgomery writes his having received news of Langlands Comeing with a Stronger party than before, that his Men think themselves a match for them I have only to inform you further that the Men in the Garrison are all Sick, Not having Above three Effective Men- I shall however do better I hope when the reinforcement Comes-

Augt. 1st. this day Capt Baley & Lieut. Clark arrived with about 1400w of Flower & 50 Bush. of Corn and 28 Men, a Small supply indeed, having about Two hundred mouths to feed daily- We Remain in hopes Yet of Corn from the falls-

I am Sir...

Robt George

JOHN DODGE TO THOMAS JEFFERSON[29]

FORT JEFFERSON August 1st, 1780.

SIR

I think it my indispensable duty to lay before you a true state of our situation in this Country since my arrival, which probably may throw some lights on the various reports, which may reach you through channels not so well acquainted with its real wants as I am.

On my arrival at the Falls of the Ohio, Colᵒ John Todd gave me instruction to proceed to Kaskaskies, in order to take charge of the goods when arrived, which were purchased

---

[29] *Clark Papers*, 435-438.

by Mr Lindsay for this department, with farther orders to divide them into two parcels, one of which for the troops, and the other to be disposed of to our friendly Indian allies: considering it better to sell them on reasonable [terms] than dispose of them in gifts— Horses and ammunition, being articles much wanted for the Troops, I contracted for and received a quantity of lead an some horses, before the arrival of the goods, and having discretionary powers, was constrained to accept of orders drawn on me for provisions which could not otherwise be obtained. Since the goods came into my hands, the troops and Inhabitants at this place not having received the expected supplies form Government, and being well assured that without some timely relief, the post and settlement must be evacuated, I was also constrained at divers times to issue quantities of the goods intended to be disposed of to our Indian allies, in order to furnish them with the means of subsistence.

The few troops that are now here are too inconsiderable to guard themselves: nor are the inhabitants much better, notwithstanding they remain in great spirits in expection of relief from Government, and have with great bravery defeated a very large party of Savages who made a regular attack on the village, at day break on the morning of the 17th ult°.

Col° Clark has divided his few men in the best manner possible so as to preserve th Country. the apprehension of a large body of the enemy in motion form Detroit towards the falls of Ohio, has called him there with what men he could well spare from this Country, before he had well breathed after the fatigues of an expedition up the Missisippi—and Colo Crockett not arriving with either men or provisions, as was expected, has really involved both the troops and settlers in much distress, and greatly6 damped, the spirits of industry in the latter, which till lately was so conspicuous—I see no other alternative, from the present appearance of our affairs, but that the few goods I have left, after supplying the troops, must all go for the purchase of provisions to keep this settlement from breaking up: and how I shall ever support my credit, or acquit myself of the obligations I have bound myself under, to those of whom I have made purchases for the troops before the arrival of the Goods, I know not—Our Credit is become so weak among the French inhabitants, our own, and the Spaniards on the opposite side of the Mississippi, that one dollars' worth of provision or other supplies cannot be had from them without prompt payment, were it to save the whole Country—by which you will perceive, that without a constant and full supply of Goods in this quarter to answer the exigencies of Government, nothing can ever be well affected but in a very contracted manner.

I observe that the distance the settlers, who come in general to this Country, have to travel, impoverishes them in a great degree. They come at the expence of their all, in full hopes and expectations of being assisted by Government. Were these hopes cherished and supplies of necessaries of all kinds furnished them in the manner of the neighboring Spaniards, to be paid in produce such as might answer for the troops or for exportation, many good consequences would be attendant. emigrants, on such encouragement, would flock to us in numbers instead of submitting to the Spanish Yoke—the principal part of their new settlements would join us. all those form the Natchez in particular, only wait the encouraging invitation to remove themselves and their properties to our settlement, preferring the mildness of our laws to the rigours of the Spanish, which they detest, notwithstanding their great offers. Such encouragement would be a spur to industry which would never die. The troops would in a little time, be solely furnished in provisions by our settlers, and in process of time, a valuable trade might be opened with the overplus.

These hints I beg leave to offer to your own better judgement conscious, that if they are worthy of notice you will direct their proper uses.

I have got a party of the friendly savages of the Kaskaskie tribe to hunt and scout for us—they are of singular service, as the provisions in store, are totally exhausted, and indeed their hunting tho', it may afford an useful, yet it is a very precarious supply.

As to the general disposition of these indians in alliance with us, it appears at present to be very peaceable; but as poverty is always subject to temptation, I fear their good intentions may be seduced by those who have it more in their power to supply their wants, being well convinced of the necessity of having proper supplys for them, which will not only keep them in our interest, but even afford us a very beneficial traffic.

The bearer of this travels to the falls of Ohio, thro' the wood. I am uncertain what the fate of my letter will be, as I know he has a dangerous and tedious journey before him—however, by the next opportunity I shall do myself the honor of writing to your Excellency a few more of my observations, begging leave once more, to remark the necessity of keeping at all times, full supplies of goods in this remote quarter, in order to forward the service of Government encourage the settlement of the frontiers, supply our troops with necessaries, provisions &c, and finally open a very profitable and extensive trade in little time.

I have the honor to be Your Excellency's most obedient and most humble servant &c &c.

JOHN DODGE

ROBERT GEORGE TO JOHN MONTGOMERY[30]

Fort Jefferson, 2nd Septem^r 1780

.Sir

I wrote you by Express the 28th past, to whom I refered you for a particular Accot of our investiture by the enemy savages I thought it then more prudent to trust the Accot. to their Relation, than to risque the whole of our Circumstances in a Letter, however, as things wesr somewhat of a better appearance at present, I shall Venture to give You a sketch of What has happened –

On Sunday morning the 20th about Sunrise, a few of Capt. Smith's Negroes having gone on the outside of the Lots, towards the Corn fields, were Chased into the Village by a party of the Savages, who finding they were likely to escape, fired on a killed a Wench within Gunshot of the Houses – Contrary to my expectations they made no particular Attack at that time, except some Shot fired at times by Small parties at the Houses in the Village, & at the Fort – about Ten OClock they made a pretty smart fire for a while at the Fort from point over the Creek, & some from up the Creek – When it was

---
[30] Seineke, 457-459.

dark, they hailed the House s in the lower end of the Town desired to know the name of the Commanding Officer – was answered Col⁰ Clark – the person who spoke said he came from Pensacola, his name Jas. or Wᵐ Whitehead, and Commanded the party That his Errand was to prevent the Savages from massacring the Women & Children, That he expected to be reinforced by a large party with Cannon, the next day or day after – That he would come the next morning and (?) speak with us in the same places, which he accordingly did (or rather another in his Stead, who was known to some of our people by the name of Colbert) he mentioned much the same as overnight, adding that his people had killed four and taken one prisoner the day before, that the prisoner had informed him of our distressed situation in every respect, of our expectation of a Boat with provision from Illinois, that they had sent fifty Men to Intercept the Boat and that as they were no strangers to our miserable Condition they were determined to starve us out; that in the Spring. some of their people had discouvered us, but took us for a Travelling party, that on their return, a stronger party had been sent to examine, who found we had setled & accordingly attacked us – That now they were come with a full Determination to drive & Destroy us, which they would certainly Effect before they left us, That his principal Errand errand was in order to protect the Women & Children (whom he pittied) from being Massacred – Capt. Helms whom I sent out, Informed him by my orders, that he was sent out to know his Demands; he answered, he was come with a strong Body of Indians, who was very much displeased at our settleing on their Lend, they had been here before, but was Now come with a full determination to have the place; that their main Body was not Yet come up, but expected it that day, or next at farthest, which Consisted of Chicasaws, Choctaws, Cherokees, & some Dellawares; who was Determined to Surround the place and starve us out if they did not take it by storm; and as he pitied our Circumstance which he knew very well he would be fond of saving the Lives of so many Women & Children, Which undoubtedly must fall a Sacrifice, provided we did not Surrender – Capt. Helms then replied, that they had not come any ways unexpected, we were well assured of their Comeing, and was prepared for their Reception, as for their Land, they had Commited Hostilities on our frontiers long before we came to this place, that we looked upon ourselves, together with the French & Spaniards to be proprietors of North America but took no Lands from our friends & allies, without purchasing; If they had a mind to become such, there was Commissioners appointed to settle much matters, but we Intended shortly to fortify ourselves on other parts of the River, and protect the Navigation & Fronteers against them, and any others of our Enemies, and as that was his Errand, it was unnecessary saying any more on the subject but tell his Savages we stood in Defiance of them or any other of our Enemies – The Gentleman with the flag said if we wanted to speak any farther, again, we would fire a Gun; & If he wanted to Speak, he would appear as he then did, with a White flag; but Capt. Helms again Informed him, he thought it unnecessary to speak any farther on that subject: they then withdrew – Just at their parting (unknown to me) some of the Indians who had ran out, and had been prevented from taking him prisoner, having got into one of the Houses, fired, as did some others, he real'd and we are sure he is killed, the Blood having been found in great quantity behind a Tree which he retired to and his Retreat being made in such a confused manner as assures us he is Dead – I must confess I cannot be much displeased at it considering the errand he came on; though it was positively contrary to my orders, it has had one good effect however; all that day we had scarce a Shot, but just at dark they made a very warm attack on Fords and Donne's Houses at the lower end of the Town, and also on the Garrison, they fired several Rounds very briskley, but did no Damage – Our people in the Village & Fort behaved with great Gallantry and killed several, however, the firing ceased and no farther attack of any Consequence Commenced till next evening, when they fired pretty warmly on the upper end of the Town & the Block House, and next morning Decamped, after killing what few sheep & Cows were left from their former Violence, & Destroying almost all of a very beautiful and large Crop of Corn and other Truck – The last evening, far from our Expectation Capt. Bailey came in, who had been out hunting with a party of his Boys, of whom four were killed and one taken: he remained hid in the Island, though they came Continually in parties, some within a Rod of him, but providentially got in undiscovered _ The Capt. says he seen four of the Savages whom we well knew, one was a Piankeshaw, and three Pittawatimies – All the Indians were well Clad in new fine Ruffled shirts – Although the Enemy appear to be gone off, I cannot certainly Determine Whiter or no – The Corn being Chiefly Destroyed has determined the Inhabitants almost to a Man to evacuate the place – They are now making preparation for the purpose of going down the River being too weak to go up –

    You, Sir, can now be the best judge, whether it will be possible, or admitting it to be possible, whether it would be most expedient to hold our Post or not – If you think it best to continue, Some Mode of supplying us with provision must be adopted, a Reinforcement of Men in lieu of the Inhabitants to Guard the Redoubts round the Fort must be send and as many Swivels as can be had – If You think it Impossible, or Rather Inexpedient to hold our post longer, a Reinforcement of Men, will yet be necessary to convey us away, as also of Craft for Transporting us up Stream, for my part I am Determined to hold out to the last son long as one ounce of provision and ammunition can be had – But as we have not only Dangerous, but Numerous Enemies to expect from every quarter, it becomes Necessary we should make such preparations for their Reception, as will convince them how little their efforts will avail against us – All the loss we have sustained During the whole is only two of the Militia slightly Wounded & one Soldier; except the few unfortunate fellows of Baileys, who fell into the Enemies hands as they Returned with the Boat form hunting – I cannot do too much Justice to the Gallantry of the few Troops under the Command of Lieut. Clark who were stationed in the Black-House, & also of the Militia, no Men could behave with greater Bravery nor with more spirit and Courage; they killed several who fell on the spot, the Bloody marks of whom we have since discouvered in many places – I hope this will reach you safe to convince you of our distressed situation & how much, I am Sir

Your Obed^t Servt

Robt. George Capt

JOHN MONTGOMERY TO CLARK[31]

FORT CLARK, Sept 22th 1780

DEAR COLO^L

SIR—I had the pleasure of Receving your Letter By Mr Glen & Exceeding hapey to hear of your Sucses & Espeshiley of your safe ARivel and now By Express send you Capt Georges Letter Which will Give the nues as Nothing Elce has happened Elce Where in this part of the Cuntrey But at his post.[1] The second nite after the atact Begun, he sent Me an Express By Jack Ash & an Indian Came To Me in four dayes at Kaskaskia Where I had just arived from kohos. I had no Trupes With Me But three officers that Came to ascort Me down I aplied to the Militia to Goin Me to Go to the Assistance of That distresed post But there answer Was they thot it their dutey to Stay and Take Care of their Wives and Children: I then had No Other Shift But to Aply To the kaskaskia indians to Go With Me as I thot it imprudent to Wate until The Trupes Could Come from kahoe I then Amediately imberked With som provision ten White Men & Sixtey five indians With a determination to fite our way into The fort But Expected to lose our provision as the thorrowfair is Dried up and not adraup of Mesepie [Mississippi] With in half Amile of the fort but When We Got there the Enemye had Quite their Atact The inhabitunts semed Much discurraged and Were all preering their Botes to start of But I preveled on them to Wate untill next Morning When I Assemleld them to Gether Telling them the Bad Consequence of Going to a strange please With out aney Thing to purchase provision & Living under a despotick Government as Liberty wos What the had Contended For telling them that Every promis you had Mead them that I then was Redey To proform in you Absence the Anser they Maide Me Wos, how Cold I Expect them or Request them to stay When their Stockes Wos intirely Lost Theire Cropes destroyed & worst of all A great party of there Fameleys Gone To the Grave of all Silance With Sickelyness; &, Sir knowing that to be a truth as Everey day I Remeaned there one tow or Three Wos Buried Which threw Humanity I Could not Compell them To stay But prevelled on som of the principal inhabitants to Remean & som others to take the Rout up to this post and the Remender went Down. as soone as I Got Matters alittle Setled I Came up to purchase a Quantity of provision as I had the The Opportunity of purchasing a Quanititey of Goods that Mr Pollock Offered us the Refusel of at A most Exorbetent prise But you know Needs Must When the devel drives As We Could noGit one Mouthful on the Credit of the state the Goods I have deposited in Capt Dodges hands With in structions to purchase Alarge Quantitey of Corn flower & Salt But I Much despair in his Giting The Quantitey desired as theire Cropes Wos Mean, I Expect to start in a few Dayes with the Balance of the trupes From Kaho to Campt Gefferson Except Capt Rogers Companey ho I have ordered TO Remean untill furder orders Sir it is imposible to Geve you a full deteall as it WOuld take a Quire of peaper But hope soone to have the favour of seeing you at
[Second Sheet Missing]

---

[31] DMs 50J58; *Clark Papers*, 456-457.

TWO LETTERS OF CAPTAIN ROBERT GEORGE[32]

TO CAPTAIN JOHN ROGERS; TO G. R. CLARK

Sir   Fort Jefferson 27th Octr 1780

    Lieut Clark goes up in order to bring us down some provision, I hope you will be of as much Assistance to him as possible; our Craft lies on Dry Ground, & we are not able to put any in the River. I have wrote to Capt. Dodge to hire a Boat (if can do no better) which if he does, You will send down as many Men as will Take her back again- & hope you will see that Good & holdsome provision is sent You may be Assured that we are in grant Distress, You will therefore Assist us all you can. Mr Clark will give You all the News that we have. hope therefore You will Excuse the shortness of my Letter

                                             & am Sir..
                                                     Robt George[33]

NB. Mr W. Clark presents his Compliments to Capt Rogers & hopes, that the want of paper will appoligize for not sending a Letter.

Capt John Rogers at Kaskaskias favd by Lt Clark

Endorsed: Capt. Robert George to Rogers 27th Octo. 80

Dr. Colo [Clark]:   Fort Jefferson, 28th of October, 1780

    Our present distress puts me under the necessity of informing you by Express the absolute necessity of your presence at this place we are Reduced to a Very small Number at present occasioned by Famine, Desertion and Numbers daly Dying; we have but a Very Small Quantity of provisions at present Col'o Montgomery on his way to New Orleans call'd on us, he says that Capt. Dodge has purchased one thousand Bushells of Corn and Ten Thousand Lb. of Flower which is all that is to Shew from a Cargoe of Eleven Thousand hard dollars worth of goods Sent by Mr. Pollock to You together with about five or six thousand Dollars worth from this place. We are informed they are Intirely Expended I Expect Capt. Philip Barbour up Every day with a Quantity of Goods for this State and Should be glad of Directions from you that they may not be Exhausted in the manner we have reason to doubt the rest was Its rather tedious to mention the Conduct at the Illinois since your departure as nothing but you r presence can Rectify it If necessity detains you from us pray send and express as soon as possible, The Inhabitants is chiefly gone down the River and what there is left is Very much distressed Lieut. Clark Sett off to Kaskaskias this morning to know the Certainty of the provisions being purchased, It appears there was a parogue Sent down Sometime ago loaded with Corn and Fower with Eight Men who deserted with it Down the River. I doubt the greatest

---

[32] Seineke, 465-466.
[33] DMs, 50J72.

part of this Batallion will soon Turn Merchants all for the want of your Presence here. If there is not Some Step taken to prevent it Lieut. Daltin is gowin down the river with Col. Montgomery in order if possible to [torn] Capt. Williams has arrived here with Col. Hohn Montgomery and assum'd the command which I Refused to give up without further orders from you, Major Harlin is out hunting but is at a loss for want of Horses. I have sent for all the State Horses at Kaskaskias but it appears there is but few, what is gone with them God knows but I believe there will be a Very disagreeable Accompt Rendered to you of them as well as many other things when called for the poor distressed remains of this little Borough Joins in prayers for Your presence once more at this place

I am Sir...

Robert George, Capt. Command'r of Fort Jefferson[34]

I have letters from Mr. Pollock to you which I omit sending for fear of Miscarriage.

ROBERT GEORGE TO CLARK[35]

FORT JEFFERSON, 28th of October, 1780.

Dr. COLO:

Our present distress puts me under the necessity of informing you by Express the absolute necessity of your presence at this place we are Reduced to a Very small Number at present occasioned by Famine, Dertion and Numbers daly Dying; we have but a Very Small Quantity of provisions at present Col'o Montgomery on his way to New Orleans call'd on us, he says that Capt. Dodge has purchased one thousand Bushells of Corn and Ten Thousand Lb. of Flower which is all that is to Shew from a Cargoe of Eleven Thousand hard dollars worth of goods Sent by Mr. Pollock to You together with about five or six thousand Dollars worth from this place. We are informed they are Intirely Expended I Expect Capt. Philip Barbour up Every day with a Quantity of Goods for this State and Should be glad of Directions from you that they may not be Exhausted in the manner we have reason to doubt the rest was Its rather tedious to mention the Conduct at the Illinois since your departure as nothing but your presence can Rectify it If necessity detains you from us pray send and express as soon as possible, The Inhabitants is chiefly gone down the River and what there is left is Very much distressed Lieut. Clark Sett off to Kaskaskias this morning to know the Certainty of the provisions being purchased. It appears there was a parogue Sent down Sometime ago loaded with Corn and Fower with Eight Men who deserted with it Down the River. I doubt the greatest part of this Batallion will soon Turn Merchants all for the want of your Presence here. If there is not Some Step taken to prevent it Lieut. Daltin is gowin down the river with Col. Montgomery in order if possible to [MS. torn} Capt. Williams has arrived here with Col. John Montgomery and assum'd the command which I Refused to give up without further orders form you. Major. Harlin is out hunting but is at a loss for want of Horses. I have

---

[34] Executive Papers, Archives Division, Virginia State Library, Richmond, Virginia; Seineke, 465-466.
[35] *Ibid.*

sent for all the State Horses at Kaskaskias but it appears there is a but few, what is gone with them God knows but I believe there will be a Very disagreeable Accompt Rendered t o you of them as well as many other things when call for The poor distressed remains of this little Borough Joins in prayers for Your presence once more at this place

I am Sir Your most Obe. & Very Humble Servant

ROBERT GEORGE
Capt. Command'r of FORT JEFFERSON

I have letters from Mr. Pollock to you which I omit sending for fear of Miscarriage.

JOHN WILLIAMS TO CLARK, October 28, 1780[36]

CAMP JEFFERSON, 28th of Oct. 1780.
SIR:

On the 23d of this Instant I arived at this poast by order of Colo. John Montgomery to take the Command but from the Carrector he at present bares Capt. George did not think proper to give him or any other person the command at this poast untill he being properly Releav'd by your order, I for my part, Seeing times so precarious and what might Insue from the least contest or Umbridge between Capt. Robt. George and myself Am determined to Remain as Retired as possible untill your arrival here. I commanded at Cahokias Since the Expedition up the Mississippi till ordered to this post and here I found both the Soldiers as well as the Inhabitants in the most dissolate Situation Immaginable not So much by Reason of Sickness as for the want of good provisions. there is a quantity of provisions purchased at present but the difficulty we Labour under now is Sickness and lowness of water prevent us getting any provisions down at this time by which Reason we are kept Constantly Starveing, As I am Convinced before the reception of this you are satisfied form Government in Regard to my Majority I would be glad you'd Give me Instructions by the first opportunity in what Manner to Act. I Expect to see you shortly at this place for other News. I refer you to Capt. Robert George's letter, and Remain with the greatest esteem, Your very Humble Servant,

JOHN WILLIAMS, Capt.
In Illinois Battalion.

LEONARD HELM TO GEORGE SLAUGHTER[37]

FORT JEFFERSON, Oct. 29th, 1780
DR. COL. Siting by Capt. Georges fire with a piece of Light wood and two Ribs of an old Bufloe which is all the meat We have Seen this many days, I congratulate your

---

[36] Executive Papers, Archives Division, Virginia State Library, Richmond; *Clark Papers*, 463.
[37] *Ibid., Clark Papers*, 466.

Success Against The Shawanahs but their never doubts when that brave Col. Clarke Commands, we will know the Loss of him at the Ilinois, I expect he is well aquainted with the Conduct of some Gen't at that place by Capt. Georges Letter, our situation is melancholy but has not time at present to acquaint. I rec^d the Agreable Balsom you sent by Maj. Harling which all that I have had this Summer the Gen't at Keskais Could not spare us about 8 or 10 Gal. Out of about 6 or 7 Hogsheads sent by Mr. Pollock to Col. Clark, the Use it was apl'd to with many other things Expect Col. Clarke will be made acquainted with if we have the happiness to see him once more at this place, I wanted badly to Come to your parts but at Capt. Georges request waits the return of Express Excuse hast as the Lightwoods just out and mouth watering for part of the two Ribs, tell Capt. Todd Henry Croucher produced Accts. against him for more than he had against him. With compliments to Madam Slaughter and all Aquaintances am with Esteem Yr. Obeident & Humble Servant,

LE^{OD} HELM

N. B. Capt. George gives his compliments but has neither Ligh nor paper

RICHARD HARRISON TO CLARK[38]

FALLS OF OHIO 7th of December 1780.

D^R COL^O

From the accounts we have had from Fort Jefferson, that place Being allmoast destitute of Men and Officers, occasioned by the Chief of them turning Merchants, and others Going down the River, I have thought it my duty to Repair to that poast Immediately. I propose leaveing this place the day after Tomorrow with my artillery and her Stoares. Capt Shannon is Likewise Takeing down a Quantity of Corn with him I hope we Shall soon Releave them there of their distresses. I am Informed by Express from there of Capt Phil. Barbours Comeing Up with a Very Large Cargoe for this State I Expect he is at the Mouth of the River by this time. The Indians are Still Troublesome to us here. Takeing of horses Killing and Takeing off prisoners from this and other adjasent Stations, we have had No arrivals as Yet from above Mr Randolph and Capt More are not Yet Come we are as You Left us Capt Worthington is Still at Harrodsburgh. I am of opinion he do Not Intend Going down this winter, If there is No Great Necessity for my Remaining at Fort Jefferson I propose being here again in the Month of February in order to Receive any Instructions You may Send forward to this place, I am Informed what few of the Inhabitants that are left at Charksville are desireous of Your Moving them down to the Iron banks or Your Order for So doing as in time of low water it is Intirely dry Between the forts and Island which makes that place Very Inconvenient what few that is there when I go down I will do all in my powere to Incourage them in order to Keep up the place for I Shall always be of the Oppinion that Some where about there will be one of the first places in this State in a very few Years

---

[38] DMs, 50J58; *Clark Papers*, 468-469.

I am Dr Col^o Your Most Obedient and Most Humble Servant

R^D HARRISON

P^S Pensacola is not as yet Taking by Reason of the Despute Between Governor Galvez and admiral of the Spanish fleat Governor Galvez had orders from the Court of Spain to have the Command of the Army Agaist Pensacola the admiral would not Give it up therefore Galvez Is Returnd again to mobeal with his army

GEORGE SLAUGHTER TO THOMAS JEFFESON[39]

Louisville 8th Decr 1780

SIR

   Inclosed are Copies of Letters from Capt George the Commanding officer at Fort Jefferson & Capt. Williams from the same place to Col. Clark, also an original letter sent by Capt Helm, by which you will learn the situation of the Officers in that Quarter. Such a number of Officers leaving their Posts, & so many of the Men Deserting together with the Conduct of the Commertial Agent & the scarcity of provisions the Crews of the Boats loaded there with having deserted & Carry'd them off that there is too much reason to fear that the post will be evacuated. I have therefore taken the Liberty of ordering the remains of the Country Store together with a large Cargo which is now on its way from Orleans for the use of this State to be brought hither. these reasons will I hope Justify me but when I inform Your Excellency of the number of Complaints against Capt. Dodge both from Officers nad Men of the shameful Misapplication of the Goods in his care, and of the Abuses Commited by him in his Department you will think it prudent to prevent this, as there is too much reason to believe he did the former Cargoes. My Men have never drawn any thing from the State but Cloth & thirty Blankets at Williamsburg are all the necessaries they have drawn since their Inlistment they [have] now no Shirts, Hats, Blankets or Breeches not having drawn Cloth for that purpose, Shoes, Stockings or Mocasons. so that they are totally unfit for duty. The Indians still are Troublesome to us having Visited us four or five times since Col^o Clark left this place, & have killed and taken 5 or 6 Men and Wounded 3 others.

I am Sir Your hum^l Servant

GEORGE SLAUGHTER.

WILLIAM SHANNON TO THOMAS JEFFERSON[40]

---

[39] DMs, 50J79; *Clark Papers*, 472.
[40] Executive Papers, Archives Division, Virginia State Library, Richmond; *Clark Papers*, 473-474.

SHANNON TO THOMAS JEFFERSON[41]

Louisville, 11th DECEM. 1780.

SIR:

As things are at present circumstanced in this Country & being so remote from the Seat of Government, must beg leave to intrude so far on your Excellencies good nature as to give statisfactory answers to the doubts I am at present in and such other Instructions you may Judge best. I would therefore be glad to know the nature of my Commission from Col'o G. Rogers Clarke on my return from Government last Spring, & must inform you that it is very difficult to execute the business I am entrusted with for want of money owing to a report prevalent that our Bills on the Treasurer have been protested which renders the Credit of the State very Trifling.

The Army in this quarter destitute of all kind of Military stores and none to be purchased; no provisions to be had except Beef, Corn & Salt and all those at most extravagant prices.

Inclosed you have the Amount of the Bills Drawn on the Treasurer this Spring & Summer.

Money is much wanting to discharge the present contracts which are payable this first day of March next as also to pay the expences of the late expedition.

I have as far as in my power supply'd Colo Slaughter's Troops and shall still continue to do so, untill further orders.

I am much at a loss how to act relative to purchasing and Issuing provisions not knowing the proper allowances

Accounts from the mouth of the River say they have been distress'd in a most extraordinary manner for want of the common necessaries of life which has occasioned many desertions

Form Orleans we have Accounts that the Spaniards have not taken Pensacola owing to a dispute wch arose between Governor Galvis and the Spanish Admiral relative to the Command of the Forces and neither giving up the point the Siege was laid aside and the Land Force are now at Mobille under the Command of Galvis.

I expect Boats down the River dayly and intend purchasing Flour for the Troops at Fort Jefferson, Corn & Salt have sent, Shall continue to draw bills for provisions till ordered to the contrary. Your Excellencys Instructions by the earliest opportunity will much oblige

Your Excellences Mo. Obt. & Humble Servant

WILL SHANNON

---

[41] Unpublished Clark Papers; *Clark Papers*, 473474.

JOHN DODGE TO OLIVER POLLOCK[42]   KASKASKIAS, 23 Decem' 1780

SIR

Altho I have had not the honor of Receiving Answers to my three last Letters which I wrote you & our Credit being so weak Amongst the Inhabitants here that we cannot get any thing without prompt Payment which we have not our Soldiers dying every day for want of the means of Subsistance and Medicine which occasions me to Inclose you the Memorandums which if you have any regard for the Troops in this Departments you will exert yourself to procure them for us, if it should happen that you could not procure the whole try to send part By the bearer of this and I will settle with him for his trouble no news but what the bearer can inform you of. I have no more to add only your Compliance with the above will render the State a Singular service and much oblige

Sir Your humb' Serv'
JOHN DODGE

CAPTAIN ROBERT GEORGE TO G. R. CLARK[43]

Dr. Colo.   Fort Jefferson 24th. Dec. 1780

I have now before me, Your, Mr. Polluck's, and Colo. Montgomery's last Letters, and am sorry to inform You, that the greatest party of the Cargoe sent to you for the use of the State was lost by a hurricane which overset the Batus- that loss compels me to purchase the Remaindr. of Captn. Barbers Goods, that was his own property, and made Bold to draw Bills for the Same, I hope it will be agreeable to You & Government, as it appears to me by Capt. Harrison's Discourse, that it's your Intintion to evacuate this Spt & Errect Another Fortification at the Iron Banks, Am now in doubt whether to begin the matter this Winter, or before Positive Instructions from You aI am certain it can be done with liss dificulty now, than in Spring- I am sore distressed with thoughts & care, to know in what manner to proceed for the best; which I doubt, without Your Arrival here Soon, will turn my yellow locks gray- Our good old friend Captn. Helm is of Infinite Service & ~~Satisfaction~~ Comfort to me at this place- Pray, forward Advice, or instructions as quick as possible- The Gent Officers seems to be desirous of moving to the Iron Banks; & petitioned Colo. Montgomery ~~to~~ before he left the Country, to evacuate this post, or move it to the I. Banks, which was prevented by the Arrival of Major Harlan. But as I keep the Command, I intend, upon the whole to keep up this post until further Orders from You: We have no news, other than, that the Governour of Orleans, had gone to the Havannah & was on his return, before Capt. Barber left Orleans; in order to raise the Siege Against Penascola.

I hope these will reach you safe, & am
Sir...
Robt. George

---

[42] Unpublished Clark Papers; *Clark Papers*, 475.
[43] Seineke, 468-469.

ROBERT GEORGE TO OLIVER POLLOCK[44]

FORT JEFFERSON 1st January 1781

SIR

I herewith send you this As a Letter of Advice, with two Sets of Exchange for two hundred and thirty seven thousand three hundred And twenty Dollars in favour of Captain Philip Barbour, who has furnished us with a Large Cargoe of Licours and Dry goods which have been the Saveing of this Poast, Other Could not have Supported it for want of Necessaries, the Sum may appear to you to be large, but I Called a Council of my Officers And Consulted them upon the matter After having Receiv'd An Invoise of the Cargoe And they with myself thought it a Reasonable Sum Considering the Deficulties he had to surmount in geting up to us when heard of Our Distresses the season was far spent and the Enemy (Indians and English) surrounded us on Every Quarter but Notwithstanding he broke through fire and Ice and Came to our assistance, the Necssaries he has brought us supply our Immediate wants And Articles to purchase provisions for sometime which Our paper Currency would by no means do. therefore most Earnestly beg you may pay the above in Gold or Silver Coin this being done it will Inable him to supply us in future, Capt Barbour will give you all the News we have in this Remote hole, hope these few Lines will suffice till we shall have something of more Importance or Clever to write You, And am sir your Obedient Humble Servant

ROBERT GEORGE Cap^n
Commandant Fort Jefferson

JOHN MONTGOMERY TO THOMAS JEFFERSON[45]

NEW ORLEANS January 8th 1781

SIR

This is to Represent the distressed situation of Fort Jefferson and the impossibility of mentaining said Post without some Speedy Relief

First the Inhabitants in Genl are leaving the Settlement for want of Subsistance and continually Harrassed by an Unmerciful Enemy the Loss of their Corn and Stock and we not being able to suport those Adventurers by reason of our Credit being so far Reduced for want of Funds

Secondly the certainty of our Soldiers deserting as numbers has already for want of provisions &c. &c

Thirdly Experience fully Shews me that if the late Attack had held a few days longer, all our Stores and Ammunition must fall into the hands of the Enemy, by reason we had nothing but Corn in the Garrison & no more then what would support us for Six days longer, it was impossible for us to Repulse the Enemy, their Force being Superior to Ours if they were certain of our Situation, we being above half a mile from the Misissippi and that thorough a Thick Wood Except where the Channel Run when the Misissippi was high, it's well known the impossibility of Transporting provisions that way to the Fort in

---

[44] Unpublished Clark Papers.
[45] *Ibid.*

time of an Invasion all these Reasons are Evidence to Every person the different advices Received of this place Minaced with Attacks from diff^t Quarters and Nations and the long time we have had no advice from Governm^t makes me represent to You the inavoidable Loss that must happen to this place if continued as it now is and the great loss to Government not only of this place with the Stores but all the Illenois Country was this Post to Fall, I further think it highly necessary that this Post may be removed to some place where an Open Communication may be kept up with the Mississpi or to remove all the State Stores Amunition &c. with the Troops where they can be provided for, They Establishing a Settlement agreeable to their intention as the Situation of this can no ways answer having no Communication with the Missisippi for better then half a Mile for one half the Year, The Bearer hereof Capt Robison can inform You the Particulars, and had it not been for the Assistance OF Mr Oliver Pollock with whom I am now present, we must undoubtedly evacuate that Post, He well knowing that Govern^t having to heart the Setling a place of so much Consequence and form those good principles he hath always Shewn Sent us Relief from time to time both Amunition and Goods in our Greatest distresses until he has Sent his All & is Still Striving to send Us further Supplies I am fully Conviced it will not be in his Power to Send further Supplies without Relief I am in hopes You will take the Speediest Method of Sending him Remittances or Providing a Fund for our future Relief, as I can See No other Method for the Preservation of the Illenois Country Pray Excuse me for takeing Such Libertys it being the true State of our Situation and in Colonel Clarks absence I think it my duty

I am Sir With Respect Your Excellencies most Obed^t Humble Servant

JN^O MONTGOMERY

ADDRESS TO INHABITANTS OF KASKASKIA FROM CAPTAIN ROBERT GEORGE[46]

At Fort Jefferson this 11th Jan. 1981.

To Messieurs the Inhabitants of Illinois in general and particularly those of Kaskaskias

My Dear friends and Fellow Countrymen- It is with the most profound regret that I have learned that you are Robbed and Pillaged by those that you call Our People. Be well assured that I greatly regret the injury, and that I will employ all my efforts towards redress of all Your Complaints and all your grievances. Monsieur Kenedy has always been duly authorized in all our Public Affairs in Your Country. He has, actually, my Instructions for making purchases of provisions for our garrison. I beg you toCredit that I have had all Confidence in his Good Conduct and his abilities particularly since for a long time he has been one of your fellow citizens. And because he has my authority, I shall make it an order that Your Complaints will always be served with attention; but now that Colonel Clark will be with us this Good Spring I am persuaded that he will give you ample Satisfaction for all the Injuries that have occurred.

---

[46] Seineke, 472-473.

Trust in an entire, And generous payment for all the Provisions that Mr. Kennedy has bought from among you, and rest assured of the Benevolence of government Toward You.

Permit me the honor of Serving you My Dear Friends and Fellow Countrymen, Your very humble and very obt. Servant and Sincere Friend

Robert George Capt. Commandant

True Copy translated by langlois at Kas 21st. Jan. 1781
                                                    Signed Giracult

THOMAS JEFFERSON TO CLARK[47]   RICHMOND Jan 13 1781

SIR
   I received last night form General Washington a letter on your subject in which he has complied with my request. as every movement will depend so much on yourself in the Western quarter I leave to yourself to determine whether you should not as soon as possible repair hither & take the ultimate measures which are necessary.[1]

I am Sir Your most obed^t serv^t

TH JEFFERSON

GEORGE SLAUGHTER TO THOMAS JEFFERSON[48]
                                           LOUISVILLE Janr 14th 1781.
SIR
   I have the Honour to inclose to your Excellency letters form tow Gentlemn at Auposte and copys of several others from Kaskaskias directed to Col^o Clark & Col^o Todd. I have taken the Depositions of three persons which corroborates with the copies of these letters & have inclosed them also, for the consideration of your Board.
   The contents of the letters form the tow French Gentlemen being a request for ammunition & understand they apprehended an attack'd upon that post, I gave orders for Capt George to send to Kaskaskias one hundred weight of powder & four hundred wt of Lead, with directions for Capt Rogers to lend what aid he can in getting across the country to Auposte & shall endeavour to send a small supply to that place immediately form here. That I thought it necessary to do as I consider it of very great importance to this place the keeping the Auposte in our favour.
   With respect to Capt Dodge the complaints against him are so general & have so good authority for his having misapplied the publick goods, and apprehending that he may

---

[47] DMs, 51J7; *Clark Papers*, 491-492.
[48] DMs 51J12; *Clark Papers* 493-494.

possibly be collecting a cargo of Peltry for the New Orleans market that I have given Capt George Orders to make enquiry as to his conduct & if any thing of this sort appears, to seize his person & what goods he may be possessed of & secure them 'till further Orders.

The Letters now inclosed with those sent some time ago will so fully inform you of the state of Affairs in the Illinois that I shall not enlarge on the disagreeable subject.

I now beg leave to mention the mismanagement of the person appointed to superintend the making salt with the countrys Kettles. [Word *illegible*] here about 50 or 60 bushels is all that has been red from the persons who has work'd them, when private adventurers has been making near 10 times the Quantity with Kettles not boiling more than one fourth as much Water, owing principally to the indolence of the man who is appointed to carry on the business.

If Sir you Board should think proper to appoint Colo Floy'd or myself to take the directions of the Kettles I am persuaded a sufficiency would be made for the Troops in this department.

I am with much respect Your Excellencys Most obd^t & very Hble Servt

GEORGE SLAUGHTER

The two letters from the French Gent. of the Auposte was by a Mistake inclosed to Col^o Clarke who will no doubt lay them before you.

I cannot Omit Mentioning tow you the three Bills which I drew late in October last in fav^y of John Williams Province one for 2205 Dollars one other for 286 Dollars & another for £2120. which I hope will be paid

Y^{rs} as before
G. S.

CLARK TO THOMAS JEFFERSON[49]

RICHMOND Jany 18th, 81

D^R S^R

I have examined your proposed Instructions I don't Recollect of anything more that is Nessary Except the Mode of paying the Expences of the Garison of Dutroit, in Case of Success, as supporting our Credit among strangers may be attended with great and good Consequences and my former Experience Induce me to wish it to be the Case whare I have the Honour to Comm^d I would also observe to your Excellency that I could wish to set out on this Expedition free from any Reluctance which I doubt I cannot do without a Satisfactory Explination of the treatment of the Virginia Delegates in Congress to me in objecting to an appointment designed for me, which your Excellency Cannot be a Stranger to I could wish not to be thought to solicit promotion and that my Duty to myself did not oblige me to transmit these Sentiments to you The Treatment I have General^{ly} met with from this State hath prejudied me as far as Consistant in her Interest and wish not to be disturbed in the Execution of her orders by an Continental Co^r that may be in the Cuntries that I have Business in, which I doubt will be the Case althought the Orders of the Commander in Chef is very positive

---

[49] Unpublished Clark Papers; *Clark Papers*, 495-496

I am Si^r with the Greatest Esttm Y^r Excellencies Very Hbl Servt

G R CLARK

P S I hope to be Honoured by a line from your Excellencie, as before

G R C

THOMAS JEFFERSON TO CLARK[50]   IN COUNCIL January 20 1781

SIR

Having cause to entertain doubts from several Letters transmitted me whether Mr John Dodge who was appointed to conduct a commerce with the Indians on behalf of this state has not been guilty of gross misapplication or mismanagement of what has been confided to him and the distance between him and us rendering it impracticable to call the examination before ourselves you are hereby authorized and desired either by yourself or such persons as you shall appoint to enquire into any part of his conduct which you may have reason to suppose unjustifiable and if it be found so to remove him from his office and take such measures as may be most effectual for bringing him to account and indemnifying the public against such malversations. Should he be removed we think it unnecessary to appoint another in his Stead.

I am Sir Your most ob^t humble servant

TH. JEFFERSON

THOMAS JEFFERSON TO CLARK[51]

IN COUNCILL Jan 22, 1781

SIR

I do myself the pleasure of inclosing you a Brigadier General's commission the laws having given us power to appoint a general officer only for special purposes and not a perpetual one, has obliged us to express the particular occasion of the appointment. besides this I thought it necessary to give you an exemplification of your former commission which was perpetual.

I wish you in every circumstance all possible success & felicity, and to believe me to be with very sincere esteem Sir

Your most obed^t & most humble serv^t
TH JEFFERSON

---

[50] DMs 51J17; *Clark Papers*, 499.
[51] DMs, 51J18; *Clark Papers*, 500.

ROBERT GEORGE TO GEORGE SLAUGHTER[52]

FORT JEFFERSON, 15th Feby 1781

Dr. SIR:-

I have the Honor to acknowledge the rec't of yours of the 23rd January last, & am happy to find the you are so abundant as you express—as out of your great abundance I shall expect to receive frequent and large Supplies—more especially in the Commissary way. The Small Supplies you have sent us, have been of infinite Service, & if you frequently repeat them they will be of singular advantage as we look to you for it, but the supplies I beg may be of a better Quality than what is yet come to hand. The Beef is really of the poorest kind—ill-cured, and not half salted—the Barrels being bad, the pickle became wasted, if ever any had been put in, and tho' the Meat does not absolutely stink, it wants little of it. The approaching Season being warm more especially require that the Troops should be victualled with the wholesomest diet. You well know the ill Consequences of bad Provisions in an Army. I shall therefor only request you w'd not put the State to the Expence of transporting any more provisions to us, as I shall not suffer such for the future to be recieved. "Twere will if all that you send was first inspected.

Major Harlan will give you the News of the place I As have to purchase Supplies in the Illinois it draws away the Liquor from me fast, besides I have to send a Supply to the Opost, & Major Linetot has made a heavy Draft on me for 6 Hogsheads & the half of my Amunition for use of the Indian Department and three Hogshead more to purchase Eight Months Provisions for 25 Men which I have sent for the protection of the Opost and under the command of Capt. Bayly—The Credit of the State is so bad that nothing can be had either there or at Kaskaskia without prompt payment, & when our little Stock is exhausted I know not what we shall do, except you take some Care of us. Send us as much Whisky as you please as we are forced to expend our Taffia for Provisions. The Enemy are approaching the Opost, & fortifying themselves at Miamis, so that the Inhabitants of the Opost have Petitioned me for an Officer & Men to uphold the Honor of the State there, which I have complied with In the Month of January I have the pleasure to inform you we were able to drink brandy, Taffia & Wine—with your good assistance Whisky too; but it has not made us saucy, but we can drink all the Whisky you can send us.

I send under the care of Major Harlan for the use of Mr. Slaughter & Mr. Roberts one hundred wt. of sugar 12lb soap and fifty weight of coffee &c agreeable to the enclosed bill.

I have the Pleasure to drink your Health in a bumper of your good Whisky and the Honor to be your most obed. & very humble Servant,

ROBT. GEORGE.

I have taken notice of your Song and learned it. It is so good I wish you had sent more of it.

I am under the necessity of putting a Stop to the Mens Rations of Liquor in order purchase provisions. Please send us a little paper by the first opportunity as we can hardly carry on business for want of that Article.

---

[52] Executive Papers, Archives Division, Virginia State Library, Richmond; *Clark Papers*, 507-507.

JOSEPTH HUNTER TO CLARK[53]　　　FORT JEFERSON April 20th 1781

DEAR GENERAL
　　It gives me the Greatest satisfaction to hear of your Advancement and that your usual Good Fortune hase attended you thro all your Enterprizes since we hade the pleasure of seeing you hear. At the same time that I Recived so much satisfaction; in these particulars I Cannot Avoid Expressing; the ueassness I feel at the prospect of Our Litle Settlement; being Broak up; and that Chiefely for want of the personal presence of its first founder and Benefactor. I doubt not your great Good Will towards us; but since a new Field is now opened for you; wherin to Exercise those Great talents; you are Possessed of; which must Invitable take off your Attention from an object so Inconsiderable; as the Incourangement of this Settlement already Broak; and Labouring under more Impediments thin if it hade never been Attemted—I am far from Reflecting the Least Blaim on you; but with Chearfulness Strugled Against Every Vissitude my Lonley Circumstances Exposes me unto hear; I lost almost all my Stock Grain &c— Nevertheless I doe not Repine; hoping through your Influence that Goverment will not Overlook me; as I may say I have born the Burding and heat of the day; what Grain I Reasd the Troops have used—tho I Cannot but in Justice Say that Cap^n George hath done the part of a Good offcir; and Likewise all the other oficers hath Treated me with all the possible Marks of Esteem; but if his Excelency General Washington Was to Comand hear; he would not please all the people—its my sincear wish that success may attend you through all your Interprizes and that God by his kind providence may preserve you from your Cruel Enimes and Crown your Endevours—and that I may be so happy to se you Return hear to se a Good settlement at the Ironbanks I am dea General with the Greatest Esteem your most Obedient Humble Sv^t

JOSEPH HUNTER

JOHN ROGERS TO THOMAS JEFFERSON[54]　　　HARODSBURG, 29th April 1781

SIR,
　　Since my arrival at the Falls of Ohio I have been much surprised to find that some Persons have wrote assertions against my Character during the time of my Comand at the Illinoys last Winter.2 Rich'd Winston & Rich'd McCarty I am informed are the Persons. in order to give you a proper Idea of those Gentlemens' Characters I must inform you that McCarty has ever since Sept. last been under an Arrest for Treason the former tho Deputy County Lieutenant for the Illinois County opposed me in all my demands for provisions for my Men & encouraged the Inhabitants at all times to refuse my requests

---

[53] DMs, 51J41; *Clark Papers*, 539-540.
[54] *Clark Papers*, 545-546.

notwithstanding my repeated applications for that purpose tho my Men were even dying for want. Colo' Montgomery having left several of his Sick men under my Care some of which died for want of wherewithal to support nature When I found the People so lost to Humanity & that I was likely to see my men starved in a Cuntary abounding in Plenty I was under the Necessity of killing now and then a Beast for their support & that but seldom as Mr. Bentley Mercht at Kask's supplied me with the greatest part of meat as well as every other necessary requisite towards reestablishing my Men in Health who were all very sickly when Col'o Montgomery left me the Comand there & as Mr. Bentley is now on hi way to Government I should do an injustice to his Character was I not to recommend him to your good Graces for the Essential Service he has rendered me and my Men in behalf of the State as he ever cheerfully furnished everything in his power to procure—Influencing the Inhabitants at all times as far as in him laid to supply us & offering himself as security for their Payment in Hard Money on allowing him to go into Govt but was always counteracted by the tow aforment'd Persons who Spirited the People so against him that they refused him the Benefit of recovering his Debts to put I out of his power to Supply me that I might be obliged to quit the Country.

The Expedition under Brigadier General Clarke being on foot prevents my waiting on you at this time in order to cleare up everything that can have been laid to my charge which I flatter Myself I can do & doubt not but you will anticipate my Innocence as was the case with reguard to Col'o Calloways Charge in 1779. I am informed they Charge me with having shot down and barbequed the Cattle on the Commons—a Charge no less villainous than false in order to convince you of the Malignity & villany of such a Charge I send pr Cap't Dodge my Cornet & Comesaries Affidavits and have all my Letters2 to Mr. Winston & the Inhabitants with theire answers which I hope to produce to you at a proper time when you will see those people in their proper Colours, I can not conclude without informing you that tis my positive opinion the People of the Illinois & Fort Vincenes have been in an absolute State of Rebellion for these several Months past & ought to have no farther Indulgence shewn them & such is the nature of those People the more they are indulged the more turbulent they grow--& I look upon it that Winston & McCarty have been principle Instruments to bring them to the Pitch they are now at

I request the favour of you to satisfy yourself with reguard to my conduct at the Illinois by every person coming form thence & to omit no opertunity to forward Copies of all Letters to my Prejudice to General Clark that I may have it in my Power to cleare myself as soon as may be as I ever hope to prove myself worthy of my present Trust & nay farther favours which Government may hereafter be pleased to Confer on me having the honour to be with the utmost Respect

Your Excellencys Most Obedient and Most Hum^l Servt

John Rogers

CLARK TO GEORGE WASHINGTON[55]   FORT PITT 20th May 1781

SIR,

Reduced to the necessity of taking Every step to carry my point the Ensuing campag^n I hope your Excellency will Excuse me in taking the liberty of troubling you with this Request, The Invasion in Virg^a put it out of the power of the governor to furnish me with the number of men proposed for the Enterprise to the west but informd me he had obtaind leave of the Baron Steuben and agreeable to your Letters for Col^o John Gibson and Regiment together with Hirths [Heath's] company to Join my forces, An addition he suposd of more worth than the malitia we were disappointed of, On consulting Col^o Broadhead he could not Conceive that he was at liberty to suffer them to go as your Instructions was pointed Respecting the troops & stores to be furnished by him, From your Excellencies letters to Col^o Broadhead I conceived him to be at liberty to furnish what me he pleased, Convinc'd he did not think as I do or other ways he would have had no objection, as he apeard to wish to give the Enterprise every aid in his power—The hopes of obtaining a grant of those troops has Enducd me to address your Excellency myself as it is too late to consult Governor Jefferson farther on the subject, Wishing to set out on the Expedition Early in June as our Stores of provisions are nearly compleat, If our force should be Equal to the task proposd I cant Conceive that this post with a very small garrison Even of malitia will be in any danger as it is attach'd to a popular country and during our time in the Enemies [country] McEntosh and weelin [Wheeling] will be useless or might also be garrisond by small parties of malitia, Those I know to be your Excellencies Ideas, If you should approve of the troops in this department Joining our forces tho they are few the acquisition may be attended with great & good consequences as tow Hundred only might turn the Scale in our favour, The advantages that must derive to the States from our proving successful is of such Importance that I think deservd a greater preparation to Ensure it, But I have not yet lost sight of Detroit, nothing seem to threaten us but the want of men, But Even should we be able to cut our way thro' the Indians and find they have Receivd no Reenforcements at Detroit we may probably have the assurance to attack it thoug^h our force may be much less than proposed which was two thousand as defeating the Indians with inconsiderable loss on our side would almost Ensure us success, Should this be the case a valuable piece [sic] with them will probably Ensue, But on the contrary should we fall throug^h in our present plans and no Expedition take place it is to be feard that the consequences will be fatal to the whole frontiers as Every Exertion will be made by the british party to Harrass them as much as possible and disable them from giving any succours to our Eastern or Southern forces, The Indian war is now more general than Ever, any attempts to appease them Except by the sword will be fruitless, Capt Randolph waits on your Excellen^y for an answer to this letter which I flatter myself you will honour me with Immediately, Col^o Gibson who Commands in the absence of Col^o Braodhead will keep the troops ready to move at an warning conducting myself as thought this Request was granted,--Impatiently waiting for the happy order

---

[55] *Clark Papers*, 551-553.

It is with gratitude I thank your Excellency for the honour you have done me in your several letters. The greatest Earthly happiness I could possible Enjoy would be to conduct myself with such propriety as to be Entitled to your Esteem

I have the Hon^r to be Your Excellencies most Devoted & Humb^e serv^t

G R CLARK B G

CLARK TO GEORGE WASHINGTON[56]   PITTSBURG 21st May 1781

SIR,

I this moment Receivd yours of the 25th of april the Intelligence is by no means alarming to me, it corresponds with my former suspicion,

I have for several years kept up a constant chain of Intelligence from the Lakes through the channel of the Illinoise inhabitants—And a few hours after yours I Receivd dispatches from the missisippi St Vincent River & the whole a confirmation of your Excellencies Hint, Except that part of their coming by the way of the Allegany River— But Rather through the western pass as more Immediately among the Indian nations whom they would wish to have with them, And what greatly favours the Idea is that upowards of one thousand Ouabash Indians have again declard themselves in our favour and of course will draw their attention that way for some time, for fear that our troops in that Quarter Reinforcd by those Indians should make a diversion on the lakes while they had drawn of their forces to pitsburg, For in part it has been the Influence of our posts win the Illinoise and Ouabash that have savd the frontiers and a great measure baffled the designs of the enemy at Detro^{it} If they get possession of them they then Command three times the number of Valuable warriors they do at present and be fully Enabled to carry any point they aim at Except we should have a formidable force to oppose them

I am well acquainted with Col^o Connely and should be happy to meet him on Equal terms, If his dependence is principally on Indians and we should fortunately get into the field before him he will probably meet with a disapointmt But should be he Independent of them our circumstances will be truly deplorable, Excep we had other means of drawing the Inhabitants of this this country to the field besides persuasive arguments which is too much our dependence at present. I wrote to the governor of pensylvania on this Subject but Receivd no answer, I cant think any thing of Importance is to be Expected by the way of the winango but much to be apprehended from the to her Quarter, I refer you to Capt Randolph for the news of this Quarter

I have the Hon^r to be yr Excell^s Devoted Servt

G R CLARK BG

---

[56] *Clark Papers*, 553-554.

WILLIAM SHANNON TO CLARK[57]

Sullivans Station　　　　　　　　　　　　　　　　　　　　May 21, 1781

Sir.

Your express by Capt Sullivan, to fort Jefferson, I forwarded as soon as it came to hand, the return of which you have inclosed. I learn by letters from tat post, that they are in a starving Condition, & am sorry to inform you, that it is almost out of my power, at present to relieve them, Maj^r Slaughter having used the provisions purchased for that post, and injured our Credit, so much in this place that I find it almost impossible to purchase any thing without money. About three weeks ago, I sent a boat to Post St Vincent with three hundred Gallons of whisky, to purchase the skins you wrote for, & expect the return of them by the time you are here. Yesterday I sent Capt Moore with two other Gent^{lm} to the countys of Lincoln, & Fayatte, with instructions to purchase what Beef Cattle, Dry, & pickeled Beef, Butter, Cheese, corn &c. they possibley could, ono the Credit of the state, Assuring them that the money woud shortly be paid—I shoud have went myself but Detained in hopes of purchasing One or two hundred bushels of Corn, for the relife of fort Jefferson, which I intend emedetly to send With about eight or ten though weight of Beef which Slaughter has not yet got into his hands.—Capt John Rogers of the Light Dragoons, arrived here and six or seven weeks ago, from the Illinois with his whole Compny, in good helth, there ware with him Messars, Dodge. Dejean, & Bently on there was to Government, with several Indians, of which Battist the Kaskaskaia Chife wase One. I can procure any quantity of salt you may want for your present expedition, it being the only article that can be purchased here on the Credit of the state. I most sincearly wish that you would inform Government, that in Case they woud furnish me with money I Could purchase provisions in this Department, at almost half the sum, I can for Credit, Instance corn & salt, If Cash, corn can be had at forty Dollars p^r Bushel, & for Credit eighty, or one hundred, If Cash salt, can be had at five or six hundred Dollars Pr Bushel, and for Credit eight hundred or One thousand, and the same case with every species of provisions, since you left this place. I think If you wase to inform Government of this that they woud remedy it, as the state is run to Double expence, in not having money to purchase with,--As Col^o Floyd writes you I shall refer you to his letters for neuws, Capt Sullivan will write you the Difficultys he labours under with regard to being furnished with the Necessary Gaurds & fattaugs [fatigues] for the men he has Imployed to build the state boats.

I am Sir With due respect. Your most, Obed^t Humb^{le} Servt

Will. Shannon Commiss^y Genl I.D.

P.O. please present my best Compliments to Capt Benjn Harrison & inform him that, I should be happy in his showing himself once more in the mess　　W.S.

N.B. Mr Veech who is Imployed to convey the present express is refered to you for pay
W.S.

---

[57] DMs, 51J52; *Clark Papers*, 554-555.

JOHN FLOYD TO CLARK[58]   May 22, 1781, Beargrass

Dear General

    As Mr Veech is going immediately to the neighbourhood of Fort Pitt, I thought it might not be amiss to write you again although I have noting of much importance to communicate since my last. The Commissaries are gone to Lincoln to purchase Cattle & other Stores for the Campaign.

    Mr Lindsay is getting a quantity of Beef dried in Fayette, where the Buffaloe are yet exceedingly numerous. He has also bought some Beeves in that County, and I think one hundred at least will be got in Lincoln, and some few in this County. The old Women seem much engaged in making Butter and Cheese for the Army. Mrs Floyd tells me to inform you she has about 200 lb of fine cheese for you & desires that you bring her a piece of Linen.

    Corn is very plenty in the upper Counties, & although it does not answer for a Campaign, it may do to send down to the Iron Bank Station, where I am informed them poor fellows are in almost a starving condition. I am about hiring some hunters to go to Drinnens Lick to lay up some Beef from whence I expect it can be brought in the Canoes from the upper Counties, as I am informed one hundred are to be furnished from those Counties.

    Salt is plenty, and many articles might be purchased with money, & for want of it the price of every article is almost double which is bought for the State, and its Credit here is really at a very low ebb.

    Nothing can be purchased for the Troops on Credit at Illinoise where I hear they have plenty. Dodge is gone to Richmond and I hear has all his accounts well authenticated. None of our Troops are yet come out by Land, I had a Letter from Gab^l Madison in which he says the Greenbrier Men would not march till the middle of April owing to the Tents, Bags, & Linen for the pack saddles being sent to Fort Pitt by mistake.

    The Indians have this year suffered us to plant corn on Beargrass unmolested; the reason of which I expect, is owing to the little Expedition you ordered against some of their Towns early this spring, which has attracted the attention of other Tribes[59] also: not one has made his appearance here for many Weeks till last Friday, they killed one of the Guard near the Falls where they were preparing Timber for the Boats—Ned Mordock was killed some Weeks ago on the West side the Ohio a little below Salt river.

    The lower McAfee's Station was attacked a few days since by about thirty Indians, they were reinforced from the neighbouring Garrisons and Sallied out & attacked the Indians in the woods: they got three Scalps wounded several, with the loss of Nathan Lynn & one other man whose name I have not heard.

    Squire boon who was badly Wounded at his Station this spring, is likely to get well. It is with much difficulty I can get any thing done by the Militia, and all for want of Officers authorized to sit on a court Martial. Do endeavour to have some blank Militia Com^{ns} sent me from Governm^t if possible, as I am greatly perplexed for want of them. I have several times wrote to Government on the Subject to no purpose. Canoes & Boats I believe will be made but not without some cursing and wrangling. I wish I could hear

---

[58] DMs, 51J53; *Clark Papers*, 556-558.
[59] Refers to expedition sent out by Colonel Broadhead.

from you as often as possible. When may we look for you here? The Drafts are made in these Counties for the Expedition, and I expect nearly ready to March. The number of Militia in this County is 354 in Lincoln 732 & Fayette 160 This at present is the whole strength of Kentuckey, and our numbers seem to decrease, as I have ordered the Surveying in the County to be stopped till the Expedition is over—I found it impracticable to complete the business of the Draft without making this streach.

May the Heaves bless & preserve you   Farewell

Jn Floyd

CLARK TO THOMAS JEFFERSON,[60] YOHOGANIA COURT HOUSE, June 10, 1781

SIR

Cap. Bently of the Illenoise attends on me with a number of bills on government for furnitures made to our troops in that country, Those that I have countersigned appear by the Accounts. Annex'd and different lettes from Gent[n] to be Sufficiently authenticated for payment, he has other Bills drawn by Col[o] Montgomery that I cannot with propriety Credit until Iam made sensible of the Justness of them, By the accot[s] of that country but they probably may be Just, your Excellency will do as you please Respecting them, I am informd that Mr Charles Gratiot hath also Bills on their way to you some of them I know must be Just as that Gen[n] as well as Capt Bently have taken great Pains to subsist our troops in that depart[mt] Perticulary paying of the Expence of an Expedition up the Illinois River which promised good Consequences—The great Bundle of draughts you mentioned in your last I have not yet seen nor can I learn who has them, Cap[t] Bently appers desirous to undertake the Suplying Fort Jefferson with provisions for a grarrison of 100 men, If it should be your pleasure to make such Contract—I don't know any person more likely to accomplish such a task. He has a universal good Charracter as a gentleman & hath suffer'd much on Acc[t] of the present Content

I have the Honor To be your Very Humble & Obet[t] Serv[t]

GR Clark

JOHN MONTGOMERY TO THOMAS NELSON,[61]
FALLS OF THE OHIO 10th AUG[t] 1781

SIR

I had the honor of addressing a Letter to Gov[r] Jefferson dated from New Orleans January 8 1781 to which I beg leave to refer you; since when after a disagreeable & dangerous voyage up the Mississippi I arrived Fort Jefferson the 1st May last, where I

---

[60] Unpublished Clark Papers; *Clark Papers*, 563-564.
[61] Unpublished Clark Papers; *Clark Papers*, 585-586.

found the Troops in a very low and Starving Condition, nor was any goods or other Property wherewith to purchase. From the Illinois nothing could be expected, the Credit of the State being long since lost there, & no supplies coming from this place, occasioned an Evacuation of that Post, which for want of provisions, took place on the 8th June last.

Since my arrival here I find things in the same Condition—not a Mouthful for the troops to eat nor money to purchase it with, & I have just reason to believe the Credit of government is wore thread bare, here also—The Counties of Lincoln & Fayette particularly tho' able to supply us, refuse granting any relief without the cash to purchase with on the Spot. I am constrained to Billet the Troops thro' the Country in Small parties for want of necessaries, except a small Guard I keep in Garrison, so that unless supplies soon arrive, I fear the Consequences will be fatal.

I am sorry to hear since my Return that Sundry Malicious aspersions have been made to my discredit; but as I am conscious of the rectitude of my own conduct, I despise the Efforts of such, & only beg leave to request your Excellency would either order me to Government for an Examination, or else appoint a Suitable Number of respectable Gentlemen in this Country to investigate my Conduct, so that such aspersions shall not have further weight with my Country. I have been in hourly expectation of Gen. Clark since my arrival here, else would have had the Honor to address your Excellency before; but my apprehensions are now really become great, seeing no reinforcements nor Supplies; especially as I learn from some prisoners who have got in from D'Troit that they are very Strong & Preparing against us.

The Enclosed copy of a Deposition will explain the matter more fully—I have only further to request your Excellency would be pleased to give me as speedy an Answer as possible with full Instructions how to proceed, as I am at the greatest Loss under my present distress'd circumstances.

I have the Honor to be Your Excellency's mo: obed^t Servt

Jno Montgomery L^t C^l

GEORGE ROGERS CLARK TO THOMAS JEFFERSON[62]

Falls of Ohio, 12th December 1802

SIR

I latterly had the pleasure of the perrusial of a letter from the Secretary of War to my brother on the Subject of the post of Fort Jefferson on the Mississippi. His answer to that letter completely described the place. A military post & Trading Town there, must be Obvious to every man of Observation that is acquainted with the Geography of the Countrey. I was the more pleased as I had Contemplated the importance of that spot from my earliest acquaintance with the Western Countrey.

When I was ordered (to) fix the garrison at or near the Mouth of the Ohio in the year (1780) I lay three weeks in the point and explored the banks of the river and Countrey

---

[62] Samuel W. Thomas, editor, *The Papers of George Rogers Clark, 1784-1818.* Unpublished Manucript on file at Locust Grove Historic Home, Louisville, Kentucky, pp. 432-433.

before I fixed on the Sot to build a Fort, and if my Instructions had not have been to place the Garrison South of the Ohio I certainly should have raised a Fortress in the point. I marked the ground the Annual inundations flooded, it is about five feet, and from that to seven feet is the depth of the water that Covers this butifull tract of bottom., which may be raised for a City of and Size, by the earth thrown Out of the Canals, Cut through the City, and those canals may be kept pure by turning the Cash River through them. I thus drew the plan and have been improveing on it frequently to the present time. What Caused me to view this ground with more attention as that the Spanish Shore opposd. so high that a Small expense would free two or three hundred acres of Land.

This Circumstance induced me to think that it would be necessary for us, at least to have a fortress in this point as a Key to the entrance of the Ohio. Those were my Ideas while on the ground. I segest to you, Sir if worthey your attention, any further information, and the best perhaps that can be Obtained of that country, may be got from my brother William, who is now Settled at Clarksville in the Indiana territory. I have long since laid aside all Idea of Public affairs, by bad fortune, and ill health. I have become incapable of persueing those enterprising & active persuites which I have been fond of from my youth. But I will with the greatest pleasure give my bro. William every information in my power to this, or any other point which may be of service to your Administration. He is well qualified almost for any business. If it Should be in your power to Confur on him any post of Honor and profit, in this Countrey in which we live, it will exceedingly gratify me. I seem to (...) a right to expect such a gratification when asked for, but what will greatly highten it is, that I am sure it gives you pleasure to have it in your power to do me a service. With the greatest assurance of your prosperity I have the honor to be your ever sincere

G R Clark

N B Mr. Hurst the gentleman whome will hand you this letter , is a young Lawyer from Vincennes a Man of integruty and a good republican whome I beg leave to recommend to you. GRC

CHAPTER 5: THE STRUCTURAL COMPOSITION OF CLARK'S FORT JEFFERSON[1]

In this chapter, archival evidence is used to demonstrate that Clark's Fort Jefferson was structurally complex and varied. It was not a "station" or a single "blockhouse." Fort Jefferson was a fortified military garrison with two bastions; it had outlying blockhouses strategically placed to protect the adjacent civilian community of Clarksville, and it was a town of several houses, cleared agricultural fields, work stations, and a cemetery. Clark planned Fort Jefferson to become a city of note, but fruition did not occur at the settlement because the location was simply too far from economic resources and supplies.

Introduction

As early as 1777, the State of Virginia planned to build a military garrison supported by a civilian settlement at or near the Mouth of the Ohio River.[2] In part, this was to solidify through physical possession Virginia's chartered claim to her western territory, but the fort and community were to be established also to check British aggression in the Illinois Country and to stop the flow of arms and munitions from the British in the north to their Chickasaw Indian allies in the south. The military presence also would deter deserters from the American cause in the East who fled down the Ohio and Mississippi rivers.

With these points in mind, Virginia Governor Patrick Henry, then Governor Thomas Jefferson, sought permission from Bernardo Galvez, the Spanish Governor in New Orleans, to build a fort and civilian community at the mouth of the Ohio River. In point of fact, Virginia was worried about possible Spanish control of the vital confluence region. So out of obligation, as well as political necessity, Thomas Jefferson wrote Galvez. Galvez gave his permission for the American presence adjacent to the Spanish territory only one mile distant across the Mississippi River.[3]

It would not be until January 1780, though, that Thomas Jefferson, acting on behalf of the State of Virginia, authorized then Lt. Col. George Rogers Clark to build the intended fort and community at the confluence of the Ohio and Mississippi rivers.[4] Clark and about 250 military and civilians descended the Ohio from the Falls area in April, 1780, arriving five miles south of the Ohio-Mississippi River confluence on April 19, 1780 to build Fort Jefferson and the civilian community of Clarksville.[5] Fort Jefferson would have the distinction of being the only military

---

[1] A version of this paper appeared in Kenneth C. Carstens and Nancy Son Carstens, *The Life of George Rogers Clark, 1752-1818: Triumphs and Tragedies*, Greenwood Publishing Group, Westport, Connecticut (in press).
[2] Letter, Patrick Henry to Bernardo Galvez, October 20, 1777, and January 14, 1778, in Lawrence Kinnard, ed., *Annual Report of the American Historical Association for the Year 1945, Vol. II. Spain in the Mississippi Valley* (Washington, D.C., Government Printing Office), 1949: 241-2; 248-250. Letter, Thomas Jefferson to Galvez, November 8, 1779, in James Alton James, ed., *The Papers of George Rogers Clark* (New York, AMS Press), 1972:362-4.
[3] James, James Alton, *The Life of George Rogers Clark* (New York: Greenwood Press), 1969:100-8.
[4] Letter, Jefferson to G. Clark, January 29, 1780, in James, ed., *Papers*, 1972:386-91.
[5] K. Carstens, "George Rogers Clark's Fort Jefferson, 1780-1781," *Filson Club History Quarterly*, (1997) 71(3).259-284. K. Carstens, *The Personnel of George Rogers Clark's Fort Jefferson and Civilian Community of Clarksville [Kentucky], 1780-1781* (Bowie, Maryland: Heritage books, Inc., 1999), and *The Calendar and Quartermaster Books of George Rogers Clark's Fort Jefferson, 1780-1781* (Bowie, Maryland; Heritage Books,

fort and settlement built in Kentucky sanctioned and authorized by the State of Virginia.

Fort Jefferson was occupied only from April 19, 1780 until its abandonment on June 8, 1781, but during that brief time (13 months and 20 days) the fort and community (comprising up to 550 persons during late summer, 1780) would participate in several military forays and defenses, would hold the western Virginian territory, and would serve as Clark's base of operations for a very important period during the American Revolution.[6] After 1781, the fort area would be re-evaluated for military occupation in 1795 by William Clark, the younger brother of George Rogers Clark, on behalf of Anthony Wayne and Henry Knox.[7] Fort Jefferson was not re-garrisoned. Wayne opted instead for the more defendable Fort Massac, located on the north shore of the Ohio River across from present-day Paducah, Kentucky. Thereafter, the Fort Jefferson area was abandoned and only vague and general references were made to its exact location with a series of 1821 land surveys.[8] During the 1860s, one of Fort Jefferson's cannon was found eroding into Mayfield Creek.[9] By first-hand descriptions of the cannon, the field piece seems to have been a French six pounder that Clark had taken earlier from old Fort des Chartres, north of Kaskaskia in 1778.[10] It is unknown if this is the same cannon that was spiked and placed in the fort's well when Fort Jefferson was abandoned.[11]

In the 1890s, the "old" Fort Jefferson area was resurveyed by the citizens of nearby Wickliffe, Kentucky, and plans were made to establish a new 19th century community to be called "Fort Jefferson," but funding fell through for the enterprise. Instead, development at the nearby towns of Wickliffe to the north and Bardwell to the south occurred, both in competition with Cairo, Illinois for economic gain in the area.[12] The old Fort Jefferson area remained rural, but in the 1960s plans were established to bring the Westvaco paper mill into the area, an industrial development that would pump new blood into far western Kentucky's economic vein. Today, the Mead-Westvaco Corporation owns the Fort Jefferson land and has a long history of supporting our research in the area.

Nineteenth- and twentieth-century histories do not describe George Rogers Clark's 1780-1781 Fort Jefferson in any detail, which is why it is important to understand the "built" or structural evidence of Clark's Fort Jefferson and community of Clarksville. What did Fort Jefferson look like? Did it have a stockade? Blockhouses? Or buildings within or without its

---

Inc., 2000); Letter G. Clark to John Dodge, April 19, 1780 in James, *Clark Papers*: 417-418.
[6] *Ibid.*
[7] John L. Loos, *A Biography of William Clark, 1770-1813* (Ph.D. dissertation, Department of History, Washington University, St. Louis, 1953); Samuel W. Thomas, "William Clark's 1795 and 1797 Journals and Their Significance," *Bulletin of the Missouri Historical Society (1969)* 25: 277-95.
[8] William T. Henderson, *A Map Showing Part of the State of Kentucky Lying West of the Tennessee River Surveyed Agreeably to an Act of the Legislature Passed on the 14th February 1820* (Lexington: University of Kentucky Library, 1820); *Military Surveys West of the Tennessee River, 1821* (Frankfort: Secretary of State's Office, 1821). See chapter 2, this volume.
[9] Dupoyster Map, *Draper Manuscripts*, 24J91 (Madison: Wisconsin Historical Society, 1860), hereafter, DMs.
[10] Letter, J. Dupoyster to L. Draper, October 25, 1886, *DMs*, 27J1; *ibid.*, October 27, 1886, 27J2; B. Stoval to Draper, September 2, 1888, 27J7; *ibid.*, October 13, 1888, 27J15.
[11] K. Carstens, *Calendar*, 206; *Unpublished Papers of George Rogers Clark*, Archives Division, Virginia State Library, Folder 20 (Richmond, June 8, 1781).
[12] *Plat of Fort Jefferson, 1891* (Wickliffe: Ballard County Courthouse Maps).

walls?

Previous histories did not have access to the necessary documentation to answer these questions. However, about 20 years of analysis of some 4,000 unpublished Fort Jefferson documents found in the Archives Division of the Virginia State Library between 1982-1984, as well as hours studying microfilm of the *Draper Manuscripts*, have provided many clues to the activities and actual structures of Clark's Fort Jefferson and Clarksville community. Of chief interest to the history and archeology of the site are references to structures found within the landscape of the fort and its associated civilian community of Clarksville. In this chapter I summarize where I think the fort is located, what activities the people of the fort and community participated in, and what is known about the structural composition (built environment) of this site which had been constructed under the direction of George Rogers Clark, and his second in command, Captain Robert George. Emphasis is placed on the "built" environment in order to understand better the physical layout and similarities/differences to other 18th-century outposts in Kentucky (Table 5.1).

Fort Jefferson, and its civilian community of Clarksville, were Revolutionary War-period sites, occupied by Americans between April 19, 1780 and June 8, 1781.[13] This military and civilian outpost was constructed five miles below the confluence of the Ohio and Mississippi Rivers on the east bank of the Mississippi River northeast of the mouth of Mayfield Creek. Until 1982, the location of the general site area, the size and composition of the garrison and civilian community's population, the detailing of the occupants' daily activities, and the structural composition of the community and outpost were largely unknown due to a lack of historic records. However, between 1982 and 1984, I made several trips to the Archives Division of the Virginia State Library, where a considerable quantity of Fort Jefferson documents were curated and not yet fully studied. Permission was obtained to duplicate all of the documents and return copies to Murray State University for study. My students at Murray State University and I then spent the next six years transcribing each of these documents and gleaning every clue about Fort Jefferson into several large computer files (the computer files were inputed and maintained by student Cathy Biby, who did a superb job throughout her four years on the project). That work resulted in the publication of two books (Carstens 1999, 2000) and numerous journal articles and conference presentations, many of which are reproduced here in this book.

Prior to 1982, the fort was believed to have been garrisoned by only 35 persons, representing only a small contingent of Clark's Illinois Battalion (see previously published Kentucky histories). Likewise, the location of the fort and community were believed to be anywhere between the Mouth of the Ohio River and 12 miles south, along the eastern bank of the Mississippi River.[14] With respect to daily activities of the personnel from the fort and community,

---

[13] Evacuation of the fort occurred on June 8, 1781, 13 months and 20 days after its founding. K. Carstens, "Fort Jefferson," *FCHQ*, (1983), 71(3) 261-262); K.Carstens, *Personnel*; K. Carstens, *Calendar*; James, ed. *Clark Papers, 417.*

[14] Draper Ms., 27J1-29; James A. James, ed. *Oliver Pollock: The Life and Times of an Unknown Patriot* (New York: Books for Libraries Press, 1970), 205; Kentucky Department of Transportation, *Environmental Assessment, Fort Jefferson, Great River Road*, (Frankfort, KYDOT 1981), 6; John E. L. Robertson "Fort Jefferson" *The Register of the Kentucky Historical Society*, 71 (2):127-138; and H. Young, W.T. Poussin, and S. Tuttle, 1821,

only one event had been recorded in various Kentucky histories, that being the greatly embellished saga of Nancy Ann Hunter. In reality, Ms. Hunter left the fort under a flag of truce and returned a straying calf to the fort[15]). Likewise, there were six different military engagements originating at, or took place at, Fort Jefferson. Two clashes occurred at Fort Jefferson, one in July, 1780 and the other in August against the Chickasaw Indians. The second battle was led by Lt. John Whitehead from Mobile, representing the British Southern Indian Department.[16] In addition, four military actions began at Fort Jefferson, including three retaliatory raids against the Chickasaw. Two short forays in September 1780 and January 1781 also occurred, and one lengthy campaign took place between July and August 1780 (Clark's Shawnee campaign). In addition, the garrison undertook a defensive action in May 1780, sending military assistance to embattled St. Louis and Cahokia.

The only published reference to structures at this site complex is found in a small book by the late M. Juliette Magee.[17] Unfortunately, Magee's map illustrating "Fort Jefferson" is actually a map of Todd's fort in Lexington, Kentucky.[18] So, in summary, prior to 1982, nothing had been published about the built environment of Clark's Fort Jefferson, and that which had been published often consisted of embellished and erroneous stories. Previous writers appear not to have followed the lead of James' two volume work published in 1912 and 1926, which reprints several dozen primary Fort Jefferson documents. More importantly, James,[19] and subsequently Swem,[20] make further reference to a large number of unpublished Clark papers, discovered in the basement of the Virginia State Library at the turn of this past century. Now known as the "Unpublished Clark Papers," this collection consists of more than 20,000 individual documents, including quartermaster ledgers, munition reports, economic invoices and vouchers, letters, dietary information, outline drawings of the fort's bastion construction, and even fragments of a musical score.[21] These documents have since been duplicated on microfilm and indexed and are now publicly available due to the efforts of Greg Holm and support from the Sons of the American Revolution and the Society for Colonial Wars. These papers should NOT be confused with what some have termed the "Virginia" papers of Clark, that is, those papers edited by James

---

Map: "Reconnaissance of the Mississippi and Ohio Rivers" (Washington D.C., Library of Congress; Map Division, 1821).

[15] Carstens, Kenneth, "The Role of Women in Kentucky's Western Colonial Frontier" *Historical Archaeology in Kentucky*, edited by Kim McBride, W. Stephen McBride, and David Pollack (Frankfort, Kentucky Heritage Council, 1995), 159; Letter, Dodge to Jefferson, in James, ed., *Papers*, 435-438, 456-457; George to Montgomery in K.W. Seineke, *The George Rogers Clark Adventure in Illinois* (New Orleans: Polyanthos Press, 1981), 457-459; Unpublished Clark Papers, Boxes 1-50.

[16] Whitehead was a senior lieutenant in Lieutenant Colonel John McGillivray's provincial West Florida Regiment in the Crown's Service, Robert R. Rea to Kenneth Carstens, November 18, 1985; also Provincial Records Office, Kew, England, *Treasury Papers*, T1/540:75.

[17] Magee, 14-15.

[18] Paul I. Chestnut, State Archivist, Personal Communication to K. Carstens (Richmond, Virginia State Library, Letter dated October 12, 1982).

[19] James, ed., *Clark Papers*: v-vi.

[20] E. G. Swem, "The Lost Vouchers of George Rogers Clarke [sic]," *Virginia Journal of Education*, 22 (1927): 424.

[21] Carstens, "Fort Jefferson" *FCHQ*, (1997), 71(3): 259-260, n.1.

through the Illinois Historical Society and published in 1912 and 1926, and reprinted by AMS Press in 1972.[22]

Of the estimated 20,000 "Unpublished Clark Papers," more than 4,000 pertain to Clark's Fort Jefferson. This archival collection represents an almost unbroken daily record of economic activities at this frontier post, including documents for 386 of the 416 days the fort was occupied. More importantly, information contained within these records provides data about the site which can be tested archaeologically--or in other cases, must rely upon archeological excavations to detail specific aspects about the site not adequately described within the papers, such as the specific type of construction used for the site's buildings.

In this chapter I provide a description of the physical characteristics of the Fort Jefferson site complex and its "built" landscape as interpreted from published and unpublished primary documents.

Physical Setting

Fort Jefferson and the civilian community of Clarksville were constructed five miles south of the Mouth of the Ohio River, immediately east of the first island below the confluence of the Ohio and Mississippi Rivers. This area, as illustrated on the 1780 William Clark map,[23] lies northeast of the mouth of Mayfield Creek, then also called Liberty Creek (Figure 2.2).[24] North and northeast of the fort and community are sandstone conglomerate bluffs rising 150 to 200 feet above the Mississippi River floodplain.

William Potter and Ken Carstens[25] reconstructed the major forest associations for the period from 1784 to 1821 from descriptions of witness trees found within the earliest recorded land surveys of the area. Bluff tops supported hickory, gum and oak associations (listed by greatest frequency first), and eventually gave rise to more interior cane brakes and open grasslands (Figure 5.1). Hill slopes north of the fort area supported hickory, ash, gum, oak, and poplar, while the secondary bottoms (the area above most flooding), on which the fort is believed to have been built, included oak, ash, hickory, poplar, and gum. The lower-lying primary bottoms and islands

---

[22] James, *Clark Papers*.

[23] Carstens, "The 1780 William Clark Map of Fort Jefferson," *FCHQ* 67(1):23-43 (1993); Draper 1M11.

[24] The location of the fort is independently confirmed by George Rogers Clark's brother's (William) map drawn in 1795 (Washington D.C.: National Archives, No. 16876), and also by Robert Todd's 1795 description of the area: "The upper point of the island is about 3 1/2 miles below the Ohio. Mayfield Creek is about the middle of the island across from an easterly direction. The country has a gradual ascent of about 150 or 200 feet. From there it has the appearance of a high, healthy country, interspersed with plains. Lands are covered with oak and hickory; dry healthy appearance. For three or four miles back is a high fertile country. A few fine springs. As to the healthfulness of the place, the sickly parts of the Mississippi are confined to the low bottoms which are over-flooded yearly in all parts. Where the high lands meet the Mississippi is healthy; as for a settlement, I think it is a spot well situated for a settlement and commerce" Robert Todd "Notes about old Fort Jefferson below the Mouth of the Ohio in 1795," (Washington D.C.: National Archives, Revolutionary Record Group, Item No. 0113, 1777).

[25] William M. Potter and Ken Carstens, "Floral Reconstruction and Early Nineteenth Century Land Surveys in Western Kentucky: A Test Case from the Fort Jefferson Area." Paper presented during the 43rd Annual Southeastern Archeological Conference (Nashville, 1986). See chapter 2, this volume.

were covered principally with cottonwoods, but swamp oaks, poplars, cypress, and grasses were present also.

In a recent publication,[26] I attempted to determine the scale and orientation of the 1780 William Clark map (Fig. 2.2). It appeared that the map scale was 10:1 and had been drawn using a 40 parts-per-inch-scale; the orientation of the map appeared to be 21 degrees west of north). Determining the preceding helped fit the William Clark map to modern topography and locate the approximate position where Fort Jefferson and the civilian town of Clarksville probably were constructed. In a re-evaluation of my 1993 Filson Club *Quarterly* publication, I no longer think the function of the 1780 William Clark map was to illustrate the fort's location as much as it was designed to illustrate "in lot locations," which were sold to newly arrived civilians looking for land adjacent to the fort.

A recent Geographic Information Systems (G.I.S.) study by Carstens, Pat Bomba, and Kristin Brown[27] demonstrated that the region northwest and west of the fort area has been severely eroded by the Mississippi River since 1880. Island One is now a part of the river's east bank, and instead of being west of the fort, is now considerably south of the site area, as illustrated on the Wickliffe 1970 U.S.G.S. 7.5-minute topographical map of the study locality (see Figure 2.13).

Therefore, the physical setting in which George Rogers Clark's Fort Jefferson was built was highly diversified: hill slopes, dissected uplands, and prairie grasslands to the north and northeast, fertile primary and secondary bottomlands to the east, south, and west, and riverine resources of rank four and five streams to the west and south, respectively. In this area, more than 550 persons established a military garrison and civilian community on April 19, 1780.[28] The post and community were short-lived, however, and were both evacuated 416 days later on June 8, 1781.

The Structural or "Built" Landscape

Data describing the presence of structures built as part of the Fort Jefferson landscape are detailed within published and unpublished documents and allow for a partial reconstruction of the fort and community's built landscape. When these documents are taken with the 1780 William Clark schematic drawing, a better approximation of the structural features at the site becomes possible and is presented in the following three sections:

---

[26] Carstens, *FCHQ*, 1993, 67(1): 23-43.
[27] Carstens, Pat Bomba, and Kristen Brown, "A Geographic Information System (GIS) Study of the Fort Jefferson Area." Paper presented at the Society for American Archeology meetings (St. Louis, 1993).
[28] Archeological research in this area has located four 18th century artifacts: 2 pieces of cream ware ceramics and two fragments of a white clay (kaolin) pipe bowl, e.g., a tavern pipe. These are the only 18th-century artifacts located in an otherwise highly disturbed environmental setting that, in the last 200+ years, has been used as a tree farm, tobacco patch, farmstead with outbuildings, tractor manufacturing area, rail depot with round table, and residential/hotel area. I feel confident about the location of Fort Jefferson because of the William Clark map and because of our finding four-18th century artifacts in the study locality. However, the exact location of Fort Jefferson will depend on locating contextual evidence in the archaeological record.

Structures within the Fort. The William Clark map clearly depicts a square fort with two protruding bastions located at opposite angles (Figure 2.2). The fort was relatively small, measuring only 100 feet per side. The walls of each bastion were twenty feet long. Unfortunately, the map neither demonstrates how the fort's walls were constructed nor the arrangement or number of structures contained within them.

According to Clark's 1779 Council of War directives six months before the construction of Fort Jefferson occurred, Clark's junior officers[29] advised that the fort should be "one hundred feet square...with bastions at each corner so proportioned that [gun fire from] one shall clear another."

Acting as president of the officers at that meeting was Capt. Robert George. Captain George became the commander at Fort Jefferson in May, 1780, when George Rogers Clark left the post to help defend Cahokia from a British/Indian raid.[30] Captain George was also in charge of the construction at Fort Jefferson.

With respect to how the fort should be built, Clark's officers[31] recommended that the fort be "built of earth dug out of an entrenchment ten feet deep, with earth thrown upon the inside of said entrenchment [forming] a wall ten feet high and eight feet thick, which with the entrenchment will form a wall twenty feet perpendicular, on the top of which there should be a wooden wall of sawed or hewn timber ten feet high, [and] twelve inches thick." It is not clear if Fort Jefferson was constructed according to Clark's Council of War directives, the recommendations of Clark's junior officers, or both. However, if the reconstructed scale of the 1780 Clark map is correct,[32] then it would appear that the directives were followed. Three other items lend support to this thinking. The first is a Fort Jefferson voucher[33] request for three pints of tafia on which is illustrated a raised bastion with pickets outlining the triangular form of the structure (Figure 5.2).

Secondly, Captain George[34] wrote to George Rogers Clark on June 4, 1780, stating, "As to our situation here, we are endeavoring to make it as strong as possible, I have got the Trenches for the Pickets ready & the inhabitants are hurrying the Pickets to me as fast as their circumstances do well admit. I hope to have the Fort enclosed within this week."

Thirdly, the artificers (engineers) who worked on Fort Jefferson left an inventory of items they constructed. One of their entries includes "covering and flooring of two bastions."[35] It would appear that the 1780 William Clark map is collaborated by the vouchers and letters within the Virginia State Library Unpublished Clark papers.

As a result, it is possible to conclude that Fort Jefferson was encircled by a ten-feet-deep trench, and that the dirt from the trench was used to build an earthen wall ten feet high and eight feet thick. On top of the dirt wall were vertically set timbers placed within a trench within the earthen embankment. The exposed portions of the sawed/split timbers were at least ten feet tall.

---

[29] James, ed., *Clark Papers*, 377.
[30] *Ibid.*, cxxvii-cxxxvii. See also J.A. James, "Significance of Attack on St. Louis, 1780," *Proceedings of the Mississippi Valley Historical Association II* (1915): 206; and John Francis McDermott, "The Battle of St. Louis 26 May 1780," *Bulletin Missouri Historical Society* (St. Louis, 1980), 132.
[31] James, ed., I: 377.
[32] Carstens, 1993, op cit.
[33] Unpublished Papers, Box 17.
[34] Unpublished Papers, Box 11; also, James, ed., *Clark Papers*: 377
[35] Unpublished Papers, Box 20.

In addition, two 20-feet-square bastions were constructed at opposite angles of the fort, in the northeast and southwest corners.

Other structures built within the fort by the artificers include a well[36] with windlass, dug on August 27, 1780 and framed for 12 feet, a powder magazine with an iron gate, a two-room necessary house of framed construction, the commandant's house with an attached fire place, a guardhouse, and three storehouses including the Agent's store (at least one of the storehouses had a basement, because in April 1781, an unusually high water-table flooded one of the basements, causing an evacuation of the items in storage to a dryer, more elevated place of storage).[37]

Major John Williams, one of several officers stationed at Fort Jefferson, maintained a private house at the post. His house apparently had a detached kitchen with [opened?] windows. It is not clear from the documents if his house was within or outside the fort's walls.[38]

Other structures inferred to be present based on activities occurring at the site and which may have been constructed within the fort include servant quarters,[39] a blacksmith's shop with bellows and anvil,[40] "flooring and covering two bastions," "eight camps or huts for the soldiery,"[41] and three gates.[42]

Structures within the Civilian Community. The reconstructed scale of the 1780 William Clark map also allows for an examination and measurement of space utilization by the post's inhabitants outside of the fort area. The civilian community of Clarksville was constructed east of the fort. It consists of 101 in lots each measuring 50 x 160 ft.,[43] but the lots are grouped by combinations of 4's, 5's, 6's, and 7's, thereby varying blocks of in lots from 200 x 160 ft., as a minimum dimension, to a maximum of 350 x 160 ft. space (Table 5.2; Figure 2.2). The in lot groups are arranged in three columns separated by two major streets. The most westerly column of in lots is numbered south to north 1 through 15. The middle column is numbered north to south, 16 through 64. The third column also is numbered north to south and contains lots 65 through 101.

The more westerly of the two north-south oriented streets measures 70 by 800 feet; the easterly street is more narrow and longer, measuring 25 by 2200 feet. The 17 groups of in lots are further separated by seven smaller, east-west streets each measuring 20 x 350 feet.[44] These lots appear to be arranged to fit the topography of the area so that relatively few lots are located on hill slopes. Also present on the 1780 Clark map is a single blockhouse, triangular in shape and measuring 30 feet per side. Numerous references in the unpublished Clark papers refer to the

---

[36] On June 8, 1781, Martin Carney, quartermaster at Fort Jefferson, signed a memorandum for Virginian materials placed in the well and left at Fort Jefferson when the site was abandoned: seven hand mills, one wagon, one six-pound ordinance (cannon?), 50 stand of old arms [muskets], one grinding stone, two 56-weight and one-28-lb grinding stones, two canoes, one brick iron, and one pair of [bellows? illeg.] belonging to John Harris [the armourer] (Unpublished Papers, 20).

[37] Unpublished Papers, 20.
[38] Unpublished Papers, 20; Draper, 56J40-41.
[39] Unpublished Papers, 20.
[40] *Ibid.*
[41] *Ibid.*
[42] *Ibid.*
[43] Carstens, 1993 67(1): 23-43.
[44] DMs, 1M11; Carstens, 1993, 38.

"blockhouse on the hill."[45] No other structural features are illustrated on the 1780 William Clark map.[46]

The unpublished Clark papers contain the names of 41 families residing within the Clarksville community (see Chapter 12, this volume), but only seven named individuals are known to have been homeowners: John Donne,[47] Joseph Ford,[48] Matthew Jones,[49], James Wiley[50], John Williams,[51] Lt. Thomas Wilson,[52] and Major John Williams[53] Although the records also indicate that several families lived together within a single dwelling, such as the Taylor and Watkins families who lived with the Joneses,[54] the degree to which housing was shared among the entire community is not known. Nor are the exact locations known for the houses, although general references to "houses in the upper end of town,"[55] "houses in the lower end of town,"[56] and "houses in the village"[57] are recorded, as are references to named households and their general location, such as Donne's house and Ford's house, which were "located in the lower end of town."[58] Mention is not made of quarters for slaves, yet at least three prominent citizens of Clarksville (as well as several military officers), maintained individual slaves and at least one family of slaves.[59]

Other Structural Features. Buildings constructed in and around the Clarksville community include three blockhouses built by artificers,[60] a boat/landing area,[61] a saw pit,[62] and a cemetery.[63] Two of three blockhouses were built north of the community on top of the hills and bluffs

---

[45] Carstens, *Calendar*, pp. 7, 17, 21.
[46] DMs, 1M11; Carstens, 1993, 38.
[47] Unpublished Papers, 15, 50; William Clark Papers, Missouri Historical Society, Forest Park, Box 1, Folder 21, hereafter MHS.
[48] Unpublished Papers, 12; MHS B1, F21.
[49] DMs, 56J41.
[50] MHS B1, F21.
[51] Unpublished Papers, 17.
[52] MHS B1, F20.
[53] DMs, 56J40-41.
[54] DMs, 56J41.
[55] MHS B1, F21.
[56] *Ibid.*
[57] Unpublished Papers, 13.
[58] *Op. cit.*
[59] John Donne (Commissary), Major John Williams, and Col. George Rogers Clark all had slaves at Fort Jefferson. More than likely, other families and officers brought slaves with them too. See Carstens, "George Rogers Clark's Fort Jefferson: An Historical Overview with Archeological Implications." Paper Presented during the 5th annual Illinois Historic Archeology Conference (Giant City State Park, Illinois, 1990). C. Alvord, *Collections of the Illinois State Historical Library, Vol. II, Virginia Series, Vol. I: Cahokia Records (1778-1790),* (Springfield: Illinois State Historical Library, 1907): xv-xvi. Alvord states that Kaskaskia's population of 1,000 persons was nearly evenly divided between whites and slaves. Although there is no indication that the slave population at Fort Jefferson was comparably large, the Kaskaskia example accurately reflects the great number of persons lost to history.
[60] Unpublished Papers, 20.
[61] *Ibid.*, 13.
[62] *Ibid.*, 20.
[63] *Ibid.*, 20.

overlooking the town and fort; a third blockhouse was built adjacent to Donne's house "in the lower end of town."[64] Whether or not all three blockhouses were triangular in shape (measuring 30' per side) like the one illustrated on the 1780 Clark map[65] is not known.

In an earlier paper I assumed that the boat landing/mooring areas at the outpost was located along Mayfield Creek instead of within the chute of the Mississippi River. I assumed this because the published Clark Papers repeatedly state that the summer of 1780 was exceedingly dry and that the citizens could walk across the chute to the island on which they farmed. During the dry summer of 1988, 200 years later, I was able to see first hand that the mouth of Mayfield Creek is quite deep—at least 65 feet.[66] If it was as deep in 1780 as it was in 1988, then Mayfield Creek could easily handle the safe mooring of boat and barge traffic for Fort Jefferson. On the other hand, the bayou or chute of the Mississippi was only seasonally available for mooring boats,[67] which would explain how the Clarksville community residents walked to and farmed 17 acres of land on Island No. 1 adjacent to the fort.

The location of the community's cemetery is not known, but it was frequently utilized by the inhabitants of the post.[68] Published and unpublished references detail the deaths of 49 individuals (military and civilian) during the 13 months and 20 days the post was occupied. One voucher in the unpublished Clark papers attests to artificers constructing coffins for 38 men, women, and children,[69] although the list included in Chapter 12 accounts for 48 military and one civilian death. The frequency of deaths in the military at Fort Jefferson was so great that Captain Robert George remarked on October 28, 1780 that, "numbers [were] daily dying."[70] It is unknown how many additional persons (children, spouses, Native Americans) actually died at the fort, and how many deaths went unrecorded. Nor is it known what type or style of coffin was used for those who died, the type of coffin furniture, or other information regarding funeral activities that occurred for military, non-military, and Native American populations living at the post. It is possible that not all of the post's deceased were buried in the cemetery, nor were all deceased individuals given coffins. As an example, several Native Americans died at the post (Piankashaws and Kaskaskia Indians) and were given only blue burial shrouds from the quartermaster stores in which to be buried; it is unknown where they were laid to rest.[71] What is important is the fact that a portion of the Fort Jefferson landscape was set aside for funerary purposes and that that area contained at least 38 coffins and possibly more than 48 individuals.

Lastly, the presence of a general work area, such as a saw pit, is implied by several vouchers

---

[64] *Ibid.*, 13, 50.
[65] DMs, 1M11.
[66] Kenneth C. Carstens, "Current Field Strategies and Hypothesis Testing: The Fort Jefferson Project Continues," *Proceedings of the Sixth Annual Kentucky Heritage Council Archeological Conference*, edited by Charles D. Hockensmith (Frankfort: The Kentucky Heritage Council, 1991), 165-174.
[67] Unpublished Papers, 12.
[68] The cemetery for fort and community may have been adjacent to the blockhouse on the hill illustrated on the 1780 William Clark map between house in lots 20 and 21. This information is corroborated by B. H. Stovall's September 22, 1888 letter to Lyman C. Draper, Draper Manuscripts, 27J7, Wisconsin Historical Society, Madison, Wisconsin.
[69] Unpublished Papers, 20.
[70] Unpublished Papers, 13.
[71] Carstens, *FCHQ*, 1997, 71(3):277-282.

that detail the sawing of 2,500 feet of plank boards, and the dismantling of 11 flat-bottomed boats used to help construct the fort and community.[72]

Table 5.3 lists the various structures present at Fort Jefferson as described in published and unpublished accounts.

Conclusion

Unlike earlier (prior to 1982) histories written about Fort Jefferson, data described in this paper clearly illustrate that the fort and civilian community were structurally-complex, spatially extensive, and highly varied, and that Clark's fort at the Mouth of the Ohio served an important, although short-lived, strategic military function, having taken part in at least six military activities, including defending itself twice against hostile attacks from the Chickasaw Indians.

The large population of the site area was socially stratified. This social stratification was probably reflected by differences in house size and house type built by the settlers (including persons of English, French, and Native American descent), and by the number of individuals living in a single-household whether single-individual, single-family, or multiple-family units. Stratification may have been further reflected in the location of one's house, such as being in either the "upper" or "lower" end of town, or whether or not a house was within or outside of the fort's walls. Social differences among the fort's population were also reflected by how, and in what, the deceased were buried. In addition, several officers and prominent citizens owned slaves, but there were also raw recruits who owned little to nothing of the material world. The military further cut across cultural and ethnic boundaries by including companies of French soldiers and Kaskaskia and Piankashaw Indian allies. The social stratification present within the civilian community was likewise similarly complex, consisting of both relatively wealthy and very poor families, such as the Donnes and Taylors, respectively.

Yet, throughout the above descriptions of fort and community, no information is given relevant to the style or type of architecture, size variability per house, or any other characteristic which might be culturally based, or which may have had an effect upon the construction of the structures at the fort (ethnic groups comprising the 550 persons at Fort Jefferson include French, English, Spanish, and Native Americans). The extent to which intra- or inter-cultural values may have influenced the layout or construction of fort and community is not known.[73] And, although a much better understanding of the day-to-day activities and fort layout and design of this important frontier outpost is now at hand, we still have an extremely limited understanding of how

---

[72] Unpublished Papers, 20.

[73] Based on my research over the last 24+ years, it is now possible to suggest that in the fort were two floored and covered bastions located at opposite angles, three storehouses, one well with windlass (planked for the initial 12 feet), one powder magazine, one privy (2-room necessary house of frame construction), eight huts or camps for the soldiers, three gates (main, water and munitions), and one blacksmith's shop enclosed within a stockade consisting of ten feet high pickets. Surrounding the fort was a ditch or moat ten feet wide and eight feet deep. Outside the fort were three blockhouses, at least one of which was on the hill overlooking the fort and community, and one was located at the south end of town near Donne's and Ford's houses. There was also a cemetery with at least 38 coffins, and one loading dock/mooring area. Within the community of Clarksville were civilian houses, including houses in the "upper end of town," and "lower end of town."

the fort and community were constructed and the exact number of those structures. If the site of Fort Jefferson can be located through archeological field studies, the plethora of historical records now available will assist greatly with the interpretation of the archeological record of this significant frontier outpost.

How similar Fort Jefferson and the civilian community of Clarksville were to other sites in Kentucky occupied at about the same time (e.g., Bryant's Station, Boonesborough, Harrodsburg, Todd's Fort in Lexington, or Fort Nelson in Louisville) is not known. As Table 5.1 illustrates, Fort Jefferson was quite small compared to other forts/stations built in Kentucky.[74] Fort Jefferson and Clarksville were also laid out differently from the French communities at Kaskaskia, Cahokia, and Vincennes, as well as being dissimilar to French-settled, and Spanish-occupied, St. Louis. When compared to the Kentucky/Virginia settlements at Boonesborough and Harrodsburg, the size of Fort Jefferson is small, but it is most similar to Todd's fort in Lexington built in 1781. Yet when considering the population of Fort Jefferson (more than 550 persons), it would seem that there must have been sizable population centers in frontier Kentucky by 1780. Population descriptions have gone largely unrecorded (much like Fort Jefferson's history until its records were found in Virginia.) Like today, the center of those populations was located in north-central Kentucky, which later formed the nucleus of Kentucky settlement and the soon-to-be established "golden triangle of Kentucky" (Louisville-Lexington-Frankfort). Like many towns in western Kentucky today, being too far from economic assistance and sustenance, Fort Jefferson and Clarksville were doomed to failure because they were located too far west of the center of the 18th-century frontier, and they had inadequate means to assure their survival. Although the attacks by the Chickasaw were relatively insignificant from a military standpoint, the physical damage accomplished by the Chickasaws (burning the settlement's corn crop and killing the livestock) proved to be insurmountable for the garrison and civilian occupants of George Rogers Clark's 1780-1781 Fort Jefferson. As a result, the fort and community were abandoned on June 8, 1781, and the site of this historic settlement became a part of the archaeological record forever.

---

[74] Nancy O'Malley, "Stockading Up: An Archaeological Evaluation of Pioneer Stations in the Inner Bluegrass Region of Kentucky." *Archaeological Report No. 127*, University of Kentucky's Program for Cultural Resource Assessment (Lexington, 1987).

Table 5.1: General Characteristics of Selected Kentucky Forts

Fort	Length	Width	No. blockhouses	Stockade
Todd's-Lexington	80	80	yes-4	yes
Harrodsburg	264	264	yes-2	yes
Boonesborough	260	150	yes-4	yes
Bryant's Station	250	600	yes-4	yes
Fort Nelson	208?	208?	yes-?	yes
Fort Jefferson	100	100	yes-2	yes

(Fort Nelson was said to contain 1 acre within its walls)

Number of Items	Description of Item	Dimension on 40 scale	Size in 10's of Feet
1	Fort	10 sq.	100' square
2	Bastions	2 sq.	20' square
101	In lots	Variable	N-S x E-W
Individual Lot		5 x 16	50' x 160'
1 Group of 4 in lots		20 x 16	200' x 160'
1 Group of 5 in lots		25 x 16	250' x 160'
1 Group of 6 in lots		30 x 16	300' x 160'
1 Group of 7 in lots		35 x 16	350' x 160'
1 Blockhouse (Triangular)		3 x 3 x 3	30' per side
2 North South Streets			
Easterly Street "A"		220 x 2.5	2200' x 25'
Westerly Street		80 x 7	800' x 70'
7 East-West Streets			
Street 1 (Top)		2 x 40	20' x 400'
Street 2		2 x 60	20' x 600'
Street 3		4 x 35	40' x 350'
Street 4		4 x 35	40' x 350'
Street 5		2 x 35	20' x 350'
Street 6		2 x 35	20' x 350'
Street 7 (Bottom)		2 x 35	20' x 350'

Table 5.2: Dimensions of Fort Jefferson and Clarksville Community Based on Measurements of the 1780 William Clark map (after Carstens 1993, 67[1]:23-43).

Table 5.3: Structures Built at Clark's Fort Jefferson and Clarksville Community

Inside Fort
    Square fort w/two bastions, 100 feet per side, 20 feet square bastions;
    Two bastions in fort are floored and covered;
    Well within fort w/windlass dug 8-27-80 and framed for 12 feet;
    Necessary house (latrine) framed w/2 rooms;
    Powder Magazine w/iron gate;
    Fort is stockaded w/pickets set in trench;
    Officers' Mess;
    Captain George house w/fireplace;
    Construction of a garrison;
    Construction of three gates;
    Fort is constructed out of earth dug out around its perimeter;
    Guard House present;
    Construction of 8 camps or huts for the soldiery;
    Construction of three storehouses or Agent's store
        (large enough to hold court of inquiry and court martial proceedings)
        (at least one of the storehouses had a basement).

Possibly Inside Fort
    Maj. John Williams house w/detached kitchen w/open windows;
    Blacksmith's shop w/bellows and anvil;
    Major John Williams' servant's quarters;

Civilian Community (named Clarksville)
    Joseph Ford's house in the lower end of town;
    John Donne's house in the lower end of town;
    (Donne's house flanks a blockhouse in the lower end of town.)
    James Wiley's house at upper end of street;
    Matthews Jones's lodge (large enough for Mr. & Mrs. Watkins & James Taylor to live
        in);
    Lt. Thomas Wilson's house;
    John Williams "has several sick people in his house;"
    "Houses in lower end of town;"
    "Houses in upper end of town;"
    "House at upper end of street adjacent to the woods;"
    "Houses in the village;"
    "Upper end of town & the blockhouse;"
    Building 5 dwelling houses (constructed by artificers);
    Clarksville consists of 101 in lots;
    Quarters for slaves implied (Col. Clark, Captain Smith, John Donne all had slaves).

Table 5.3 (continued):

Other Structures
- "helping to build and finish three blockhouses;"
- "the blockhouse on the hill" (note blockhouse illustrated on 1780 William Clark map is triangular in shape);
- "Lt. Clark's blockhouse on the hill;"
- "Captain Kellar's blockhouse;"
- "Captain Edward Worthington's company stationed at the blockhouse;"
- Lt. Richard Clark's three men at the blockhouse;"
- "John Donne's home flanks the lower blockhouse;"

Boat dock/landing...
- Saw pit (sawed 700 feet of poplar plant; 1800 feet of plank; dismantling 11 flat-bottomed boats for public service for building barracks;

Cemetery containing coffins for 38 men, women and children.

Other Use Areas:
- 17 acres on island west of fort farmed;
- Cornfields east of town (east of the town lots);
- Turnip garden;
- T. Phelps intercropped his garden with beans;

21 farmers farmed 45.75 acres, raising 1,125 bushels of corn, averaging 2.118 acres/farmer; 9 farmers worked 16 acres collectively.

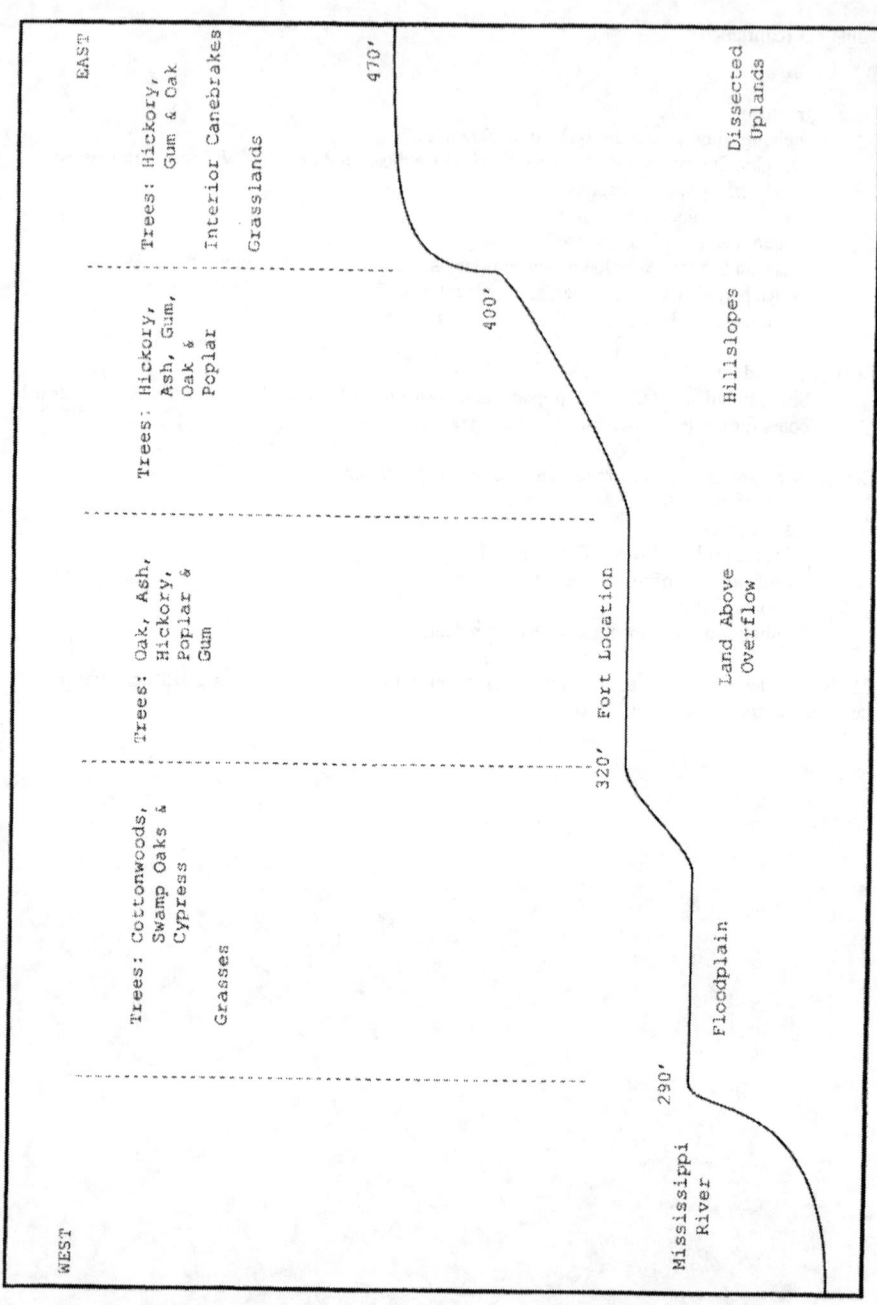

Figure 5.1 Cross-section of Fort Jefferson Physiography.

Figure 5.2 Illustration of Fort Jefferson Raised Bastion from Unpublished Clark Papers, Archiv Division, Virginia State Library.

CHAPTER 6:   ISSUES AT FORT JEFFERSON, 1780-1781: THE
QUARTERMASTER BOOKS OF JOHN DODGE AND
MARTIN CARNEY[1]

Fort Jefferson and its associated community of Clarksville were built near the mouth of the Ohio River in 1780 so Virginia could physically claim her western "paper" boundary. The fort and community were short-lived, both being evacuated during June of 1781, only 14 months after being established. Foremost among the reasons cited by historians for the evacuation of Fort Jefferson and Clarksville have been the notions that the fort and community were poorly supplied and that the fort and community were under constant threat of Indian attack. This chapter includes an examination of the three surviving Fort Jefferson quartermaster books and what those books reveal about the brief history of Fort Jefferson.

Introduction

Prior to James Alton James's publishing his two seminal volumes of Clark papers in 1912 and 1926 (reprinted by AMS Press in 1972), additional "lost papers" papers of George Rogers Clark had been found in the basement of the Governor's house in Richmond, Virginia. These were the papers John Dodge had carried to Richmond in April, 1781.[2] Not studied by James in his 1912 volume, portions of these documents were included in James's second volume of Clark papers. Amounting to more than 20,000 documents, these vouchers and pay records were the documents that Clark had personally sent back to government in 1781 under the care of John Dodge. Richmond must have been a very busy place in 1781, what with the war in the East raging and the moving of the governor's house and capitol from Williamsburg to Richmond. Stashed away in the basement of the governor's house, George's pay records and receipts would be "lost" until rediscovered at the turn of the 20th century.[3] Described generally as "bundles" of papers, no detail was given to these documents by James. In the 1920s, the boxes of documents were moved from the Governor's house in Richmond, next door to the newly created State Library and State Archive, where again the documents sat unstudied and unused until the anniversary of the Bicentennial, when several of the documents with

---

[1] A version of this paper first appeared in the *Selected Papers from the Fifth and Sixth George Rogers Clark Trans-Appalachian Frontier History Conferences* edited by Robert J. Holden, Eastern National Park & Monument Association and Vincennes University, 1990: 54-75, and in Kenneth C. Carstens's *The Calendar and Quartermaster Books of George Rogers Clark's Fort Jefferson, 1780-1781* (Heritage Books: Bowie, Maryland, 2000). A version of that paper is published here with the permission of Vincennes University and the Eastern National Park & Monument Association. Funding for the original publication came from the Eastern National Park & Monument Association.
[2] James Alton James, ed. *Papers of George Rogers Clark*, Vols. I & II, AMS Press, New York, 1972; Kenneth C. Carstens, *Calendar and Quartermaster Books of George Rogers Clark's Fort Jefferson, 1780-1781*. Heritage Books, Bowie, Maryland, 2000. "Fort Jefferson, A Summary of Its History," this volume.
[3] E.G. Swem, The Lost Vouchers of George Rogers Clarke [sic]. *Virginia Journal of Education*, XXII: 424, 1927.

Clark's signature were sent to Indiana for display.[4] In 1983 I received a grant from Murray State University to verify the content of the documents and determine if any pertained to Clark's Fort Jefferson. To my surprise, I estimated about 4,000 of those documents contained information about Fort Jefferson. Indeed, of the 416 days that Fort Jefferson was occupied, there was paper work for 387 of those days,[5] an almost unbroken daily record of documents that included quartermaster books, pay vouchers, a portion of a musical score, a portion of a diagram of Fort Jefferson, playing cards, letters, medical inventories, and military rosters. This was in short, a day-to-day history of Clark's Fort Jefferson and civilian community of Clarksville. My friend and fellow NWTA re-enactor Greg Holm also visited the collection and decided to contact organizations that would preserve these valuable, yet fragile, pieces of American history before they deteriorated beyond readability. Greg contacted the Sons of the American Revolution and the Society for Colonial Wars (in Cincinnati). Both organizations raised money necessary to have each of the 20,000 documents microfilmed and made accessible to other libraries. Now available on 13 reels of 35mm microfilm, this portion of the Clark papers is permanently preserved for posterity.

Permission from the Virginia State Library (Archives Division) was granted in 1983 and 1984 for me to make photoduplicate copies of each Fort Jefferson document before they were microfilmed. These documents were then brought back to Murray State University, where for six years teams of undergraduate and graduate students spent countless hours transcribing the 18th-century handwritten documents, typing duplicate copies, and creating computer data files as part of the Fort Jefferson Archival Research Project. That project resulted in the writing and publishing of more than 30 conference papers and two monographs.

The following paragraphs summarize only certain aspects of the quartermaster books from Clark's Fort Jefferson. Space does not allow reproducing each of the 4,000 written Fort Jefferson entries, but now, because of microfilming and publishing, copies of these rare historical documents are publicly available. The following pages address only the quartermaster books (John Dodge and Martin Carney) of Clark's Fort Jefferson. Other quartermaster books were written, but only these three have survived, offering unplumbed insight into the day-to-day life of the 18th-century person and military garrison.

Prior to 1983, an understanding of the history of Fort Jefferson prior to 1983 was based for the most part upon a limited number of published documents. The presentation of a large collection of previously unpublished historical papers is very exciting because of its potential contribution to history. The quartermaster Books from Fort Jefferson, which include John Dodge's book and Martin Carney's books "1E " and "1F" (makes you wonder what's missing in Carney's books "1A-1D"!), provide very detailed data about the Illinois Battalion at Fort Jefferson for the 1780-1781 period. The contents of these ledgers add considerably to the previously published papers and letters of Clark and throw new light on the history of the frontier during the American Revolution.

---

[4] Mary Jane Meeker, Original Vouchers in the George Rogers Clark Bicentennial Exhibition. *Indiana History Bulletin*, 53(6), 1976.
[5] Carstens, 2000.

John Dodge and Martin Carney were private citizens. Although more is known about Dodge than Carney, that which is known about Dodge is not flattering.[6] Henry Hamilton, the infamous "hair buyer," dismissed Dodge as an "obscure person...unprincipled and [a] perjured renegade."[7]

John Dodge was born on July 12, 1751 in Connecticut. He was named after his father, who was a blacksmith. Dodge left Connecticut and began a trading business among the Indians around Sandusky, Ohio, prior to 1770.[8] Along with an associate, William Tucker, Dodge purchased a house and a lot in Detroit on April 4, 1776, where he apparently continued his trading activities among the Indians of the Detroit region.[9] He was arrested by the British for allegedly spying and other non-loyal activities, and was imprisoned in Quebec, escaping in October of 1778.[10] Fleeing to Boston, Dodge gave information to generals Gates and Washington relevant to American operations against Canada.[11] For that, Dodge should be praised as an outstanding citizen of the early United States. In January 1779, Dodge wrote a letter to John Montour detailing Dodge's plight during his captivity, later expanding the detail and writing "A Narrative of Mr. John Dodge During his Captivity at Detroit," which was first published in Philadelphia in 1779 and reprinted in England the following year. Dodge was subsequently recommended to Thomas Jefferson by Washington as a person who might be useful in the West.[12]

It is probable that Dodge and George Rogers Clark first met at Fort Pitt, as both individuals spent time in that area. Dodge served Clark first as Indian Agent for the Western Department, and later as quartermaster for the Illinois Battalion.[13] Subsequent references to Dodge as "Captain" seem unfounded, however (see especially the discussion by Alvord),[14] but may have been a courteous title applied to a person's name.[15] Agents and quartermasters, however, were paid at the rate of six shillings per day, the same pay as a captain.[16] Dodge may have extended the rationale of "rate of pay' to one of rank, which would be in keeping with Dodge's personality as described by Alvord[17] and James,[18] and as expressed by persons at Fort Jefferson who knew him on a

---

[6] Clarence W. Alvord, *Collections of the Illinois State Historical Library, Vol. II: The Cahokia Records, 1778-1790.* Published by the Trustees of the Illinois State Historical Library, Springfield, 1907; *Collections of the Illinois State Historical Library, Vol. V: The Kaskaskia Records, 1778-1790.* Published by the Trustees of the Illinois State Historical Library, Springfield, 1909; James, ed. 1972.
[7] James, ed. 1972, I: 202.
[8] John Dodge, *Narrative of Mr. John Dodge During His Captivity at Detroit.* Reproduced in facsimile from the second edition of 1780. Introductory note by Clarence Monroe Burton, Cedar Rapids, Iowa, The Torch Press, 1909.
[9] *Ibid.*
[10] *Ibid.*
[11] *Ibid.*, 6-9; 56.
[12] Clarence Alvord, *The Illinois Country 1673-1818.* Reprinted in 1965 in the American West Series by Loyola University Press, Chicago, edited by J.F. Bannon, 1922.
[13] Alvord, 1922: 352; Alvord 1907, II: xcv.
[14] Alvord, 1907: xcv, n.1; cxii-cxiii.
[15] Donald Carson to Ken Carstens, personal communication, September 19, 1999.
[16] William W. Hening, *The Statutes at Large: Being a collection of All the Laws of Virginia from the First Session of the Legislature in the Year 1619*, Vols. I, IX, X. Reprinted in 1969 for the Jamestown Foundation by the University Press of Virginia, Charlottesville.
[17] Alvord, op cit. xcvi-xcvii, xcix, 620; 1909: 156, 215, 219-220; 644.
[18] James, ed. 1972, I: 338, n. 1; 472.

daily basis.[19] Subsequent accusations challenging Dodge's character and honesty are found in surviving letters.[20] Military and civilians alike at Kaskaskia, Vincennes, and Fort Jefferson question Dodge and his associates (especially the double agent Thomas Bentley), and Dodge's lack of scruples.[21] Yet Clark must have believed totally in him, as it was to Dodge that Clark entrusted his vouchers and pay records.[22] No accusations against Dodge's younger brother Israel seem to exist, however, nor are there questions about Martin Carney's character, John Dodge alone appears to have play a questionable role at Fort Jefferson and Kaskaskia during the occupation of Fort Jefferson and after.[23] Indeed, a State of Illinois interpretative sign at Fort Gage (above Kaskaskia, where John Dodge lived after 1781) refers to John Dodge as a "freebooter," that is to say, a person who pillages or plunders.

Little is known about Martin Carney. He worked as quartermaster in Dunmore county, Virginia, for the 8th Virginia Regiment.[24] He may have come into contact with Clark or one of Clark's associates who recruited from the Holston Valley of Virginia for the Illinois Battalion. Carney was in the Louisville area (Falls of the Ohio) by early March, 1780, purchasing equipment for Colonel Clark for Fort Jefferson. He was at Fort Jefferson as Deputy Quartermaster from at least May 22, 1780 until June 7, 1781. After Fort Jefferson's abandonment, Carney returned to Louisville, where he continued his quartermaster duties at Fort Nelson. It remains unclear what happened to Carney. John Dodge apparently lost track of Carney by 1785. Writing to William Clark (the cousin of GRC, not the brother) at the Falls of the Ohio, John Dodge asked, "Pray Let me Know if Mr. Carney is in that Quarter or whare [sic] the Little Heron is."[25] What Dodge meant by "Little Heron" is unclear, unless it referenced Carney as a slender, bird-like figure of a man. Although Carney was granted land after the war for his service to Virginia, the acreage was subsequently disallowed by the Western Commissioners at the end of the war.[26]

The Supply System of the Western Department

According to the laws of Virginia, quartermaster positions were given to individuals who, in addition to posting a bond, could read, write, do simple arithmetic, and swear an oath that they would be honest with all accounting practices.[27]

The quartermaster procurement and issuance system in the Western Department depended heavily upon both local and non-local sources for its supplies. Even on the frontier, settlements in the middle Mississippi Valley were tied to world markets through

---

[19] Draper Manuscripts, Wisconsin Historical Society, Madison: 56J22, 56J29.
[20] Alvord 1922: 352-353; Kathrine Seineke, The George Rogers Clark Adventure in Illinois (1981): 474, 478, 480, 481.
[21] *Ibid.*, Alvord, Seineke.
[22] Carstens, "Fort Jefferson History," this volume.
[23] Seineke, 68-75.
[24] National Archives, Revolutionary Record Group, Item No. 16876, Voucher Receipt, Dated 4 November 1777.
[25] Alvord, 1909:376.
[26] William H. English, *Conquest of the Country Northwest of the River Ohio, 1778-1783 and Life of General George Rogers Clark*, Vols. I and II. Reprinted in 1991 by Heritage Books, Inc., Bowie Maryland, 1896, II: 840, 1072; James, ed., 1972, II.
[27] Hening IX: 14: X: 256.

major port cities, such as new Orleans. The long-distance trade with New Orleans brought dry goods, fabrics, liquors, and equipment; more local trade provided perishable items (food supplies primarily). Products received from long-distance trade were often used to procure items from the more immediate markets (especially corn and flour). That is, it was not uncommon to trade dry goods or liquors received from world markets for perishable foods in local markets.

The major frontier areas controlled by the Americans included Cahokia, Kaskaskia, Fort Jefferson (including Clarksville), Vincennes, the Falls area (including the Bear Grass Stations), and the central Kentucky forts and stations of the Inner bluegrass region, like Boonesborough and Harrodsburg, or Logan's (St. Asaph's Station) Fort. Although French and Spanish assistance was available from the Mississippi and Wabash settlements, American credit, the devaluation of Virginian currency, and prior demands placed upon the French and Spanish settlement by Clark's forces made it mandatory for the Virginian government to assist with the support of its western outposts. But, Virginia could not and did not assist. This created an economic system, therefore, that was doomed for failure.

By 1780, Virginia was not in a position to provide support. Goods procured for the Western Department through long-distance trade were shipped from two principal sources, Fort Pitt and New Orleans, through the efforts of men like Oliver Pollock.[28] Local trade came from the French settlements of Ste. Genevieve, Kaskaskia, Cahokia, and Vincennes, and from other Anglo settlements in Kentucky, e.g., Harrodsburg, Boonesborough, and the Falls of the Ohio. Fort Jefferson's survival depended upon an unbroken flow of goods from these settlements to the mouth of the Ohio, and the post reciprocated by providing the Illinois, Wabash, and Falls settlements with European and Caribbean goods it received from New Orleans (Figure 6.1).

Although seemingly sound on paper, the scheme did not work. The flow of supplies did not always follow the prescribed path.[29] Goods directed to Fort Jefferson from Fort Pitt were sometimes redirected en route to the central Kentucky stations or were appropriated by officers at the Falls of the Ohio for their own use. Foods were often ill-cured and poorly packed, which also compounded the problem. On several occasions the inhabitants of Fort Jefferson, initially overjoyed at the arrival of food from the Falls, were disappointed when the supplies turned out to be too ill-preserved to be consumed. In his February 15, 1781 letter from Fort Jefferson to George Slaughter, Commissary at the Falls of the Ohio, Captain Robert George, Commandant at Fort Jefferson, writes:

...The Small Supplies you have sent us, have been of infinite Service, & if you frequently repeat them they will be of singular advantage as we look to you for it, but the supplies I beg may be of a better Quality than what is yet come to hand. The Beef is really of the poorest kind—ill-cured, and not half salted—the Barrels being bad, the pickle became wasted, if ever any had been put in, and tho' the Meat does not absolutely stink, it wants little of it...'Twere well if all that you send was first inspected.[30]

---

[28] Light T. Cummins, Oliver Pollock and George Rogers Clark's Service of Supply: A Case Study in Financial Disaster in *Selected Papers from the 1985 and 1986 George Rogers Clark Trans-Appalachian Frontier History Conferences*, edited by Robert J. Holden. Eastern National Park & Monument Association and Vincennes University, Vincennes, Indiana, 1988: 1-16; James Alton James,.Oliver Pollock: *The Life and Times of an Unknown Patriot*. Originally published in 1937, Books for Libraries Press, New York.
[29] J. G. Randall, George Rogers Clark's Service of Supply. *Mississippi Valley Historical Review*, 8: 250-262.
[30] James, ed. 1972, I:50-6.

Fort Jefferson's major source of supply was New Orleans (Figure 6.2). Unfortunately, most of the supplies reaching fort Jefferson from that port were dry goods and liquor, which did little to compensate for the loss of foodstuffs from the Illinois settlements, Fort Pitt, or the Falls of the Ohio area. Even when the quartermaster at Fort Jefferson sent loads of dry goods and rum to other posts to trade for food, only small amounts of food were found;[31] moreover, the Illinois towns were ready to revolt, because the French towns had grown tired of supporting the Americans.

Four individuals at Fort Jefferson occupied positions of authority associated with the distribution of goods and foods: John Dodge, Israel Dodge, Martin Carney, and John Donne. Occasionally Patrick Kennedy or James Finn from Fort Clark (Kaskaskia), or Zephaniah Blackford from Fort Patrick Henry (Vincennes), would arrive to assist or take over in the absence of one of the former purveyors. The Dodge brothers and Donne appear to have been associates while at Fort Pitt in 1779.[32]

Despite the presence of numerous vouchers, letters, and other records belonging to Israel Dodge and John Donne in the Fort Jefferson papers, only John Dodge and Martin Carney left quartermaster books among the unpublished Clark papers in Virginia.[33]

The John Dodge quartermaster book consists of 144 pages, each bound page measuring six inches wide by nine inches long. Each page was made from blank sheets of paper measuring six by eighteen inches. The pages of the book were hand-ruled by its owner to facilitate bookkeeping. The exterior of the Dodge book consists of a plain weave, coarse-linen fabric that covers pressed pages of coarse paper. The binding of the book consists of a single loose stitch with a coarse linen thread (eleven stitches, varying from one-quarter of an inch to one inch in length). The stitching bound the pages and cover together to form the book.

The majority of the pages in the Dodge book[34] contain itemized charges, which are entered sequentially by the individual being charged. Each entry specifies whether or not the issue was due that person by law (i.e., clothing allowance by rank and time served), or if the individual had charged the purchase against his personal account (i.e., overdrawn). The quantity and price per item were given for supplies whose cost recovery was necessary.

Dodge's quartermaster book contains 1,718 separate entries. The number of entries varies per page. The book is organized into sections that list issues to officers (generally in order of rank), military companies, and different specialized departments (such as the Indian department, interpreters, and the surgeon, among others). Dodge concludes his book with copies of letters, testimonies, and statements important to his career, such as his letter of appointment as Agent, and various inventories of goods that were lost during shipments to or from Fort Jefferson for which he would not take fiscal responsibility or be accountable.

---

[31] Ibid., I: 461-3, 473-475, 506-7.
[32] National Archives, Revolutionary Record Group, Item No. 0113; Consul W. Butterfield, *History of George Rogers Clark's Conquest of Illinois and the Wabash towns 1778 and 1779.* Reprinted 1972 by Gregg Press, Boston, 746.
[33] Unpublished George Rogers Clark Papers, Archives Division, Virginia State Library, Richmond, Boxes 48-50.
[34] *Ibid.,* Box 48.

The entries of the John Dodge book name 204 individuals, including men, women, and children of the military, civilian, and Indian communities. The genealogical significance of that listing is very important. From an anthropological, economical, or historical perspective, the ultimate significance of the Dodge book lies in the completeness of the accounting record and the insight that that information provides the research of late 18th-century frontier life.

The Martin Carney quartermaster books consist of two volumes labeled "1E" and "1F."[35] Books "1A" through "1D" are, apparently, missing.[36]

Carney's book "1E" measures six and one-half inches long by five and one-half inches wide. The cover and the first three numbered pages of the book are missing; 52 pages of the book survive. The paper of the Carney book, like that of the Dodge book, is folded in half and sewn down the middle. Blank pages were hand-ruled as necessary for accounting purposes. No apparent organization of Martin Carney's book "1E" exists other than individual page headings. Book "1E" records issues of ammunition (powder, lead, and flints), arms and accoutrements (muskets, swivels, rifles, bayonets with belts, swords, axes, kettles, and tents), and commodities (sugar, tobacco, and soap). In addition, Carney inventories items he purchased for the establishment of Fort Jefferson and provides information in some cases as to how those items would be used (such as the flat-bottomed boats purchased in Louisville "for sake of the plank to build a garrison and barracks"). Lastly, in the 823 line entries of Carney's "1E.," 74 additional individuals and families are identified for being at Fort Jefferson in addition to the people named by Dodge in his quartermaster book.

Carney's book "1F" consists of 80 pages, each measuring five and one-half inches wide by seven and one-half inches long. Like the other quartermaster books, the pages of book "1F" were originally blank, but were hand-ruled to create forms necessary for accounting. The front and back covers are missing from this book.

The subject matter of book "1F" consists almost entirely of commodities: rum, sugar, tobacco, and soap. Fifty-four individuals are named in its 190 entries (five persons listed were not previously named by Dodge or Carney in their other books). In total, the quartermaster books from Fort Jefferson contain 2,731 line item entries. They identify more than 283 persons and make references to the comings and goings of various military companies at Fort Jefferson. They identify the Clarksville militia, name and specify quantities of arms, accoutrements, munitions, commodities, and dry goods issued to officers, members of their companies, members of the militia, and the friendly Indian allies. And, they offer an approximation of family size and activities pursued by men, women, and children while serving in a support capacity at Fort Jefferson and the civilian community of Clarksville.

The quartermaster books also reflect major activities occurring within and without the fort area, and they provide very specific information about the presence and absence of certain structures associated with the fort and community, ownership of those

---

[35] *Ibid.*, Boxes 49-50.

[36] Maybe not "missing, " maybe simply not yet found like the other Clark papers. Present within the Unpublished Clark Papers are a series of oversize, (2 foot x 3 foot) ledgers. Several of the ledgers correspond to Carney's 1E and 1 F. The missing Carney books maybe duplicated on the oversize ledgers that are in the possession of the Archives Division, Virginia State Library.

buildings, building function, and in several cases, even the type of wood used to build the structures, e.g., "cherry wood used for flooring".

The quartermaster books of John Dodge and Martin Carney are extremely significant. They provide a better understanding of life and activities at Fort Jefferson, and they enlighten our previous misconceptions about frontier history during the American Revolution.

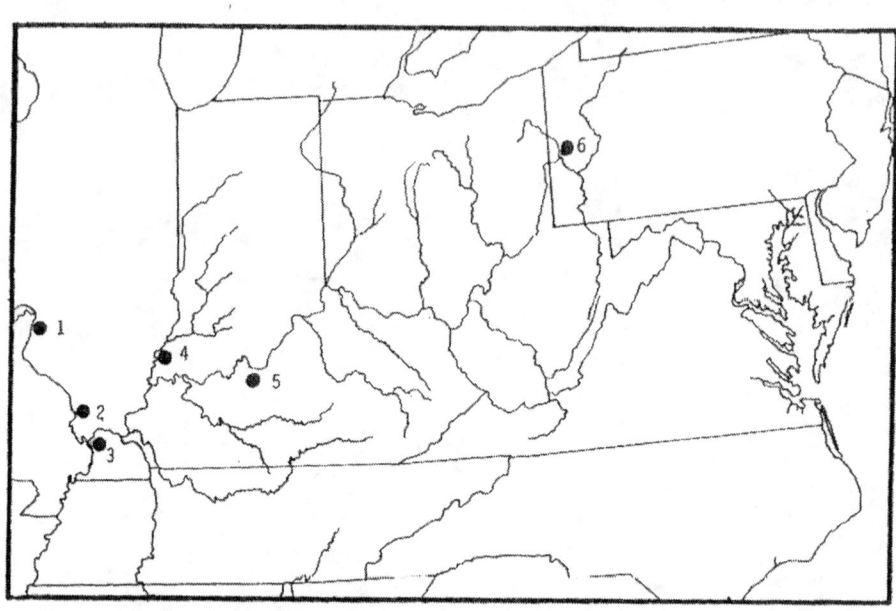

Figure 6.1: The Western Department, 1780-1781: 1, Fort Bowman (Cahokia); 2, Fort Clark (Kaskaskia); 3, Fort Jefferson/Mouth of the Ohio; 4, Fort Patrick Henry (Vincennes); 5, Louisville (Falls of the Ohio); and 6, Fort Pitt (Pittsburgh).

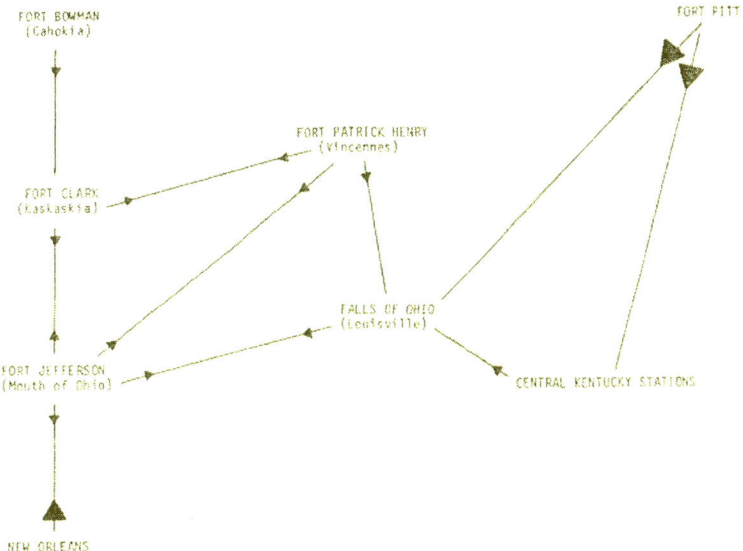

Figure 6.2; Distribution Diagram of Food, Dry Goods, and Other Supplies throughout the Western department (large triangles denote major source locations; small triangles depict regional sources as well as "departure" of goods through population movement, i.e., civilian moving and/or military desertions).

CHAPTER 7: MUNITION SUPPLIES AT GEORGE ROGERS CLARK'S FORT JEFFESON[1]

The kind, amount, and distribution of arms and munitions between 1780 and 1781 at Clark's Fort Jefferson are examined in this chapter. As the economic and redistribution center for Clark's Illinois Battalion, Fort Jefferson received and supplied other key military sites with large quantities of arms and munitions in support of Virginia's efforts to secure her claim to her western border.

Introduction

Unlike the popular 1941 phrase uttered by Chaplain Howell M. Forgy, "Praise the Lord and Pass the Ammunition," few people have heard about George Rogers Clark's Fort Jefferson.[2] Clark's name is associated more closely with his successful military campaigns at Kaskaskia and Vincennes[3] than it is with Fort Jefferson. Yet Clark—in conjunction with Patrick Henry—planned the construction of Fort Jefferson in 1777 and set into motion a series of events that would lead to the acquisition of the Northwest Territory by the United States.[4]

Previous studies by J.G. Randall,[5] James Alton James,[6] Light T. Cummins,[7] and Greg Holm[8] have presented overviews of Clark's line-of-supply logistics. This chapter shall do so, too, but shall be more particularistic in scope, examining ONLY munition supplies and armament of Clark's Fort Jefferson for the years (April) 1780 through (June) 1781, the duration of Fort Jefferson (April 19, 1780 to June 8, 1781). The research

---

[1] A version of this paper titled, "Praise the Lord and Pass the Ammunition: Munition Supplies at George Rogers Clark's Fort Jefferson, 1780-1781" was published in 1991 as part of the *Selected papers from the 1989 and 1990 George Rogers Clark Trans-Appalachian Frontier History Conferences*, edited by Robert J. Holden and published jointly by the Eastern National Park & Monument Association and Vincennes University in 1991. Funding for that publication came from the Eastern National Park & Monument Association. Permission to republish this paper came from the George Rogers Clark National Historical Park and Vincennes University.

[2] John Bartlett, editor, *Familiar Quotations*, p. 994b, 13th and Centennial Edition, Little Brown and Company, Boston, Mass.

[3] Wilshire Butterfield, *History of George Rogers Clark's Conquest of the Illinois and Wabash Towns 1778-1779*. Printed originally in 1904. Republished by Gregg Press, 1972.

[4] William Hayden English, *Conquest of the Country Northwest of the River Ohio 1778-1783 and Life of Gen. George Rogers Clark*, Vols. I and II, Bowen-Merrill Company, Indianapolis, Ind. Letter, Governor Patrick Henry to Governor Bernardo de Galvez, 1777. Archivo General de Indias, Seville, Estante 87, Cajon 1, legajo 6.

[5] J.G. Randall, George Rogers Clark's Service of Supply. *Mississippi Valley Historical Review*, 8: 250-262.

[6] James Alton James, Oliver Pollock, Financier of the Revolution in the West. *Mississippi Valley Historical Review*, 16:67-80.

[7] Light T. Cummins, "Oliver Pollock and George Rogers Clark's Service of Supply: A Case Study in Financial Disaster." *Selected Papers from the 1985 and 1986 George Rogers Clark Trans-Appalachian Frontier History Conferences*. Robert J. Holden, editor, Eastern National Park and Monument Association, George Rogers Clark national Historical Park and Vincennes University, Vincennes University Printing Center, Vincennes, Ind.

[8] Greg Holm, "Supply Issues of the Illinois Regiment Under George Rogers Clark." *The Life of George Rogers Clark, 1752-1818: Triumphs and Tragedies*, edited by Kenneth C. Carstens and Nancy S. Carstens, Westport: Greenwood Publishing Group, 2004.

in this chapter represents the first attempt to reconstruct the actual numbers of munitions and armaments for one of Clark's Illinois Battalion forts. How many muskets and pieces of artillery did Clark's troops have at Fort Jefferson? How much powder and lead were they issued? How much did they expend? And, how much did they distribute to other Illinois Battalion forts? This study provides some specific insights into Clark's military supplies at Fort Jefferson that have not been addressed previously by other researchers. Furthermore, in this paper the student of Clark gains a glimpse into one aspect of Clark's logistical considerations: the actual number of Fort Jefferson's munitions which were used by Clark's Illinois Regiment. From these data, one may better generalize the extent to which Clark's Illinois forces were outfitted during the war in the West, and, therefore, provide for a better assessment of the military characteristics of the Illinois battalion in general.[9]

Background

Fort Jefferson was a military garrison and civilian community constructed near the Mouth of the Ohio River in April 1780.[10] As a settlement, Fort Jefferson represented Virginia's attempt to physically claim her western boundary and maintain her political and economic interest in the West. Although more easterly located settlements at Harrodsburg and Bonnesborough previously had existed within Virginia's West, neither had been initiated at the request of the Virginia government. Only Fort Jefferson was a product of the Virginia government, an executive act of Patrick Henry put into effect by Thomas Jefferson. Fort Jefferson was, for all practical purposes, a fortification and a community planned and sanctioned by the Executive Branch of Virginia's government.[11]

When Clark left the Falls of the Ohio River (Louisville) in April 1780 to travel to the Mouth of the Ohio to build Fort Jefferson, he reportedly took with him, "perhaps 120 men...well Cloathed [sic] except in the article of Linens."[12] This quote has been interpreted previously as representing the total number of persons present at Clark's Fort Jefferson.[13] Recent studies have demonstrated that many more individuals were present at the fort.[14] It also has been demonstrated that the population density for Fort Jefferson

---

[9] Kenneth C. Carstens, "At the Confluence of the Ohio and Mississippi Rivers: Virginia's Claim to the West." Paper presented at the Second Annual Ohio Valley History Conference, 1986, Murray State University, Murray, Ky. Kenneth C. Carstens, "Fact vs. Fiction: Military Engagements at Fort Jefferson, 1780-1781." Paper presented at the Seventh Annual George Rogers Clark Trans-Appalachian Frontier History Conference, 1989. Meetings co-sponsored by the George Rogers Clark National Historical Park and Vincennes University, Vincennes, Ind., Kenneth C. Carstens, "Issues at Fort Jefferson, 1780-1781: The Quartermaster Books of John Dodge and Martin Carney." *Selected Papers from the 1987 and 1988 George Rogers Clark Trans-Appalachian Frontier History Conferences*, 1989. Robert J. Holden, editor. Eastern National Park and Monument Association, George Rogers Clark National Historical Park and Vincennes University, Vincennes University Printing Center, Vincennes, Ind.
[10] Carstens, 1986, *op cit*.
[11] James Alton James, editor, *George Rogers Clark Papers 1771-1783, Vol. 1*: 386-391. Originally published in 1912 and 1926, Trustees of the Illinois State Historical Library, Springfield. Reprinted, 1972, AMS Press, New York, N.Y.
[12] *Ibid.*: 417-418.
[13] Kathryn M. Fraser, "Fort Jefferson: George Rogers Clark's Fort at the Mouth of the Ohio River, 1780-1781." *The Register of the Kentucky Historical Society*, 1983, 81: 1-24, Frankfort, Ky.
[14] Carstens, 1986, op cit. Kenneth C. Carstens, *The Personnel of George Rogers Clark's Fort Jefferson and Civilian Community of Clarksville [Kentucky]: 1780-1781*. Heritage Books, Bowie, Maryland, 1999.

varied greatly, from as few as 100 to a maximum of 565 persons.[15] Within that population range were members of the Illinois Battalion (representing several companies), the Clarksville Militia, numerous civilians (including many [40 or more], named families, and several Indian ally groups, especially 65 of the Kaskaskia Indians.

Among the major activities at fort Jefferson between 1780 and 1781 that generated documentation about armament and munitions supplies were six military engagements (including two battles at the fort), the outfitting of numerous hunting parties, and the issuance and redistribution of various supplies directed to and received from other posts.[16] And, although it has been assumed that Clark's forces left the Falls of the Ohio fully-equipped militarily, no specific documentation to that effect ever has been reported. However, records from Fort Jefferson indicate that a full range of supplies must have been brought from the Falls of the Ohio to the Mouth of the Ohio in April 1780, in order for Fort Jefferson to exist. Supplementary shipments of other goods were received at Fort Jefferson from Spanish-held New Orleans in December 1780, and January 1781.[17] And, although the supplements were primarily liquid (tafia), shipments to Fort Patrick Henry at Vincennes and Fort Clark at Kaskaskia included substantial quantities of munitions in return. Those supplies came not from Fort Pitt or elsewhere in the East, but from New Orleans by way of Fort Jefferson.[18] Fort Jefferson was Clark's redistribution center and economic hub during 1780-1781.[19]

Munition Supplies

The two most significant munition supply items at Fort Jefferson were gunpowder and lead. As illustrated in 7.1, more than 3,200 pounds of gunpowder and 3,600 pounds of lead were shipped to Fort Jefferson. These 6,800 pounds of munitions originated in New Orleans through the supervision of Oliver Pollock.[20] Although 6,800 pounds may seem like a large quantity of munitions, it is not, especially when taking into account individual issues given to each soldier, the allotment made to the artillery, and the amounts redistributed to other posts (principally forts Clark, Patrick Henry, Bowman, and Nelson) from Fort Jefferson.

As an example, almost one-third of the total gunpowder issued (1,001 of 3,235 pounds) went to the militia and state troops at Fort Jefferson. The other two thirds (2,105 pounds) was redistributed from Fort Jefferson to Fort Clark at Kaskaskia and Fort Patrick Henry at Vincennes. Likewise, only 37% of the lead received at Fort Jefferson was issued to the soldiery at that post; the remaining amount of lead was sent to Kaskaskia and Vincennes. Minor amounts were issued to individuals going express among the various Illinois garrisons (Clark, Bowman, Patrick Henry, and Falls). It should be noted that the totals from lead issued and distributed do not, however, when taken together, equal the amount of lead received at Fort Jefferson (7.1). Therefore, it could be suggested that the

---

Kenneth C. Carstens, *The Calendar and Quartermaster Books of George Rogers Clark's Fort Jefferson, 1780-1781*. Heritage Books, Bowie, Maryland, 2000.

[15] Carstens, *ibid.*, 1999.
[16] Carstens, *op cit.*, 1986.
[17] Carstens, *op cit*, 1986; *op cit.*, 2000.
[18] Unpublished George Rogers Clark Papers, Boxes 1-50, Virginia State Library, Archives Division, Richmond, Va. (hereafter, VSA, Box No.).
[19] Carstens, *op cit.*, 1989.
[20] Unpublished Clark Papers, Boxes 48-50.

Fort Jefferson garrison must have arrived with full or partial munition stores, at least at the individual level. If they did not, then either an error in bookkeeping at Fort Jefferson by Martin Carney or John Dodge occurred, or the Fort Jefferson archival record is incomplete and receipts for "received amounts" are under-represented in the records that remain.

Similarly, even the difference between the total amount of gunpowder received and the total issued (Table 7.1: Issued at Fort Jefferson plus distributed to other posts from Fort Jefferson) is amazingly low (only about 129 pounds). It's doubtful that a quartermaster would intentionally issue stores of munitions to other posts that could place his own fortification in jeopardy. However, it is possible that simply a shortage of gunpowder existed at Fort Jefferson. Yet the larger quantities of gunpowder shipped to other posts FROM Fort Jefferson indicates to me otherwise. I believe the only logical conclusion is that full or partial munition stores MUST have been brought with the personnel from the Falls when they established Fort Jefferson in April 1780, even though an inventory of those stores has not been located.

These observations become increasingly important when the number of individuals present at the fort is taken into account. A "standard issue" of powder and lead per individual is not defined clearly within the voucher records at Fort Jefferson. However, a ratio allotment of one-to-two is generally apparent in the Fort Jefferson vouchers; that is, one pound of powder usually was issued for every two pounds of lead. One pound of gunpowder usually permits the manufacture of 24 to 30 musket cartridges.[21] Although these small numbers hardly seem to impact the 1,001 pounds of gunpowder issued at Fort Jefferson, their numerical significance becomes substantially great when the total number of issues is taken into account. The following description of the military population at Fort Jefferson will demonstrate this point.

At its maximum, Fort Jefferson contained nine companies of infantry totaling 182 men, along with one company of Dragoons totaling 34 men, 46 men of the Clarksville Militia and 24 miscellaneous military personnel. In addition to these 286 men, this post also contained a company of artillery. As illustrated by 7.2, the artillery complement at Fort Jefferson was considerable, consisting of five swivels (possibly one-pounders), a two-pounder swivel, a four-pounder (possibly a light-four pounder brass field piece), and a six-pounder iron cannon.[22]

If calculations are made for the amount of gunpowder consumed per shot for each of the above artillery pieces (figured at the charging rate of one-fourth of the shot's weight for each item)[23] a single simultaneous shot fired from the six swivels and two cannon would consume 4.25 pounds of gunpowder. In addition, a single mass volley fired from each of the 286 muskets, calculated at 0.04 pounds per cartridge, would require 11.44 pounds of gunpowder. Collectively, a single combined volley of artillery and musketry would use 15.69 pounds of powder. That being the case, only an estimated 64 volleys could be fired from Fort Jefferson before the 1,001 pounds of gunpowder would be exhausted. Or so it would seem in theory.

---

[21] Captain George Smith, *An Universal Military Dictionary: A Copious Explanation of the Technical terms &tc. Used in the Equipment, Machinery, Movements, and Military Operations of an Army*, p. 58. Printed for J. Millan, near Whitehall, London: 1779. Reprinted, Museum Restoration Service, 1969, Ottawa.
[22] VSA, Boxes 12, 13, 17, 20, 50.
[23] John Muller, *A Treatise of Artillery: 1780*. Republished, 1972, Museum Restoration Service.

A figure as low as 64 volleys probably indicates a biased underrepresentation of the actual amount of gunpowder at Clark's fort. If that is true, such would further strengthen the argument that Clark's forces arrived at Fort Jefferson from Louisville with partial to full munition stores.

Other Armament

The kind of arms carried by Clark's Illinois Battalion has been a matter of contention among historians and historical re-enactors for quite some time. Did they use the Committee of Safety musket? The French Charleville? The Spanish fusil? What about using a captured British Brown Bess? And, what about rifles? Were they used? If so, to what degree? Lastly, did Clark's troops carry swords and were they issued scalping knives?

Several of these questions can be addressed by information contained within the voucher records from Fort Jefferson for the period of 1780 to 1781. (It is important to emphasize that the Fort Jefferson documents pertain to this period ONLY, because Clark's line of supply varied greatly by time. Generalizations that retrofit Fort Jefferson data to previous Clark campaigns are greatly discouraged.)

It is hoped that sufficient data has been presented to demonstrate that Clark's troops were at least partially equipped with munitions and arms when they settled Fort Jefferson. By December 1780, they received an additional supplementary shipment of 120 muskets from New Orleans. These muskets came complete with 120 bayonets, 422 bayonet belts, 261 cartridge boxes with belts and one "Spanish musket and bayonet" (Table 7.2). In addition Clark's men received four fusils, nine carbines, and eight rifles. Both the fusils and the carbine are, generally speaking, light-weight shorter muskets designed primarily for use by the artillery, light infantry, or cavalry.[24] All three unit types were present at Fort Jefferson, and references made to these various "specialized" musket forms indicate that Clark's forces for 1780-1781 were equipped well and equipped properly. (It should be noted, too, that although Captain John Rogers' Company of Dragoons, or cavalry, had the right kind of gun, there were no horses to be issued at Fort Jefferson. As a result, the "Light Horse" were literally "light of horse" and served instead as Light Infantry.)

Rifles, although present at Fort Jefferson, were not distributed widely. They were, however, extensively used for procuring meat for the garrison. Even a broken rifle from Vincennes carried a $500 hard-money price tag at Fort Jefferson. After such a rifle was fixed by the post armorer, the Clarksville sheriff confiscated the rifle for use by the civilian community.[25]

Last but not least, a grand total of 100 swords—of unknown type—was received from Spanish New Orleans. Captain Robert George, the fort commandant at Fort Jefferson in the absence of Clark, was the first to receive a sword from the allotment. The remaining 99 swords were not issued until January 1781.[26] Scalping knives were

---

[24] M.L. Brown, *Firearms in Colonial America*, 1980. Smithsonian Institution Press, Washington, D.C. Harold L. Peterson, *The Book of the Continental Soldier*, 1968. Stackpole Book Company, Harrisburg.
[25] VSA, Box 12.
[26] VSA, Box 15.

issued on a daily basis from the moment Fort Jefferson was first settled in April of 1780 and throughout its duration.

In conclusion, it is clear that the soldiery at Clark's Fort Jefferson were armed quite well with cannon, swivels and musketry. It is NOT clear if Clark's soldiers had enough gunpowder to use the armament effectively. Further research with the archives from the Falls of the Ohio, Kaskaskia, and Vincennes settlements should determine whether or not Clark's forces brought munition supplies with them. If they did, then Fort Jefferson must have been more than adequately supplied, having received additional supplies from New Orleans later in the year. If, however, they did not bring munition supplies with them in April 1780, then the supplies received from New Orleans at Fort Jefferson were precariously few in number and sorely needed.

Table 7.1 Pounds of Gunpowder and Lead Received, Issued, and Distributed at Fort Jefferson, 1780-1781.

	Gunpowder	**Lead**
Received at Fort Jefferson		
1780	3,235 pounds	3,095 pounds
1781	---	506 pounds
Totals	3,235 pounds	3,601 pounds
Issued at Fort Jefferson		
1780	681.75 pounds	1,009.50 pounds
1781	319.50 pounds	321.50 pounds
Distributed to other posts from Fort Jefferson		
1780	1,320 pounds	1,683 pounds
1781	785 pounds	746 pounds
Totals	2,105 pounds*	2,429 pounds**

Notes: * 128.75 pounds remaining
**-159 pounds (an apparent deficit)

Table 7.2 Armament and Munitions Received and Issued at Fort Jefferson, 1780-1781.

	Received 1780	Received 1781	Issued 1780	Issued 1781
Small Armament				
Muskets	157	0	16	20
Bayonets with belts	422	0	0	7
Spanish musket w/bayonet	1	0	0	0
Fusil	0	0	0	4
Carbines	0	0	9	0
Rifles	8	0	20	0
Flints	0	0	294*	622**
Swords	100	0	1	99***
Cartridge boxes w/belts	261	0	0	0
Large Armament				
Swivels	5	0	5	0
Two-pounder (swivel)	1	0	1	0
Four-pounder (cannon)	0	0	1	0
Six-pounder (cannon)	0	0	1	0
Yards flannel (for cannon)	12	0	66	7

Notes: *only 2% (6) issued to the Indians
**77% (480) issued to the Indians
***approximately 11% (11) issued to Indians

CHAPTER 8: SUBSISTENCE STRATEGIES ON THE WESTERN FRONTIER[1]

Introduction

Subsistence (food-getting) activities at Fort Jefferson are examined in this chapter. Food-getting processes were accomplished differently by different ethnic groups on the frontier as illustrated at other archaeological sites on the 18th-century frontier (French, Spanish, British, Native American). Fort Jefferson was settled April 19, 1780,[2] but was on June 8, 1781.[3] The chief reason why the fort and community were abandoned, according to Lt. Col. John Montgomery, was the lack of food.[4] From his position at the Falls of the Ohio, Montgomery wrote Virginia Governor Thomas Nelson on August 10, 1781:

> I arrived at Fort Jefferson the 1st of May last (1781), where I found the Troops in a very low and Starving Condition, nor was any goods or other Property wherewith to purchase. From the Illinois nothing could be expected, the Credit of the State being long since lost there, & no supplies coming from this place, occasioned an Evacuation of that Post, which for want of Provisions, took place on the 8th June last.[5]

Despite the brief existence of this post (13 months and 20 days), invaluable information about the late 18th-century frontier is contained within the Fort Jefferson papers that I recently edited,[6] within the Clark papers edited by James Alton James,[7] and within the Fort Jefferson court records preserved in the Draper Manuscripts.[8] These sources contain a record of vital activities about the fort's economic

---

[1] A previous version of this paper was published as, "What's for dinner? Late 18th Century Subsistence Strategies at George Rogers Clark's Fort Jefferson and the Civilian Community of Clarksville, 1780-1781" in Vol. 7 of *Current Archaeology in Kentucky*, edited by Charles Hockensmith and Kenneth Carstens, Kentucky Heritage Council, Frankfort, Kentucky, 2004. A revised version of that paper is published here with the permission of the Kentucky Heritage Council.

[2] George Rogers Clark letter to John Dodge, April 20, 1780, in James Alton James, ed. *The Papers of George Rogers Clark*, I: 417-418, AMS Press, New York, 1972.

[3] Colonel John Montgomery letter to Governor Thomas Nelson, August 10, 1781. James, ed., I: 585-586.

[4] Ibid.

[5] Ibid.

[6] Kenneth C. Carstens, *The Calendar and Quartermaster Books of George Rogers Clark's Fort Jefferson, 1780-1781*. Heritage Books, Bowie, Maryland, 2000. Kenneth C. Carstens, *The Personnel of George Rogers Clark's Fort Jefferson and Civilian Community of Clarksville [Kentucky], 1780-1781*. Heritage Books, Bowie, Maryland, 1999.

[7] *Op cit.*, Vols. I and II.

[8] Lyman Draper, *Draper Manuscripts*, esp. Series J., Wisconsin Historical Society, Madison, Wisconsin.

and subsistence systems, as administered by the fort's quartermasters, John Dodge and Martin Carney, and the fort's commissary, John Donne.[9]

Information about Fort Jefferson's subsistence practices will be presented in this chapter and a comparison will be made to the potential availability of natural resources near the fort.[10] This post's subsistence system will be studied in light of other 18th-century Midwestern frontier settlements in order to better delineate the Fort Jefferson food procurement system.

Background

A minuscule amount of published data exist that describe late-18th-century culinary practices in use throughout the western Virginia frontier (principally Kentucky, but also the Ohio Valley and general Midwest). Several 18th-century sites in the Midwest have received archeological and archival investigations. Among those are Elizabeth Scott's[11] analysis of subsistence patterns at 18th century French- then-British-held Fort Michilimackinac; Charles Orser's[12] work at Fort DeChartres II and Bonnie Gums'[13] study at the French village of Cahokia, both in west central Illinois; Nancy O'Malley's[14] work at Fort Boonesborough in east central Kentucky; and lastly, Virgil Nobel's,[15] Judy Tordoff's,[16] and Terrance J. Martin's[17] work at the French outpost Fort Ouiatenon in north central Indiana.

---

[9] Carstens, 1999.

[10] William L. Potter and Kenneth C. Carstens, 1986, "Floral Reconstruction of the Fort Jefferson Area." Paper presented at the 1986 Southeastern Archeological Conference, Nashville.

[11] Elizabeth Scott, 1985, *French Subsistence at Fort Michilimackinac, 1715-1781: The Clergy and the Traders.* Archaeological Completion Report Series, Number 9, Mackinac Island State Park Commission, Mackinac Island, Michigan.

[12] Charles Orser, Jr., 1976, *The 1975 Season of Archaeological Investigations at Fort de Chartres, Randolph County, Illinois.* University Museum, Southern Illinois University, Carbondale.

[13] Bonnie L. Gums, 1988, *Archaeology at French Colonial Cahokia. Studies in Illinois Archaeology No. 3*, Illinois Historic Preservation Agency, Springfield.

[14] Nancy O'Malley, 1989, *Searching for Boonesborough.* Archaeological Report 193, Program for Cultural Resource Assessment, University of Kentucky, Lexington. Terrance J. Martin, 1989, "Preliminary Report on Animal Remains from Block C of the Fort Area at Fort Boonesborough State Park, Kentucky." In O'Malley, 1989.

[15] Vergil Noble, 1983, *Functional Classification and Intra-Site Analysis in Historical Archaeology: A Case Study from Fort Ouiatenon.* Ph.D. dissertation, Michigan State University, University Microfilms, Ann Arbor.

[16] Judy Tordoff, 1983, *An Archaeological Perspective on the Organization of the Fur Trade in Eighteenth Century New France.* Ph.D. dissertation, Michigan State University. University Microfilms, Ann Arbor.

[17] Terrance Martin, 1986, *A Faunal Analysis of Fort Ouiatenon, An Eighteenth Century Trading Post in the Wabash Valley of Indiana.* Ph.D. dissertation, Michigan State University, University Microfilms, Ann Arbor.

Throughout the last 25 years, locating contextual—archaeological--evidence of Fort Jefferson has been difficult. Therefore, the subsistence model described here is based only upon 18th-century historical data, biomass statistics from the site's immediate five-kilometer radius, and from an interpretation of excavated Midwestern 18th-century sites.

Archeological Record

Elizabeth Scott[18] recognizes that at Fort Michilimackinac there were two different patterns of food procurement that characterize the two major cultures present at the fort: French (1715-1761) and British (1761-1781). The French period is subdivided into a French mission period (1715-1730), and into two subsequent units called first French (1730-1744) and second French (1744-1761). All four periods (mission, first French, second French, and British) are recognized stratigraphically and contextually in the archeological record at Fort Michilimackinac. Comparable raw data for the two cultures come from sheet middens (layered garbage), not features (subsurface pits). According to Scott,[19] "the overwhelming majority of meat contributed to both French and British diets is from mammals, with the fish contribution a distant second." She notes a sampling bias, however, against birds and fish, which are underrepresented for the French deposits, where many more bird and fish remains were recovered than in the British levels. These remains, however, were not identified as to species. Her data further demonstrate that domestic animals were eaten more frequently by the Michilimackinac British (69.8% domestic to 30.2% wild) than by the French (54.8% domestic to 45.2% wild) who relied upon a larger number of wild animals to supplement their diet.[20] Chief among the animals exploited by both French and British settlers were cow (*Bos taurus*), pig (*Sus scrofa*), white-tailed deer (*Odocoileus virginianus*), river otter (*Lutra canadensis*), mink (*Mustela* cf. *vison*), ferret/mink/weasel (*Mustelidae*), black bear (*Ursus americanus*), wolf/dog (*Canis sp.*), porcupine (*Erethizon dorsatum*), and beaver (*Castor canadensis*). Birds included Canada goose (*Branta canadensis*), various ducks (*Anatinae*), hawk (*Accipitrinae*), domestic chicken (*Gallus gallus*), ruffed grouse (*Bonasa umbellus*), turkey (*Meleagris gallopavo*), and passenger pigeon (*Ectopistes migratorius*). Fish included lake sturgeon (*Acipenser fulvescens*), lake whitefish (*Coregonus clupeaformis*), lake trout (*Salvelinus namaycush*), pike/pickerel/muskellunge (*Esox sp.*), walleye/sauger (*Stizostedion sp.*), and freshwater drum (*Aplodinotus grunniens*).[21] Scott's[22] analysis further notes that the French raised corn while the British grew squash.

---

[18] Scott, *op cit*.

[19] Scott, *ibid*., 191.

[20] *Ibid*.

[21] *Ibid*., 189-190.

[22] *Ibid*., 167.

Bonnie Gums[23] (1988) observed that at the French village of Cahokia (1699-1790), the French civilians sought both domestic and wild animals for subsistence. However, chief among the large mammals were white-tailed deer, comprising 45.9 % of the identified specimens and 41.5% of the total biomass;[24] cattle/bison comprised only 10% of the sample identified. Other mammals exploited included black bear, beaver, pig, and dog/wolf. In addition, the French hunted birds, including Canada goose, wild turkey, and sandhill crane. Gums notes an underrepresentation of waterfowl in her sample (e.g., only three Trumpeter swans [*Cygnus buccinator*]). Cahokia's geographical position near a wetland area and in the middle of the Mississippi flyway predicts a greater potential for waterfowl exploitation, but such was not represented in the archeological record. Other species exploited for food at Cahokia included the snapping turtle (*Chrysemys sp.*), catfish (*Ictalurus sp.*), buffalo fish (*Ictiobus sp.*), and sucker (*Catostomidae sp.*).[25] Botanical remains of three domestic species were found: corn, wheat, and apple, while wild plant remains were represented by hickory (*Carya sp.*) and walnut (*Juglans*). Gums[26] states that the French diet reveals a distinct preference for wild animal resources, especially white-tailed deer, while some domesticated animals (cattle, pig, and chicken) constitute less than 14% of the sample. Gums[27] further states,

> ...the early French subsistence pattern incorporated bison, black bear, beaver, large birds, aquatic turtles, and fish... The pattern that emerges is one in which French families [living] outside major French settlements (e.g., Kaskaskia or Fort de Chartres) were more self-sufficient regarding the acquisition of provisions. Even when domestic animals were maintained, the rich wildlife habitats...were seemingly perceived as too bountiful to ignore. Cattle, pigs, and chickens served as supplements to a local Native American diet which had been adopted by the French.

Charles Orser's[28] excavations at Fort de Chartres II found faunal remains in Feature 40 (a large black stain near the east barracks of the fort). Associated with the animal bones were English Whieldon-type earthenware ceramics manufactured during the period of 1750-1775. The faunal remains were analyzed by Elizabeth A. Cardinal.[29] In her report, Cardinal[30] states that "cow appears

---

[23] Bonnie Gums, 1988, *Archaeology at French Colonial Cahokia. Studies in Illinois Archaeology No. 3*, Illinois Historic Preservation Agency, Springfield.

[24] *Ibid.*, 224-234.

[25] *Ibid.*, 228-229; Table 11.

[26] *Ibid.*, 230.

[27] *Ibid.*, 233-234.

[28] Charles Orser, Jr., 1976, *The 1975 Season of Archaeological Investigations at Fort de Chartres, Randolph County, Illinois.* University Museum, Southern Illinois University, Carbondale.

[29] Elizabeth Cardinal, 1976, Appendix B.: Faunal Remains from Fort de Chartres. *The 1975 Season of Archaeological Investigations at Fort de Chartres, Randolph County, Illinois*, University Museum, Southern Illinois University, Carbondale.

to have been the most important source of food at [Fort de Chartres II]..., supplemented with deer, birds, and fish."[31]

In Terrance J. Martin's analysis of the 1717-1761 French trading post, Fort Ouiatenon, in north central Indiana, Martin[32] concluded that:

1. Wild animal species were prevalent in the subsistence economy...[and that] white-tailed deer was by far the most significant [wild]...species [and that] waterfowl (including swan, geese, and ducks), wild turkey, and raccoon were also important food animals.

2. Domesticated animals, which include cattle, pig, horse, and chicken, together comprised only a supplement to the subsistence economy.

In Kentucky, Nancy O'Malley[33] located the remains of Fort Boonesborough. Although this post is 300 miles east of Fort Jefferson (on the northern banks of the Kentucky River in Kentucky's central Blue Grass region), it is, nonetheless, socially, culturally, and politically similar to Fort Jefferson, because of its Virginian roots. Terrance J. Martin[34] analyzed the excavated faunal remains from Fort Boonesborough. Martin's study revealed that both wild and domesticated animals were hunted, especially the black bear, pig, white-tailed deer, bison/cattle, turkey, and channel catfish. Of these animals, the most popular was deer, followed by bison/cattle. Large birds, such as turkey, represented the third most popular species exploited by the inhabitants of Boonesborough.

Fort Jefferson

The habitat surrounding the Fort Jefferson area is both diverse and rich in plant and animal life. Inhabitants of the post had access to four major biological zones, all within an easy five- kilometer walk of the fort: riverine resources (Mayfield Creek and the Mississippi River), rich bottomlands and islands in the Mississippi, forest hill slopes, and upland forests and prairies (Figure 8.1). As listed in Table 8.1, these biomes could support a wide array of animals and plants which could be exploited easily by the 18th-century hunter, gatherer, and fisherman. Chief among these animals were white-tailed deer, black bear, elk, raccoon, passenger pigeon, wild turkey, beaver, opossum, various terrapins, rabbits, snapping turtles, river otter, prairie chicken, geese, ducks, and buffalo. From the forest could be collected walnut, pignut, and other naturally-occurring forest fruits and vegetables. This 18th-century frontier provided a cornucopia of foods.

---

[30] *Ibid.*, 174.

[31] *Ibid.*, 165, Table 10.

[32] Martin, 1986: 341-346.

[33] O'Malley, 1989.

[34] *Ibid.*, 123-126.

Based on the listing of animal species in Table 8.1, more than 20 billion calories of food energy were available annually to the residents of Fort Jefferson within a five-kilometer radius of the post. Even without fishing, more than 93,850,487 calories could be obtained from the natural environment around the fort without depleting the animal populations. If the average 18th-centruy adult male[35] required 2,358 calories per day, and the average adult female[36] required 1,858 calories per day, and if, on the average, there were 110 men and 20 women at the post throughout the fort's existence, then 296,540 calories would have been necessary to feed the post daily. Based on the calories available in the natural environment from animal species alone, excluding fish (Table 8.1), the Fort Jefferson population could sustain itself for nearly a year (316 days) and meet calorie requirements.

Unfortunately, the Fort Jefferson research project has no excavated faunal remains with which to compare archeological records with the aforementioned forts and outposts. However, more than 5,000 Fort Jefferson documents have been found and studied recently.[37] These records provide insight into the daily activities at this frontier post. It is upon these papers that the following data are based.

The Fort Jefferson dietary record can be divided into five classes of food: meat, vegetables, condiments, beverages, and other (e.g., breads, or references to food-procuring activities, e.g., "five men out hunting animals" or "harrowing the fields"). In this chapter, only the first four classes will be discussed.

At least six types of meat were recorded as being consumed by the inhabitants of Fort Jefferson between April 19, 1780, and June 8, 1781. These meats include domestic beef (cow), buffalo, deer, bear, pig, and sheep. Other types of meat, e.g., fish, waterfowl, or small mammals, are not quantified in the Fort Jefferson papers. (That is not to say that such animals were not consumed. They probably were. For example, there were issues of fishing seines to the soldiers in March and April, 1781, as well as fishing line, but no record of types or numbers of fish caught were reported.) Of the recorded meats, domestic beef and buffalo constitute the majority recorded, representing 49.8 and 41.7 percent of the total 16,064 pounds of meat (Table 8.2).

The only vegetables described in the Fort Jefferson papers are corn, "cornmeal," turnips, and a reference to private gardens with squash. However, only the corn and cornmeal were quantified because they were issued by the commissary agents at the post. Slightly more than 1,431 bushels of corn were issued to the military and civilian inhabitants. An additional 300 bushels of cornmeal also were issued. Clarksville civilians planted and raised more than 45 acres of corn, which, had they

---

[35] According to Professor Sally Duford, Home Economist and Dietary Specialist at Murray State University, the average 18th century male was between 60-66 inches tall and weighed about 140 pounds.

[36] *Ibid.*, The average 18th century female was between 56-60 inches tall and weighed about 125 pounds.

[37] Carstens, 1999, 2000; Kenneth C. Carstens, 1994, "Fort Jefferson, 1780-1781: A Summary of Its History." *Selected Papers from the 1991 and 1992 George Rogers Clark Trans-Appalachian Frontier History Conference*, edited by Robert J. Holden, Vincennes University and the National Park Service, Vincennes, Indiana (See this volume, Chapter 3). Kenneth C. Carstens, 1993, "The 1780 William Clark Map." *The Filson Club History Quarterly*, 67(1): 23-431 ; Kenneth C. Carstens ,1991a, "Praise the Lord and Pass the Ammunition: Munition Supplies at George Rogers Clark's Fort Jefferson, 1780-1781." *Selected Papers*, edited by Robert J. Holden (See chapter 7, this volume); Kenneth C. Carstens, 1991b, "The Structural Composition of George Rogers Clark's Fort Jefferson, 1780-1781: An Assessment." Paper Presented at the 1991 Society for Historic and Underwater Archeology, Richmond, Virginia (See chapter 5, this volume)..Kenneth C. Carstens, 1990, "Issues at Fort Jefferson, 1780-1781: The Quartermaster Books of John Dodge and Martin Carney." In *Selected Papers*, edited by Robert J. Holden (see chapter 6, this volume).

reached maturity, would have yielded another 1,115 bushels of corn.[38] Unfortunately, the Chickasaw attack of August 28-30, 1780, destroyed the corn crop. What amount of corn was recovered from those burned fields is not known, but some salvaging by the Fort Jefferson militia did occur.[39]

Condiments of sugar and salt were furnished for many different purposes to the population at Fort Jefferson. More than 3,012 pounds of sugar and 20.56 pounds of salt were issued. Condiments had many uses. As an example of non-food use, more than 153 pounds of sugar were issued to sick persons as a homeopathic medicine to combat malaria during the month of September (the daily dose was two pounds of sugar per adult per day and one pound per child per day).[40]

Lastly, beverages as food sources, as well as intoxicants and stimulants were given. At least four milk cows were present at the post between September and November, 1780. But milk was not the mainstay of the post. Nor was coffee, although more than 418 gallons of coffee were issued. Soldiers and civilians alike were allotted alcoholic beverages including, in descending order: tafia (watered-down rum) 1660.76 gallons; an unspecified liquor 254.22 gallons; rum (unwatered-down) 150.49 gallons; whiskey 3.41 gallons; and wine, 3 gallons. In total, more than 2,071 gallons of alcoholic beverages were issued at Fort Jefferson (Table 8.3).

The Fort Jefferson records show that meat, corn, and alcoholic drink had the greatest impact on the inhabitants of Fort Jefferson. Table 8.4 exhibits the monthly distribution for those three items.

Disbursements of meat and alcoholic drink reflect similar bimodal patterns of distribution, although the reasons for those patterns are different. The distribution of meat, which was done so sporadically throughout the fort's 14 months, peaked during September and October, 1780, and again in March, 1781. The issuance of alcoholic drink peaked during September and October, 1780, and again in January and February, 1781.

At the end of August (specifically the 27-30), 1780, Chickasaw Indians attacked Fort Jefferson, burning the corn crop and killing much of the fort's stock. The greatest amount of meat distributed to the fort's inhabitants occurred in the months immediately following that incident. Also, as a result of that attack, settlers would not leave their homes to hunt for themselves. They chose to live instead from the meat taken off the carcasses of the domestic beef. In addition, there was the buffalo, deer, and bear meat which the friendly Kaskaskia Indians brought to the garrison in November, 1780. These measures helped the settlers prepare for the winter.

The larder would not be filled again until March, 1781, when additional beef, buffalo, and pork were received from the surrounding regions. Fishing also was important in March and April of 1781. A small quantity of domestic meat (beef and pork) was issued again in June, just prior to the evacuation of the post. Such action possibly was taken to ready the inhabitants for their move to Fort Nelson in Louisville.

The distribution of alcoholic drink peaked in October, 1780, and January, 1781. These dates coincide with the arrival of two cargo boats (bateaux) from New Orleans, captained by Philip Barbour, who arrived the first time near the end of September and the second time just after the new year.

---

[38] September 2, 1780 report, William Clark and Leonard Helm to Capt. Robert George, Draper Ms: 1M8-11.

[39] Carstens, Chapter 3 this volume.

[40] Carstens, 2000.

Libations ensued and continued until all spirits had been fully consumed two months later. Coffee had been drunk in September, prior to the arrival of Captain Barbour's first cargo. Corn was disbursed principally between August and December, 1780, following the major battle. But this autumn date also coincides with the normal availability of freshly harvested corn from other sources such as the Illinois country, central Kentucky settlements, and New Orleans. It may not be coincidental that large quantities of corn were issued during the fall arrival of Captain Barbour's New Orleans shipments. Otherwise, corn was present only at the origin of the post in April, 1780, when a shipment of 250 bushels of cornmeal accompanied Clark's Illinois Battalion from the Falls of the Ohio.

Calculating amounts of meat, corn, condiments, tobacco, and alcohol dispensed to each individual is highly problematic, but it has its purpose. If, as Lieutenant Colonel Montgomery stated, the fort's inhabitants were near starvation in May, 1781, which caused the evacuation order, then examining the amounts of known food quantities becomes important to understanding the daily subsistence patterns at this frontier settlement. In order to calculate daily food allotments, it is necessary to have a firm population estimate. Unfortunately, the exact size of the garrison and civilian population on a daily basis is *not* known. The Fort Jefferson record reflects that only an approximate 200 persons (civilian and military) initiated the founding of the fort in April, 1780, but by June, 1780, the numbers had swelled to 565 persons (all named military, civilian, and Kaskaskia Indians).[41] By August, 1780, only about 200 inhabitants again were present (many civilians and soldiers had deserted the post; other military had gone with Clark on his Shawnee campaign into Ohio); by January, 1781, the fort's numbers had lessened to 150. (These numbers are based upon an inventory of civilians still present, and upon quantified disbursements of tafia rations to members of the Illinois Regiment.) Based on the foregoing, it can comfortably be stated that the combined average population of Fort Jefferson and the civilian community of Clarksville was approximately 150 persons, 130 being adults.

Based on the preceding information and the realization that the post and community were quartered for 416 days, it becomes possible to examine food allotments on a "per-person-per-day" basis at Fort Jefferson (Table 8.5).

The data in Table 8.5 show that the inhabitants of Fort Jefferson daily received an average of 1/4 pound of meat, 1.5 pints of unprocessed corn, four ounces of cornmeal, almost three pounds of sugar, and about one gill of alcoholic drink. Caloric food value for this "daily" meal is more than 7,700 calories, but it is extremely low in fiber, folacin, and vitamin C, which also are needed for survival.[42]

It can be concluded that the Fort Jefferson diet was excessively lean. The residents diet must have been supplemented with other foods in order for the population to have survived. But the biases of written records do not record those other foods. Only the archeological record may contain that information.

The food resources present were not equally distributed throughout the year, nor was the quality of those foods received necessarily dependable. Take, for example, the following letter from Capt. Robert George, the commandant of Fort Jefferson. In his writing of February 15, 1781, to Col. George Slaughter in Louisville, George stated:[43]

---

[41] Carstens, 1999.

[42] Duford, *op cit.*, personal communication.

[43] James, ed. *Clark Papers*, 506-507.

>...out of your great abundance I shall expect to receive frequent and large Supplies--more especially in the Commissary way. The Small Supplies you have sent us, have been of infinite Service, & if you frequently repeat them they will be of singular advantage as we look to you for it, but the supplies I beg may be of a better Quality than what is yet come to hand. The Beef is really of the poorest kind--ill-cured, and not half salted--the Barrels being bad, the pickle became wasted, if ever any had been put in, and tho' the Meat does not absolutely stink, it wants little of it.

Sustenance at Fort Jefferson was either feast or famine. Clark apparently did not heed Gov. Thomas Jefferson's statement that the post's population would have to be self-reliant:

>...the less you depend for supplies from this Quarter, the less will you be disappointed by those impediments distance & a precarious foreign Commerce[44]

The population at Fort Jefferson was not self-reliant. The problem became worse when too few edible resources were delivered from Virginia stores to Fort Jefferson. Meager offerings did little more than sustain a people who would not hunt regularly for themselves, would not collect, or would not exploit the richness of their local environment for themselves for fear of Indian depredations. Such occurrences led to the abandonment of Fort Jefferson due to poor leadership and poor economic planning.

How does the Fort Jefferson subsistence pattern compare to other 18th-century forts and settlements on the frontier? Both Martin[45] and Tordoff,[46] in their discussions of the comparability of faunal assemblages between Midwestern sites, suggest that in addition to observable differences in diet preferences between cultures (e.g., a French or a British frontier diet), a difference may be accentuated by a post's economic position. That is, a greater similarity exists between large, geopolitical hubs of different cultures (or what Tordoff calls regional distribution centers), than among smaller, local distribution centers. Forts Michilimackinac and de Chartres II are regional distribution centers. At these two important sites, diets consisted mainly of cow, but the similarity between French and British ends there. Primary supplements to the French diet focused on wild game from the local environment. The British augmented their diet with greater quantities of lesser-sized domesticated animals (e.g., pig and chicken) and less of wild game species, just the opposite of the French custom.

The small French village Cahokia, the French trading post of Fort Ouiatenon, and the American settlement of Fort Boonesborough all displayed dietary patterns expected for smaller, local distribution centers, where emphasis is placed upon wild resources supplemented with a handful of domesticated ones. From that vantage then, even an ethnically British-related site such as Boonesborough reflects an exploitation pattern geared not to the urban centers, but to the local environment. Such would be

---

[44] T. Jefferson to G. Clark, January 29, 1780, in James, ed., *Clark Papers, I*: 389.

[45] T. Martin, 1986, 306-331.

[46] J. Tordoff, 1983, 140.

expected for Fort Jefferson, too, because of its cultural and geographical similarities to Boonesborough, but for a plethora of reasons, Fort Jefferson does not fit the mold.

Instead, the dietary pattern of Fort Jefferson mirrored that of the large regional distribution centers and not a local allocation center (See Table 8.2). Was Fort Jefferson an American frontier regional distribution center? One could make arguments in support of that position.[47] The Fort Jefferson outpost did serve Virginia as a major dissemination site for the middle Mississippi and lower Ohio River valleys.[48] Then, again, it may be argued that the Fort Jefferson subsistence and economic pattern does not follow the dietary pattern of other regional centers. This may be due to its analysis being based upon archival records, not upon an archeological record as was the case with other Midwestern sites in this study.

Yet another difference may be explained by Thomas Jefferson's January 29, 1780, directive to Clark, wherein the post was advised to be self-sufficient. Unfortunately, the people of the post were not self-sufficient due to the constant threat of Chickasaw attack. If settlers and soldiers left the fort, they never came back, by chance or by choice. Indeed, during the month of September, 1780, more than half of the 44 families at Fort Jefferson left for other settlements because they feared additional Indian depredations as well as the prospect of a difficult winter without their corn crop or animal stock.[49] Shipments of supplies from New Orleans, Kaskaskia, Vincennes, and Louisville to Fort Jefferson simply were too few and were too infrequent. When shipments arrived, they consisted of dry goods, military accoutrements, spoiled foods, and alcoholic beverages. Dealing with a terrible credit rating throughout the Illinois country, facing 1000% inflation in the cost of goods, realizing a depreciating Virginian currency, Fort Jefferson was doomed to economic failure.[50] Thus, on June 8, 1781, Lt. Col. John Montgomery, in noting that no new supplies or assistance were imminent and that there existed few prospects for a positive future, decided to forsake Virginia's claim to her westernmost lands.

---

[47] Carstens, 2000; L.T. Cummins, 1986, "Oliver Pollock and George Rogers Clark's Service of Supply: A Case Study in Financial Disaster." In *Selected Papers of the 1985 And 1986 George Rogers Clark Trans-Appalachian Frontier History Conferences*. Edited by Robert J. Holden, Eastern National Park and Monument Association, Vincennes, Indiana.

[48] Carstens, 1999; chapter 6, this volume.

[49] Carstens, 1999, 2000; chapter 3 this volume.

[50] James, ed., *Clark Papers*, I: cliv, 173, 379, 388, 444, 561.

Animal	Predicted No. Species	Potential Pounds Meat Available	Approximate Calories Per Pound	Potential Calories Available
Bison	9	6,408	572	3,665,376
Elk	4	1,300	572	743,600
Deer	427	32,597	572	18,645,484
Black Bear	3.66	655	1306	855,430
Raccoon	456	4,163	1306	5,436,878
Mustelids	11	132	1306	172,392
Opossums	307	1075	1306	1,403,950
Beaver	219	7,690	1306	10,043,140
Muskrat	154	561	1306	732,666
Gray Squirrel	2189	2191	572	1,253,252
Cottontail Rabbit	1331	1797	989	1,777,233
Terrapin sp.	9696	2851	572	1,630,772
Snapping Turtle	4678	36,024	572	20,605,728
All Fish	141 pounds per acre	278,858	720	2×10^{10}
Passenger Pigeon	25,731	2149	400	859,600
Prairie Chicken	45	9.32	400	3728
Wild Turkey	212	1545	1308	2,020,860
1% All Ducks	13,304	18,626	1300	24,213,800
1% All Geese	125,000	5688	2015	11,461,320
TOTALS		404,319.32		20.1×10^9

Table 8.1: Estimate of Annual Biomass for Selected 18th-Century Animal Species within a Five-Kilometer Area of Fort Jefferson (after T. Martin 1986: 347-439).

Meat Consumed	Amount in Pounds	Percent
Domestic Beef	8006	49.8
Buffalo	6695	41.7
Deer	745	4.6
Pig	342	2.1
Bear	246	1.5
Sheep	30	0.02
Totals	16,064	99.72

Table 8.2: Recorded Consumption of Meat at Fort Jefferson, 1780-1781.

Beverage	Amount Gallons	Percent/Total	No. Issues
Coffee	418	16.79	57
Tafia	1660.76	66.70	590
Unsp.Liquor	254.22	10.21	49
Rum	150.49	6.04	7
Whiskey	3.41	0.14	1
Wine	3.00	0.12	1
Totals	2489.88	100.00	705

Table 8.3: Beverages Issued at Fort Jefferson, 1780-1781.

Month (1780-1781)	Meat (Pounds)	Corn (Bushels)	Alcoholic Bev. (Gallons)
April, 1780	---	250 cornmeal	---
May	70	---	0.63
June	50	2.5	38
July	10	---	33.75
August	88	102 bushels & 50 bu. cornmeal	---
September	1005	666.05	205.25
October	4667	269	265.38
November	6407	126.75	2.00
December	---	245	52.44
January, 1781	30	---	608.39
February	---	---	557.01
March	3058	19	111.77
April	30	---	74.32
May	623	0.75	122.94
June	---	---	---
Totals	16,064 lbs.	1731.05 bu.	2071.88 gal.

Table 8.4: Schedule of Disbursement for Meat, Corn, and Drink at Fort Jefferson, 1780-1781.

Issue	Total Issue	Per Person	Ration/Day
All Meat	16,064 lbs.	107.09 lbs	0.257 lbs./day
Corn	1411.3 bushels	9.4 bushels	.023 bu./day
Corn Meal	300 bushels	2.0 bushels	4 oz./day
Sugar	3012.5 lbs.	20.08 lbs.	2.77 lbs./day
Tobacco	2108 lbs.	14.05 lbs.	0.53 oz./day
Alcohol	2071.88 gals.	13.81 gals.	0.033 gal./day

Table 8.5: Projected Theoretical Disbursements per Person per Day Based on a Population Estimate of 150 Persons for 416 Days at Fort Jefferson, 1780-1781.

Figure 8.1: Five Kilometer Site Catchment Area Around Fort Jefferson

CHAPTER 9: GENDER ROLES AT FORT JEFFERSON[1]

Fort Jefferson was short-lived, lasting only 416 days (April 19, 1780 to June 8, 1781). During that brief span of time the garrison and community participated in the construction of a fort with numerous buildings in and outside of its stockaded walls, created an agriculturally based civilian community, cleared and farmed at least 45 acres of land, buried at least 49 of their deceased men, women, and children (38 in coffins), took part in six different military actions (including two major assaults on the fort and community by Chickasaw Indians), held and conducted at least eight different courts of inquiry and court martial proceedings, and participated in other daily activities of late 18th century life including, but not limited to, excessive drinking and merriment. In these, and in other activities, the Fort Jefferson and Clarksville population of 565 persons participated. In this chapter, I examine the gender/work-related roles and activities of the Fort Jefferson population.

Gender-Based Roles

Two of the major problems encountered while conducting studies of 18th-century American frontier life and our understanding of its gender-based roles are lack of primary documentation and the perpetuation of historical myths and half-truths.

The former, lack of primary documentation, is not a problem for Fort Jefferson studies, but the perpetuation of historical half-truths and falsifications is. Earlier histories about Fort Jefferson often state that no more than 35 individuals were present at the post, and that the fort and community were not important to the American Revolution. Indeed, supposedly the only real "hero," or more correctly stated "heroine," of Fort Jefferson was 15- year-old Nancy Ann Hunter. Nancy, as myth records,[2] sneaked out of the fort while it was under siege by "one thousand Chickasaw Indians," her voluminous ballroom dress being riddled with arrows and bullets. Bravely she found her way to the Mississippi River, swam the river, killed a buffalo, floated the buffalo back to the fort and saved the fort's inhabitants from starvation. She was truly the heroine of the day. In fact, Nancy left the post while under a flag of truce and retrieved a straying cow and calf back into the fort. This was hardly the Amazonian-like action subsequent history created, but nonetheless, a deed important to the survival of the fort's inhabitants.

The Nancy Ann Hunter scenario is a classic example of our biased recollection of pioneer or frontier history, especially the feminine role in that history. Many Americans, when asked to name women who participated in the American Revolution, provide two names: Betsy Ross and "Molly Pitcher" (the latter being a colloquialism for two specific camp followers: Margaret Corbin and Mary Hays).[3] These individuals, as well as many,

---

[1] A version of this paper was published as, "The Role of Women in Kentucky's Western Colonial Frontier," pp. 157-167, *Historical Archaeology in Kentucky* by Kenneth C. Carstens, edited by Steven McBride, Kim McBride and David Pollack, The Kentucky Heritage Council, Frankfort, Kentucky, 1995.
[2] M. Juliette Magee, *Old Fort Jefferson. The Advance-Yeoman*, Wickliffe, Kentucky, 1975: 28; Frederick Palmer, *Clark of the Ohio*. Dodd, Mead and Company, New York, 1929: 416; John E.L. Robertson, *West to the Iron Banks*. Master's thesis, Department of History, University of Louisville, Louisville, Ky, 1961: 46, 48.
[3] Linda Grant De Pauw, *Founding Mothers: Women of America in the Revolutionary Era*. Houghton Mifflin Company, Boston.

many others, performed important tasks that history has either forgotten completely or has embellished elaborately.

The historical perspective of gender-based roles has been contradictory. Historians sustain conflicting ideas about sex roles during the late 18th-century. An older school of thought argues that the 18th century was a "golden age" for females.[4] American women were simply better off than either their English counterparts or their 19th-century descendants.

> ...scarce in the colonies, and all hands—male or female—were needed to sustain the growing settlements...*Rigid sex role distinctions could not exist under such circumstances*...and female colonists could engage in whatever occupations they wished [emphasis added].[5]

The antithesis to the "golden age" hypothesis has been presented by Norton. In her study of two geographical extremes (New England and Maryland Chesapeake), Norton deduces that there was a strong division of labor between the sexes in the late 18th-century.[6]

The surviving Fort Jefferson records contain many references to gender roles; therefore, they can be used to clarify the role of gender as it was perceived on the frontier during the late 18th century. Also they can be used to examine the importance of the division of labor in frontier communities as a test of Dexter's[7] and Norton's[8] ideas about late 18th century division of labor standards.

Numerous references to the day-to-day activities of both sexes are contained within the surviving Fort Jefferson documents.[9] The economic and civilian records of this military and civilian outpost include written justifications for every payment for any goods or services exchanged through the post quartermaster, as well as many transcripts of court martial and inquiry proceedings. Each economic transaction required a formal written request. The request was penned by the individual initiating the transaction, if he or she was literate, or by the officer responsible for that individual if the person was not literate. All written requests were signed or "marked" by the individual making the request and by the fort commandant. These stringent rules of economic echelon helped insure the proper use of all material goods, drink, and food supplies. Similarly, the reverse side of each receipt contained an itemized listing of materials actually received, with careful notations of any substitutions or other changes to the initial request.

---

[4] Elisabeth Anthony Dexter, *Colonial Women of Affairs*. Boston, 1931; Herbert Moller, Sex Composition and Correlated Culture Patterns of Colonial America. *William and Mary Quarterly, 1945*, 2: 113-153; Richard B. Morris, *Studies in the History of American Law, with Special Reference to the Seventeenth and Eighteenth Centuries*, New York, 1930.

[5] Mary Beth Norton, The Evolution of White Women's Experience in Early America. *The American Historical Review*, 1984, 89(3): 593-619.

[6] *Ibid.*

[7] Dexter, *op cit.*

[8] Norton, *op cit.*

[9] Unpublished George Rogers Clark Papers, Boxes 1-50, Archives Division, Virginia State Library, Richmond.

Women, as well as men, participated in this economic system. Insight into the daily economic activities of the inhabitants of Fort Jefferson can be gleaned from these economic records. As an example, the following are typical quartermaster ledger entries for women and men at the post:[10]

June 16, 1780, 1 silk handkerchief paid Rachel Yates for making 3 ruffled shirts.

August 29, 1780, paid Nicholas Canada for his account of Smith work, 40£.

Do the Fort Jefferson records indicate all of the activities of the post's military and civilian personnel? Probably they do not, but it is safe to say that the records provide a quantifiable accounting of both male and female activities. If we assume that the fort's economic "books" were not purposefully fabricated or altered, then these records are an accurate accounting of the recorded economic history of the post and an unembellished sample of, and insight into, late-18th-century frontier life (and gender roles on the western (Kentucky-Virginia) frontier).

Fort Jefferson Population Composition

More than 565 people lived at Fort Jefferson throughout the 13 months and 20 days the post was garrisoned.[11] Even so, that number fluctuated greatly, and at times there were probably fewer than 125 men, women, and children at the fort and community. Of the individuals present, the accounting records indicate 267 named adult males in Clark's Illinois Battalion at Fort Jefferson (including officers up to the rank of colonel, and enlistees from private to non-commissioned officers). A portion of the Illinois Battalion at Fort Jefferson consisted of a company of French men from the Kaskaskia-Cahokia region. Forty-six adult men comprised the Clarksville civilian militia. Most of these men were married and varied in social status, but they were primarily farmers.

Sixty-three adult women were present, and were either married, recently widowed, or a part of the military retinue (likewise representing a variety of social classes), along with at least 33 children. Additionally, there were 65 male Kaskaskia Indians who were American allies (only one Kaskaskia woman is mentioned as being present; it is unclear whether other native American women were at the fort).

Also present were 24 members of the commissary and quartermaster corps and Indian department, 67 unmarried adult males, and an unspecified number of male and female black slaves belonging to the officers of Clark's Illinois Battalion.[12] The economic records include the names for two of these adult male slaves: Caesar (who belonged to Col. Clark [Bogert asserts that Caesar was a free Blackman and artificer]),

---

[10] *Ibid.*, Box 48.
[11] Kenneth C. Carstens, *The Personnel of George Rogers Clark's Fort Jefferson and Civilian Community of Clarksville [Kentucky], 1780-1781.* Heritage Books, Bowie, Maryland.
[12] Cf., Pen Bogert, Clark, the Illinois Battalion and the Slave Trade, in *The Life of George Rogers Clark, 1752-1818: Triumphs and Tragedies,* edited by Kenneth C. Carstens and Nancy Son Carstens, Greenwood Publishing Group, Westport, Ct., in press.

and Cato Watts (who belonged to John Donne, a deputy commissary agent at the post).[13] Several of the black males functioned as artificers (engineers) during the construction of the fort.

For the purpose of this study, only the work assignments described in the economic records for the white adult males (n=404) and the white adult females (n=63) are compared. The data include the recorded tasks of the "highest" through "lowest" social positions for the two genders that appear to have been worthy of economic compensation. This comparison should indicate whether there was indeed equality of labor as a result of an inequality in sex ratios (6.41:1), as suggested by Dexter's 1931 "golden age" hypothesis, or whether the gender roles were maintained despite a relative numeric imbalance, as suggested by Norton's 1984 study.

Gender Roles Recorded at Fort Jefferson

Nineteen different activities are described in the economic records for white adult males (Table 9.1). These activities include sewing, clearing fields, planting fields, carting, warring, hunting, going and coming express, seine making, net making, or serving in special capacities such as armourer/blacksmith, doctor, recruiter, sheriff, court martial member, boat crew member, artificer, secretary, or commissary ("drinking" as a social activity is also documented, but was not included in the tabulation of economic activities).

Of the 19 male activities, six are shared with females, include sewing, clearing and planting fields, court martial activities, making fishing nets, and serving in the capacity of Indian interpreter. Of these, sewing activities for women are noticeably more varied and include making linen and leather shirts, suits of clothes, military waistcoats, military trousers, and miscellaneous soldier clothing. As a measure of the intensity of female sewing activities, 41 women made 497 linen shirts in less than one year. In total, more than 529 separate economic entries were made in the Fort Jefferson records for white adult women. Of that number, the majority of those entries (97% or 513/529) were for payment in return for sewing activities.

The records indicate that only four kinds of tasks were performed exclusively by white adult women: serving as washerwomen for three military companies, providing care for widower's children, and serving as a nurse and as a kitchen servant to one of the officers. Of the 23 different total activities described for the two genders, only six activities (26.1 percent) were shared (Table 9.1). Only two of those six (interpreter and court testimony) are not directly related to procuring food. Male-dominated activities (56.5 percent of the total tasks) consist of skilled and unskilled physical tasks that pertain to positions of authority, specialization, non-specialization, and food procurement. Female-based tasks however, were strictly hearth-centered (17.4 percent). Sewing seems to be THE activity in which the majority of the females participated for economic compensation. It is undoubtedly a learned skill, but one that is primarily domestic. In

---

[13] Kenneth C. Carstens, At the Confluence of the Ohio and Mississippi Rivers: Virginia's Claim to the West. Paper presented at the Second Annual Ohio Valley History Conference, Murray State University, Murray, Kentucky, 1986; Unpublished George Rogers Clark Papers, Archives Division, Virginia State Library, Boxes 48-50, Richmond.

other words, the majority of the females at Fort Jefferson spent the major portion of their workdays sewing for economic compensation. Male work for economic compensation was more varied and less domestic.

Based on the foregoing information, it would appear that equality in gender roles was not a part of the colonial frontier social system at Fort Jefferson. Norton's 1984 rebuttal of Dexter's 1931 "golden age" theory appears to hold true for the Fort Jefferson situation. Dexter's 1931 statement that inequality in numbers will cause a breakdown in the division of labor (resulting in an equality of gender roles) *is not supported by the Fort Jefferson data*, even when an extremely unbalanced sex ratio of 6.4:1 is present (404 men to 63 women).

A valid question to ask of the Fort Jefferson data and the above interpretations is whether or not a bias is present within the economic documentation. Just how well is the TOTAL population of Fort Jefferson represented in the economic transactions and the court records?

James Deetz's book, *In Small Things Forgotten*,[14] makes the point that recorded history does not adequately explain the common, everyday aspect of life. History can be very vague when one looks for descriptions dealing with the "non-elite" and "non-important" events. Might the vast quantities of economic and testimonial records from Fort Jefferson have overlooked work assignments specific to gender role that were uncompensated and mundane, or which may have been taken for granted or performed by a minority segment of the population (i.e., female and male black slaves, Indians, or adolescent or indigent whites)?

The answer could be strongly affirmative. As an example, throughout all of the economic vouchers and ledger entries, letters, notes, etc., not one reference mentions candle production (or any source of lighting other than "light wood").[15] Yet someone or some group of persons at Fort Jefferson must have supplied the inhabitants with candles. (Candles are listed on the economic inventories at Kaskaskia [Fort Clark] and Vincennes [Fort Patrick Henry]). Did slaves, Indians, or children make the candles at Fort Jefferson? If they did, was it simply a "mundane" chore that did not merit description or reward from the fort's quartermaster or in his economic records? Or, was candle making a chore expected of both genders and not a part of the fort's economic system? We may never know, but it is clear that ALL aspects of Fort Jefferson life were NOT recorded in the fort's economic records. Yet, our current understanding of gender roles at Fort Jefferson is more complete now than for most frontier forts and outposts, and Fort Jefferson archival research allows us to delve deep into the reconstruction of life at this western frontier outpost.

---

[14] James Deetz, *In Small Things Forgotten: The Archaeology of Early American Life*. Anchor Books, New York, 1977.

[15] James Alton James, editor, The George Rogers Clark Papers, Vol. I, pg. 466, AMS Press, New York, 1972.

Table 9.1: Activities of Men and Women at Fort Jefferson, 1780-1781.

Activity	Women only	Men Only	Shared
Making fishing nets	No	No	Yes
Sewing	No	No	Yes
Clearing fields	No	No	Yes
Planting fields	No	No	Yes
Indian interpreter	No	No	Yes
Provided testimony	No	No	Yes
Serving as doctor	No	Yes	No
Secretary	No	Yes	No
Fishing w/seines	No	Yes	No
Artificer/construction	No	Yes	No
Hunting	No	Yes	No
Sheriff	No	Yes	No
Carting	No	Yes	No
Cartridge making	No	Yes	No
Commissary/quartermaster	No	Yes	No
Military recruiting	No	Yes	No
Armorer/blacksmith	No	Yes	No
Express (messenger)	No	Yes	No
Boat crew member	No	Yes	No
Kitchen servant	Yes	No	No
Child nursery	Yes	No	No
Serving as nurse	Yes	No	No
Military washerwoman	Yes	No	No
Totals	4	13	6

CHAPTER 10: FORT JEFFERSON LEGAL MATTERS, 1780-1781

A legal system, albeit a military one, was present at Fort Jefferson. In support of that legal system was a strong military code of conduct, as well as a well-defined system of operation, including the physical means to incarcerate (jail with iron gate), and a method for hearing legal cases (courts of inquiry and court martial). The following paragraphs provide insight into an often overlooked area of frontier life that blended both civil and military activities. A typical system of punishment included physical torture, as evidenced by a penal system that used "lashes well laid on" as a deterrent.

Introduction

If attacks on the fort by Chickasaw Indians were not enough to upset the peace and tranquility of a frontier setting, then the difficulties of a military justice system, replete with accusations against fellow officers and a court of inquiry system, must have seemed very disturbing indeed. Disrespecting an officer in the presence of others, questioning the correctness of command and authority, investigating abuses to servants and fellow citizens, robbing, and allegations of dereliction of duty, all took place at Fort Jefferson and were heard by its legal system. These charges were investigated through courts of inquiry and court martial activities. The following transcriptions of sworn testimony provide insight into the day-to-day experiences of life on the western frontier, a life that combined military and civil activities, the struggle of classicism, and conflicts rising from the social order of the 18th-century. Maybe several of these investigations stemmed from the inexperienced command of junior officers, maybe others were due to the absence of Clark's leadership, and still other offenses seem like "boys-being-boys" in a frontier setting at Fort Jefferson (yet punishable by 50 lashes on a bare back "well laid on"). Maybe, too, the accusations resulted from the psychological pressures of living within a frontier setting that included eking out a living on a daily basis, trying to survive when the next day was doubtful, the continual lack of food, the possibility of hostile Indian attack, all coupled with heavy drinking and gambling among the officers and different social classes of 18th century society. No doubt, jealousies originated between the haves and have-nots and among different ethnic classes at Fort Jefferson, including racism and racial slurs. Each of these known reasons and possibly others gave rise to the testimony recorded below. It makes for interesting reading and provides considerable insight into the legal and social systems operating on the western frontier in early American society. These testimonies are recorded in the Draper Manuscripts of the Wisconsin Historical Society in Madison. The handwritten documents have been transcribed as accurately as possible. Gross spelling errors and gross punctuation have been corrected. Syntax and grammar have been kept in the original. Where text is missing due to a torn manuscript, such is noted in the text, or if a word was illegible, it too, is noted. The testimonies include allegations against Capt Dodge for speaking disrespectfully to Capt. George; allegations by Major George Slaughter against Capt. Worthington; allegations against

Capt. McCarty by Capt. John Dodge; allegations against Capt. Rogers while on command at Fort Clark in Kaskaskia; allegations against David Allen and James Taylor for robbing Captain Williams and treating his servants poorly; and allegations against Capt. Worthington for dereliction of duty.

The processesy which Courts of Inquiry were conducted have been uniform in U.S. military history. Although the following examples come from the American Revolution, compare the following processes of courts of inquiry to that described by Colonel H.L. Scott in 1864.[1] According to Scott,

> In cases where the general or commanding officer may order a court of inquiry to examine into the nature of any transaction, accusation, or imputation, against any officer or soldier, the said court shall consist of one or more officers, not exceeding three and a judge-advocate, or other suitable person as a recorder, to reduce the proceedings and evidence to writing, all of whom shall be sworn to the faithful performance of duty. This court shall have the same power to summon witnesses as a court-martial, and to examine them on oath. But they shall not give their opinion on the merits of the case, excepting they shall be thereto specifically required. The parties accused shall also be permitted to cross-examine and interrogate the witnesses, so as to investigate fully the circumstances in the question. The proceeding of a court of inquiry must be authenticated by the signature of the recorder and the president, and delivered to the commanding officer, and the said proceedings may be admitted as evidence by a court-martial, in cases not capital, or extending to the dismission of an officer, provided that the circumstances are such that oral testimony cannot be obtained.
> The court may be ordered to report the facts of the case, with or without an opinion thereon. Such an order will not be complied with, by merely reporting the evidence or testimony; facts being the result, or conclusion established by weighing all the testimony, oral and documentary, before the court. . .court may sit with open or closed doors, according to the nature of the transaction to be investigated. The court generally sits with open doors. The form of proceeding, in courts of inquiry, is nearly the same as that in courts-martial: the members begin assembled, and the parties interested called into court, the judge-advocate, or recorder, by direction of the president, reads the order by which the court is constituted. . .ccusation is then read, and the witnesses are examined by the court; and the parties accused are also permitted to cross-examine and interrogate the witnesses, so as to investigate fully the circumstances in question. . .examination of witnesses being finished, the parties before the court may address the

---

[1] Colonel H. L. Scott, *Military Dictionary: Comprising Technical Definitions; Information on Raising and Keeping Troops; Actual Service, including Makeshifts and Improved Material; Law government, Regulation, and Administration Relating to Land Forces.* D. Van Nostrand, New York, 1864, pp. 210-212.

court, should they see fit to do so; after which the president orders the court to be cleared. The recorder then reads over the whole of the proceedings as well for the purpose of correcting the record, as for aiding the memory of the members of the court. After mature deliberation...they proceed to find...

Draper Manuscripts: 56J22

A Court of Inquiry at Camp Jefferson,
July 13, 1780, Ordered by Col. Montgomery, Capt. George and Jno. Dodge, Agent.

Fort Jefferson, July 13, 1780

At a Court of Inquiry held by order of Lt. Col. John Montgomery, by the complaint of Capt. R. George, to inquire into some disrespectful language Capt. Dodge had made use of in regard to his character.

President Major John Williams
Capt. Jno. Rogers, Capt. Keller
Ens. Jarret Williams, Ens. Lawrence Slaughter
Lt. Girault Acting-Judge Advocate
Court met according to Order

    Capt. George complains that Capt. Dodge spoke disrespectfully of his character and wrongfully accused him of making forcible entries into the Public Store.
    Doctor Andrew Rey, being sworn, said that being in the Public Store he asked Capt. Dodge his reason for refusing to give the officers who were present their full quotas of clothing as he had already done to others. Capt. Dodge answered that if he had done it, he had been forced to it by Capt. George's orders.
    Ensign Slaughter, being duly sworn, said that being in the store he inquired of Capt. Dodge why he refused to give him his quota as he had done to other officers, to which Capt. Dodge answered he had been forced by Capt. George to give more than he otherwise would have done.
    Capt. Dodge acknowledges that what is deposed by the above named gentlemen is true.
    Capt. James Piggott of militia, being sworn said that some time after Col. Clark's departure, Capt. Dodge asked him if he was present when his brother asked Capt. George to sign a receipt for clothing to his troops. He said he was present and that Capt. George refused signing it saying it was unnecessary as he had sent an order for them which was entirely sufficient. Capt. Dodge told him that Col. Clark had desired him to tell Capt. George that he intended the clothing might be equally divided among the officers and that Capt. Dodge told this deponent at the same time that Col. Clark had taken but a part of his quota such as he thought might come to the share of

each of the officers, that Capt. Dodge said that he thought the men ought better to be employed in repairing the fort or bastions than working out and that he had found a sentinel asleep.

That Capt. George had taken several articles out of the store for his [illeg.] use which he thought would not be approved of by Col. Clark, that Capt. George had sent orders which he refused.   Everything being contrary to his instructions from government.

Capt. Dodge asked the deponent if Cap [document torn]
[illeg.] at the time of refusing to sign the [document torn]
in him to ask a receipt of a commanding officer [document torn]
Capt. George said he thought Capt. Dodge ought to [document torn]
told Capt. Dodge's brother said he would sign a receipt in a [doc. torn] kept one, but he would not sign a loose one a [document torn] be laughed at, that Capt. Dodge said he thought [document torn] guards to escort individuals when he could not have [document torn]

Capt. Smith being sworn said that Capt. Dodge had said everything   that he knew of the matter now in hearing. Mr. Joseph Hunter being sworn says that Capt. Dodge told him [that he] numbered out a certain quantity of shirts for Capt. George and that Capt. George had found one less and demanded another which he refused as they had counted out, and that Capt. George took one and gave no voucher therefore.

Ezekial Johnson being sworn said that he heard Capt. Dodge say that Capt. George was neglectful of his duty; he asked him in what manner and he said he did not keep his soldiers in order and that the sentry, mounted without ammunition or flints.

Mr. Carney, quartermaster, being sworn and being asked by Capt. Dodge and his brother, did he not deliver him a gun which he took from a sentry who was asleep [?], and he answered "yes." And being asked if the sentry was ever confined to his knowledge, he said "not." And being asked if he ever caught a sentry asleep? He said he did. Capt. Dodge asked if the deponent did not hear him speak to Capt. George about it, he said he did not.

James Sherlock being sworn said that he never heard Capt. Dodge say anything against Capt. George or that was in any manner prejudicial to his character.

Mrs. Mary Smith being sworn says that as she presented to Capt. Dodge an order of Capt. George's he threw it from him saying he accepted orders from no such fellow and afterwards recalled it saying as it was by order Col. Clark and he would on that account except it, but he knew no right Capt. George had to draw any, and that some time ago Mr. Israel Dodge had asked this deponent if she would make 15 shirts for him and his brother, that her daughter said she had been too badly paid for making some before on which Mr. Dodge had taken; he had a great quantity to make for him and his brother and that they would be well paid in linen or anything else required which they sent. They did want everybody to know of it gave her some coarse linen, some beads and a [illeg.] and some [illeg.] the said [illeg.] work [illeg.], and she heard he had given 15 other shirts [illeg.] Capt. Dodge asked Mrs. Smith if she did [illeg.] of the first [illeg.] said that [illeg.] asking for it [illeg.]

[Document torn] that Capt. Dodge then swore [document torn] saying he had no right to act in that [document torn] told Mrs. Smith she was very welcome to the [document torn] not have said what he did only the Indian agent [illeg.] to appear sharp before him.

[Document torn] [After] mature consideration the court are of [document torn] that [document torn] Capt. Dodge has said nothing to hurt Capt. George's character [document torn].   (Signed)   Jno. Williams President

                    Approved
                    Girault Ja   Jno. Montgomery

The foregoing taken from the original delivered me by Lt. Girault 18th, Dec. 1780.

                    Richard McCarty Judge Advocate

August 15, 1780. Incomplete document: Captain John Rogers and Captain Abraham Kellar sign a court martial order for John Carnes.[2]

Draper Manuscripts: 56J27

At a court of inquiry held at Fort Jefferson on Monday the 26th of Feb. 1781 by order of Capt. Robert George to examine into sundry allegations laid against Capt. Worthington by Major George Slaughter.

                    Capt. Rogers, President

                    Members

Capt. Kellar	Capt. Roberts
Lt. Girault	Lt. Calvit
Lt. Clark	Cornet Thruston

William Clark, Judge Advocate

The court having met proceeded to business. The Judge Advocate produced a letter from Major Slaughter [which] contained the allegations against Capt. Worthington as follows.

From the unparalleled conduct of Capt. Edward Worthington of the Illinois Regiment, I have hereby thought expedient to desire you to put him under an arrest and detain him at your fort until the return of Col. Clark, at which time, with the assistance of Col. Crockett's officers we shall be enabled to hold a general court

---
[2] Unpublished Clark Papers, Archives Division, Virginia State Library, Richmond, Box 17.

martial for the trial of all such offenders as comes within their jurisdiction. When Capt. Worthington will have a chance to acquit himself with honor, if he has conducted himself consistent with the character of a gentleman officer, which I have reason to doubt he cannot; from the following charges laid against him (i.e., retailing liquors to the soldiery and others, frequent disobedience of orders, gambling with the soldiers of his own company and feloniously carrying off an auger and broad axe, the property of Francis Adams).

Capt. Worthington in his defense, says, that the liquor which he retailed, was for the advantage of the recruiting service, and was done at the request of Col. Clark. And with respect to disobedience of orders, says, he does not know of being guilty of any such offense.

The third charge, for gambling with soldiers he looks upon to be groundless, or no offense as he was a recruiting officer. The fourth charge, for feloniously taking an auger and broad axe, utterly denies; and says when he was setting off from the Falls of Ohio, he received an auger and axe of the quartermaster, or commissary at that post to repair some part of his boat, that the tools was left on board; and it being late at night when he started, had not an opportunity of returning them. And at his arrival at this place, he acquainted the commanding officer how he had brought away the tools, and expressed his desire of having them sent back by the first opportunity. And further says he never was guilty of gambling with a soldier but once, which was at Christmas last and then only took in a soldier as a partner, when another could not be had, to play a game at cards for a goose.

Lt. Calvit being sworn, saith, that he and Capt. Worthington went on board late at night when they were leaving the Falls of Ohio, and found an auger and axe which had been used in repairing the boat, and Capt. Worthington asked him what was best to do with them that he told Capt. Worthington, if they were put on shore, 'twas likely they might be lost, and thought it best to take them down the river, and return them by the first opportunity. And when we arrived here, Capt. Worthington desired me to put the tools into the possession of the quartermaster, that they might be returned by the first opportunity.

Sergeant Miles being sworn, says, there was no opportunity of returning the tools when the boat started from the Falls, and he often heard Capt. Worthington say he would send them back to Capt. Roberts.

Robert Davis being sworn, gives evidence corresponding with that of the other two witnesses.

Capt. Worthington called upon Capt. Roberts to acquaint the court of his conduct, respecting disobedience of orders; who after being sworn, says, that he never knew Capt. Worthington to be guilty of disobedience of orders, other than, being [remainder of document missing].

Draper Manuscripts: 56J29

Court of Inquiry, Feb. 28, 1781

Proceedings of a court of inquiry held at Fort Jefferson on Wednesday the 28th of February 1781 by order of Capt. Robert George, to inquire into a complaint lodged against Capt. Richard McCarty by Capt. John Dodge, agent for State of Virginia.

     Captain Robert George President
Members
Capt. Kellar   Capt. Roberts
Lt. Girault   Lt. Calvit
Lt. Clark   Cornet Thruston

William Clark, acting as Judge Advocate

  The Court met according to order, and being sworn proceeded to business, Capt. McCarty appeared before the court, and the following charges are exhibited against him; Viz. speaking disrespectfully of the service, for which he was arrested, and other behavior since his arrestment, unbecoming an officer under such circumstances.
  Capt. Kellar being sworn saith, he was ordered from cohos [Cahokia] by Col. Montgomery, to come to the assistance of this place during the last attack by the savages. A little before he was ready to embark he sent a message to Capt. McCarty desiring him to come to the river and set off. The messenger returned and told him that Capt. McCarty said he had some little business to settle first and about half an hour after, Capt. McCarty came down, and ordered the men on board, as soon as he was obeyed, the boat sprang a leak, which obliged them to unload. Whereupon Capt. McCarty seemed angry, damned such service, and them that occasioned it to be so, adding, if proper methods had been taken, things would have been in better order; and wished his limbs had been broke before he entered into such a service; and said, they are now going to send us to have our throats cut or brains beat out.
  Capt. Dodge's question to Capt. Kellar: Did not Capt. McCarty, when he set off, take the best of the men in his own boat and leave you the weakest to bring up the rear with the provision?

Answer. Capt. McCarty did take the best of the men; but do not believe he did it designedly, as he made no inquiry about the disability of the men, neither did I know it myself, till we were setting off, when I found several of the men was drunk, otherwise able enough.

Question. If there had been proper inquiry made, and the men properly divided, don't you think you might have got further that night than you did?

Answer. I believe I could.
Question. Do you not think Capt. McCarty delayed his time when coming down to the relief of this place?
Answer. We might have got further the first evening, had Capt. McCarty known the

circumstance of the rear, but he not knowing how far it was behind, stopped before night, which I believe was in order to let the rear come up; and after we got [illeg.][to] misire[Missouri], Capt. McCarty delayed about three hours, the reason of which I do not remember at this time; but after that there was no time lost.

Capt. McCarty's question. Did you go to the Mississippi [illeg.] Officer [illeg.]. [Line illeg.] from the village of Cohos [Cahokia], before me, or did we go together?
Answer. I went first myself.
Question. Was not I present with yourself and Ensign Slaughter, when the boat was loaded, and the men on board?
Answer. I think you came down some time after the boat was loaded, but before the men was on board.
Question. Was not the men in confusion having taken a dram extraordinary at leaving their friends?
Answer. I believe half the men was.
Question. When I called to the men to jump over board and save the provision, did they seem dilatory in doing it?
Answer. No.
Question. Did not I throw a club among them to be heard?
Answer. Not that I remember of.
Question. Was not the boat sinking with all our provision on board?
Answer. It was likely to sink, and had it not been expeditiously unloaded, I believe it would have sunk in a few minutes.
Question. In what tone of voice did I speak when I cursed the service?
Answer. Like a person both confused and angry.
Question. Did you think I spoke it through vexation to see the boat, or ill will to the service and state?
Answer. I believe the boat being likely to sink occasioned you to make the expressions.
Question. Was it not very difficult to get boats, and did there not come several Frenchmen claiming their canoes?
Answer. Yes.
Question. Did not I, in conjunction with you and Ensign Slaughter, advise to hurry off, to prevent hearing so many complaints from the people for their canoes.
Answer. I believe you did, a little before the canoes (which we had pressed was loaded).
Question. Was it not agreed, that I should camp at the Marramack[3] to wait for you?
[Answer]. Not that I remember of.
Question. Did I pick out or choose the men for my boat?
Answer. Not to my knowledge.
Question. Did I not leave Ensign Slaughter with you for an assistant, as you were unwell?
Answer. Yes.
Question. Did you land with me at Mesire[4] [Missouri]?

---

[3] Merrimack River.

Answer. Yes.
Question. How long did you stay there?
Answer. About fifteen minutes.
Question. Did you not apply to me for leave to go to Kaskaskia on your own business, and was it not granted, ordering you to join at the mouth of Kaskaskias River where I proposed camping that night?
Answer. I did apply for such liberty, which was granted, with orders to join at the proposed place of encampment.
Question. What time did you join me that evening?
Answer. About half an hour after dark.
[Question]. Was not the Mississippi very low at that time, and very dangerous for our small [boats to c]ome down in the night or do you think we could have got down sooner [than we] did?
[Answer. The rive]r was very low and could have been dangerous for us to have proceeded [illeg.]

[Five lines missing].

in the night, but believe we might have got down three or four hours sooner, if no time had been lost at Mesire [Missouri], and the first evening we encamped.

Question by the court. Do you think the time that was delayed by Capt. McCarty at Mesire [Missouri] was done through contempt of the service, or was there any necessity for that delay?
Answer. I think I recollect, 'twas in order to get something to cover our provision, which was very necessary.

Capt. McCarty's Question. Did you ever hear me say anything disrespectful of the State of Virginia, or any other since I have been in the service?
Answer. Nothing more than what I have already declared.
The court adjourns 'till tomorrow at eight o'clock. Thursday, March 1st.

The court met according to adjournment.

James Finn being sworn;

Capt. Dodge's question: What expressions did you hear Capt. McCarty make use of, when he was embarking at Cohos [Cahokia] to come to the assistance of this place?
Answer. Capt. McCarty at setting off seemed to get in a passion, on account of the remissness of the soldiers, and while they were making ready to set off, he sat down and damned such service and them that was the occasion of it

Question by the court. Did you conceive by Capt. McCarty's behavior, 'twas the

---

[4] Ste. Genevieve, Missouri.

passion he was in which occasioned him to make such expressions; or do you think he did it out of contempt to the service?

Answer. I think the passion that Capt. McCarty was in, on account of the remissness of the soldiers, occasioned him to make the expressions, and not contempt of the service.

Capt. McCarty's question. Do you recollect whether the men was on board, the boat leaking and likely to sink when I made them expressions?

Answer. Some of the men was on board, and I heard them say the boat was leaking, and I heard you ask if the flour was likely to get wet in the boat and some of the men answered yes, for the boat would sink before it could get two hundred yards.

Question by the court. Did you ever hear Capt. McCarty speak anything prejudicial to the service since he was in it, or know of his behaving himself anyway unbecoming an officer, other than what you have already declared?

Answer. No.

James Sherlock being sworn, says he was in company with Capt. Dodge at Kaskaskia, when Capt. McCarty came into the room and fell in conversation with Capt. Dodge, during which, Capt. McCarty said he was going to Cohos [Cahokia], and would resign, and if he did, his men would leave the service also. Upon which Capt. Dodge said such expressions was enough to break an officer and Capt. McCarty made answer and said he would think it more honor to be broke than to serve the State of Virginia.

Capt. McCarty's question to James Sherlock. Are not you in the Indian Department under Capt. Dodge?

Answer. I am in the Indian Department and act under my Commanding Officer or Agent for the State of Virginia.

Question. Was you not in his service on the 28th of Sept. last, and did you not reside with Capt. Dodge?

Answer. Yes.

Question. Did you not look on Capt. Dodge and myself as particular friends, and treat each other as such before that time?

Answer. I always looked upon you as particular friends before that time.

Question. Have you not often heard us discoursing familiarly, touching many things public and private, as two particular friends?

Answer. I do not recollect hearing any very particular discourse between you, but you always appeared as friends to each other.

Question. Was you present at the time I said I intended to resign if things did not change?

Answer. I never heard you say anything about resigning more than I have already declared; and then you made no reserve that I remember of.

Question. Do you remember of hearing me mention the distresses of my soldiers for want of provision, or have you heard it from any other person, at or about that time?

Answer. I have heard you many times mention the distresses of your soldiers but don't remember of hearing anything about it at the time the dispute happened between you and Capt. Dodge.

Question. When Capt. Dodge said we will not let you resign, you are liable to be broke for what you have said, and I answered, I had as leave be broke as serve the State of Virginia; What do you think I meant by it?

Answer. I cannot undertake to determine what prompt you to make the expression as you appeared to be in a passion.

Question. Did you think I spoke with disrespectful to the State, or to personal misconduct of people that had the direction of state property in hand?

Answer. I cannot say which.

Question. When Capt. Dodge and myself had this dispute, do you remember if we had been drinking, or did I seem intoxicated with liquor?

Answer. I think you was a little in liquor.

Question. Did I say I would take my men away with me, or that I thought they would not stay after I resigned?

Answer. I think you said you would leave the service and your men would go too.

Question. Did I appear angry or had Capt. Dodge and I any quarrel before Capt. Dodge's mentioning that I had lost time in fetching Succor to Camp Jefferson?

Answer. Not to my knowledge.

Question. Have you known me any considerable time?

Answer. About two years.

Question. Have you been long in the Indian Department, and under whom?

Answer. I have been near three years in the Department, have acted under different agents, but chiefly under Capt. Helm.

Question. Have you occasionally been under my command at the outposts?

Answer. Yes.

Question. In what manner have I given speeches to Indians?

Answer. Much in behalf of the State which I have to show.

Question. Have you any knowledge of my furnishing of my own property to keep peace.

End of document.

Draper Manuscripts: 56J45

Fort Jefferson 9th March 1781

At a Court of Inquiry held by order of Robert George Capt Commandant at the request of Capt Rogers to inquire into Capt. John Roger's conduct during his Command at Kaskaskia:

        Capt. Kellar President
        Capt Roberts   Lieut. Girault
        Lieut Clark   Lieut. Carney
        Cornet Thruston
        William Clark, acting as Judge Advocate

The Court met according to order & being sworn, proceeded to inquire into the cause in hearing------------

The Court having made examination, and finding no proof of any misconduct in Capt Rogers, & there being no allegations exhibited against him, but frivolous reports, do acquit him.------

              Abrm Kellar prs^{dt}
              Approved of---
         Robt. George Capt Commd^t

Draper Manuscripts: 56J40

Fort Jefferson the 20th March 1781

Proceedings of a Court Martial held this day at ten O Clock by Order of Captn. Robert George Commandant for the Trial of all the prisoners in the Quarter Guard, Edward Marthis Excepted---

Captain Kellar President
Members
Capt. Roberts Liet^t. Clark
Lieut^t. Carney Cornet Thruston Lieut^t. John Girault, Acting Judge Advocate
The Court met according to order and after being duly sworn proceeded to business---

     David Allen and James Taylor, both prisoners confined by Major Williams for having robbed his kitchen, beat his servants, and abusing him after being confined---
   The prisoners say they are not guilty of crimes laid to their charges---

Rachel Yeats being Sworn saith that being in Major Williams kitchen some persons came to the window of said kitchen and then flashed a gun, and threw chips and bones at her and darted needles or pins fixed with hair thro' a cane reed at her, by which they wounded her and put her in fear of her life to such a degree that she was forced to make her escape; that they repeated this inhuman behavior several times---and saith that she verily believes that they the prisoners were among those who so treated her. She particularly saw David Allen and knew James Taylor by his voice----She further declares that the above named Taylor has, at several different times, abused and ill used her, particularly last Saturday---that while she was out of the kitchen, she suspects they stole a blanket from her, having missed it at her return, and found it this morning in the said James Taylor's quarters---

Rachel Kennedy being sworn says that she heard the prisoners say that Major Williams by his behavior appeared to have been raised in a Negro Quarter -- and that he was a Raccoon Hunter---with many other disrespectful words regarding him, which she does not particularly remember--neither does she remember if they both abused him or which of them in particular did.

Philip Hupp being Sworn says, that being last night in company with Boston Damewood, he saw him fixing pins with hair to shoot through the window of Major Williams kitchen in order (illeg.) to (illeg.) Rachel Yeats and that afterwards he saw Damewood go to the window and he believes he did then dart them in at her, and that he saw a soldier of the Light Horse Company who had flashed one of his pistols at the said window, also that he heard it said among those who were concerned in the fray that Damewood's wife threw the bone, or something in at the window.

Valentine Balsinger---Being sworn says that being sentry at the Guard
House he heard the prisoners or one of them (but he knows not which),
say, there is the raccoon hunter, and at same time he perceived Major Williams had just walked across the Fort; being asked by the Court if he could in no ways recollect which of the prisoners made the above expression, he answered he thought it was Allen but was not certain---

John Daugherty being sworn says that he is positively certain that James Taylor was not in the fray mentioned above, having been in company with him until it was over---

Elizabeth Watkins being sworn says that not agreeing with Mrs. Yeats, she went to lay at Jones's where Taylor lodges, and being there, sent her husband for their bedding; in Major Williams's kitchen who thro' mistake brought a blanket belonging to said Mrs. Yeats which she came and took away a short time afterwards----

Boston Damewood being sworn---Question, Are you positively certain that David Allen was not concerned in the fray that happened at Major Williams Kitchen last night---Answer: I am---

The Court after deliberation are of the opinion that James Taylor is not guilty of any of the charges laid against him and order that he shall be immediately released from his confinement---After having maturely examined the tenor of the evidences the Court are of opinion that David Allen is acquitted of the charges laid against him of robbery and of the fray committed at Major Williams kitchen, but that he is guilty of speaking disrespectfully of Major Williams for which the Court by Majority order he shall receive fifty lashes on his bare back well laid on---

Abr. Kellar Pres^d.
Approved of Robt. George Capt. Commd^t.

Draper Manuscritps: 56J25

Ordered by Col^o. Clark (when set off to government) to proceed immediately to Fort Jefferson; When Capt Worthington was directly taken sick, which prevented his coming down at that time according to his orders---

The Court having considered the several charges exhibited against Capt Worthington, & his Defense, are of opinion that as there is no person to prove anything against him, that his trial ought to be deferred 'till his accusers can be present

Jno Rogers Pres^d.
W. Clark Judge Adv^c.

The Commanding Officer
approves of the above---
Robt. George Capt. Commdt.

At a Court of Inquiry held at Louisville on Monday the 16th. Of July 1781 by order of Col^o. John Montgomery, to examine into the nature of a complaint exhibited against Capt Edward Worthington by Major Geo. Slaughter:

		Capt Robert George President
Members:	Capt Rogers	Lieut Calvit
	Capt Brashear	Ensn. Williams
	Capt Roberts	Cornet Thruston

The Court having met proceeded to business---
Capt. Shannon being sworn, saith: on or about the first of
January last at night, he happened in at John Nelson's, a soldier in the Illinois Regiment, and to his infinite surprise found Capt Worthington at cards with said Nelson and two others, and understood they were playing for whiskey---And further said, in the month of April 1780, on his return from government to this place, he went on board of Col^o. Clark's boat (which then lay along side of the sandy island) in order to deliver dispatches he had from government from him & other business---during which time, he heard Capt Worthington apply for leave to go to Harrodsburg, which, after some time was granted him on proviso he would be sure to repair to Fort Jefferson with him, the said Shannon, which was to be in the latter part of that, or the beginning of, the ensuing month, which orders Capt Worthington disobeyed, he not repairing to the place of rendezvous until the month of January 1781---at which time, he, the said Shannon, was informed By Mr. Geo. Wilson that he had reason to believe that Capt Worthington intended carrying off a broad axe & auger with him, the property of Francis Adams, an inhabitant of this place (Louisville), which he, the said Wilson, borrowed for repairing Capt Worthington's boat, and desired that I would see that the tools were stored, as the owner would be considerably damaged by their being taken away, it being impossible

to procure such other tools in the country, on which he, the said Shannon, spoke to Capt. Worthington & Lieut Calvit, setting forth how much the owner would be injured by so doing, they (the tools) being his chief support; to which Capt Worthington pledged his word and honor in presence of Mr. Geo Wilson & Willis Green that he would send them back---from the foot of the Falls by a soldier. [But the] tools were carried to Fort Jefferson without the least respect to his promise to me---

  The Court having made examination, have stated the facts as proved in the above, & at a Court of Inquiry held at Fort Jefferson on Monday the 26th of February 1781, on the said Complaints---

    Robt. George Capt. &
    President

   I think by the evidence & the proceedings of the Court that Capt Worthington should be acquitted from the charges laid against him with honor, except Genl. Clark makes something appear against him in regard of retailing liquor.

Given under my hand this 16th. July 1781--
Jno. Montgomery L^{t}Colo^l Commadant

CHAPTER 11: MEDICAL CONCERNS ON THE WESTERN FRONTIER[1]

James A. Lucy and Kenneth C. Carstens

Eighteenth-century medicine, especially as practiced on the western frontier, is a subject with few extant primary sources from which to draw for serious research. The ledgers kept by Francis Connard, a frontier physician and surgeon, lend valuable insight into the manner in which the art of medicine was practiced on the frontier. As Connard was also a military surgeon, his ledgers give a glimpse into the daily professional life of a regimental surgeon of George Rogers Clark's Illinois Battalion.

Introduction

Bleedings, noxious mixtures of sulfur, fantastic herbal decoctions, and non-anesthetic amputations are all part of eighteenth-century medicine. Were physicians of this period merely stumbling along in blind ignorance, blithely unaware of the harm and pain they were causing their patients? Or were they just beginning to realize the real possibilities which the medical profession could and would realize in the years to come? Francis Connard was a frontier physician of the late eighteenth century in Kentucky and the Illinois country (primarily Fort Clark in Kaskaskia). He was engaged by General George Rogers Clark's Illinois Battalion as Surgeon from 1779 to 1781.[2] In this chapter, we examine late-eighteenth-century medical practices based upon Francis Connard's medical accounts ledger, a list of medical applications and surgical procedures contained within the collection of unpublished George Rogers Clark papers in the Archives Division of the Virginia State Library in Richmond.[3]

Dr. Connard of Kaskaskia was, in June, 1779, engaged to attend to the soldiers of Captain Harrison's Company, and in 1782, sent to attend to Clark's garrison at the Falls of the Ohio. He served General Clark, Col. Montgomery, Captain Rogers, Captain Harrison and other officers. He worked with Dr. Andrew Ray, Surgeon Major of Clark's Regiment from 1778 to 1781.[4]

The guiding principle of 18th-century medicine was that of balance.[5] The body and all of its constituents must be in proper harmony in order for good health to be maintained. The Greek medical concept of "humors" as the central component of the body's chemistry was still the accepted standard of physiological science in the 18th century. These humors included the body fluids of blood, phlegm, black bile, and yellow bile.[6] The proper balance of these humors was considered essential to healthy existence.

---

[1] This chapter, originally titled "An Analysis of Medicines Used on the Late Eighteenth Century Frontier in Kentucky and Illinois," was published by the Kentucky Heritage Council in their volume, *Current Archaeological Research in Kentucky, Vol. 5.*" The paper is reprinted here with changes/additions with the permission of the Kentucky Heritage Council.
[2] Draper Manuscripts, 60J265, Wisconsin Historical Society, Madison, Wisconsin.
[3] Box 48, Unpublished George Rogers Clark Papers, Archives Division, Virginia State Library, Richmond, VA.
[4] Draper, *op cit.*
[5] C. Keith Wilbur, *Revolutionary Medicine*. The Globe Pequot Press, Chester, Connecticut, 1980.
[6] Barnest Barker, *Greek Medicine*. J. M. Dent and Sons, London, 1929.

Therefore, the practices of 18th-century medicine were designed to keep humors in balance.

Eighteenth-century medical practice was far removed from its modern counterpart. Medical schools were not the primary route to becoming a physician. By far the most popular route was through apprenticeship. During a three-to-six year period, the apprentice was given "on–the-job" training by his mentor. After successfully completing his apprenticeship, the apprentice was awarded a certificate of proficiency, which at the time, carried the same credence as a medical school degree.[7]

Only larger cities had the facilities suited to formal medical instruction. The first recorded anatomy lecture in the Colonies, with dissection, occurred in 1750 in New York. Using the corpse of an executed murderer, Hermanus Carroll exposed his students[8] to the internal structures of the human body, much to the distress of the general public. The windows of the dissection rooms were often destroyed by angry mobs.[9]

The only statutory requirement for medical practice was the possession of a certificate of proficiency from an apprenticeship or a degree from a medical school. However, the enforcement of these requirements was haphazard at best. Often a person could engage in the practice of medicine with no formal training whatsoever, and no questions would be asked regarding his qualifications.

The etiological environment of the 18th-century was one that was extremely challenging to the practitioners of "physic," as medicine was termed in the 18th-century.[10] The lack of understanding of the modern area of bacteriology and virology made for a morass of theory and practice aimed at defeating the diseases that were so misunderstood.

The most common ailments of the 18th-century included gout, hydrops (or dropsy), the tympany, diabetes mellitus, consumption, asthma, jaundice, nephritis (or kidney stones), palsey, hemiplexia, St. Vitus's Dance, apoplexy, scrofula, epilepsy, leprosy, pruritis, plague, smallpox, and the ague (or malaria).[11] Sanitary conditions, horrendous by modern standards, were prime producers of outbreaks of diseases such as cholera, typhus, and plague. The lack of a standardized vaccination process also led to outbreaks of diseases such as small pox.

Some attention should be given to the contrasting roles of the apothecary and the physician. The apothecary's position was primarily that of mixing and dispensing the medicines, which were prescribed by the physician, who was the primary diagnostician. One may draw parallels to modern pharmacists based upon this; however, these comparisons are not entirely valid. The apothecary, did at times, practice medicine. Often a physician's order was countermanded by the apothecary, sometimes at the patient's request, at other times because the apothecary simply disagreed with the physician's diagnosis.[12]

The apothecary's arsenal, although lacking in modern antibiotics and pain killing drugs, nonetheless had no fewer than ten different classifications of drug treatments. Each of these treatments had its own place in the natural pharmacopoeia of the 18th

---

[7] Wilbur, *op cit.*, 1.
[8] *Ibid.*, 2-3.
[9] *Ibid.*
[10] Kenneth Dewhurst, *Thomas Dover's Life and Legacy*. The Scarecrow Press, Methuen, New Jersey, 1974.
[11] Dewhurst, 37.
[12] Wilbur, 21.

century. Anodynes, such as opium and laudanum, were used to relieve pain; however, they were not useful for relieving other symptoms. Antiarthritics, such as Epsom salts and Peruvian (Jesuit's) Bark, which contains quinine, were used to treat the ague (or malaria). Antidysentery treatments included pulverized Brazil root and paregoric. Antipyretics or febrifuges, were used to treat fevers.[13]

Emetics formed a fifth group of treatments. Emetics, including tartar and ipecac, produced immediate vomiting and were popular treatments with physicians, although their popularity among patients is debatable. Muscular antispasmodics, such as hard liquor and oil of amber, were used to relax muscles. Purgatives and cathartives, or laxatives, such as rhubarb, castor oil, and Epsom salts, were used to induce diarrhetic evacuation of the bowels. Salivation inducing medicines, such as oil of mercury, were used to stimulate the production of saliva, as well as act as an intestinal counterirritant. Diaphoretics, such as camphor and rhubarb, were used to induce sweating, especially after intestinal symptoms had been resolved. Diuretics of all kinds were employed to increase the flow of urine, especially in cases of dropsy or (edema), thereby ridding the body of excess fluids.[14]

These medicines were prepared and administered in several different ways. The preferred manner was oral administration. Another popular methods was "clysters," which were rectal infusions similar to an enema.[15] Blisters and cataplasms (or poultices, were often applied directly to the skin to counteract irritation. One of the more popular blisters was cantheride, known today as "Spanish Fly."[16]

Civilian trauma tended to be of the more common variety, such as sprains, strains, fractures, the occasional gunshot wound, and other traumatic injury to soft tissue. In this regard, 18th-century medical practice was little different from today.

The military, however, faced drastic trauma. Gun and cannon shot wounds were common, as were injuries from sword and bayonet.[17] Treatment priorities also differed between civilian and military situations. In the military, less emphasis was placed on saving a damaged limb. The surgeon near the battlefield was more inclined to stop bleeding first through the use of a tourniquet, then amputation of the limb. This course of action was simply more expeditious given the large number of wounded that had to be tended.[18]

Surgeons of the 18th-century were not the esteemed group of professionals that they have become today. Once again, the medical world followed the lead of the ancient Greeks, to whom the distinction between a physician, who practiced medicinal cures, and a surgeon, who enacted physical repair, was nonexistent.[19] The role of the military surgeon and surgeon's mate were mandated by law.[20] Every military regiment was to have a surgeon, as well as a surgeon's mate, whose task it was to assist the physician in

---

[13] Wilbur, 11-12.
[14] *Ibid.*
[15] *Ibid.*
[16] *Ibid.*
[17] *Ibid.* 34.
[18] *Ibid.*, 27.
[19] Barker, 1929.
[20] William Waller Hening, ed., *Statutes at Large, Vol X*. University Press of Virginia for the Jamestown Foundation, Charlottesville, Virginia, 1969.

the completion of his duties. Often this entailed holding patients immobile for procedures such as amputations and bullet extractions.

Surgical procedures were carried out without benefit of anesthesia. Often the wounded soldier was given a musket ball to bite to aid in enduring the pain of the procedure, thus giving rise to the modern express, "bite the bullet."[21] Surgeons were also limited in the scope of what they could accomplish by surgery. Compound fractures, deeply imbedded bullets, frost-bitten digits, and gangrene were often cases for the amputation knife.

Medical practice on the frontier was different from the practice of medicine in the cities, primarily because medicines were difficult to come by on the frontier. Because of this, frontier practitioners were forced to rely more heavily upon native medicines than upon imported ones. For example, *Belladonna* (or Deadly Nightshade), was a common plant in use by 18th-century physicians. Atropine, which could be extracted from the leaves and roots of *Belladonna*, was a useful antispasmodic drug. Also, *Hellebore*, a plant from American swamps and meadows, produced a root which could be decocted into a diuretic, cathartic, and a circulatory stimulant.[22]

Different types of trauma were also present on the frontier. Perhaps the most widely known was that of scalping. Scalping was not pursued by Native Americans alone; many Euro-Americans practiced this activity with great enthusiasm. Even at Fort Jefferson, "scalping knives" were issued on a regular basis to soldiers and citizens alike.[23] The only treatment for scalping was to dress the wound and allow the scalp to regenerate itself. Often this would work, although the scalp would be totally devoid of hair in the affected region.[24]

Connard's Ledgers

The medical ledgers kept by Francis Connard as a running account of his expenditures, are a fascinating record of frontier medicine in the latter half of the 18th-century. They describe in detail medicines and treatments prescribed for the members of General Clark's Illinois Battalion while they were under Connard's care. For example, the ledgers show that from June 27, 1879 to May 16, 1780, Connard prescribed 72 purgative decoctions.[25] This is in keeping with the practice of the day—that of using laxatives to remove intestinal irritation. Therefore, one may see that in this particular arena, Connard followed typical 18th-century protocols.

Rum was used in medicines quite often. From July 10, 1779 to April 13, 1780, a total of 21 gallons and 29 bottles of unknown capacity were distributed to the men of the Illinois Battalion for medicinal purposes. It was standard practice in the army to issue no more than one half pint of rum per soldier per day.[26] Rum was usually considered to be detrimental to the soldiers' health and well-being. However, when mixed with camphor,

---

[21] Wilbur, 38.
[22] *Ibid.*
[23] Unpublished George Rogers Clark Papers, Boxes 48-50, Archives Division, Virginia State Library, Richmond.
[24] Wilbur, 39-40.
[25] *Op. cit.*, Box 48.
[26] Wilbur, 55.

it was considered useful for treating a variety of illnesses, including malaria.[27] In keeping with this practice, Connard issued 38 doses of an unspecified diuretic decoction and sixteen doses of emetic, two additional methods of removing fluids from the body.

Connard also issued 165 bottles of sudorific decoction. Sudorifics were used to instigate perspiration and were one way to rid the body of fluids detrimental to good health, thereby keeping the "humors" in balance.[28] Also issued were four doses of an unspecified diuretic decoction and sixteen doses of emetic for removing fluids from the body.

Mercury, or quicksilver (a poison), was also prescribed as a medicine. Connard issued seventy-six does of mercurial pills to the Illinois Battalion. Mercury was thought to be useful in the treatment of smallpox (as a purgative),[29] and in the treatment of "the itch" (or syphilis), and is present in surprisingly large quantities. A total of 125 ounces of mercurial ointment were issued to the men of the Illinois Battalion, an interesting commentary on their off-duty activities.

Poultices were common to Connar's practice, and the available literature tends to indicate that poultices were fairly common in 18th-century medical practice. Plasters were also fairly common in Connar's Ledger. Plasters were used as an irritant or a blister to produce an irritation that would counter irritation elsewhere in the body.[30] Connard issued 44 plasters.

Surgical procedures comprise a surprisingly small portion of Connard's Ledger entries, possibly because he was working in concert with Surgeon Major Andrew Rey. It is possible that combat-related procedures went unremunerated, while non-combat pharmacological distributions were reimbursed (hence, the ledger may be biased toward reimbursable actions vs. non-reimbursable actions). There is precedent for this assumption, as evidenced by the Continental Army policy charging officers and men alike for treatment of any venereal disease they contracted.[31] Too, Connard's term of service for the duration of the ledger was primarily at Fort Clark in Kaskaskia, not at Fort Jefferson. As far as we know, Connard's did not see military action at Kaskaskia, whereas Surgeon Rey at Fort Jefferson did. Unfortunately, we do not have Surgeon Rey's Ledger from Fort Jefferson for comparison.

Of the surgical procedures listed by Connard, bleeding comprises the greatest frequency, with eleven entries. Bleeding, through the use of a lancet, was a popular procedure, as it was generally considered the premier method for the removal of impure blood from the body.[32] Contrary to popular belief, there are very few references to leeches being used in the military medical literature of the 18th-century. Perhaps this is due to the slowness with which a leech removes blood from the body, or accessibility to the leeches themselves.

Next, in order of frequency of ledger entries, was the extraction of teeth. Connard performed a total of seven tooth extractions. The drawing of teeth was likely to be a source of mixed emotion for the soldier. To be sure, application of the wrench-like

---

[27] Wilbur, 15.
[28] Wilbur, 12.
[29] Wilbur, 14.
[30] Wilbur, 11.
[31] Wilbur, 16.
[32] Wilbur, 10.

tooth extractor was painful; however, the relief from the pain of the diseased tooth may have mitigated the pain of the extraction.[33]

Last in the field of surgical procedures were the setting of fractures and the excision of tumors. Fracture reductions occurred three times. The excision of tumors, of which two are listed, is simply surgical removal of growths (whether the growth were benign or malignant is not stated).

Examination of Connard's Ledger demonstrates no extraordinary illnesses attributed to the Illinois Battalion, with the possible exception of a small outbreak of either smallpox or consumption, and syphilis, as evidenced by the presence of medicinal mercury. The large distribution of rum represented may have resulted from a laxness in discipline, which may have occurred as a result of extended service on the frontier.

Most curious was what was not mentioned in Connard's Ledger. Of primary significance is the absence of Peruvian (Jesuit's) Bark, which was used to combat malaria or ague.[34] This drug played a very significant role on the Kentucky/Illinois frontier and was issued to officers at Clark's Fort Jefferson, where Captain Robert George declared that men "were daily dying."[35] However, it must be remembered that just because an item was not listed in the ledger does not mean the men did not have access to it. Interestingly, at Fort Jefferson, the Jesuit Bark issued came from the Quartermaster Department and not through Dr. Rey.[36] As an example, Captain Leonard Helm at Fort Jefferson wrote the following voucher request of the Quartermaster Department at Fort Jefferson on March 13, 1781: "Leonard Helm requests 3 pints of tafia to put with Jesuit Bark to cure a fever."[37]

The purpose of Dr. Connard keeping his ledger was to be reimbursed by the State of Virginia after the war. To that end, the Western Commissioners made the following statements about Dr. Connard's accounts: "The Commissioners having examined Doctor Connard's accounts find that his Bills No. 1, 2, 6, 8, 10 are for medicines and Services and ought to be protected…The Commissioners are of the opinion that Dr. Connard ought to be allowed for one years' service as Surgeon to the Troops in the Illinois County, commanded by Col. [John] Montgomery [at Kaskaskia], the sum of 270 pounds, 50 pounds for medicines furnished, 75 pounds 2 shillings for flour, tafia, sugar, etc., furnished…The medicines are said to be furnished Col. Montgomery [and] the Board cannot judge of, as no prices are fixed, but are of the opinion the articles marked were necessary, [but] the quantity of many of them too great for the number of men."[38]

Following his service at Kaskaskia, Dr. Connard returned to Fort Nelson at Louisville where he and Dr. Rey would assist the men of Clark's Illinois Battalion in 1782 until the end of the war.[39]

---

[33] Wilbur, 40.
[34] Wilbur, 34.
[35] James Alton James, *George Rogers Clark Papers*, AMS Press, New York, 1972.
[36] Kenneth Carstens, *The Calendar and Quartermaster Books of George Rogers Clark's Fort Jefferson, 1780-1781*. Heritage Books, Bowie, Maryland, 2000.
[37] Unpublished Clark Papers, Box 17. Carstens, 2000:175.
[38] James, ed., II: 396-397.
[39] *Calendar of Virginia State Papers*, entry for January 7, 1782, Richmond, VA: 29

Conclusion

We conclude that Francis Connard was a competent practitioner of medicine, given the state of the art in the late 18th-century. His medical documentation reveals a frontier physician operating within a medical establishment. He dealt with diseases and injuries common to the less developed parts of the continent. There is no conclusive evidence of epidemic or widespread disease, other than the presence of smallpox, consumption, and syphilis, all of which are implied from the type of pharmacopoeia issued. Otherwise, Clark's Illinois Battalion appears to have been quite healthy (this, in spite of the unbalanced diet that they had—see Chapter 8, this volume). It is interesting to note the overlapping of medicinal issues between the Quartermaster (Jesuit's Bark) and Medical Corps. In Chapter 8, it was also noted that great quantities of sugar were issued from the Commissary Corps to help combat "the ague," as much as two pounds of sugar per day. Medicinal aid on the western frontier, therefore, came from many quarters, not simply the trained or educated within the medical profession.

1779

A list of four mixtures Ligaments and medecines which I have made and furnished to the Regiment of the Illinois under the command of Colonel Clark and Mr. Mongomery Lt. Colonel Wiki

June 24 to one fracture complicated and ending into a wound 30
to two medecines composed of manna Seni Rhubarbe and glauber salts at 4 Dr. ... 8
to Lint for the wounded 5
to a Bottle Camphird ammoniac brandy
to a Bottle of febrifuge medecine
to a Bottle of apperitif & Refreshing potion
to one do
to one do

27 to three bleedings 4
to two composed medecines 8
to one Bottle of apperitif and astringents 4
to two ounces of camphir two ounces Salt ammoniac .. 4
to Divin Salt 4
to one aromatique Infusion 5
to four intermixed medecines 10
emplastrum Sciaticum 6
to two purgatif glisters 4

July 2 to two Bottles of Sudorific ptisane 6
to two ounces of camphir two ouin Salt ammoniac 4
unguentum Divinum .... 1 ½
to a Load of wood
to one Bottle febrifuge mixture 3
to one Bottle Sudorific composition 5

? to two glisters 1
to one Sudorific mixture 3
to one once camphir one once Salt am moniac .. 2
to two Bushels grounded corn 4

Table 11.1: An Excerpt from Dr. Connard's Medical Ledger, June 24, 1779-May 30, 1780 (Unpublished George Rogers Clark Papers, Archives Division, Virginia State Library, Richmond, Va, Box 48).

CHAPTER 12: FRIVOLITY AT FORT JEFFERSON

M. Dorothy George[1], Robert Hutchinson,[2] and W. Howland Kenney[3] all document that life in the 18th-century was not always serious, that frequently bawdiness, drunkenness, music, and frivolity relieved the day-to-day stresses of life and the seriousness of living on the frontier. The following excerpts from the Fort Jefferson records, although brief, clearly demonstrate that the inhabitants of Fort Jefferson knew how to have a good time. They celebrated holidays--sometimes to an extreme with liquid refreshment, sometimes carried a practical joke too far, and enjoyed making music. With a sex ratio of six men for every woman at Fort Jefferson, it is not surprising there is a reference by Capt. Leonard Helm stating, [I'm] in "good health with a Bottle of Taffeta at my elbow [but] my greatest want is a woman to crown my joys at night."[4] The Unpublished Clark Papers[5] and the published letters of Fort Jefferson[6] clearly exhibit two activities meant to ease the stress of frontier life: drinking and playing cards. With respect to the latter, decks of playing cards were present among the officer corps at Fort Jefferson; when writing paper ran short, officers wrote requests (often for alcoholic beverages) to the quartermaster on the front and reverse sides of playing cards.[7] I would assume, although I have no direct evidence, that playing cards were present throughout the entire Fort Jefferson population. Although decks of cards do not appear in the ledgers of the quartermasters, several direct and indirect references to card playing occur within the Fort Jefferson letters and papers. The same is true about music. Apparently, hand-written musical scores were exchanged among the officer corps at different military outposts (Figure 12.1).[8] At Fort Jefferson, Commandant Robert George enjoyed playing the fiddle and exchanging musical scores with his friend George Slaughter in Louisville.[9] To that music is added a fifer and two drummers who were members of Captain Edward Worthington's Company.[10] Music must have filled the boring labors of the frontier evenings. Singularly, though, the greatest vice shared by many of the Fort Jefferson inhabitants was that of drinking. Table 8.3 clearly documents that more than 2,071 gallons of various alcoholic beverages (1660.76 gallons tafia, 254.22 gallons liquor, 150.49 gallons rum, 3.41 gallons whiskey, and 3 gallons wine) were consumed at Fort Jefferson. Assuming the average adult population at Fort Jefferson numbered 110 persons for the 416 days the fort was garrisoned, each individual drank 2.5 quarts of alcoholic beverages per day! And that implies that every adult drank the 2.5 quarts a day.

---

[1] M. Dorothy George, *London Life in the 18th Century*, Alfred Knopf, New York, 1926.
[2] Robert Hutchinson, *Joe Miller's Jists or, the Wits Vade-mecum, a facsimile of the original "Joe Miller" (1739), the most popular humor book of all time*, Dover Publications, Inc., New York, 1963.
[3] W. Howland Kenney, *Laughter in the Wilderness: Early American Humor to 1783*, Kent State University Press, Kent, Ohio, 1976.
[4] Helm quoted in John Bakeless, *Background to Glory: The Life of George Rogers Clark*, Philadelphia, J.B. Lippincott Company, 1957:255. Bakeless attributes quotes to Unpublished Clark Papers in Virginia.
[5] Unpublished George Rogers Clark Papers, Archives Division, Virginia State Library, Boxes 1-50.
[6] Principally, James, ed., *Clark Papers*, 1972; also Katherine Wagner Seineke, *The George Rogers Clark Adventure in the Illinois and Selected Documents of the American Revolution at the Frontier Posts*. New Orleans: Polyanthos Press, 1981. See chapter 4, this volume.
[7] Unpublished Clark Papers.
[8] Unpublished Clark Papers, March 23, 1781, Box 17.
[9] Captain Robert George to George Slaughter, October 29, 1780 letter, in James, ed. I:506-7.
[10] Unpublished Clark Papers.

With only half of the adults imbibing, drinkers consumed 5 quarts of booze a day! That's quite an average when you consider that they also consumed 418 gallons of coffee and untold gallons of water. Captain Robert George wrote further, "In the Month of January, I have the pleasure to inform you we were able to drink brandy, Taffia & Wine-- with your good assistance Whisky too; but it has not made us so saucy, but we can drink all the whiskey you can send us."[11] As documented in several of the quotes below, excuses were plentiful when it came to requesting justifications to the quartermaster as to why a person should be issued something to drink, including entertaining friends. With respect to the latter, Captain George wrote Quartermaster Martin Carney on January 23, 1780, "Sir: Issue to Mr. Donne, deputy conductor, Twelve pounds of Sugar, for a particular occasion, being to celebrate a festival of his. Your humble servant, Robert George, Capt./Commandant."[12]

Just what do you do with 12 pounds of sugar? Pull taffy? Distill it? Even prisoners got into the act: Mr. Dejean was issued six quarts of tafia. Other quotes/descriptions demonstrate frustrations of life, and a philosophical statement penned by an anonymous author at Fort Jefferson looks at life and simply ponders. All of these quotes put a human face on the Fort Jefferson population.

"I have taken notice of your Song and learned it. It is so good I wish you had sent more of it" (Robert George to George Slaughter February 15, 1781)[13]

April 26, 1780
If paper was plenty, I would attempt a description of our uncomfortable situation—with a Xantippe[14] of a Landlady, something like a Petruchio[15] from Shakespeare and a Nabal[16] for a landlord, their Dirty children, leaky boat, Drunkenness &c., but I am by no means equal to the task.[17]

September 5, 1780
John Martin writes on the reverse of a voucher between John Donne and John Dodge, "a man of understanding will be governed by reason."[18]

December 24
Captain Harrison informed Captain George that it is Clark's intent to evacuate Fort Jefferson and erect another fortification at the Iron Banks. George states that his "yellow locks" will turn gray if Clark does not arrive soon to clarify his intentions.[19]

---

[11] *Ibid.*
[12] Unpublished Clark Papers, Box 15.
[13] *Ibid.*
[14] Socrates' famously shrewish wife.
[15] A leading character in the comedy, *Taming of the Shrew* by William Shakespeare.
[16] "A rich but churlish biblical figure" (Ted Brown, MSU English professor, personal communication to Ken Carstens, July 13, 2004, e-mail).
[17] Daniel Smith writing to Clark about his experience coming to Fort Jefferson from the Falls of the Ohio.
[18] *Ibid.*, Box 13.
[19] Missouri Historical Society, Box 1, Folder 23.

December 25th
Artillery command expends 60lbs gunpowder, seven lbs. lead, and six yards flannel by five swivels and one four pounder both in town and garrison per verbal orders by Captain Robert George.[20]

December 31st, 1780
New shoes issued to Ensign Slaughter, Martin Carney, Leonard Helm, Lt. John Girault, Major John Williams, Ensign Jarrett Willis, Captain Richard Brashears, Captain Richard Harrison, Captain Richard Clark, and Captain John Bailey.[21] Rank has its privileges.

January 1, 1781
Martin Carney (Quartermaster) issued James Sherlock (Indian Dep't.) six pounds tobacco to the Indians.[22] Celebration of New Year.

Captain Leonard Helm: "I am in good health with a Bottle of Taffia at my Elbow, & my greatest want is a Woman to Crown my Joys by night, as my Bottle does by day."[23]

Captain Kellar's blockhouse on hill issued eight lbs gunpowder and five lbs lead.[24] Celebration of New Year.

February 28, 1781
Please to let me have one bottle tafia; Lord how Dry I am![25] John Williams

Let your humble serve have a bottle of the Best to make his heart Glad.[26] John Williams

March 3, 1781
Please to issue one bottle of tafia for my use; I am very dry.[27] John Williams

March 9, 1781
I have much Company to beg you well if possible, open the Spicket as I have not been Troublesome. I expect Indulgence with three pints of Tafia.[28] John Rogers

If you would be so kind to Let me have one Case Bottle of Tafia as it is a Cold Morning…"[29] James Finzi

---

[20] Unpublished Clark Papers, Box 14.
[21] *Ibid.*
[22] *Ibid.*, Box 15.
[23] Bakeless, op. cit.
[24] *Ibid.*, Box 50.
[25] *Ibid.*, Box 16.
[26] *Ibid.*, Box 16.
[27] *Ibid.*, Box 17.
[28] *Ibid.*, Box 17.
[29] *Ibid.*, Box 17.

One bottle tafia for my throat[30] John Williams

March 17, 1781
Edward Worthington signs a request to the quartermaster for one quart tafia to Saint Patrick, who is "almost dead."[31]

Leonard Helm and Robert George sign a request to the quartermaster for three pints tafia for "the sake of St. Patrick."[32]

Lt. Girault signs a request to the quartermaster for one quart tafia for "the use of St. Patrick."[33]

James Sherlock and Robert George sign a request to the quartermaster for one quart tafia, for Sherlock's use to "drink to St. Patrick's health."[34]

March 18, 1781
James Sherlock and Robert George sign request to the quartermaster for one quart tafia for Sheal's sake; she being the wife of St. Patrick.[35]

March 19, 1781
John Donne requests Martin Carney issue one bottle tafia on Donne's account, for an unnamed individual who has made a pair of shoes for Mrs. Donne. Donne also states the quantity of tafia received from Carney (the quartermaster) yesterday was insufficient, because Donne had several visitors.[36]

March 20, 1781
David Allen and James Taylor, prisoners, robbed Major Williams' kitchen, beat his servants, and [verbally] abused Major Williams...Rachel Yeats testifies while she is in Major Williams' kitchen, individuals (David Allen, James Taylor) came to kitchen window, flashed a gun, threw "chips" [manure?] and bones at her and darted needles or pins fixed with hair through a cane reed at her by which they wounded her and put her in fear of her life;...Phillip Hupp...in company with Boston Damewood said he saw Damewood fix pins w/hair to shoot through the window of Major Williams' kitchen [at Rachel Yeats].[37]

---

[30] *Ibid.*, Box 17.
[31] *Ibid.*, Box 17.
[32] *Ibid.*, Box 17.
[33] *Ibid.*, Box 17.
[34] *Ibid.*, Box 17.
[35] *Ibid.*, 17.
[36] *Ibid.*, 17
[37] Draper Manuscripts, 56J40.

March 21, 1781
Leonard Helm and Robert George sign a request to Martin Carney for one quart tafia to "drive away all sorrow."[38]

March 26th
Issue 2 bottles of tafia to make my heart glad and give contentment to my friends.[39] John Williams

Letter from Lt. Girault of Fort Jefferson to Col. Clark. Girault requests to go on any expedition with the troops from Fort Jefferson. Girault feels he could be of greater service in any place other than Fort Jefferson. Girault mentions that there have been several disputes since Clark's departure.[40]

"Phlegm, phlegm question phlegm, may be propounded by a fool, for no wise man can Answer for his soul." Anonymous, Fort Jefferson.[41]

Robert George signs a request to the quartermaster for six gallons tafia to Mr. Dejean, a prisoner of war.[42]

June 6, 1781
For God's Sake, let Me have two pounds of sugar for use[43] John Williams

---

[38] Unpublished Clark Papers, Box 17.
[39] *Ibid.*, 17.
[40] William Clark Collection, Missouri Historical Society, Box 2, Folder 2.
[41] *Op cit.*, 17.
[42] *Ibid.*, Box 17.
[43] *Ibid.*, Box 20.

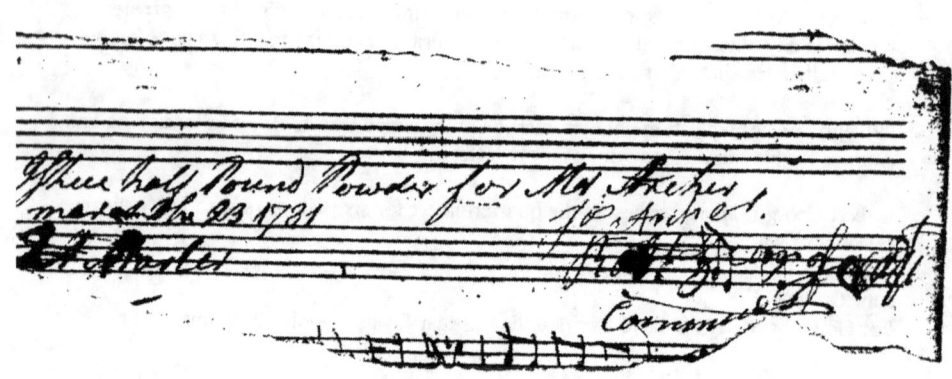

Figure 12.1 : A Portion of a Musical Score from Fort Jefferson, Dated March 23, 1781 (Unpublished Clark Papers, Archives Division, Virginia State Library, Richmond). Is this part of the song Slaughter sent George as mentioned in the February 15 letter?[44]

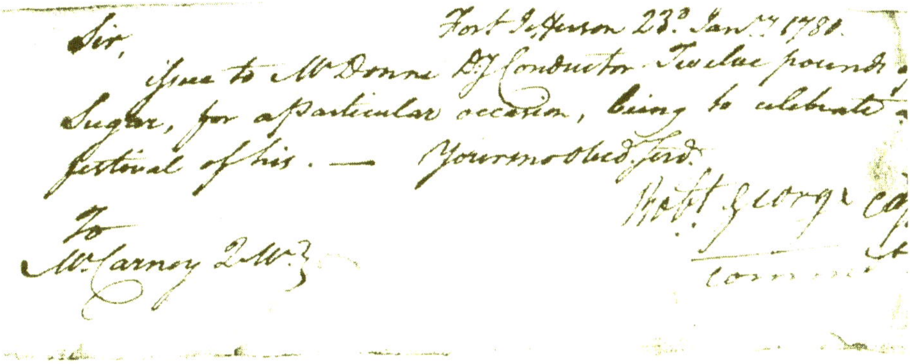

Figure 12.2 A Hand-written Request for 12 Pounds of Sugar "for a festival."

CHAPTER 13: FRIENDS AND FAMILY DEATH AND DYING

Friends and family, death and dying. Some things never change. So, too, it was on the western frontier more than 200 years ago. For some people, who are descendants of the families who were at Fort Jefferson, this is a happy chapter. Their ancestors are listed here. The Fort Jefferson documents and sources, when taken together, permit a collective reconstruction and listing of 40 families present at the fort who formed the nucleus of the civilian community of Clarksville. Many of these people, until their names have become public, have been lost to history, hitherto only players in history who filled the gap of time. But now they are known. These were some of Kentucky's first frontier settlers, every bit as important as the George Rogers Clarks or Daniel Boones of the world, for they lived the day-to-day moment and permitted the great plans of the leaders to become reality. But as enlightening and rewarding as this list of friends and families is (Table 13.1), it is also sad for the listing of those individuals, military and civilian (Table 13.2) who gave the ultimate sacrifice for the cause of freedom and the establishment of Fort Jefferson and civilian community of Clarksville.

As complete as the Fort Jefferson documents are, they do not tell the whole story, nor do they give the names of all the persons or families present. An examination of Table 13.1 illustrates this point precisely. When first names of husband or wife are known they are given. Even so, of the 40 families, 11 first names of married women are not known. In several instances, women were referred to simply as "widow," as in "the Widow Meredith," or the "Widow Asher." We do not know their first names, but we know to whom they were married and whether or not they had children. In some instances, we even know the names of the children (such as the McMeans: Mary, John James, Isaac, Jane, Robert, and Anne). A large family to be sure, especially on the frontier. How typical was this pattern for the other families? In several instances we know only of the number of children in the family and not the names, and sadly for others, we know not if there were any children at all. Yet, compared to personnel histories for other late 18th century stations, forts, and settlements, the Fort Jefferson documentation is surprisingly complete.

Last Name	Wife's Name	Husband's Name	Family	Children
Asher	Widow	William	Unknown	Unknown
Brashears	Unknown	Richard	Unknown	Unknown
Breeding	Hanah	Francis	Unknown	Unknown
Bryan	Unknown	John	Yes	Unknown
Burks	Elizabeth	John	Unknown	Sarah
Dalton	Hannah	Valentine	Unknown	Unknown
Damewood	Mary	Boston	Unknown	Unknown
Daughterty	Unknown	John	Yes	2-children
Donne	Martha	John	Unknown	Unknown
Elms	Ann	(See note #1)	Yes	1-daughter
Hellebrant	Mary	Peter	Yes	Unknown
Hughes	Martha	Unknown	Yes	Unknown

Hunter	Marah	Joseph	Yes	Nancy & Mary
Hutsel	Widow	John	Yes	Unknown
Johnston	Ann	Ezekiel	Unknown	Unknown
Jones	Elizabeth	Matthew	Yes	Unknown
Kennedy	Rachel	Patrick	Unknown	Unknown
Lockard	Unknown	Archibald	Yes	Unknown
Lunsford	Mary	Anthony	Yes	Unknown
McAuley	Mary	Patrick	Unknown	Unknown
McCormack	Unknown	John	Unknown	Unknown
McMeans	Ann	Andrew	Yes	Mary, John, James, Isaac, Jane, Robert, Anne
Mains	Unknown	Patrick	Yes	1-child
Mayfield	Unknown	Micajah	Yes	Unknown
Meredith	Widow	Daniel	Unknown	Unknown
Meredith	Luvana	(See note #2)	Unknown	Unknown
Miles	Deceased	Michael	Yes	1-son
Murray	Unknown	Matthew	Unknown	Unknown
Oiler	Unknown	Unknown	Yes	7-children
Owens	Charity	George	Yes	Unknown
Phelps	Elizabeth	Thomas	Yes	6-children
Piggott	Eleanor	James	Yes	Levi & William
Quirk	Unknown	Thomas	Yes	2-children
Rion/Ryan	Unknown	Lazurus	Unknown	Unknown
Shilling	Mary	Jacob	Yes	Unknown
Smith	Mary	Henry	Yes	Sarah or Sidy
Trent	Sarah	Beverly	Unknown	Unknown
Watkins	Elizabeth	Samuel	Unknown	Unknown
Witzel	Widow	Unknown	Unknown	Unknown
Young	Margery	James	Unknown	Unknown

Note 1: Her husband may be William, John, or James Elms.
Note 2: Her husband may be Laurence or James Meredith.

Table 13.1: A List of Known Fort Jefferson/Clarksville Families.

For the name data in Table 13.2, individuals are listed chronologically by the date of death, name, cause of death, the military company to which they belonged (or civilian), and the specific references used to confirm the death information. This listing provides clues, or implies clues, about other information associated with the deaths. Where there is variation in last name spelling, both variations are given (such as Ker, which several authors have recorded as Ilor, or Snowden/Sworden). Table 13.2 lists 49 deaths, but within these "deaths" are terms that imply how the individual may have died or circumstances surrounding the death. That is, clear distinctions were made when recording deaths if the individuals was "killed" or had passed away to natural causes ("deceased" or "dead" or "died"). Of the 49 listed who died, 23 are listed as "killed." When the "killed" dates are matched to the dates of known military assaults on Fort Jefferson by Chickasaw Indians, an interesting correlation appears. By the same token, the pattern of "dead," "deceased," or "died" reflects a more random pattern dispersed throughout the duration of fort occupancy. More than likely, these are deaths due to malaria or ague. In a letter to George Rogers Clark, Captain Robert George made the statement that "Numbers [are] daly [sic] Dying."[1] Interestingly, when Fort Jefferson was abandoned on June 8, 1781, the coffin maker at Fort Jefferson billed the State of Virginia for making "38 coffins for men, women, and children at Fort Jefferson." Surprisingly, none of the 49 names listed in Table 13.2 are names of children, and only two women are listed in the table (a Black slave and Mrs. Michael Miles). Not listed also are the friendly Kaskaskia Indians who died at Fort Jefferson. Based on the quartermaster books of the post, a blue burial shroud was issued for one "friendly Kaskaskia Indian." Was he, or his compatriots, buried at Fort Jefferson? I do not know. I would conclude, therefore, that the list of deaths at Fort Jefferson/Clarksville is probably abbreviated.

Lastly, where was the Fort Jefferson cemetery? No one knows for sure, but according to the B. Hardy Stovall 19th-century map of Fort Jefferson,[2] the Fort Jefferson cemetery was located on the hill north of the fort and adjacent to the blockhouse overlooking the community and fortification below. The William Clark map[3] (1M11) would place the northern blockhouse between house in-lot rows 20 and 21 (see Chapter 2, this volume). Perhaps that is the location of the Fort Jefferson cemetery. Only additional archaeological studies will determine the actual location.

Date	Individual	How Died	Military Company	Reference (ref/pg.no.)
6/2/80	Estes, J.	Killed	Worthington	2:53
6/2/80	Gilmore, G.	Killed	Worthington	2:47
6/3/80	March, J.	Deceased	George	2:29-30
6/7/80	Certain, P.	Killed	Worthington	2:47, 53
6/7/80	Ker, C.	Killed	Owen's Militia	2:48-49; 3:464, Ilor?
6/7/80	Ker, H.	Killed	Owen's Militia	2:48-49; 3:464, Ilor?

---

[1] See Chapter 4, this volume; James Alton James, ed., *George Rogers Clark Papers*, Vol. I., AMS Press, New York, 1972: 461.
[2] *Draper Manuscripts*, 27J17-22, Wisconsin Historical Society, Madison, Wisconsin.
[3] *Ibid.*, 1M8.

Date	Name	Status	Unit	Reference
6/7/80	Ker, M.	Killed	Owen's Militia	2:48-49; 3:464, Ilor?
6/8/80	Haul, H.	Killed	George	2:30, 31
7/15/80	Dean, J.	Killed	Worthington	2:53
7/17/80	Aldar, J.	Killed	Owen's Militia	1(26J28) 2:49; 3:465 6:13
8/12/80	Blair, J.	Deceased	Brashear	2:51
8/27/80	Female Slave	Killed	Smith	5:21
8/27/80	Snowden, J.	Deceased	Worthington	2:47; 2:53, Sworden?
8/27/80	Hutsill, J.	Killed	Owen's Militia	2:49; 3:465
8/27/80	Hatton, C.	Killed	Worthington	2:47; 2:53
8/28/80	Laney, T.	Killed	George	2:30, 32
9/4/80	Fair, E.	Deceased	George	2:31, 32
9/5/80	Whitacre, D.	Killed	George	2:30
9/23/80	Rubido, F.	Deceased	Brashear	2:51
9/24/80	Unnamed soldier	Dies	Rogers	6:13
9/28/80	Robeson, William (also Robson)	Deceased	Worthington	2:53 2:47
9/30/80	Unnamed soldier	Dies	Kellar	6:13
10/4/80	Brown, J.	Killed	Worthington	2:47
10/4/80	Thorington, J.	Killed	Worthington	2:53
10/4/80	Ditterin, J.	Deceased	George	2:32
10/5/80	Wilson, E.	Killed	Owen's Militia	2:48; 3:464
10/7/80	Decker, J. (also Deckar)	Deceased	Kellar	2:24
10/10/80	Crawley, J.	Died	Kellar	2:24
10/10/80	Villier, F.	Killed	McCarty	2:27
10/10/80	Papin, J.	Killed	McCarty	2:46
10/14/80	Hardin, F.	Deceased	Bailey	2:46
10/17/80	Davies, J.	Deceased	Kellar	2:24
10/20/80	Thompson, J.	Deceased	Kellar	2:24
10/20/80	Waggoner, P.	Deceased	George	2:30
10/25/80	Allen, J. (also listed as killed on 11/22/80)	Killed	Kellar	2:24 6:14
11/2/80	Harrison, R.	Deceased	Brashear	2:51
11/9/80	Williams, D. Daniel	Dead	Worthington	2:47
11/12/80	Morris, J.	Deceased	Brashear	2:51
11/19/80	Turpin, R.	Deceased	George	2:30
12/26/80	Horn, J.	Deceased	George	2:30
1/2/81	Smith, G.	Died	George	2:30
1/15/81	Fever, W.	Died	George	2:32
1/24/81	Carr, W. (also Kerr)	Deceased	Bailey	2:46
3/28/81	Piner, J.	Killed	McCarty	2:27

4/12/81	Cooper, J.	Died	Kellar		2:23
5/28/81	Slaughter, L.	Killed	Bailey		2:45
6/2/81	McCarty, R.	Killed	McCarty		2:27
6/5/81	Murray, E.	Deceased	Bailey		2:46
3/28/81-6/7/81	Miles, Mrs. Michael (several dates given)	Deceased	Civilian		6:20

Table 13.2   A Listing of Known Deceased Individuals at Fort Jefferson, 1780-1781

References for Table 12.2:
1. *Draper Manuscripts*, State Historical Society of Wisconsin, Madison.
2. Margery Harding, *George Rogers Clark and His Men: Military Records: 1778-1784* (Frankfort: The Kentucky Historical Society, 1981).
3. James Alton James, ed. *George Rogers Clark Papers* (New York, AMS Press, 1972)
4. *William Clark Papers*, Box 1, Missouri Historical Society, Forest Park, St. Louis.
5. *Steamboat Files* (Genealogical History of the Piggott Family), Missouri Historical Society, Forest Park, St. Louis.
6. Unpublished George Rogers Clark Papers, Boxes 1-50, Virginia State Library, Archives Division, Richmond.

CHAPTER 14: INVENTORY OF MILITARY COMPANIES

The following rosters of men (and women) are based on information contained primarily within the unpublished George Rogers Clark papers from the Archives Division of the Virginia State Library in Richmond. In most instances, the rosters were created from lists that were used by military unit captains to note which of the men in their unit had received their clothing issue/allotments. In other instances, an individual may have been identified for having done something for the garrison at Fort Jefferson, and his unit affiliation is noted on the voucher. Where noted, a reference to the "box" (e.g., VSA Box 17) from which that particular reference can be found in the original hand-written notation is given. Other references used to generate these lists of company rosters include Margaret Harding's 1981 *George Rogers Clark and His Men* (a book of published rosters)[1] and the William Clark collection in the Missouri Historical Society in St. Louis. For the later, both "box" number and "folder" number are given. No attempt has been made to correct spelling as spellings for specific names varied in different contexts, and although a preferred spelling may be suggested, the actual spelling of the person's name may never be known. Many of the recorded names were simply spelled phonetically. This chapter is important from the standpoint of understanding military strength on the western frontier, and it is important because the listing of names demonstrates that the males of families, whether fathers and sons, brothers, or paternal cousins, often enlisted together, maybe with the idea that doing so would result in a paying job when none else were to be found on the frontier, or, more importantly, that, should they survive the war, they would be awarded *land*. In many instances, the latter was the driving force behind both recruiting and enlisting. As you read the names below, an interesting comparison can be made to William Hayden English's list of individuals who were awarded, or denied, claims of land following the war in the Indiana tract for serving in Clark's Illinois Battalion.[2] Ironically, should two persons have served in the same capacity during the war, only one was awarded land for his service by the Board of Western Commissioners[3] a very unfair and unjust system.

Captain Robert George's Company of Artillery (VSA Box 50)
Captain Lt. Richard Harrison
Joseph Andrews
G. Armstrong
John Ash
Daniel Babu
John Bakly
Valentine Balsinklee
Daniel Bolton
John Brian
Charles Burk

---

[1] Margaret Harding, *George Rogers Clark and His Men*, The Kentucky Historical Society, Frankfort, Kentucky, 1981.
[2] William H. English, *Conquest of the Country Northwest of the River Ohio, 1778-1783 and Life of General George Rogers Clark*, 2 volumes, Bowen-Merrill Company, Indianapolis, 1897.
[3] James Alton James, *George Rogers Clark Papers*, Vol. II, AMS Press, New York, 1972: 413-472.

Drury Bush
John Bush
Martin Carney
Cesar (free? Black artificer)
Andrew Clark
Bostin Damewood (also Dance)
John Daughterty
Thomas DeLany (also Lany)
Mary DeMore (washerwoman)
Jacob Ditterin
William Fabers (also Fever)
Edmund Fair
John Gilbert
J. Grimshaw
Michel Hacketon
John Hacker
John Hazard
Jeremiah Hern
Richard Hopkins
Phil Hup
Matthew Jones
Lazarous Kennada
Lawrance Kenon
Ryon Layarous
Francis Little
Philip Long
Patrick McCalley
James McDaniel
J. McMullen
Patrick Marr
E. Mathews
John Megarr
Abraham Miller
William More
C. Morgan
Matthew Murray
Buckner Pittman (Boatmaster)
William Posey
William Postin (also Pastin)
Isaac Pruit
Paul Quibes
James Ramsey
Patrick Rogers
George Smith
John Smothers
Travis (?), Taylor

Michel Tinklee
Richard Turpin
Thomas Win
Peter Wagner
Jacob Wheat
William White

Captain Richard Brashear's Company (VSA Box 11)
Ensign Jerret Williams
Isaac Allen
Samuel Allen (Sgt.)
William Bartholomew
John Blair
John Boils
James Brown
John Cowen
James Curry
Patrick Curry
James Dawson
James Elms
John Elms
William Elms (Sgt.)
James Flarry
Peter Howell
John Joins (Sgt.)
Lois LePaint
John Mackever
Macajah (Cagy) Mayfield
John McMichael
Joseph Moneral
Charles Morgan
James Morris
Charles Ouneler
Joseph Ross
Francis Rubedo
Jake (Jache) Rubedo
Thomas Snellock (also Snarlock)
Daniel Tyger
David Wallis

Captain John Rogers, Virginia Light Dragoons (VSA Box 12)
Lt. James Merriwether
Coronet John Thurston
Robert Barnit

Henry Blankinship
Travis Bootin
William Bootin
Francis Bredin
Casper Cailer
William Campbell
Rice Curtis
Frederick Dohaty
William Frogget
Mikiel Glass
William Goodwin
William Bruin
James Hammit
Joseph Irwin
John Jones
George Key
Thomas Key
William Leer
Charles Martin
David McDonald
Nathaniel Mershom
William Meriwether
John Murphey
Mikel O'Harrah
David Pagan
George Snow
Francis Spillman
James Spillman
Dominick Welch
Barney Wigins
Kendal Williams

Captain Edward Worthington's Company of Regulars[4]
Lieutenant Richard Clark
David Allen
John Anderson
John Bowdery (fifer)
William Brading
James Bryant
Thomas Cox
William Crump
Henery Dewit (also DeWitt)
James Estis
Charles Evans
George Gilmore

---

[4] William Clark Collection, Missouri Historical Society, Box 1, Folder 20.

John Hargis
Francis Harris
Christopher Hatton (also Hutten)
John Jewell
Andrew Johnson (also Johnston) drummer
Edward Johnson (corporal)
Reubin Kemp (also Camp)
James Kerkely
George Leviston
Archibald Lockart
Moses Lundsford
Mordiack McKensey
John Moore (Sgt.)
Enoch Nelson
John Nelson
Moses Nelson
John Robison
Page Sertain (also Certain)
Lawrance Sutherland
Johnathan Swordkin
Josias (Joseph) Thornington
John Tulfor (also Tulford)
John White
Daniel Williams
Zachariah Williams
Jacob Willis
John Wilson
Isaac Yeates
John Yeates (drummer)

Captain Richard McCarty's Company[5]
Lieutenant John Girault
Lieutenant Michael (?) Perrault
Jean Andre (Sgt.)
Francis Bennoit
(?), Blanchard
Jacque Gagnus (also Gagnier)
Louis Gagnus (also Gagnier)
Francis Grolet (father)
Francis Grolet (son)
James Harrison
(?), Laform
Francois L'Enfant
John La Marine
John LaRichardy

---
[5] Unpublished Clark Papers, Box 13; Margaret Harding, *GRC and His Men*, 1981:21-22.

Richard Lovin (also Loving)
Charles McLaughlin
John Metivce
Ps. Metivce
William Mulboy (also Mulby)
Peter (?), or John, Pepin
Jesse Piner
(?), Pursley
Francis Villier (Sgt.)

Captain Abraham Keller's Company[6]
James Brown (Sgt.)
John Chappel
Barney Cooper
Joseph Cooper
John Crawley
James Davis
Jacob Decart
Jacob Dasker
Haymore Duly
Philip Duly
Harmon Eagle
Thomas Hays
George Hoit
David Humber
James or John Kearns
John Kellar
Francis Laycore
Anthony Montroy
Joseph Panther
James Pritchet
Baptist Raper (also Rahr?)
David Russill
John Shank
George Smith
James Thompson

Captain John Bailey's Company[7]
Lieut. William Clark (cousin to GRC)
Ensign Laurence (also Lawrence) Slaughter
Larken Ballenger
William Bell
William Brayly

---

[6] Unpublished Clark Papers, Box 12.
[7] *Ibid.*

William Buchanan
Nicholas Burk
William Bush
William Carr
John Clark
John Conner
Frances Horden
James Hays
James Jarril
John Johnson
Anthony Lunsford
George Lunsford
Graves Morris
Edward Murray
Edward Parker
Henery Philaps
David Shaver
Peter Shepard
Levi Theel
William Thomson
Beverly Trent (Sgt.)
Nicholas Tuttle
John Vaugh
Robert Waitt
Randel White
Robert Whitehead
William Whitehead
Hugh Young

Captain Jesse Evans Company (men discharged at Fort Jefferson)[8]
Lou Brown
Richard Chapman
Andrew Clark
Joshua Hollis
Jacob Huffman
John Lastly
John McGuire
James Potter
Leonard Shoemaker
Joseph Smith

Captain George Owens (also Oins) Company of Militia[9]
John Aldar
Joshua Archer

---

[8] *Ibid.*
[9] James Alton James, ed., *Clark Papers*, I: 464-465.

James Barnet
John Burk
Francis Ciblet
Samuel Cooper
Robert Craten
John Ford
Joseph Ford
Robert Ford
Daniel Graffen
Jacob Groats
Silas Harlan
Peter Hellebrandt
Joseph Hunter
John Hutsil
William Hutsil
John Johnston
Conrad Ker (also Ilor)
Henry Ker (also Ilor)
Jonas Ker (also Ilor)
Mark Ker (also Ilor)
Charles King
James King
Moses McCan
John McCormack
Andrew McMeans
James McMeans
Daniel Merridith
Nicholas Nedinger
Anthony Phelps
Georg Phelps
Josiah Phelps
John Phister
William Reid
Jacob Shilling
Edmund Smith
Enoch Springer
Henry Steward
James Wiley
Edward Wilson
John Wilson
Michael Wolf
James Young
John Young

Captain Isaac Taylor's Company Discharged at Fort Jefferson[10]
John Anderson
William Bell
William Brawly
Peter Freeman
Miles Hart
James Hayes
Josiah Meadows
Thomas Murray
Samuel Oater
Richard Senet (also Sinnat)
Edward Taylor
Richard Tennell
William Thomson
Christopher Tiburn
Nicholas Tuttle
Daniel Tygar
Mordicai Wicks
John Willson (Sgt.)

Other Soldiers who spent time at Fort Jefferson (several enlisted men below traveled to FJ for discharge):

Lt. Colonel John Montgomery
Major Thomas Quirk (also Kirk)
Major John Williams
James Ballenger
John Cox
Joseph Duncan
William Hall
Samuel Johnston
John Ozala (Captain?)
Lewis Pines
John Roberts
Ebenezer Suverns
Daniel Tolley
Samuel Watkins

Quartermaster/Commissary Corps[11]
John Dodge (to be paid at rate of Captain)
Zephaniah Blackford
Martin Carney
Valentine Thomas Dalton (also in Indian Department)

---

[10] Unpublished Clark Papers, Box 12; Harding, 1981:13.
[11] Unpublished Clark Papers, Box 50.

Israel Dodge
John Donn
James Finn (also Finz)
Patrick Kennedy (assistant deputy conductor)
Joseph Lindsay
Benjamin Roberts (Captain in George Slaughter's Quartermaster Corps)
William Shannon (Captain, Conductor)

Artificers
Gasper Butcher
Caesar (also Sezor, Cesar; also listed in Capt. Robert George's Company)
Andrew Clark (also listed in Capt. Robert George's Company)
Joseph Thornton (also listed in Capt. Edward Worthington's Company)

Indian Department/Affairs, Leonard Helm, Superintendent
Valentine Thomas Dalton
Hannah Dalton (wife of Valentine; interpreter)
James Sherlock (interpreter for French and Indians)

Armorer and Smithy
John Harris
John White (listed also in Captain Worthington's Company)

Tailor
John Bryan
Mrs. (no first name) Bryan (also O'Brian and OBryan)

Prisoners at Fort Jefferson
David Allen
Mr. (no first name given) Dejean
James Taylor
Thomas Wilson (Lieutenant)

Friendly Indians
Baptisst (Chief of Kaskaskia Indians)
"Joseph," a friendly Indian
65 unnamed Kaskaskia Indians
Unspecified number of friendly Delaware and Piankashaw

Slaves
George Rogers Clark's slaves (unspecified number)
Captain (no first name given) Smith's slaves (unspecified number)

Doctors at Fort Jefferson
Andrew Ray (also Rey), Surgeon Major
Samuel Smyth (Surgeon)

CHAPTER 15: WHAT THEY WORE

I have always been interested in historical re-enactment. Next to archaeology (my profession), historical re-enactment is the next best thing to time travel and a viable way of attempting to recreate and understand, as best we can, what it must have been like to live in the 18th century. During the 1980s, I was a member of the Northwest Territorial Alliance, or NWTA. I joined the 42nd Royal Highland Regiment (I'm sorry, that is a British unit!), not as a soldier, but as a civilian surveyor. I acquired the proper clothing and the proper accoutrements that would have been used by an 18th-century surveyor. Original items that I couldn't find to buy, I made or had made. Of paramount importance to our regiment, and to all of the members of the NWTA, was the historical research that went into our character development AND our costuming. Whether you are a member, today, of the NWTA or Brigade of the American Revolution (BAR), both organizations emphasize the importance of wearing the correct fabric, the correct color, so on and so forth. The following paragraphs are taken from the John Dodge Quartermaster Book as retained in Box 48 of the Unpublished George Rogers Clark Papers in the Archives Division of the Virginia State Library. These ARE the fabrics issued and the clothes made at Fort Jefferson, and yes, they were all hand stitched (see Chapter 9, this volume) by both men and women assigned to that western frontier outpost.

According to Hening's statutes of Virginia law, every officer of the State of Virginia was entitled to the following yearly allotment of clothing, "and no more."[1] It is interesting to make two comparisons with the following information between the allotted and recommended issues for the officers, and the differences between what officers received and what enlisted men received. If an enlisted man received a new shirt or a pair of shoes, he was lucky. Officers received much more, actually receiving enough fabric so they could have regular changes of clothing, or clothing for certain seasons of the year. Not the enlisted man. The statement that "rank has its privileges" was very true in the 18th-century and clothing did much to reflect the classes of society within 18th-century culture.

According to the Virginia statutes, an officer is to receive:

Six yards cloth 7/4 wide w/trimming for suit of clothes
"Stuff" for six summer vests and breeches
Linen for six shirts
Cambric for rules for shirts
Buttons
Six (neck) stocks
Three pair of silk hose and three pair of thread hose
Six handkerchiefs
Two pair of good shoes
One hat
"AND NO MORE"

---

[1] William Waller Hening, *The Statutes at Large; Being a Collection of all the Laws of Virginia from the First Session of the Legislature, in the Year 1619*, Vol. X, 1779-1781, pg. 25. Richmond, 1822. Facsimile reprint 1969, Jamestown Foundation, University Press of Virginia, Charlottesville.

But these are the issues given at Fort Jefferson by Captain John Dodge, quartermaster (original spellings retained):

Lt. Col. John Montgomery

Item of clothing	Type of Material
neckstock	cambric
shirt	linen-white
ruffling	Holland-fine
breeches	casernone (white), thickset, cotton velvet (spotted), dimete (corded), seysays, calendry, chince
waistcoat	(same as breeches)
socks	thread hose (linen)
knee garters	issued
handkerchiefs	silk, Indian, and linen

lining was done with coarse & damaged linen
buttons were issued

Majors (John Williams, Richard McCarty)

Hat	issued
Neckstock	fine Holland; muslin
Shirt	white linen
Ruffling	Holland, cambric
Breeches	callendry, corded dimete, & thickset (also cottonade, seysays, cotton velvet [spotted], cotton seyree, seloon, camblet, callominco, toil grise, and chince)
Waistcoat	same as breeches
Knee garters	issued
Socks	thread hose (linen)
Handkerchiefs	silk, Indian, linen

Coarse linen issued as lining material.
Buttons issued.

Captains (Rogers, Kellar, Bailey, & Brashears)

Hat	issued (all but one, termed "fine hatt")
Neckstock	muslin (3), fine Holland (2), cambric (1)
Ruffling	fine Holland (6), cambric 1
Shirts	White linen (4); linen (unspecified 2), 1 cambric
Breeches	Seysay (6), callendry (3) thickset (7), chintz (3), corded dimity (2), toile grise (3), spotted flannel (2), corduroy, spotted Persian, unspecified grey cloth [wool], calemenaco, checked linen, cottonade, casemore
Waistcoats	thickset (4), chintz (4), saysay (3), callendry (3), toile grise (2), spotted flannel (2), cottonade (2), corded dimity, blue Persian, grey cloth [wool?], checked linen, calemenco, camlet, casemare, corduroy, spotted Persian
Socks	thread hose [probably linen-6], silk hose 1.
Shoes	1 pair issued
Overcoats	blue bath coating (3)
Lining Material	coarse linen (4), damaged linen, unspecified linen
Trousers	checked linen
Breech cloth	blue bath coating
Handkerchiefs	silk (7), Indian (6) Linen (unspecified, 5), checked linen (2), cambric, red cotton

Lieutenants (Girault, Perrault, Clark & Merriwether)

Hat	5 issued
Neckstocks	6 muslin
Shirts	white linen (3), fine linen (1), unspecified linen (1)
Breeches	toile grise (4), callender (3), camblet (3), chintz (3),

	Waistcoats	checked linen (3), spotted flannel (3), fustian (2) and 1 each: callemenco, casemore, shalloon, unspecified gray cloth [wool?], corded dimete, spotted velvet, seysays toile grise (3), spotted flanne (4), calendar (3), camblet (3), chintz (3), checked linen (2), and 1 each: dimette, callemenco, casemore, shalloon, calendry, gray cloth unspecified [wood?], fustian, corded dimete, spotted velvet, seysays.
	Ruffling	fine Holland (4), white Holland (1), cambric (1)
	Knee garters	2 pair issued
	Socks	5 pair thread hose (linen?)
	Trousers	1 issued (toile grise)
	Handkerchiefs	silk (6), Indian (5), checked linen (3), linen unspecified (3)
	Lining material	coarse linen (3), shalloon (1), damaged linen (1), unspecified linen (1)
	Metal buttons	large buttons, small buttons

Ensigns (Jarrett Williams, Lawrence Slaughter)

	Socks	thread hose (1)
	Breeches	gray cloth (wool, 2), checked linen (2), one each: callender toile grise, calamanco (black), thicksett, calendar, seysays, chintz
	Waistcoats	gray cloth (wood, 2), one each: callender, toile grise, checked linen, thickset, calendar seysays, chintz, calamanco
	Handkerchiefs	silk (2), Indian (2), Linen (2)
	Hat	2
	Neckstocks	muslin (2)
	Shirts	White linen (1), linen (1) not specified
	Ruffling	Holland fine (2)

	Lining material	Coarse linen

Doctors/Surgeons (Andrew Ray and Samuel Smyth)

	Socks	thread hose
	Breeches	one each: casemore, chintz, spotted flannel, camblet, shalloon, toile grise, check linen, spotted cotton velvet, spotted Persian, checked gingum
	Waistcoat	one each: casemore, chintz, spotted flannel, camblet, shalloon, toile grise, check linen, spotted cotton velvet, spotted Persian, checked gingum
	Handkerchief	silk (2), checked linen, Indian, linen (unspecified).
	Hat	one
	Neckstock	muslin (1), cambric (1)
	Shirts	muslin (1), linen unspecified (1)
	Overcoat	blue bath coating (1)
	Ruffling	fine Holland (1), cambric (1)
	Lining material	linen unspecified (1), damaged linen (1),
	Knee garters	one
	Trousers	linen unspecified, (1)
	Breech cloth	blue bath coating
	Leggings	white half thicks

French & Indian Interpreter
(James Sherlock, Capt. Helm-superintendent Indian affairs)

	Socks	thread hose (2)
	Breeches	gray cloth unspecified [wool?] 1), chintz (1), corded dimity (1), cotton sachque (1), toil grise (1), thickset (1)
	Waistcoat	gray cloth unspecified [wool?] 1), corded dimity (1) cotton sachque (1), cottonade (1), camblet (1)
	Handkerchief	linen unspecified (1), silk (2), Romall (1), checked linen

Hat	(1), Indian (1) two
Neckstock	cambric (1)
Shirts	linen unspecified (1), ruffled shirt (1)
Overcoat	brown broad cloth (1), shalloon (1), scarlet cloth [wool ?] (1), coarse damaged linen (1)
Ruffling	damaged linen
Lining material	linen unspecified (1), linen damaged (1)
Knee garters	one
Buttons	unspecified
Trousers	cottonade (1)
Chapeau	gray cloth unspecified (1), silk ferreting (1)
Summer coat	chintz (1)

Quartermaster Corps
(J. Dodge, I. Dodge, M. Carney, J. Donne, J.Finn, P. Kennedy, Z. Blackford, W. Shannon)

Socks	thread hose (2), silk (1)
Breeches	cashmere (2), corduroy (1), chintz (2), thickset (5), cottonade 93), checked linen (1), toile gris (3), spotted velvet (2), spotted cotton (1) syseys (1), white linen (1), corded dimity (1)
Waistcoat	cashmere (2), corduroy (1), chintz (3), thickset (3), spotted Persian (1), cottonade (3), unspecified linen (1), toile gris (1), spotted velvet (1), spotted cotton (1), syseys (3), spotted Persian, calendry (1)
Handkerchiefs	linen unspecified (3), silk (6), red cotton (2), Indian (4), checked linen (5), blue cotton (1), Romall (1)
Hat	five
Neckstock	fine Holland (3), cambric (2), Britainies (1), muslin (2)
Shirts	linen unspecified (6), white

Overcoats	linen (1)
	silk (1), toile gris (1), blue bath coating (1), camblet (1)
Ruffling	fine Holland (4), cambric (1)
Lining material	linen unspecified (4), damaged linen (2), coarse linen (1)
Knee garters	four
Shoes	one
Metal buttons	2
Trousers	cottonade (1), checked linen (3), toile gris (2)
Breech cloth	blue bath coating (1)

Slaves (belonging to G. Clark: 1 Negro man, 1 Wench, 1 boy):

Shirt	oznaberg (1)
Trousers	oznaberg (1)

Company Issues
(includes issues to Col. Montgomery, Capt. Quirk, Kellar, Bailey, Worthington, Brashears, Rogers, and McCarty)

(Total "N" for 8 military units)

Blue cloth	230 yds
Coarse Combs	11
Fine Combs	11
Ruffled Shirts	29
Plain Shirts	212
Black Persian for stocks	11 yds
Fine linen for stocks	15.5 yds
Check handkerchiefs	1 to a Sgt.
Flannel	21 yds
Buttons (unspecified)	4 doz.
White flannel	178.5 yds
Cloth (unspecified)	80.5 yds
Shirts (unspecified)	21
Shirts (linen)	8

CHAPTER 16: ARCHAEOLOGICAL STUDIES PERFORMED IN SEARCH OF FORT JEFFERSON, 1980-2004

The search for Clark's Fort Jefferson has been filled with irony. Here I am an archaeologist. I deal in dirt, artifacts, and subsurface context of those artifacts. One would think that finding the archaeological remains of a fort and civilian community as large and as structurally diverse and extensive as Fort Jefferson and Clarksville would be no problem. Indeed, where most problems are encountered in historical archaeology is in the lack of historical documentation and not in locating the sites. Just the opposite is true with the Fort Jefferson project. I've got the documents but not the fort! But all is not lost, nor have we given up trying to find the physical remains of the fort.

I began the Fort Jefferson research project in 1979, primarily because one of my students, Bob Bell, gave me a little green book written by the late M. Juliette Magee entitled *Old Fort Jefferson*.[1] Magee was a native of Ballard County, Kentucky and a publisher of *The Advance-Yeoman*, a local county newspaper published in Wickliffe, Kentucky. She also claimed ancestry from a member of Clark's Illinois Battalion and therefore had a personal interest in the history of Fort Jefferson and in particular, Ballard County.

Magee's book intrigued me. In 1979 I was beginning the Murray State University archaeology program, and I was looking for a long-term project with which I could involve Murray State students and simultaneously build an archaeology program. I had always been interested in both colonial and frontier history, but I had been trained as a prehistorian investigating the origins of Native American plant domestication. Most of my research had taken place in the western Great Lakes and in the caves of Kentucky during my graduate days at Washington University in St Louis. As I grew up in the Saginaw Valley of Michigan, my parents took my older brother and younger sister and me frequently to Fort Michilimackinac and Fort Mackinac in northern Michigan. There, teams of archaeologists, principally from Michigan State University, conducted historical archaeological digs and interpreted frontier historical sites through the Mackinac Island State Park Commission. Little did my parents know they were influencing both my career and my future research interests—the reason why this book is dedicated to them.

Magee's book teased me. The book told me enough about the history and location of Fort Jefferson that I thought, just maybe, a long-term archaeological project, like that at Michilimackinac, could be centered about the fort and Clarksville civilian community—if they could be found. The few historical records and references I could find about Fort Jefferson in 1979 were of little help. As it turns out, Magee's book, which illustrated "Fort Jefferson," actually depicted Robert Todd's 1781 fort built in Lexington, Kentucky.[2] That was a disappointment, but that setback simply meant additional research would need to be conducted to find out what Fort Jefferson actually looked like, and where it might be located. As Sherlock Holmes said many times, "the chase was on."

If you're going to study any aspect of George Rogers Clark, you have to become familiar with three main sets of reference works: the Draper Manuscripts in the

---

[1] M. Juliette Magee, *Old Fort Jefferson*. Wickliffe, The Advance-Yeoman, 1975.
[2] Paul Chestnut, head archivist, Virginia State Library, letter to Ken Carstens, October 12, 1982.

Wisconsin Historical Society,[3] the writings of Clarence W. Alvord (Kaskaskia and Cahokia papers, principally),[4] and the many books and journal articles of James Alton James.[5] At Murray State University's Pogue Library (a special collections library focusing on regional history and genealogy) during the late 1970s and 1980s, you also needed to be acquainted with Dr. Keith Heim. Keith could find any reference you were looking for, even the obscure ones. Keith let me search the catacombs in Pogue Library. I came up with an out-of-the-way reference by E.G. Swem from the 1920s,[6] who had published an article in a Virginia education journal (not a history journal!). The reference gave information about a large collection of George Rogers Clark papers that had been found at the turn of the 20th century in the governor's basement in Virginia, and which had been taken to the Archives Division of the Virginia State Library, located next door to the governor's mansion in Richmond.[7] These were the lost vouchers of George Rogers Clark—the reason Virginia had never made good on her debt to George Rogers Clark. Virginia had lost Clark's vouchers, but now, 200 years later, had found them. George had kept the records as required of him as he said he had, and he had returned them to Virginia, but the records had become lost during the construction of the new capitol at Richmond, or as they say, "hidden in plain sight" as the Virginia capitol was moved from Williamsburg to Richmond. Poor George.

In 1982 I wrote a Committee on Institutional Science and Research (CISR) grant proposal at Murray State University to travel to Virginia and to examine the references, and, if possible, secure permission to duplicate the Fort Jefferson records and return a copy of them to Murray State University. Sure enough, more than 20,000 documents (I'm guessing at that total) were there, of which almost 4,000 documents detailed the history of Fort Jefferson. Indeed, of the 416 days Fort Jefferson existed (April 19, 1780- June 8, 1781), I recovered information for 387! An almost unbroken daily record of life at Fort Jefferson and Clarksville. An historian's dream!

There's the irony. For most frontier archaeological sites there are no, or at least, very few, historical records, but the site of the settlement has been found and it takes the archaeologist to unravel the "unwritten" history of the site. Me? I've got the historical records but no archaeological site. Well, at least not yet. But then, throughout the last 24 years of doing Fort Jefferson research, I've only spent 30 field days doing archaeology in the area, excavating 13 different test excavation units (usually 2-meter squares or smaller), conducting augering and coring studies, and conducting three magnetometer studies and a metal detecting survey. In all, we've been very efficient with the use of our time, but we have seen a very limited amount of the ground's content beneath its surface.

---

[3] *Draper Manuscripts*, Wisconsin Historical Society, Madison, Wisconsin.
[4] Clarence W. Alvord, *Collections of the Illinois State Historical Library. Virginia Series, Vol. 1, Cahokia Records, 1778-1790*. Illinois State Historical Library, Springfield, 1907; *Collections of the Illinois State Historical Library, Vol. 5, Kaskaskia Records, 1778-1790*. Illinois State Historical Society Library, Springfield, 1909.
[5] James Alton James, *George Rogers Clark Papers, 1778-1784*, 2 vols., AMS Press, 1972; *The Life of George Rogers Clark*, Greenwood Press, New York, 1969.
[6] E.G. Swem, Lost Vouchers of George Rogers Clarke [sic]. *Virginia Journal of Education*. Richmond, June, 1927.
[7] This was the same governor's mansion and state capitol that had been built between 1780-1781 when Clark's papers were sent back to "government in Virginia." The capitol had been moved from colonial Williamsburg to Richmond. There, Clark's papers had been misplaced for 200 years, having been taken there during the height of the construction.

I do know, based on the historical documentation, that the site of Fort Jefferson is *not* where the state historical markers have located it (on top of "Fort Jefferson hill"). I also know that the site is somewhere in the more elevated "secondary bottoms" and not the bottoms subject to *overflow* by the flooding of the Mississippi River or Mayfield Creek. And although I have not yet found contextual archaeological evidence for Fort Jefferson (buried artifacts in their original position), my student research teams have recovered four 18th century artifacts from the study area (two pieces of creamware, a late 18th-century ceramic for which we have inventories at Fort Jefferson), and two fragments of kaolin (tavern, ball clay) pipe bowls (also prevalent in the 18th century). We also have documented great numbers of 19th- and 20th-century disturbances to the 40-acre Fort Jefferson research area. The following paragraphs describe the surface collections, test excavations, augering projects, and remote sensing (magnetometer, conductivity and metal detecting) studies that we have conducted between 1980 and 2004.

The Archaeology

Between 1980 and 2004, several different but inter-related field strategies were employed to conduct the archaeological investigations in the Fort Jefferson research area. In the 24 years of our research time frame, the land cover of the project area has changed dramatically, as it did during the 200 years from the inception of the fort until the beginning of my research program.

When I first began investigating Fort Jefferson, the primary surface features of the 40-acre research area included a bluff area to the north, hill slopes, and two types of bottomlands: an elevated bottoms that connected to the hill slopes and a lower bottoms that occasionally flooded from overflow from both Mayfield Creek and the Mississippi River. In other words, there was an elevated area in the north, with drainage and a decrease of elevation toward the south. Separating the two types of bottoms were the twin rail beds of the Illinois Central and Mobile & Ohio railroads that traversed the area on a southeast-to-northwest angle. On the southern edge of the bluffs was a recent (post-1970) asphalt road that carried Westvaco Mill traffic from the plant site east of Kentucky Highway 51 to the Mississippi River. Both sets of bottoms (primary and secondary) had been used for agricultural purposes since the abandonment of Fort Jefferson. In addition, according to the Stovall Map (see Chapter 2, Figure 2.10, this volume), a rail turntable and associated outbuildings for the late-19th-century rail system were located to the southwest of the fort area. Lastly a grove of trees located just north of the rail line, and on the border between the primary and secondary bottoms half-way between Kentucky Highway 51 and the Mississippi River outlined a historic structure associated with what folk tradition (and the Chiles Terrell map of 1830) called "Webb's Old Hotel."

Today, the bluff area to the north remains wooded, although some dirt removal in support of local construction projects has taken place. The eastern portion of the research area is defined by Kentucky Highway 51 and a property fence belonging to what is now the MeadWestvaco Industrial Complex. The secondary bottoms east of Webb's hotel and north of the rail line beds is now a tree farm with 30-foot-tall hybrid sycamore trees. The secondary bottoms west of Webb's hotel and north of the rail lines is grass-covered. On the south side of the rail lines is grassland, and west of Webb's hotel south of the rail lines is an additional tree farm.

In 1980, when the project began, all of the areas were open farm lands (marked as research areas 1, 2, 3, and 4 on Figure 16.1). Areas 1 and 4 were open and were surface-collected (artifacts collected from the surface of the ground). Artifacts collected include a range of prehistoric (Late Woodland, post-A.D. 500, and Mississippian, A.D. 1000-1350) artifacts, including prehistoric ceramics (grog-tempered wares [plain and cord-marked exterior surfaces], prehistoric lithics (chipped stone unifacial and bifacial knives and scrapers), and non-utilized chipped stone artifacts made mostly from local chert material available in the loess-covered hilltops and as collovium and alluvial deposits within the study area. This very large (ca. 40-acre) prehistoric site complex was first reported by Drs. William Funkhouser and William S. Webb (their site No. 3),[8] but later reported by Dr. R. Berle Clay in 1963 as 15Ba10 as part of his master's thesis study.[9]

Also present throughout the research area were a series of 19th-century artifacts that reflected the post-Fort Jefferson occupation and use of the site, including white ware ceramics, earthenware ceramics, coal cinders, rail road spikes, bolts, and many other odds and ends associated with both the farming industry and the rail industry during the 19th-century.

Most importantly, near Webb's hotel, were two fragments of cream ware (a late-18th-century "uppe" class ceramic, for which we have inventories from the Fort Jefferson economic vouchers; 12 cream ware plates were issued to George Rogers Clark[10]), and two pipe bowl fragments of a white clay (kaolin) tavern pipe (Figure 16.2). Are these artifacts from Clark's Fort Jefferson, or are they curated artifacts associated with Webb's hotel? Webb's hotel probably dates from 1830. Most cream ware had been replaced by Pearl Ware and White Ware by 1830, unless of course, the cream ware had stayed in the Webb family for more than a generation or two. We will probably never know if these artifacts belonged to Fort Jefferson or Webb's hotel, because the artifacts were found on the surface of the ground, outside of archaeological context (the ground had been plowed and therefore the context was disturbed). In popular forensic parlance, the crime scene had been disturbed, which limits the conclusions that can be drawn by the detectives (archaeologists). Yet, it's nice to think that these artifacts are from Clark's Fort Jefferson, and not the (early) 19th-century Webb hotel.

One of the difficulties of doing the field archaeology for this project has been reconciling the historic maps (18th through 20th century), all of which use different scales or use no scale at all (1780 William Clark map, the 1795 William Clark map, 1830 Chiles Terrell map, Dupoyster's two maps, the B. Hardy Stovall map, or the U.S.G.S. 7.5 minute Wickliffe topographical map—see chapter 2 this volume). Characteristics or certain features on each of these maps have caused our research program to change gears

---

[8] William D. Funkhouser and William S. Webb, *Archaeological Survey of Kentucky. Reports in Archaeology and Anthropology, Vol. II.* Department of Anthropology, University of Kentucky, Lexington, 1932.
[9] R. Berle Clay, *Ceramic Complexes of of the Tennessee-Cumberland Region in Western Kentucky.* Master's Thesis, Department of Anthropology, University of Kentucky, Lexington, 1963.
[10] Unpublished George Rogers Clark Papers, Archives Division, Virginia State Library, Richmond, Box 48, John Dodge Quartermaster Book.

and thinking many times, to create new hypotheses, and to revise hypotheses as each was tested and either accepted or rejected.

For various reasons, not necessary to expand upon here, we have conducted archeological field investigations (including surface collecting and hand excavation) in each of the four study area subdivisions. Mechanical coring in the lower bottoms of areas 1 and 2 (Figure 16.1) revealed that the lower bottoms (bottoms subject to overflow) were, indeed, lower in A.D. 1000-1350. Prehistoric Mississippian-aged ceramics were pulled from a 12-foot-deep level of the lower bottoms, indicating that the A.D. 1000-1350 surface was much lower in elevation 1000 years ago. Were the 18th-century elevations much lower than present elevations also? When we conducted our first excavations during the summer and fall of 1980, we thought we had uncovered a part of a buried stockade wall. But upon controlled excavations of the buried feature by Dr. Kit Wesler, and geoarchaeological analysis by Dr. Julie Stein,[11] it was determined we had uncovered the top of a buried swamp. Our estimation, prior to the augering project on the north edge of areas 1 and 2 was that if Fort Jefferson existed south of the rail lines in 1780, it could be buried by as much as 20 feet of overburden—or more. But then, how does one reconcile the fact that J.C. Dupoyster found a spiked cannon eroding out of the north bank of Mayfield Creek in 1861?[12]. Was not the fort's spiked cannon left in the fort's well as stated in the unpublished Clark papers[13]? Or was there a second spiked cannon that history does not record, the one that Dupoyster found in 1861. After all, there were two cannon at Fort Jefferson, a four-pounder and a six-pounder (see chapter 7 this volume); if one was the Dupoyster cannon, then the other spiked cannon should still be in the fort's well. But where is the well?

Hand excavations were also conducted on the north side of the rail lines. Undisputed 19th–and 20th-century artifacts were recovered from those excavations, but no 18th-century artifacts were found, unless a charred plank found in test unit three on March 22, 1986 by Bill Potter was 18th-century in origin. Unfortunately, we could not date the charred plank and associated burned feature. Although cultural material superimposed on top of the plank was 19th-century, no historic cultural material was found beneath the plank. Hence, the *terminus ante quem* (date before which) could not be established, and only the *terminus poste quem (date after which)* date for the plank could be ascertained. For that matter, the burned piece of wood could be prehistoric and not even historic. That cultural feature remains a mystery. Future excavations around that feature are planned.

Likewise, in 1983 NASA flew a low-altitude reconnaissance over our Fort Jefferson study area as part of a remote sensing project we were conducting in western Kentucky through the Mid-American Remote Sensing Center at Murray State University.[14] The color infra-red imagery of that scene for the whole study area (reproduced here in black and white, Figure 16.3), clearly revealed portions of the prehistoric site 15Ba10, but also a rectangular anomaly in our research area 4 that has, in

---

[11] Julie K. Stein, Kenneth C. Carstens, and Kit W. Wesler, "Geoarchaeology and Historical Archaeology: An Example from Fort Jefferson, Kentucky." *Southeastern Archaeology*, 1983, 2(2):132-144.
[12] J.C. Dupoyster to Lyman C. Draper, letter and map, October 21, 1888, Draper Manuscripts, Wisconsin Historical Society, Madison, Wisconsin, 27J1.
[13] Unpublished Clark Papers, Box 20.
[14] Tom Kind, Neil Weber, Burl Naugle, and Ken Carstens, "Using Thematic Mapper Data for Finding Archaeological Sites in Western Kentucky." Grant conducted for NASA, Bay St. Louis, Mississippi, 1982.

its southwestern corner, a distinctive triangular feature that looks like an 18th-century bastion (see Figures 5.2 and 16.3). Is the anomaly in the aerial photograph the ground signature of Fort Jefferson? It looks both like the fort illustrated on the 1780 William Clark map (Figure 2.1) AND the bastion drawn on a tafia request penned at Fort Jefferson on March 4, 1781 (Figure 5.2).

Two independent magnetometer studies and a conductivity study were conducted on this infra-red anomaly; once at the direction of Dr. James Foradas,[15] then a graduate student of Dr. Ralph von Frese at Ohio State University (1985), and a second time (May-June 2004, magnetometer and conductivity studies) by Dr. R. Berle Clay[16] of Cultural Resources Analysts of Lexington, Kentucky. Limited archaeological test excavations in the areas of several of the magnetic "hits" from the 1985 study revealed only 19th- and 20th-century metallic objects (wire, railroad spikes, etc.) or concentrations of manganese within the soil (2004). Studies are now underway to coincide the 1985 and 2004 studies and redirect the archaeological excavations through deep testing with a backhoe or solid core augering. Both Foradas and Clay recommend deep testing. Only by removing the upper layers of the soil will we hope to locate the buried archaeological deposits associated with Clark's Fort Jefferson.

Lastly, an attempt was made in 1990 by one of my students, Buddy Dowdy, to locate the civilian community of Clarksville.[17] The civilian community, according to the 1780 William Clark map, lies east of Fort Jefferson, stretching from the bluffs in the north to the bottoms in the south. In total, more than 101 in lots (house lots) appear on the William Clark map. References to houses "in town," in "the southern part of town," "Donne's home," "Ford's home" and "blockhouse in the southern end of town," all indicate that civilian (and perhaps military) houses were built throughout that study area.[18] On the 1983 NASA color infra-red photograph of the study area, several areas of what appeared to be "midden" (human garbage or waste areas) were visible as "new growth" or "hot areas" visible in red on the color infra-red photo. It was determined that because the southern portion of the study area also had been planted in trees (with a 12-foot-square grid system), we could use the grid as a control for a metal-detecting survey. In total, more than 3.44 hectares, or 39,284 square meters were surveyed by our research teams, but again, no 18th-century metal was found, only that belonging to the 19th and 20th century, and a prehistoric Native American midden belonging to the Mississippian period, A.D. 1000-1350.

As a result of our limited archaeological studies, we can state that we know where the fort is *not* located, but that we still do not know where the fort *is* located. We know from our historical studies that the site is not located on top of Fort Jefferson hill. We have ample historical documentation, including maps, that place the fort in the bottoms and not on top of "Fort Jefferson hill," one mile to the north of the project where historical road markers indicate the fort's location. And, we have found four 18th-century

---

[15] James Foradas, "Magnetometer Study of a Suspected Site of Fort Jefferson, 1780-1781." Ohio State University, Columbus.
[16] R. Berle Clay, "Geophysical Survey of 400 Square Meters of the Fort Jefferson Archaeological Site, Ballard County, Kentucky." Cultural Resource Analysts, Inc., Report 04-106, Lexington, 2004.
[17] William P. Dowdy, *A Spatial Distribution Study in the Fort Jefferson Research Area, with an Assessment of the Utility of a Metal Detector as a Research Tool*. Senior Thesis, Murray State University Honors Diploma, Murray State University, Murray, Kentucky, 1992.
[18] Unpublished Clark Papers, Boxes 1-50.

artifacts from the *upper* bottoms that could be associated with the fort's occupation. In this area, too, we have the eyewitness 1795 accounts of William Clark (the younger brother), his map, and his description of the fort area, and we have the descriptions and maps drawn half to three-quarters of a century later by Dupoyster and Stovall documents preserved in the Draper Manuscripts. The archeological studies we have conducted all demonstrate that the research area is very complex geologically. There are both colluvial (hill slope) and alluvial (riverine) deposits within the study area, some of which amounts to very deep deposit. Our coring in one portion of the area demonstrated a portion of a late prehistoric site, 15Ba10, to be buried by as much as 12 feet of deposition. Could Fort Jefferson be as deeply buried? If so, this might explain why it has been so difficult to identify the fort's exact location. Only future, deeper, archaeological excavations in the area will reveal the precise position of this very significant archaeological site.

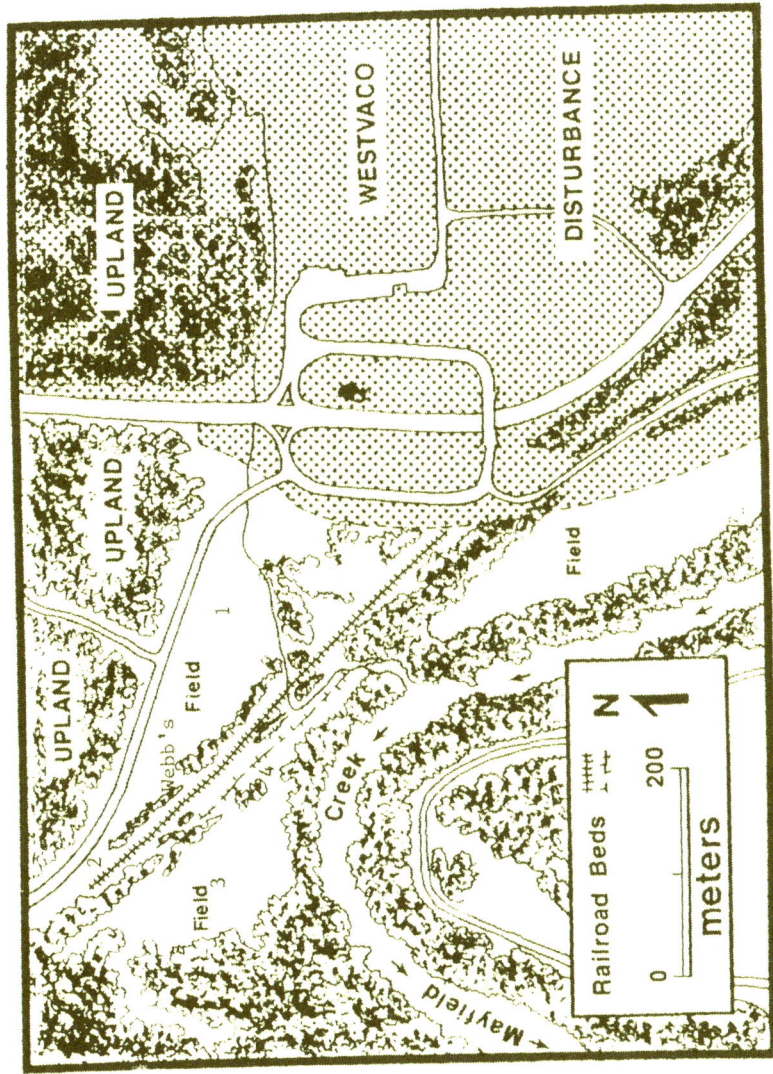

Figure 16.1: Research Regions in the Fort Jefferson Study Area (after Stein Carstens, and Wesler, 1983).

Figure 16.2: Photograph of Four Possible 18th-Century Artifacts from the Fort Jefferson Research Area.

Figure 16.3: NASA-flown Low Altitude Color Infra-red Photograph of Fort Jefferson Anomaly (arrow points to anomaly).

CHAPTER 17: FORTS, FAMINE, AND FAILURE?

One of the problems of writing a regional history is that it tends to stay very narrow in scope and in assessment of significance. Historians have unfortunately, for years, paid little attention to Clark's Fort Jefferson, most considering it an out-of-the-way frontier settlement that never amounted to anything. Yet, as has been demonstrated in this book, nothing could be further from the truth. In this chapter, I will place Fort Jefferson in a broader perspective to assess its significance and importance during the American Revolution.

On a very localized level of significance, Fort Jefferson was the first Anglo settlement in western Kentucky (then, extreme western Virginia). There, in what would become Ballard County, Kentucky, more than 550 persons lived, died, cleared and planted fields, and defended their territory. To them, it was a new start, a beginning that meant leaving the war in the East and wrestling a new land from Mother Nature and defending it from Native Americans who saw this settlement as another encroachment upon their land and their culture. This new enterprise, although daunting, was probably seen by the settlers as the lesser of two evils (war in East or fighting Indians); more importantly, the settlers saw it as a new beginning. With it came the prospect for obtaining land. In the East, the land had already been taken through centuries of bartering and buying by the landed gentry. Here, in the West, it was possible for a people with less-than-gentry-status to obtain land, providing they (and their families) could survive the term of their enlistment. It was a new beginning and a new start in life. The lure of land brought all social classes westward, but it probably gave the greatest hope to those who had little or nothing. To get the land, they had only to defend and make their mark on a piece of paper. For these reasons, Fort Jefferson and Clarksville are important to local history. These settlements represent the base from which all future settlement and development in western Kentucky would take place. Although the area would not be free and legally available for white settlement until after Jackson's Purchase in 1818, the roots of Anglo settlement began in western Kentucky in 1780-1781 with Fort Jeffreson. These hardy pioneers blazed the trail for all future settlement. Fort Jefferson, therefore, represents the foundation from which future development, land ownership, land speculation, and trade would take place, even though it was never garrisoned after 1781.

Settled in April, 1780, the fort and community were constructed by June of 1780, and shortly thereafter contested by the Chickasaw and the British. Military actions took place at the fort, and several significant campaigns (Battle of St. Louis, Shawnee expedition) were supported by the troops from Fort Jefferson. But it was the battles at Fort Jefferson that spelled its doom, along with its distance from supplies and government. Fort Jefferson was, "beyond the frontier." Fort commandant Captain Robert George referred to Fort Jefferson as, "this remote hole."[1]

The crippling attacks by the Chickasaw in the summer of 1780 killed very few soldiers and settlers. But their assaults harassed the inhabitants of the post and, more importantly, took away their source of winter food when the Chickasaw burned the newly grown corn crop and killed the settlers' livestock. With the Indians continually lurking in

---

[1] Robert George letter to Oliver Pollock, January 1, 1781, Unpublished Clark Papers, Archives Division, Virginia State Library, Richmond. Published in James Alton James's *George Rogers Clark Papers, 1771-1781*, 496-497. AMS Press, 1972.

the region, it was never safe to venture outside the confines of Clarksville to hunt, or so the settlers felt. Hunting for the garrison was accomplished by 65 friendly Kaskaskia Indians. Occasionally, militia, led by Major Silas Harlan, would venture outside the immediate area and hunt for buffalo and venison, but all too often, the settlers and garrison went without rather than put their lives in jeopardy trying to fend for themselves. As a result, stories survive, greatly blown out of proportion, about the heroics of the settlers, such as the story of Nancy Ann Hunter, who actually retrieved a straying calf under a flag of truce—but subsequent historians had swimming the Mississippi and dragging back a buffalo to save the starving fort!

In the correspondence from the fort (chapter 4, this volume), it is clear that Jefferson warned Clark that Fort Jefferson must be self-sufficient or it would perish. To that end, attracting civilians to the community would promote gardening and farming activities that would see the fort through the scarce months when supplies from government would be few in number. Indeed, the supplies that arrived (munitions, dry goods, and liquor), were used as barter with other posts (Kaskaskia, Cahokia, and Vincennes) to secure food supplies for the starving and sickly population at Fort Jefferson, because Virginia credit was no longer accepted in the Illinois country. But food that arrived from Louisville and Fort Pitt was ill-cured and often ruined before arrival. It was, therefore, of little consequence. Yet, wild food abounded in the fields, hilltops, and bottoms around the fort but few would venture to retrieve it for fear of Indian reprisals and ambush. As stated earlier, it took Lt. Col. John Montgomery's arrival from Fort Clark in Kaskaskia with 65 Kaskaskia Indians to come to the (food) relief of Fort Jefferson.

Sickness was another difficulty. An examination of the muster rolls from Fort Jefferson and Clarksville community reveals as many persons "dying" as from being "killed." What was the main killer at Fort Jefferson? It was the ague: malaria. As Captain Robert George commented in October of 1780, "numbers [were] daily dying." The bottomland on which Fort Jefferson was built was, indeed, the "sickly bottoms."

The winter months passed without incident. In December and January, supplies from New Orleans arrived; unfortunately, none of the supplies were food, but they could be used to barter for food from other Illinois (Kaskaskia) and Wabash (Vincennes) country posts. But speculation by the quartermaster corps (principally John Dodge), led some to suggest that the fort's command had turned highway robbers, motivated only by personal reward and self-interests. Even Captain Philip Barbour, who, having brought a load of supplies from New Orleans and realizing the deplorable state of Fort Jefferson, inflated the price of the cargo from $25,000 to $230,000![2] Moreover, he demanded payment in hard specie and not worthless Virginia paper currency, which had inflated to more than 1000%. Knowing that Barbour's cargo brought with it the possibility of barter for food, Captain George and his officers concurred that Barbour's outrageous price should be paid. Captain George would subsequently be called to task for this decision. But what was he to do, turn away the cargo? I think not.

Part of Barbour's cargo was liquid refreshment—rum! Between January and March, 1781, exceedingly large amounts of liquor were consumed by the citizenry of Fort Jefferson, especially during March in observance of St. Patrick's day (for the entire month!). By no coincidence, the majority of surviving court records at Fort Jefferson

---

[2] *Ibid.*

stem from this month; patience had run short, accusations emerged everywhere, and multiple court of inquiry took place. Were these courts simply the outward frustration of the failure of the settlement by the settlement's inhabitants and officers? It would appear so. Many of the accusations were found to be without merit, a venting of steam, anger, and frustration. But the damage was done. There was no more camaraderie. The fort and the inhabitants no longer worked in unison or as a team. There was no more unity. Fort Jefferson was coming apart at the seams throughout its command structure. First, there was the stress of settling an area beyond the frontier; logistically Fort Jefferson was a nightmare by any stretch of the imagination. It was "beyond" the frontier, a frontier that stopped in Louisville and at Harrodsburg. Secondly, there were the Indian depredations throughout the summer of 1780. By fall, malaria had taken its toll. At least 50 persons from the fort's population (of which there is a record, the number is probably greater than that) lay buried in the fort's cemetery, a combination of malaria and killings by Indians. Obviously, Fort Jefferson was becoming a difficult place to sustain and maintain.

By the end of May, 1781, after a failed attempt to take the command away from Captain Robert George by Lt. Col. Montgomery (there apparently was no love lost between George—a distant relative of George Rogers Clark--and Clark's right-hand man on the frontier, John Montgomery), Montgomery took the command and called for the evacuation of Fort Jefferson. The records are unclear what words or actions transpired between Captain George and Lt. Col. Montgomery in May of 1780 when Montgomery returned from a trip to New Orleans, but Montgomery prevailed. On very short notice the few settlers who were left, along with the Fort Jefferson garrison, evacuated Fort Jefferson on June 8, 1781, heading back to Louisville to newly constructed Fort Nelson, a sister fortification of Fort Jefferson.

Or, was the evacuation of Fort Jefferson a planned action? Planned by George Rogers Clark who was, in the spring of 1781, still detailing his plans to attack the British at Fort Detroit, having secured permission to do so from George Washington (see letters in chapter 4)? Or, was the evacuation of Fort Jefferson the result of both its internal failures and Clark's plan to regroup in Louisville prior to an assault on Detroit? Again, we may never know.

On a larger scale of significance, Fort Jefferson was the only Kentucky fort and settlement constructed expressly at the command of the Virginia government. All other sites, e.g., Boonesborough or Harrodsburg, were the acts of land companies or private individuals. Fort Jefferson and Clarksville were proposed to, and authorized by, Patrick Henry, then Thomas Jefferson. Fort Jefferson was, therefore, an attempt by Virginia to secure and hold its westernmost boundary. In the 18th century, having only a token representation in an area held that ground on behalf of its government. Fort Jefferson was no exception. It held, albeit briefly, Virginia's westernmost property between 1780 and 1781.

On a more theoretical level, the presence of Fort Jefferson supposedly kept the British from encroaching upon Virginian territory, although the British-led assault against Fort Jefferson occurred at the end of August 1780 but was thwarted. Did the presence of Fort Jefferson keep arms and munitions from traveling from the British north to the Chickasaws in the south? Not during the summer of 1780. However, it is interesting to note that there were no Chickasaw attacks on Fort Jefferson from January until June of 1781--the very period during which Fort Jefferson was at its weakest. One must ask why? Was it because the three assaults on Fort Jefferson during the summer of 1780 proved unsuccessful from the standpoint of not breeching the fort's stockade, yet successful in destroying the fort's source of winter sustenance, not to mention the psychological effect the three battles with the Chickasaw had on the fort's population (half the civilians, 20 families' worth, deserted the fort after the third and final Chickasaw attack)?

On an international level the significance of Fort Jefferson becomes more speculative. By the end of 1780, Clark controlled Fort Jefferson, Fort Clark in Kaskaskia, Cahokia across from Spanish-held Pancore (St. Louis), Fort Patrick Henry in Vincennes, Fort Nelson in Louisville, and the remaining Kentucky forts and settlements. This was in essence, the expanse of the Illinois country and the Kentucky settlements, of which Fort Jefferson was a part. Moreover, Clark's control of that country was strong enough to permit offensive forays into the Ohio country to squelch the British-supported Shawnee Indians. Much has been said about Clark's "conquest" of the Illinois country. Had he really conquered it, or had he simply wrested its political and military control from the British to the Americans?

The national/international significance of Fort Jefferson lies in the fact that it was a part of Clark's (Henry's, then Jefferson's) plan to wrest control of the area northwest of the Ohio from the British. And Clark *did* do that. Therefore, placing Fort Jefferson in the broadest of all perspectives, Clark is credited with "conquering" the Old Northwest (Michigan, Ohio, Indiana, Illinois, Wisconsin, and parts of Minnesota). But did he? Of course he didn't. But that's not the point. It's a matter of who was in control of the area that's important. Both sides of the argument have been made. Clark was in control (having "conquered" the [southern] Illinois and Indiana country). He did not control Ohio (the Shawnee and Delaware were never displaced from their lands in Ohio during the American Revolution). Nor did Clark control Michigan, although he did psych-out the British to move their wooden fort from Michilimackinac to Mackinac Island, where they built a stone fort in anticipation of Clark's arrival. But Clark never attacked Detroit, the focus of British occupation in the Great Lakes. Nor did Clark conquer Wisconsin, or even the slightest portion of Minnesota. What can be said is that Clark captured the communities of Kaskaskia, Cahokia, and Vincennes, and established forts Jefferson and Nelson, all focusing on the southern one-third of the Illinois country. And, more importantly, he retained physical control over Fort Nelson in Louisville. But, that was more control than what the British out of Detroit exerted. And, Benjamin Franklin argued during the Paris peace talks that Virginia (the United States) *was* in control of the lands northwest of the Ohio and that Clark should be given credit for "conquering" that area--meaning Fort Jefferson *did* play a strategic role from 1780-1781. When Dwight Smith weighed the two sides of the coin in 1976, he found himself in a gray area of history, with no clear-cut decision as to Clark's final contribution (and therefore the contributing of Fort Jefferson is left in limbo, too). As Smith says, "on the one extreme it is asserted that 'British power in the West was broken,' on the other hand it is said that "the war ended without a rebel having set foot in the greater part of the territory north of the Ohio." Whether reading James,[3] English,[4] Thwaites,[5] Alvord,[6] Carey[7] or Van Tyne,[8]

---

[3] James Alton James, "To What Extent Was George Rogers Clark in Military Control of the Northwest at the Close of the American Revolution?" *Annual Report of the American Historical Association for the Year 1917* (Washington: [U.S. Government Printing Office], 1920: 315-329.

the final decision is inconclusive. Clark was in "control" (to use the word loosely) of the territory north of the Ohio, but had he "conquered" it? Whatever the case, "the Old Northwest as secured to the United States in the preliminary articles of peace were signed in Paris, November 30, 1782. Ratifications were exchanged, and the treaty became official on April 15, 1783. The definitive treaty was proclaimed January 14, 1784."[9]

So was Fort Jefferson a failure? No, it was not. It was short-lived, and the logistics for the outpost were poorly planned, but for the 416 days the post was occupied, it proved to be Clark's hub of action, economic redistribution center, and staging area for several key military campaigns. To say that Fort Jefferson was a failure is to acknowledge that little information was known about the garrison and civilian community prior to 1983. Today, with the discovery of 387 days worth of information about this Virginia outpost, a clearer understanding of this site, and its significance, has come to light. Fort Jefferson played a truly important role during the American Revolution for Virginia, for Kentucky, and for the young United States. This significant role has been interpreted by some as having had both national and international consequences. Fort Jefferson logistics left much to be desired, and there was famine and sickness at Fort Jefferson, but Fort Jefferson was far from being a failure. It, along with forts Clark, Bowman, Patrick Henry, Harrodsburg, Nelson, etc., gained an important foothold in lands controlled by the British and British-Indian allies. In the end, the spoils went to the victors. Whether or not Clark's action can be viewed as a "conquest," he *was* "in control" of the outposts northwest of the Ohio at the time of Yorktown. For that, he and his followers have been honored by the great rotunda in Vincennes as a mute testimonial to their bravery, and indeed, their audacity, for taking the fight *to* the British and establishing a foothold, no matter how tenuous, in the Old Northwest.

---

[4] William Hayden English, *Conquest of the Country Northwest of the River Ohio 1778-1783 and Life of General George Rogers Clark.* Indianapolis: Bowen-Merrill Company, 1897, II, 761-66.
[5] Reuben gold Thwaites, *How George Rogers Clark Won the Northwest and Other Essays in Western History*, 6th ed., Chicago: A.C. McClurg & Company, 1931: 71-72.
[6] Clarence W. Alvord, "Virginia and the West: An Interpretation." *Mississippi Valley Historical Review, III* 1916-17:34.
[7] Lewis J. Carey (trans. and ed.), "Franklin Is Informed of Clark's Activities in the Old Northwest," *Mississippi Valley Historical Review, XXI,* 1934-35:375-78.
[8] Claude Halstead Van Tyne, *The American Revolution 1776-1783* (New York: Harper & Brothers, 1905), 284.
[9] Dwight L. Smith, The Old Northwest and the Peace Negotiations," *The French , The Indians, and George Rogers Clark in the Illinois Country: Proceedings of an Indiana American Revolution Bicentennial Symposium*, Indianapolis: Indiana Historical Society, 1977: 95, 102.

CHAPTER 18: A FORT JEFFERSON RESEARCH BIBLIOGRAPHY

The following bibliography represents a collection of Fort Jefferson-related materials I have collected or have placed in my Fort Jefferson research library over the last 24 years. It consists of publications about the late-18th-century frontier in the Midwest and upper Midsouth. These publications either discuss information specifically about Fort Jefferson or address contemporary settlements and military installations with whom Fort Jefferson may have interacted. Unfortunately, a bibliographic listing such as this will always be incomplete and out of date by the time it is published, but the bibliography is meant to be a beginning point for persons doing research into Fort Jefferson history or frontier history in the Midwest and upper Midsouth.

Manuscript Materials:

Archivo General de las Indies. Mss., Seville, Spain (transcripts in Ayer Collection, Newberry Library), 1777-1783.
Collections of the Pioneer Society of the State of Michigan Together with Reports of County Pioneer Societies, Michigan Pioneer Collections, Second Edition, 1885-1891.
Croghan Family Papers. Library of Congress.
DeLeyba Papers. Missouri Historical Society, St. Louis.
Draper Manuscripts. Wisconsin State Historical Library.
Durrett Collection. University of Chicago, Chicago.
George Rogers Clark Collection. Missouri Historical Society, St. Louis.
Haldimand Manuscripts. British Museum.
Haldimand Manuscripts (copies). Canadian Archives.
Illinois Papers. Virginia State Library: Archives Division.
Innes Papers. Letters Relating to Kentucky Discontent, 1789-91, National Archives.
James Piggott Papers. Illinois State Historical Library.
Kaskaskia Manuscripts. Circuit Clerk's office, County of Randolph, Illinois.
Manuscripts in Archivo General de Indias. Seville, Spain.
Morgan, George. Letter Books, Carnegie Institute, Pittsburgh.
"Pollock Papers." Papers of the Continental Congress, Library of Congress, Washington D.C.
Revolutionary War Records. National Archives.
Temple Bodley Papers. Filson Club, Louisville.
Unpublished G.R. Clark Papers. Locust Grove Historic Home, Louisville, Kentucky.
Unpublished (microfilm) G.R. Clark Papers, Virginia State Library, Archives Division.
Washington Manuscripts, Library of Congress, Washington, D.C.
William Clark Papers, Missouri Historical Society, St. Louis.

Published Books and Article Sources:

Abernethy, Thomas Perkins. *Western Lands and the American Revolution.* N.Y.: Russell and Russell, 1959.

Alvord, C. W. "Eighteenth Century French Records in the Archives of Illinois," *American Historical Association, Annual Report, 1905.* Washington, 1906.

--- "Cahokia Records," *Illinois State Historical Library Collections* II., Virginia Series, II. Springfield, 1909.

--- "Kaskaskia Records." *Illinois State Historical Library, Colections*, Virginia Series, II. Springfield, 1909.

--- "Virginia and the West; An Interpretation." *Mississippi Valley Historical Review* 3 (1916): 19-38.

--- *The American West: The Illinois Country: 1673-1818.* Chicago: McClurg and Co., 1922.

Anonymous. "A Suit Against George Rogers Clark." *Indiana Magazine of History* 4 (1908).

Anonymous. "Dedication of George Rogers Clark Memorial." *Register of Kentucky History* 33 (1935): 52-69.

Armour, David A., and Weider, Keith R. *At the Crossroads: Michilimackinac During The American Revolution.* Mackinac Island State Park Commission, 1978.

Adams, Evelyn Crady. "Dr. Richard Ferguson (1769-1853), Pioneer Surgeon of Louisville, Attended General George Rogers Clark." *Filson Club History Quarterly* 36 (1962): 177-83.

Bakeless, John. *Background To Glory; The Life of George Rogers Clark.* Philadelphia: Lippincott, 1957.

Baldwin, Carl R. *Captains of the Wilderness.* Belleville, Il: Tiger Rose Publishing Company, 1986.

Bannon, John Francis. "The Spaniards and the Illinois Country, 1762-1800." *Journal of the Illinois State Historical Society* 69 (1976): 110-18.

Barnhart, John D. "A New Evaluation of Henry Hamilton and George Rogers Clark." *Mississippi Valley Historical Review* 37 (1951): 643-52.

--- "The Blue Licks Monument." *The Register of Kentucky State Historical Society* 26 (1928): 289-310.

Barnhart, John D., ed. *Henry Hamilton and George Rogers Clark in the American Revolution with the Unpublished Journal of Lieutenant Governor Henry Hamilton.* Crawfordsville, Indiana: R.E. Banta, 1951.

Bearss, Edwin C. "George Rogers Clark: Vincennes Sites Study and Evaluation." Washington D.C.: National Parks Services, 1967.

Beers, Henry Putney. *The French and British in the Old Northwest: A Bibliographic Guide to Archive and Manuscript Sources.* Detroit: Wayne State U P, 1964.

Belting, N.M. *Kaskaskia Under the French Regime.* Springfield: U of Illinois P, 1948.

Bense, Judith A., editor. *Archaeology of Colonial Pensacola.* University Press of Florida, Gainesville, 1999.

Benton, E.J. *The Wabash Trade Route in the Development of the Old Northwest.* Baltimore: John Hopkins U P, 21 (1903).

Blanco, Richard L. ed. *The American Revolution, 1775-1783: An Encyclopedia.* New York: Garland Publishing Inc, 1993.

Boatner, Mark Mayo III. *Encyclopedia of the American Revolution.* New York: David McKay Company, Inc, 1966.

Bodley, Temple. *George Rogers Clark: His Life and Public Service.* Boston: Houghton Mifflin Company, 1926.

---. "Clark's 'Mason Letter' and 'Memoir'." *Filson Club Historical Quarterly* 3 (1929): 163-70.

---. "George Rogers Clark: A Toast." *Filson Club History Quarterly* 26 (1952): 109-11.

Boggess, A.C. *The Settlement of Illinois, 1778-1830.* Chicago Historical Society Collections 5. Chicago, 1908.

Boyd, C.E. "The County of Illinois." *American Historical Review* 4 (1899): 623-35.

Boyd, Julian P., ed. *The Papers of Thomas Jefferson.* Princeton: Princeton U P, 1950-1951.

Brennan, George A. "De Linctot, Guardian of the Frontier." *Journal of the Illinois State Historical Society* 10 (1917): 323-66.

Bridwell, Margaret M. "George Rogers Clark Park." *Filson Club History Quarterly* 23 (1949): 140-45.

Brookes-Smith, compiler. *Master Index to Virginia Surveys and Grants, 1774-1791.* Frankfort, 1976.

Brown, J.M. *The Political Beginnings of Kentucky.* Louisville: Filson Club Publications 6, 1889.

Butler, Mann. *A History of the Commonwealth of Kentucky.* Louisville: Wilcox, Dickerman, 1834.

Butterfield, C.W. *History of George Rogers Clark Conquest of the Illinois and the Wabash Towns 1778 and 1779.* 1904. Boston: Gregg Press, 1972.

Calendar of Virginia State Papers. 11 vols. Richmond, 1875-1893.

Calloway, Colin. *The American Revolution in Indian Country.* Cambridge: Cambridge U P, 1995.

Cannon, J.T. "Index to Military Certificates." *The Register of the Kentucky State Historical Society* 22 (1924): 2-20.

Cannon, Mrs. J.T. "The Kentucky Active Militia -1786." *The Register of the Kentucky State Historical Society* 32 (1934): 224-73.

Carstens, K.C. "The Structural Composition of George Rogers Clark's Fort Jefferson, 1780-1781: An Assessment of the Historical Records." Unpublished manuscript, n.d.

1984 "In Search of Fort Jefferson: Past, Present and Future Studies." Symposium on Ohio Valley Urban and Historical Archaeology 2, 1984.

--- "At the Confluence of the Ohio and Mississippi Rivers: Virginia's Claim to the West." Paper presented to the 2nd Annual Ohio Valley Historical Conference, Murray State U, 1986.

--- "In Pursuit of Ft Jefferson: A Summary of Investigations, 1980-1986." Paper presented to the 43rd Southeast Archaeological Conference. Nashville, 1986

--- "British Allies and American Enemies: The Chickasaws of the Mississippi River Valley." Paper presented at the 5th Ohio Valley Historical Conference: Murray, KY, 1989.

--- "George Rogers Clark's Fort Jefferson: An Historical. Overview with Archaeological Implications." Paper presented to the 5th annual Illinois Historical. Archaeological Conference. Giant City State Park, 1990

--- "Issues at Fort Jefferson, 1780-1781: The Quartermaster Books of John Dodge and Martin Carney." *Selected Papers George Rogers Clark Conference.* Robert J. Holden. Ed. Vincennes, 1990.

--- "The Fort Jefferson Research Project: The First Decade of Work Closes. Paper. Southeastern Archaeology Conference. Mobile, 1990.

--- "'Praise the Lord and Pass the Ammunition': Munitions Supplies at George Rogers Clark's Fort Jefferson, 1780-1781." *Selected Papers George Rogers Clark Conference*, Robert J. Holden, ed. Vincennes, 1991.

--- "Unraveling the Mysteries of Fort Jefferson: An Interdisciplinary Study of George Rogers Clark's 1780-1781 Fort at the Mouth of the Ohio River." Paper. Alpha Chi Honor Society Distinguished Lecture. Murray State University. Mar., 1991.

--- "Current Field Strategies and Hypothesis Testing: The Fort Jefferson Project Continues." *Studies in Kentucky Archaeology*. Charles D. Hockensmith ed. The Kentucky Heritage Council, Frankfort, 1991.

--- "The 1780 William Clark Map of Fort Jefferson." *Filson Club History Quarterly* 67 (1993): 23-43.

Carstens, K. C., ed. "Life on the 18th Century Frontier: The Narrative of Anne Macmeans Jamison." Paper. George Rogers Clark Conference. Vincennes University, Vincennes, Indiana. 1993.

--- "Fort Jefferson, 1780-1781: A Summary of Its History." *Selected Papers from the 1991 and 1992 George Rogers Clark Trans-Appalachian Frontier History Conferences* (hereafter, *Selected Papers GRC Conf.*), Robert J. Holden ed. Vincennes, 1994.

--- "The Fort Jefferson Research Project: A Summary of the Program, 1980-1995. Paper. Annual Meeting of the Central States Anthropology Society. Indianapolis, 1995.

--- "The Role of Women in Kentucky's Western Colonial Frontier." *Historical Archaeology in Kentucky*. K. McBride, W. McBride, and D. Pollack, Eds. Kentucky Heritage Council, Frankfort, 1995.

--- "George Rogers Clark's Forts Jefferson, 1780-1781." *Filson Club History Quarterly* 71 (1997): 259-84.

--- "What's for Dinner? Late 18th Century Subsistence Strategies at George Rogers Clark's Fort Jefferson and the Civilian Community of Clarksville, 1780-1781." *Current Archaeology Kentucky*. Charles Hockensmith and Kenneth C. Carstens. Eds. The Kentucky Heritage Council, Frankfort, 2001.

. Carstens, K. C., ed. *The Personnel of George Roger's Clark's Fort Jefferson and the Civilian Community of Clarksville [KY], 1780-1781*. Bowie, Md.: Heritage Books Inc., 1999.

--- ed., *The Calendar and Quartermaster Books of General George Rogers Clark's Fort Jefferson, 1780-1781*. Bowie, MD: Heritage Books, Inc., 2000.

Carstens, K. C. and Nancy Son Carstens. "George Rogers Clark's Fort Jefferson: An Historical Overview with Archaeological and Ethnic Considerations and Implications." *Current Archaeology*. Charles Hockensmith and Kenneth C. Carstens, eds. The Kentucky Heritage Council. Frankfort, 2001.

Carstens, K. C. and Nancy Son Carstens, eds. *The Life of George Rogers Clark, 1752-1818: Triumphs and Tragedies*. Greenwood Publishing Group, Westport, CT. 2004.

Carstens, K. C., P. Bomba, and K. Brown. "A Cartographic GIS for the Fort Jefferson Archaeological Research Area." Ms. On File Mid-America Remote Sensing Center, Murray State University. Murray, KY. 1993.

Carstens, K.C. and W. P. Dowdy. "Searching for Fort Jefferson's Civilian Community with a Metal Detector." Paper. 1992 Kentucky Heritage Council Annual Archaeological Meetings, Murray, Ky. 1991.

Caughey, John W. "Willing's Expedition down the Mississippi." *The Louisiana History Quarterly* 15 (1932).

Chinn, G.M. *Kentucky: Settlement and Statehood, 1750-1800*. Frankfort: Kentucky Historical Society, 1975.

Clark, T.D. *A History of Kentucky*. Lexington: John Bradford Press, 1960.

--- "Reuben T. Durrett and His Kentuckiana Interest and Collection." *Filson Club History Quarterly* 56 (1982): 353-78.

Coker, William S. and Robert R. Rea, Eds. "Anglo-Spanish Confrontation on the Gulf Coast during the American Revolution." Gulf Coast History and Humanities Conference. 9, 1982.

Coleman, Christopher B. "Kaskaskia and Vincennes: An Anniversary Enterprise." Transactions. *Illinois State Historical Society* 32 (1925).

Coleman, J. W., Jr. *The British Invasion of Kentucky*. Lexington, KY: Winburn Press, 1951.

Collet, Oscar W. "Notes and Criticisms: DeLeyba and Clark." *Magazine of Western History* 4 (1951).

Collins, Lewis and Richard H. *History of Kentucky*. 2 vols. Covington, KY: Collins and Co., 1874.

Collins, Richard H. and W.R. Jillson. "The Siege of Bryan's Station." *The Register of the Kentucky State Historical Society* 36 (1938): 15-25.

Conkwright, Bessie Taul. "Captain Leonard Helm." *Indiana History Bulletin* 10 (1933).

Cook, Minnie G. "Virginia Currency in the Illinois Country." *Transactions, Indiana Historical Society*. (1912).

Corr, Paul B. "George Rogers Clark: Conquest of the Northwest–Fort Gage Sesqui-Centennial Observance." *Journal of the Illinois State Historical Society* 21 (1928): 260-72.

Corr, Paul B. "George Rogers Clark: Sesqui-Centennial Observances–Trail from Fort Massac to Kaskaskia." *Journal of the Illinois State Historical Society* 21 (1928).

Cotterill, R.S. *History of Pioneer Kentucky*. Cincinnati: Johnson and Hardin, 1917.

Craig, O.J. *Ouiatanon*. Indianapolis: Indiana Historical Society Publications, 1895.

--- *The Olden Time*. (2 vols.) Cincinnati: J.W. Cook, 1876.

Cummins, Light T. "Olive Pollack and George Rogers Clark Service of Supply: A Case Study in Financial Disaster." *Selected Papers of George Rogers Clark Conference*. Robert J. Holden, ed. Vincennes, 1988.

Dann, John C., ed. *The Revolution Remembered: Eyewitness Accounts of the War for Independence*. Chicago: U of Chicago P, 1977.

Davidson, A. and B. Stuve. *A Complete History of Illinois*. Springfield: Illinois Journal Co., 1874.

Davis, Burke. "George Rogers Clark." Williamsburg Galaxy. Colonial Williamsburg, Inc., 1968.

Dean, Lawri C. and M. K. Brown. *The Kaskaskia Ms. 1714-1816. A Collection of Civil War Documents in Colon. Ill.* Randolph County, IL, microfilm, 1981.

Derleth, August. *Vincennes: Portal to the West*. New York: Prentice-Hall, 1968.

Dillon, J.B.A. *History of Indiana*. Indianapolis, Iowa: W. Sheets and Co., 1859.

Dodderidge, Joseph. *Notes on the Settlement and Indian Wars of Virginia and Pennsylvania*. 1824. New York: Garland Pub., 1977.

Dodge, John. *Narrative of Mr. John Dodge during His Captivity at Detroit. Reproduced in Facsimile from the 2nd edition of 1780*. Cedar Rapids: The Torch Press, 1909.

Donnelly, Joseph P. *Pierre Gibault, Missionary, 1737-1802*. Chicago: Loyola U P, 1971.

Douglas, W. B. "Jean Gabriel Cerre, A Sketch." *Transactions, Illinois State Historical Society*, 1905. Springfield, 1906.

Dowdy, William P. "A Spatial Distribution Study in the Fort Jefferson Research Area with an Assessment of the Utility of a Metal Detector as a Research Tool." Honors Paper, Department of Geosciences. Murray State University. Murray, KY, 1992.

Dunnigan, Brian Leigh. *The Post of Mackinac, 1779-1812*. Master's Thesis, State University of New York College at Oneonta at its Cooperstown Graduate Program, New York, 1979.

Eckberg, Carl. *French Roots in the Illinois Country: the Mississippi Frontier in Colonial Times*. Urbana, IL: U Illinois P, 1998.

Eckenrode, H.J. *Colonial Soldiers of Virginia*. Richmond: Richmond D. Bottom, 1917.

English, Sara J. "George Rogers Clark." *Journal of the Illinois State Historical Society* 20 (1928): 523-46.

English, W.H. *Conquest of the Country Northwest of the River Ohio and Life of George Rogers Clark*. 2 vols. Indianapolis: Bowen-Merrill Co., 1896.

Evans, Emory G. "The Colonial View of the West." *Journal of the Illinois State Historical Society* 69 (1976): 84-90.

Every, Dale Van. *A Company of Heroes: The American Frontier, 1775-1783*. New York: William Morrow and Co., 1962.

--- *Forth to the Wilderness: The First American Frontier, 1754-1774*. New York: William Morrow and Co., 1961.

Farrell, D.R. "Mobilizing for War: Logistics and the British War Effort in the West, 1775-1783." *Selected Papers George Rogers Clark Conference*. Robert J. Holden, ed. Vincennes, 1985.

Ferling, John, ed. *The World Turned Upside Down: The American Victory in the War of Independence*. New York: Greenwood Press, 1988.

Filson Club History Quarterly. "Thruston Memorial Number." *Filson Club History Quarterly* 21 (1947): 101-69.

Foradas, James G., P.S. Curran and K.C. Carstens. "Archaeomagnetic Reconstruction of a Suspected Site of Fort Jefferson, A Revolutionary War Fort in Western Kentucky." Report. Ohio State University and Murray State University, 1990.

Ford, Paul L., ed. *The Writings of Thomas Jefferson*. 10 vols. New York: G.P. Putnam's Sons, 1892-1899.

Fraser, Kathryn M. "Fort Jefferson: George Rogers Clark's Fort at the Mouth of the Ohio River, 1780-1781." *The Register of the Kentucky State Historical Society* 81 (1983): 1-24.

Friend, Craig Thompson, ed. *The Buzzel About Kentucky*. Lexington, KY: U P of Kentucky, 1999.

Frost, Linda. "George Rogers Clark." *The Register of the Kentucky State Historical Society* 61 (1963): 339-43.

Grange, Roger T. *Excavations at Fort Mackinac: 1980-1982: The Provision Storehouse. Archeological Completion report Series, No. 12*. Mackinac Island State Park Commission, Mackinac Island, Michigan, 1987.

Green, James F. *Major Silas Harlan: His Life and Times*. Cleveland: Gates Legal Publishing Co., 1964.

Gums, B.L., ed. "Archaeology at the French Colonial Cahokia." *Studies in Illinois Archaeology* 3 Springfield, 1988.

Halchin, Jill Y. *Excavations at Fort Michilimackinac, 1983-1985: House C of the Southeast Row House, The Solomon-Levy-Parant House. Archaeological Completion Report Series, No. 11*. Mackinac Island State Park Commission, Mackinac Island, Michigan, 1985.

Hamilton, T. M., and K.O. Emery. *Eighteenth-Century Gunflints from Fort Michilimackinac and other Colonial Sites*. Archaeological completion Report Series, No. 13, Mackinac Island State Park Commission, Mackinac Island, Michigan, 1988.

Hammon, Neal O. *Early Kentucky Land Records, 1773-1780*. Louisville: The Filson Club, 1992.

--- "Early Louisville and the Beargrass Stations." *Filson Club History Quarterly* 52 (1978): 147-65.

--- "Pioneers in Kentucky, 1773-1775." *Filson Club History Quarterly* 55 (1981): 268-83.

--- "Research Note: Did George Rogers Clark Close the Kentucky County Land Office?" *Filson Club History Quarterly* 70 (1996): 317-325.

Hammon, Neal O. and James Russell Harris, eds. "In a Dangerous Situation: Letters of Col. John Floyd, 1774-1783." *The Register of the Kentucky State Historical Society* 83 (1985): 202-36.

Harding, Margery H. *George Rogers Clark and His Men: Military Records, 1778-1784*. Frankfort, Kentucky Historical Society, 1981.

Harrison, L.H. "George Rogers Clark and the Revolution in the West." The Society of Colonial Wars in the State of Ohio. Presentation. 81st General Council Meeting. Ohio: 6 May, 1977. 1982.

--- *George Rogers Clark and the War in the West.* Lexington, KY: U P Kentucky, 1976.

--- *Kentucky's Road to Statehood.* Lexington, KY: U P Kentucky, 1992.

Harrison, L.H. and J.C. Klotter. *A New History of Kentucky.* Lexington, KY: U P Kentucky, 1997.

Havighurst, Walter. *George Rogers Clark in the West.* New York: McGraw-Hill, 1952.

Haynes, R.V. *The Natchez District and the American Revolution.* St. Louis: U P Missouri, 1976.

Healy, Katharine G. "Calendar of Early Jefferson County, Kentucky, Wills –Will Book No. 1, 1784-1813." *Filson Club History Quarterly* 6 (1932): 1-37.

--- "Calendar of Early Jefferson County, Kentucky, Wills –Will Book No. 2. 1813-1833 –part 2, 1825-1833." *Filson Club History Quarterly* 6 (1932): 1-37.

Heldman, Donald P. *Archaeological Investigations at French Farm Lake in Northern Michigan, 1981-1982: A British Colonial Farm Site. Archaeologieal Completion Report Series, No. 6.* Mackinac Island State Park Commission, Mackinac Island, Michigan, 1983.

Heldman, Donald P., and William L. Minnerly. *The Powder Magazine At Fort Michilimackinac: Excavation Report. Reports in Mackinac History and Archaeology, No. 6,* Mackinac Island State Park Commission, Mackinac, Michigan, 1977.

Hening, W.W. *The Statutes at Large, Being a Collection Of the Laws of Virginia (1619-1792).* 13 vols. Richmond: Samuel Pleasants, junior, printer to the commonwealth, 1819-1823.

Henry, Patrick. "Letter to Governor Galvez [New Orleans]." *Archivo General De Indies,* Seville, 1777.

Henry, W.W. *Patrick Henry; Life, Speeches and Correspondence.* 3 vols. New York: Charles Scribner's Sons, 1891.

Holm, Gregory F. "The Uniform of George Rogers Clark's Illinois Reg. of Virginia State Forces from October 1778- February 1779." [The period of the attack on Vincennes]. Unpublished ms. on file at George Rogers Clark National Historical Park, Vincennes, 1995.

Horsman, Reginald. "Great Britain and the Illinois Country in the Era of the American Revolution." *Journal of the Illinois State Historical Society* 69 (1976): 100-109.

Indiana Historical Society. *The French, the Indians, and George Rogers Clark in the Illinois country : Proceedings of an Indiana American Revolution Bicentennial Symposium, Vincennes University, Vincennes, Indiana, May 14 and 15, 1976.* Indianapolis: Indiana Historical Society, 1977.

"Intercepted Letters and Journal of George Rogers Clark, 1778-1789." *American Historical Review* 1 (1895): 90.

James, James A. "Significant Events during the Last Year of the Revolution in the West." *Proceedings*, Mississippi Valley Historical Association 6 (1900).

--- "Indian Diplomacy and the Opening of the Revolution in the West." *Proceedings*, State Historical Society of Wisconsin, 1909.

--- "Some Problems in the Northwest in 1779." in *Essays in American History Dedicated to Frederick Jackson Turner*, Guy Stanton Ford, ed. New York: Henry Holt and Co., 1910.

--- "Detroit the Key to the West during the American Revolution." *Transactions. Illinois State Historical Society 14* (1910).

--- "George Rogers Clark and Detroit, 1780-1781." *Proceedings*, Mississippi Valley Historical Association 1910.

--- "French-American Diplomacy, 1795-1797." *Annual Report*, American Historical Association, 1911.

--- "Government in Illinois during the American Revolution." Paper, Chicago Historical Society, 1912. (Copy in James Alton James Collection, University Archives, Northwestern University.)

--- "Illinois and the Revolution in the West, 1779-1780." *Transactions*, Illinois State Historical Society, vol. 15, 1912.

--- *George Rogers Clark Papers 1771-1784*, 2 vols. Illinois State Historical Library, Collection, 8, Virginia Series 3. Springfield, 1912, 1926.

--- "French Diplomacy and American Politics, 1794-1795." 1911. *Annual Report*, American Historical Association, vol. 1, 1913.

--- "Some Phases of the History of the Northwest, 1783-1786." *Proceedings*, Mississippi Valley Historical Association, (1913-1914).

--- "Louisiana as a Factor in American Diplomacy, 1795-1800." *Mississippi Valley Historical Review 1* (1914): 44-56.

--- "The Significance of the Attack on St. Louis, 1780." *Proceedings,* Mississippi Valley Historical Association, 2, 1915.

--- "George Rogers Clark and Detroit, 1780-1781." *Proceedings.* vol. 3, Mississippi Valley Historical Association, 1916.

--- "Spanish Influence in the West during the American Revolution." *Mississippi Valley Historical Review 4* (1917): 193-208.

--- "The Value of the Memoir of George Rogers Clark as an Historical Document." *Proceedings,* Mississippi Valley Historical Association, 9, 1918.

--- "To What Extent Was George Rogers Clark in Military Control of the Northwest at the Close of the American Revolution." in *Annual Report for 1917*, American Historical Association, Washington, DC, 1920.

--- "French Opinion as a Factor in Preventing War between France and the United States, 1795-1800." *American Historical Review* 30 (1925): 44-55.

--- "The Significance of the Sesqui-Centennial Celebrations of the American Revolution West of the Alleghany Mountains." *Journal of the Illinois State Historical Society 19* (1927).

--- "George Rogers Clark Civilian." *Transactions.* Illinois State Historical Society, 1928.

--- *Life of George Rogers Clark.* Chicago: University of Chicago Press, 1928.

--- "Oliver Pollock, Financier of the American Revolution in the West." *Mississippi Valley Historical Review 14* (1929): 80-83.

--- "An Appraisal of the Contribution of George Rogers Clark to the History of the West." *Mississippi Valley Historical Review 17* (1930): 98-115.

--- "Oliver Pollock and the Winning of the Illinois Country." *Transactions,* Illinois State Historical Society, vol. 41, 1934.

--- "The Northwest: Gift or Conquest?" *Indiana Magazine of History 30* (1934): 1-15.

--- "Oliver Pollock and the Free Navigation of the Mississippi River." *Mississippi Valley Historical Review 24* (1937): 384-385.

--- *Oliver Pollock: The Life and Times of an Unknown Patriot.* Reprint, New York: Books for Libraries Press, 1970.

Jefferson, Thomas. *Writings*. P.L. Ford, ed. 10 vols. New York, G.P. Putnam and Sons, 1892-1899.

Jefferson, Thomas. *Writings*. H.A. Washington, ed. 9 vols. Philadelphia, 1853.

Jelks, Edward B., Carl Ekberg, and Terrance J. Martin. *Excavations at the Laurens Site: Probable Location of Fort de Chartres I. Studies in Illinois Archaeology No. 5*, Illinois Historic Preservation Agency. Springfield, 1989.

Jillson, W.R.

--- "A Bibliography of the Lower Blue Licks." *The Register of the Kentucky State Historical Society* 42 (1944): 127-129.

--- "Battle of Blue Licks." *The Register of the Kentucky State Historical Society* 47 (1949): 265-93.

--- "Index of Minute Book A [1780-1783] Jefferson County Court, Virginia." *The Register of the Kentucky State Historical Society* 53 (1955): 37-57.

--- *Pioneer Kentucky*. Frankfort: The State Journal Co., 1934.

--- "The Siege of Bryan's Station." *The Register of the Kentucky State Historical Society* 36 (1938): 15-25.

Jillson, W.R., ed. *Kentucky Land Grants*. Louisville: The Standard Printing Co. Inc., 1925.

Kellogg, Louise Phelps. *Frontier Advance on the Upper Ohio*. Madison: The Society, 1916.

--- "France and the Mississippi Valley." *Mississippi Valley Historical Review* 18 (1932): 3-22.

--- "Indian Diplomacy during the Revolution in the West." *Transactions, Illinois State Historical Society*, vol. 36, 1929.

--- "Recognition of George Rogers Clark." *Indiana Magazine of History* 25 (1929): 40-46.

Kellogg, Louise Phelps, ed. *Frontier Retreat on the Upper Ohio, 1779-1781*. Madison: The Society, 1917. [also Wisconsin Hist. Collection, vol. 24, Draper series, vol. 5.]

Kenton, Edna. *Simon Kenton: His Life and Period, 1755-1836*. Garden City, N.J.: Country Life Press, 1930.

Kinkead, Ludie J. "How the Parents of George Rogers Clark Came to Kentucky in 1784-1785." *Filson Club History Quarterly* 3 (1928): 1-4.

--- "Minute Book No. 1, Jefferson County, Kentucky, 1785-1785 –Part 1, April, May, 1784." *Filson Club History Quarterly* 6 (1932): 38-71.

Kinkead, Ludie J. and K.G. Healy. "Bond and Power of Attorney Book No. 1, Jefferson County, 1783-1798. Part 3" *Filson Club History Quarterly* 7 (1933): 154-69.

Kinkead, Ludie J. and K.G. Healy. "Calendar of Bond and Power of Attorney Gook No. 1, Jefferson County, Kentucky, 1783-1798." *Filson Club History Quarterly* 7 (1933): 34-56; 94-116; 154-169; 170.

Kinnaird, Lawrence. *American Penetration into Spanish Territory, 1776-1803*. Doctoral Dissertation, Department of History. Berkley: University of California, 1928.

--- "Clark-Leyba Papers." *American Historical Review* 41 (1935): 92-112.

--- "Spain in the Mississippi Valley, 1765-1794." *Annual Report, American History Association. 1945.* Washington, D.C., 1949.

--- "The Western Fringe of Revolution." *Western History Quarterly* 7 (1976).

Kleber, J., T.D. Clark, L.H. Harrison, and J.C. Klotter, eds. *The Kentucky Encyclopedia*. Lexington, KY: U P Kentucky, 1992.

Lafferty, M.W. "The Destruction of Ruddle's and Martin's Forts in the Revolutionary War." *The Register of Kentucky History* 54 (1956): 297-338.

Lambert, Joseph I. (Major). "Clark's Conquest of the Northwest." *Indiana Magazine of History* 36 (1940): 337-350.

Lansden, John M. "Fort Jefferson and Bird's Point." *A History of the City of Cairo, Ill.* 1910. Carbondale, Illinois: SIU P, 1976.

Lockridge, Ross F. *George Rogers Clark: Pioneer Hero of the Old Northwest*. Chicago: World Book Co., 1927.

Loos, John L. *A Biography of William Clark, 1770-1813*. Doctoral Dissertation, Department of History. Washington University, St. Louis, 1953.

Lucy, James A. and K.C. Carstens. "An Analysis of Medicines Used on the Late 18th Century Frontier in Kentucky and Illinois." *Current Archaeology in Kentucky*, David Pollack, ed. The Kentucky Heritage Council, Frankfort, 1996.

Lutz, Peak V. "Facts and Myths Concerning George Rogers Clark's Grant of Land at Paducah." *The Register of the Kentucky State Historical Society* 67 (1969): 248-53.

Magee, M. Juliette. *Old Fort Jefferson*. Wickliffe, KY: Advance-Yeoman, 1975.

Marshall, Humphrey. *History of Kentucky*. 2 vols. Frankfort: G.S. Robinson, 1824.

Martin, Terrance Martin. "Preliminary Report on Animal Remains from Block C of the Fort Area at Fort Booonesborough State Park, Kentucky." *Searching for Boonesborough* (1989), Nancy O'Malley, Archaeological Report 193, Program for Cultural Resource Assessment, University of Kentucky, Lexington.

Martin, Terrance Martin. *A Faunal Analysis of Fort Ouiatenon, An Eighteenth Century Trading Post in the Wabash Valley of Indiana.* Ph.D. dissertation, Michigan State University, University Microfilms, 1986.

Mason, E.G. "John Todd's Papers." *Chicago Historical Society, Collection 4.* Chicago, 1890.

--- "John Todd's Record-Book." *Chicago Historical Society, Collection 4.* Chicago, 1890.

--- "Rocheblave Papers." *Chicago Historical Society, Collection 4.* Chicago, 1890.

Mason, Kathryn Harrod. *James Harrod of Kentucky.* Baton Rouge: Louisiana U P, 1951.

Mayfield, R.N. "Roll of Lincoln Militia." *The Register of the Kentucky State Historical Society* 29 (1931): 220-21.

McAllister, J.T. *Virginia Militia in the Revolutionary War.* Hot Springs, Va.: McAllister Pub. Co., 1913.

McCarthy, C.H. "The Attitude of Spain During the Revolution." *Catholic History Review* 2.

McDermott, John F. "The Battle of St. Louis, 26 May 1780." *Bulletin of the Missouri Historical Society, St. Louis,* (1980), 16 (3): 131-42.

McDermott, John F., ed. *Frenchmen and French Ways in the Mississippi Valley.* Champagne: U of Illinois P, 1969.

McDowell, Sam. *Index to the Calendar of the George Rogers Clark Papers of the Draper Collection of Mississippi.* Utica, KY: McDowell Publishing, 1985.

McNeil, Floyd A. "Fort Jefferson –The Extreme Western Post of the American Revolution." *Bulletin of the Missouri Historical Society* 6 (1929).

Meeker, Mary Jane. "Original Vouchers in the George Rogers Clark Bicentennial Exhibition." *Indiana Historical Bulletin* 53 (1976): 87-93.

Mese, William A. "Colonel John Montgomery." *Illinois Catholic Hist. Review* 5 (1922).

Michigan Pioneer and Historical Society, Colections, 36 vols. Lansing, 1877.

Miller, J. Jefferson II, and Lyle M. Stone. *Eighteenth-Century Ceramics from Fort Michilimackinac: A Study in Historical Archaeology*. Smithsonian Institution Press, Washington, 1970.

Monette, J.W. *History of the Discovery and Settlement of the Valley of the Mississippi*. 2 vols. N.Y., 1846.

Morehead, J.T. *The First Settlement of Kentucky*. Frankfort: A. G. Hodges, state printer, 1840.

Nasatir, A.P. "St. Louis during the British Attack of 1780." *New Spain and the Anglo-Am. West*. George P. Hammond, ed. Los Angeles: Priv., 1932. Reprinted. New York: Kraus Reprint Co., 1969.

--- "The Anglo-Spanish Frontier in the Illinois Country during the American Revolution, 1779-1783." *Journal of the Illinois State Historical Society* 21 (1928): 291-358.

Nassaney, Michael S., and William M. Cremin. "Realizing the Potential of the Contact Period in Southwest Michigan Through the Fort St. Joseph Archaeological Project." Copy of paper in possession of author, n.d.

Nassaney, Michael S., William M. Cremin, and Daniel P. Lynch. The Archaeological Identification of Colonial Fort St. Joseph in Michigan. Copy of paper in possession of author, n.d.

Nobel, Virgil. *Functional Classification and Intra-Site Analysis in Historical Archaeology: A Case Study from Fort Ouiatenon*. Ph.D.. dissertation, Michigan State University, University Microfilms, Ann Arbor.

Nobles, Gregory H. "Breaking into the Backcountry: New Approaches to the Early American Frontier, 1750-1800." *William and Mary Quarterly* 46 (1989):641-670.

O'Malley, Nancy. *Searching for Boonesborough*. Archaeological Report 193, Program for Cultural Resource Assessment, University of Kentucky, Lexington, 1989.

O'Malley, Nancy. *Stockading Up*. Program for Cultural Resource Assessment, University of Kentucky, Lexington., 1986.

Orser, Charles E., Jr. The 1975 Season of Archeological Investigations at Fort de Chartres, Randolph County, Illinois. University Museum, Southern Illinois University, Carbondale, 1976.

Palmer, Frederick *Clark of the Ohio: A Life of George Rogers Clark*. New York: Dodd, Mead & Co., 1929.

Pease, T.C., and M.J. Pease. *George Rogers Clark and the Revolution in Illinois, 1763-1787: A Sesquicentennial Memorial*. The Ill. State History Library and the Illinois State Historical Society, 1929.

--- *The Story of Illinois*. 3rd edition. Chicago: U of Chicago P, 1940.

Perkins, Elizabeth A. *Border Life: Experience and Memory in the Revolutionary Ohio Valley*. Chapel Hill N.C.: N. Carolina U P, 1998.

Perrin, W.H., J.H. Battle, and G.C. Kniffin. *Kentucky: A Hist. of the State*. Louisville, F. A. Battey, 1887.

Peterson, Charles E. "Notes on Old Cahokia," *French American Review* 1 (1948).

Phillips, Paul C. "American Opinions Regarding the West, 1778-1783," *Proceedings. Mississippi Valley Historical Association* 7 (1920).

--- "The West in the Diplomacy of the American. Revolution." *University of Illinois Studies in Social Sciences*, II. Urbana, 1913.

Pieper, Thomas I., and James B. Gidney. *Fort Laurens, 1778-79: The Revolutionary War in Ohio*. Kent State University Press, Kent, Ohio, 1976.

Pirtle, Alfred. *James Chenoweth: The Story of One of the Earliest Boys of Louisville and Where Louisville Started*. Louisville: The Standard Printing Company, 1921.

--- "Colonel Cuthbert Bullitt's Personal Recollections of General George Rogers Clark," *Filson Club History Quarterly* 2 (1927): 177-178.

--- *Col. George Rogers Clark's Sketch of his Campaign in the Illinois in 1778-9* (Ohio Valley Hist. Ser., no. 3) Cincinnati, 1869.

--- "Mulberry Hill, the First Home of GRC in Ky.," *The Register of the Kentucky Hist. Soc.* 15 (1917).

Pittman, P. *The Present State of the European Settlements on the Mississippi. London, 1770*. Second edition, F. H. Hodder, ed. Cleveland: A. H. Clark Co., 1906.

Potter, William H. *Redcoats on the Frontier*. M.A. Thesis, Dept. of History, Murray State University, 1988.

--- "Redcoats on the Frontier: The King's Reg. in the Rev. War," *Selected Papers GRC Conference*. Robert J. Holden, ed. Vincennes, 1985.

Potter, William H., and K.C. Carstens. "Floral Reconstruction and Early 19th Century Land Surveys in Western Kentucky: A Test Case from the Fort Jefferson Area."

Paper. 1986 Southeastern Archaeological Conference. Nashville, 1986.

Quaife, Milo M. "Marking the Site of Old Fort St. Joseph." *Journal of the Illinois State Historical Society* 6 (1914): 490-95.

--- "The Ohio Campaign of 1782." *Mississippi Valley Historical Review* 17 (1931): 515-29.

--- "When Detroit Invaded Kentucky," *Filson Club History Quarterly* 1 (1927): 53-68.

Quaife, Milo M., ed. *Capture of Old Vincennes.* Indianapolis: The Bobbs-Merrill Co., 1927.

--- *Conquest of the Illinois.* Chicago: R. R. Donnelly and Sons Co., 1920.

Ranck, G. W. *Boonesborough.* 1901. New York: Reprinted Arno Press, 1971.

Randall, J.G. "George Rogers Clark Service of Supply." *Mississippi Valley Historical Review* 8 (1921): 250-263.

Rankin, Hugh F. *"George Rogers Clark and the Winning of the West."* Virginia Independent Bicentennial Commission, Richmond, 1976.

Reager, Allen M. "George Rogers Clark—A Mason," *Filson Club History Quarterly* 16 (1942): 187-190.

Resolutions, Laws, and Ordnances Relating to the Pay, Half Pay, Commutation of Half Pay, Bounty Lands, and Other Promises Made by Congress to the Officers and Soldiers of the Revolution; To the Settlement of the Accounts between the U.S. and the Several States; and to Funding the Rev. Debt, 1838. Reprint, N.Y., N.Y., Research Reprints, Inc., 1970.

Reynolds, J. *My Own Times, Embracing also the History of my Life.* Chicago: Chicago Historical Society, 1879.

--- *The Pioneer History of Illinois.* Chicago, Fergus Printing Co., 1887.

Rice, Otis K. *Frontier Kentucky.* Lexington: U P Kentucky, 1993.

Riley, Franklin. "Spanish Policy in Mississippi after the Treaty of San Lorenzo" *Publication of the Mississippi Historical Society I,* 1898.

Robertson, James R., compiler. *Petitions of the Early Inhabitants of Kentckky to the General Assembly of Virginia, 1769-1792.* Louisville: John P. Morton & Co., 1914.

Robertson, John E.L. "Fort Jefferson," *The Register of Kentucky History* 71 (1973): 127-38.

--- "The Chickasaw's Role in the Contest for Empire in North America between France and England." Paper. 5th Ohio Valley Historical Conference. Murray, Kentucky, 1989.

--- *West to the Iron Banks*. M.A. Thesis, Dept. of History, U. of Louisville, 1961.

Roosevelt, T. *The Winning of the West*. New York and London: G.P. Putnam and Sons, 1920.

Scheer, G.F., and H.F. Rankin. *Rebels & Redcoats: The American Revolution through the Eyes of Those Who Fought and Lived It*. Cleveland: World Pub. Co., 1957.

Schrodt, Philip. *George Rogers Clark: Frontier Revolutionary*. Bloomington: Buffalo Wallow Press, 1976.

Scott, Elizabeth. *French Subsistence at Fort Michilimackinac, 1715-1781: The Clergy and the Traders*. Archaeological Completion Report Series, Number 9, Mackinac Island State Park Commission, Mackinac Island, Michigan, 1985.

Seineke, Kathrine W. *The George Rogers Clark Adventures in the Illinois and Selected Documents of the American Revolution at the Frontier Posts*. Polyanthos, 1981.

Selby, John E. *The Revolution in Virginia, 1775-1783*. Williamsburg: Colo. Williamsburg Found., 1988.

Shaw, Helen Louise. *British Administration of the Southern Indians. 1756-1783*. Doctoral Diss., Dept. History, Bryn Mawr College, 1931.

Shaw, Janet P., "Francis Bosseron," in *Indiana Magazine of History* 25 (1929): 204-11.

Shaw, Janet P., ed., "Account Book of Francis Bosseron," *Indiana Magazine of History* 25 (1929): 213-41.

Siebert, William H. "Kentucky's Struggle with Its Loyalist Proprietors." *Mississippi Valley Historical Review* 7 (1920): 113-126.

Sioussat, St. George L. "The Journal of General Daniel Smith, one of the Commissioners to Extend the Boundary Line between the Commonwealths of Virginia and North Carolina, August, 1779, to July, 1780," *in Tennessee History Magazine*, vol. 1, 1915.

Skaggs, D.C., ed., *The Old Northwest in the American Revolution: An Anthology*. The StateHistorical Society of Wisconsin, Madison, 1977.

Smith, Z.F. "George Rogers Clark," in *Register of the Kentucky Historical Society*, vol. 7, 1906.

Snyder, J.F. "Fort Kaskaskia," *Journal of the Illinois State Historical Society* 6 (1913).

--- "The Armament of Ft. Chartres," *Transactions, Illinois State Historical Society*, 1906.

Sprague, Stuart S. "Kentucky Politics and the Heritage of the American Revolution: The Early Years, 1783-1788," *Register of the Kentucky State Historical Society* 78 (1980): 98-114.

State Hist. Soc. of Wisconsin, *Calendar of the Ky Papers of the Draper Coll. of Mss.* Madison, 1925, Reprinted by McDowell Pub., Utica, Ky, n.d.

--- *The Preston and Virg. Papers of the Draper Collection of Manuscripts.* Madison, 1915, Reprinted by McDowell Pub., Utica, Ky, 1979.

Stein, J. K., K. C. Carstens, and K. Wesler, "Geoarchaeology and Historical Archaeology: An Example from Fort Jefferson, Ky," in *Southeastern Archaeology*, vol. 2, 1983.

Stevens, Paul L. "To Invade the Frontiers of Ky"? The Indian Diplomacy of Philippe de Rocheblave, Britain's Acting Commandant at Kaskaskia, 1776-1778," *Filson Club History Quarterly* 64 (1990): 205-46.

Stone, Lyle M. *Fort Michilimackinac, 1715-1781: An Archaeological Perspective on the Revolutionary Frontier. Publications of the Museum*, Michigan State University, East Lansing, in cooperation with Mackinac Island State Park Commission, Mackinac Island 1974.

--- *Archaeological Investigations of the Marquette Mission Site, St. Ignace, Michigan 1971: A Preliminary Report.* Reports in Mackinac History and Archaeology, No. 1. Mackinac Island State Park Commission, Mackinac Island, Michigan, 1972.

Sutton, Robert M. "George Rogers Clark and the Campaign in the West: The Five Major Documents." *Indiana Magazine of History* 36 (1980): 334-35; rev. 367-68.

Swem, E.G. "The Lost Vouchers of George Rogers Clark." *Virginia Journal of Education.* 22 (1927).

Talbert, Charles G. "A Roof for Kentucky," *Filson Club History Quarterly* 29 (1955):

145-65.

--- *Benjamin Logan: Kentucky Frontiersman.* Lexington: U of Kentucky P, 1962.

--- "John Logan, 1747-1807." *Filson Club History Quarterly* 36 (1962): 128-50.

--- "Kentucky Invades Ohio, 1779," *The Register of Kentucky History* 51 (1953): 228-35

--- "Ky Invades Ohio, 1780," *The Register of Kentucky History* 51 (1953): 315-27

--- "Kentucky Invades Ohio, 1782," *The Register of Kentucky History* 53 (1953): 288-97.

--- "Kentucky Invades Ohio, 1786," The Register of Kentucky History 54 (1956): 203-13.

Tanner, Helen Hornbeck, ed. *Atlas of Great Lakes Indian History.* U of Oklahoma P, 1987.

Tapp, Hambleton. "A George Rogers Clark Memorial in Kentucky." *Filson Club History Quarterly* 15 (1941): 159-64.

--- "Colonel John Floyd, Kentucky Pioneer," *Filson Club History Quarterly* 15 (1941): 1-24.

--- "George Rogers Clark, A Biographical Sketch." *Filson Club History Quarterly* 15 (1941): 132-51.

--- "Memorials for Kentucky." *Filson Club History Quarterly* 15 (1941): 105-108.

Teggart, Frederick J. "The Capture of St. Joseph, Mich., by the Spaniards in 1781." *Missouri Historical Review* 5.

Thatcher, Marian H., "George Rogers Clark Memorial Bridge," in *Filson Club History Quarterly,* vol. 23, (1949): 111-16.

Thomas, Daniel H. *Fort Toulouse: The French Outpost at the Alabamas on the Coosa.* The University of Alabama Press, Tuscaloosa, 1989.

Thomas, Lowell. The Hero of Vincennes, The Story of George Rogers Clark. Boston: Riverside Press, 1929.

Thomas, Samuel W. "Letters to the Editor," *The Register of the Kentucky State Historical Society* 68 (1970): 265-68.

Thomas, Samuel W. "The Removal of George Rogers Clark's Remains from the Locust Grove Graveyard," *Filson Club History Quarterly* 41 (1967): 35-39.

---- "William Croghan, Sr. [1752-1822]." *Filson Club History Quarterly* 43 (1969): 30-61.

--- "The Croghan Papers," unpublished ms., on file at Locust Grove Historic Home, Louisville, KY, 1967

--- "The Face of the Founder," unpublished document, *The Filson Historical Society*, file accession 1929.8 , Louisville, Ky.

Thomas, Samuel W., ed. "The Papers of George Rogers Clark 1784-1818," unpublished ms., on file Locust Grove Historic Home, Louisville, Kentucky, 1967.

Thomas, Samuel W., and E.H. Conner, "George Rogers Clark (1752-1818), Natural Scientist and Historian," *Filson Club History Quarterly* 41 (1967): 202-26.

Thomas, Samuel W., and E.H. Conner. "The History and Restoration of 'Locust Grove' Near Louisville, KY, Built ca. 1790," *The Register of the Kentucky State Historical Society* 65 *(1967)*: 271-77.

Thruston, R.C. Ballard. "After the Death of George Rogers Clark," *Filson Club History Quarterly* 15 (1941): 152-58.

--- "Rachel Eastham, Not Mary Byrd or Bird, was the Wife of John Rogers, the Grandfather of George Rogers Clark," *Filson Club History Quarterly* 14 (1940): 174-75.

--- "Some Recent Findings Regarding the Ancestry of General George Rogers Clark," *Filson Club History Quarterly* 9 (1935): 1-34.

--- "The Grave of General George Rogers Clark," *Filson Club History Quarterly* 10 (1936): 203-30.

Thwaites, R.G. *How George Rogers Clark Won the Northwest and Other Essays in Western Hist.* A.C. McClurg & Co., 1903, Reprinted Corner House Publ.ications, Williamstown, MA, 1978.

--- *The Revolution on the Upper Ohio.* Madison, 1908, reprinted Port Washington, NY: Kennikat Press, 1970.

--- *Descriptive List of the Ms. Coll.*, State Hist. Soc. Wis. Madison, 1906.

Thwaites, R.G., and Kellogg, L.P. *Dunmore's War.* Harrisonburg, VA.: C. J. Carrier Co., 1905.

--- *Frontier Defense on the Upper Ohio*. Madison: Wisconsin Historical Society, 1912.

--- *Revolution on the Upper Ohio, 1775-1777*. Madison: Wisconsin Historical Society, 1908.

Tillson, Albert H., Jr. *Gentry and Common Folk: Political Culture on a Virginia Frontier 1740-1789*. Lexington: U P Kentucky, 1991.

Turner, Frederick J., ed. "George Rogers Clark and the Kaskaskia Campaign, 1777-1778." *American Historical Review* 8 (1903): 491-505.

--- "The Policy of France toward the Mississippi Valley," *American Historical Review* 10 (1904): 249-79.

Van Every, D. *A Company of Heroes: the American Frontier, 1775-1783*. New York: Morrow, 1962.

--- *Forth to the Wilderness: The First American Frontier 1754-1774*. New York: William Morrow and Co., 1961.

Van Tyne, C.H. *The American Revolution* (American National Series, IX) New York: Harper and Brothers, 1905.

Waller, George M., "George Rogers Clark and the Am. Rev. in the West." *Indiana Magazine of History* 72 (1976): 1-20.

Waller, George M., "Target Detroit: Overview of the American Revolution, West of the Appalachians," *The French, the Indians, and George Rogers Clark in the Illinois Country, Proceedings. Indiana American Revolution Bicentennial Symposium*, Indianapolis, Indiana Historical Society, 1977.

--- *The American Revolution in the West*. Chicago: Nelson-Hall, 1976.

Walthall, John A., ed. *French Colonial Archaeology: The Illinois Country and the Western Great Lakes*. Chicago: U of Illinois P, 1991.

Walthall, John A., and Elizabeth D. Benchley. *The River L'Abbe Mission. Studies in Illinois Archaeology, No. 2.*, Illinois Historic Preservation Agency, Springfield, 1987.

West, J. Martin, "George Rogers Clark and the Shawnee Expedition of 1780," in *Selected Papers GRC Conference*, Robert J. Holden, ed. Vincennes, 1994.

Whitaker, Arthur Preston, *The Spanish American Frontier: 1783-1795*. New York: Houghton Mifflin Company, 1927.

---. "The Spanish Intrigue in the Old Southwest," *Mississippi Valley Historical Review* 13 (1929): 365-86.

White, Richard. *The Middle Ground: Indians, Empires and Republics in the Great Lakes Region, 1650-1815.* New York: Cambridge U P, 1991.

Whitely, W.H. "Lincoln County Militia, 1780-1783," *The Register of the Kentucky State Historical Society* 25 (1927).

Wilson, S.M. *Battle of the Blue Licks, August 19, 1782.* Lexington, KY: 1927.

---. "George Washington's Contacts with Kentucky." *Filson Club History Quarterly* 6 (1932): 215-260.

Wilson, William E. *Big Knife: The Story of George Rogers Clark.* New York: J.J. Little and Ives Co., 1940.

Winsor, Justin. *Westward Movement.* New York: Houghton Mifflin and Co., 1897.

Wisconsin State Historical Society. Coll., 20 vols. Madison, Beginning 1854.

Withers, A.S. and R.G Thwaites, eds. *Chronicles of Border Warfare.* 1895. New York: Reprinted Arno Press, 1971.

Wood, Gordon S. *The Radicalism of the American Revolution.* New York: Vintage Books, 1993.

Wright, J. L., Jr. *Britain and the American Frontier 1783-1815.* Athens: U Georgia P, 1975.

Yater, G. H. *Two Hundred Years at the Falls of the Ohio: A History of Louisville and Jefferson County.* Louisville: The Heritage Co., 1979.

Young, Chester R., ed. *Westward into Kentucky: The Narrative of Daniel Trabue.* Lexington, KY: U P of Kentucky, 1981.

INDEX

Advance-Yeoman, 200
Alcohol (over indulgence at Fort Jefferson), 34
Aldar, John, 189
Alder, J., 181
Allen, David, 2, 186, 192; Isaac, 185; J. 181; Samuel, 185
Alvord, Clarence W., 201, 213
Anderson, John, 186, 190
Andre, Jean, 187
Andrews, Joseph, 183
Archer, Joshua, 31, 189
Armstrong, G. 183
Armorer-Smithy, 192
Artifacts, 192, 202-203
Ash, John 183
Asher, Widow, 178; William, 178

Babu, Daniel, 183
Bailey's Company, 181-182, 188-189, 199
Bailey, John, 194
Bakly, John, 183
Ballard County, Kentucky 3, 12
Ballenger, James, 191; Larken 188
Balsinger (also Balsinkee), V. 160, Valentine 183
Baptisst, writes Clark, 54
Barbour, Philip 33, 211
Bardwell, Kentucky 91
Barnet, James, 189
Barnit, Robert 185
Bartholomew, William 185
Battle of St. Louis, 30, 210
Bell, Bob, 200; William 188, 191
Bennoit, Francis, 187
Biby, Cathy, 92
Blackford, Zephaniah, 191, 198
Blair, J., 181, John 185
Blanchard, (?) 187
Blandville, Kentucky, 11
Blankenship, Henry, 185
Blockhouses 180, 205
Board of Western commissioners, 183
Boatmaster, see Pittman, 184
Bogert, Pen, 144
Boils, John 185
Bolton, Daniel, 183

Bootin, Travis, 186, William, 186
Bowdery, John (fifer), 186
Brading, William, 186
Brain, William, 186
Brashear's Company, 181, 185, 194, 199
Brashear, Richard, 178
Brawly, William 191
Brayly, William, 188
Bredin (also Breeding), Francis 178, 186, Hanah 178
Brian, John 183
Brigade of the American Revolution (BAR), 193
Britain and allies, 214
British attack St. Louis, 4
British Southern Indian Department, 32
Broadhead, Daniel 30; writes Clark 49, 57
Brown, J. (also) James, 181, 185, 188; Lou 189
Bryan, (also O'Brian and OByran) John, 178, 192, Family 178, Mrs. 192
Bryant, James 186
Buchanan, William, 188
Buffalo, 211
Burk, Charles, 183, John, 190, Nicholas, 189
Burks, Elizabeth, 178, John 178, Sarah 178
Bush, Drury, 183, John 183, William 189
Butcher, Gasper, 192

Cahokia, 1, 29, 127, 201, 211, 212
Cailer, Casper, 186
Calvit, Lt., 152
Campbell, William 186
Candles 146
Carey, Lewis, 213
Carlisle County, Kentucky, 12
Carnes, John ,152
Carney, Martin, 109, 114, 184, 191, 198; quartermaster book, 114-115
Carolina Charter of 1665, 1, 5
Carr (also Kerr), W., 181, 189
Certain, Page, 180
Cesar (free Black artificer; also Caesar), 144, 184, 192
Chain of Forts, 27
Chapman, Richard, 189
Chapel, John 188
Chillicothe (old), 4
Christmas at Fort Jefferson, 33
Ciblet, Francis, 190
Civilians 1
Clark, Andrew, 184, 189, 192

Clark, Benjamin, 5
Clark, George Rogers 1, 9, 27, 180; controls Northwest 213-214; conquests 213; grant of land 46-47; registration of land 47; writes John Todd, 48; land warrants for soldiers 50-51; writes John Dodge upon arrival at Fort Jefferson, 54; writes Oliver Pollack for supplies at Fort Jefferson, 55-56; writes George Washington, 83-84; 85; builds Fort Jefferson, 90; writes Jefferson, 78-79; 87-89.
Clark, John, 189
Clark, Richard, 186
Clark, William (brother), 5; map of 1780, 13, 203
Clark, William (cousin), 5, 7, 8, 9, 152, 195 ; map of 1795, 14, 188, 203, 205
Clarksville, 4; Trustees, 30; Petition for new Virginia county, 30; 59-61; 201; built landscape of, 97
Clay, R. Berle, 205
Clothes (trimmings), 193-199
Coffins, 180
Colbert, James, 32
Committee on Institutional Science and Research at Murray State University, 201
Company Clothing Issues, 199
Connard, Dr. Francis 163-166
Conner, John, 189
Cooper, Barney, 188; Joseph, 182, 188; Samuel, 190
Corbin, Margaret, 142
Corps of Engineers, U.S. Army, 11
Council of War of 1779, 28
Coup against Captain George, 33
Courts of Inquiry, 34; defined, 149; against John Dodge, 150; against Ed Worthington, 152, 160, 161, against Richard McCarty, 153, against John Rogers 158.
Court Martial, 159; against David Allen and James Taylor, 159-160
Cowen, John,185
Cox, John 191; Thomas, 186
Craten, Robert, 190
Crawley, J., 181, 188
Crump, William, 186
Cummins, Light T., 118
Curtis, Rice, 186
Curry, James 185, Patrick 185

Dalton, Hannah, 178, 192; Valentine Thomas 178, 191, 192
Damewood (also Dance) Bostin, 160, 178, 184; Mary 178
Dasker, Jacob 188
Daughterty (also Daugherty), John 160, 178, 184; children, 178
Davies, J., 181
Davis, James 188
Dawson, James 185
Dean, J., 181
Decker (also Deckar or Decart), Jacob, 181, 188

Deetz, James 146
Defeat British and Indians at St. Louis, 30
DeJean, Mr. (prisoner) 192
Delorme 3 D Map, 25
DeLang (also Lang), Thomas, 184
DeMore, Mary (washerwoman), 184
Deserters 1
Detroit, 212
Dewit (also DeWitt), Henery 186
Discharged men at Fort Jefferson, 191
Ditterin, Jacob, 181, 184
Doctors, surgeons, 192
Dodge, John 191, 194, 211; biography 110-11; quartermaster book, 113-115; writes Jefferson, 62-64; writes Oliver Pollack, 74; Israel, 191, 198
Dohaty, Frederick, 186
Donne, John 144, 178, 191, 198; Martha 178; home at Fort Jefferson, 205
Dowdy, Buddy, 205
Draper Manuscripts, 200
Drummer, 187
Duly, Haymore 188; Philip 188
Duncan, Joseph, 191; William Butler, 10
Dupoyster, Joseph C., 10; maps, 12; map no.1, 10, 23; map 2, 10 203; Mercer, 21; canon 204

Eagle, Harmon, 188
Elms, Ann, 178, James, John, William, 179, 185; child 179
English, William Hayden, 213
Estes, J. (also James), 180, 186
Evans, Charles, 186; Jesse, 189
Evan's Company, 189

Fabers (also Fever), William, 181, 184
Fair, Edmund, 184
Falls of the Ohio, 29, 30, 119
Fifer, 186
Finn (also Finz), James 191, 198
Flarry, James, 185
Floyd, John, writes Clark about supplies for Fort Jefferson, 86-87
Foradas, James, 205
Ford, John, Joseph, Robert, 190
Ford's home, 205
Forgy, Howell M, 118
Forsythe, William (map of 1855), 10, 20
Forts
    Bowman, 1, 4, 214
    Clark, 1, 4, 31, 211, 212, 214

Jefferson (also called Clarksville, Iron Banks, Fort at the Iron Banks, Fort at Mouth of Ohio, Camp Jefferson, and Clark's town), purpose 1, military actions, 1, supplies, 1, corruption 2, jealousies, 2, discipline, 2, land records, 3, earliest surveys 4, destruction of livestock, 4 destruction of corn, archaeological site, 4, location 6, 8, 9, 10, 12, , summary of history, 27-36, stockade, 30, economic hub, 34 items left at, 36, account books taken to Richmond, 34, physical setting, 94-95, built landscape, 95-96, structural features , 98, population composition, harrowing fields, 131, vegetables and farming, 131, 144 alcohol consumption at 132, diet spectrum, 133, infrequent supplies 135, legal matters 148-162, lashes given, 148, courts of inquiry, martial, 148-162,, frivolity 171-177, drinking 171, festivals, 177, paying cards 171, music 171, 172, Shakespeare 172, drinking to St. Patrick, 174, philosophies, 175, darting, 174, Christmas 33, issues at, 108-117, food at, 140, meat eaten 137, beverages consumed, 138, gender activities, 142-147, biomass of, 136, public store at 150, attempted coup at 33, civilians 178-180, cemetery, 36, 99, 180, men discharged at, 191, "hill" 202, 205; houses at 205; remote hole 210, "out of the way," 210 relief of 211, court records, 211;sickly bottoms 211, malaria, 211-212; significance of 210-214 , archaeology of, 200-209, hub of Clark's; killed at Fort Jefferson, 180

activities, 214, failure (?), 214; comparison to other Kentucky forts, 100

    Harrodsburg, 4, 214
    Mackinac, 200
    Nelson, 4, 36, 169, 213, 214
    Ouiatenon, 127
    Patrick Henry,1, 4, 212, 214
    Pitt, 30
    Sackville, 28
Franklin, Benjamin 213
Freeman, Peter, 191
Frogget, William, 186
Frontier History Bibliography, 215-240
Funkhouser, William D., 203

Gagnus (also Gagnier), Jacque, 187; Louis, 187
Galvez, Bernardo, 90
George, Robert, 2, 180, 211; in charge of Fort Jefferson, 29; writes Clark, 58-59; 68-69; 69-70; writes Clark about possible evacuation, 74; writes Pollack 75; writes inhabitants of Kaskaskia, 76-77; writes Slaughter 80; describes Indian attack, 61-62; write Montgomery and describes Indian attack, 64-66, writes Rogers 68
George's Company, 180, 183
Gilbert, John 184
Gilmore, G., 180, 186
Girault, John 35 (seeks reassignment), 150, 187, 195
Glass, Mikiel, 186

Goodwin, William 186
Graffen, Daniel 190
Grimshaw, J., 184
Groats, Jacob, 190
Grolet, Francis (father), 187, Francis (son), 187
Gums, Bonnie, 127

Hacker, John, 184
Hacketon, Michel, 184
Hall, William, 191
Hamilton, Henry, 28
Hardin, F., 181
Harding, Margaret, 183
Hargis, John, 186
Harlan, Silas, 190, 211
Hammit, James, 186
Harris, Francis, 187; John 192
Harrison, James, 187; Richard, 181, 183; writes Clark, 71-72
Hart, Miles 191
Hatton (also Hutten), Christopher., 181, 187
Haul, H., 181
Hays (also Hayes), James, 189, 191; Mary, 142; Thomas 188
Hazard, John, 184
Heim, Keith, 201
Hellebrant, Mary, 178; Peter, 178, 1980
Helm, Leonard, 32, 192, 197; writes Slaughter 70-71
Henderson Map, 6, 16
Henderson Survey, 12
Henderson, William, 6, 9
Hening's Statutes, 193
Henry, Patrick, 1, 4, 27, 90, 212; writes Galvez, 37-38; proposes Fort Jefferson, 37-38
Hern, Jeremiah, 184
Hoit, George, 188
Hollis, Joshua, 189
Holm, Greg 93, 118
Hopkins, 184
Hordin, Frances, 189
Horn, J., 181
Howell, Peter, 185
Hughes, Marth (and family), 178
Huffman, Jacob, 189
Humber, David, 188
Hunter, Joseph, 30, 151, 179, 190; writes Clark, 81; Marah, 179; Mary, 179; Nancy, 92, 142, 179, 211
Hup (also Hupp), Phil (also Philip), 159, 184
Hutsill, J., 179, 181 190; widow and children, 179; William, 190

Illinois Battalion, 1
Illinois Central Rail Road, 202
Illinois-Wabash posts, 211
Ilor (also Ker), 190; Mark, 30
Indian Department, 191, 192
Indians
    Baptisst, 192
    Cherokee, 28
    Chickasaws, 1, 4, 30, 31, 32, 180, 210, 212
    Delaware, 192
    Friendly, 192
    Joseph, 192
    Kaskaskia, 1, 180, 192, 210
    Piankashaw, 192
    Prehistoric, 203, 204
Indian Interpreter, 192, 197
Irwin, Joseph, 186
Island No. 1, 6, 11

Jackson's Purchase, 3, 6, 210
James Alton James, 118, 213
Jarril (also Jarrel), James, 189
Jefferson, Thomas, 5, 28, 90, 212; writes Galvez, 40; writes Martin, 41-42; writes Clark, 42-45, 51-53, 77, 79 ; writes Walker, 46; writes House of Delegates, 60-61; writes Dodge, 79
Jewell, John, 187
Johnson, (also Johnston), Andrew (drummer), 187; Edward, 187
Johnston, Ann, 179; Ezekiel, 30, 179; John, 189, 190; Samuel, 191
Joins, John, 185
Jones, John, 186; Matthew, 179, 184; Elizabeth and children, 179

Kaskaskia, 1, 2, 27, 201, 211, 212
Kearns, James or John, 188
Kennada, Lazarous, 184
Kennedy, Patrick, 179, 192; Rachel, 159, 179
Kenon, Lawrance, 31, 184
Kentucky Secretary of State's Office, 7
Kellar, Abraham, 150, 152, 188, 194; John, 188
Kellar's Company, 181, 182, 188, 198, 199
Kemp (also Camp), Reubin, 187
Kentucky County, 29
Kentucky Settlements, 213
Ker, Conrad., 180, 190; Henry., 181, 190; Jonas, 190; Mark., 181, 190; see also Ilor, 180
Kerkley, James, 187
Kerr, see Carr, 181

Key, George, 186; Thomas, 186
Kindall, William, 186
King, Charles, 190, James, 190
Knox, Henry, 91

L & C Railroad, 10
Land, 27
Land, awarded 183

L'Enfant, Francois, 187
Laform, (?), 187
LaMarine, John, 187
Land Speculation, 1
Land Warrants, 29
Laney, T., 181
LaRichardy, John 187
Lastly, John, 189
Layarous, Rynon, 184
Laycore, Francis, 188
Leer, William, 186
LePaint, Lois, 185
Leviston, George, 187
Lindsay, Joseph, 192
Liquor, over indulgence at Fort Jefferson, 2
Little, Francis, 184
Lockard, Archibald, 179, 187; family, 179
Long, Philip, 184
Lost Vouchers, 201
Lovin (also Loving), Richard, 187
Lunsford, Anthony, 179; George, 189; Mary and family, 179; Moses, 187

Mackever, John, 185
Mackinac Island, 213
Mackinac Island State Park Commission, 200
Maines, Patrick, 179; child 179
Magee, M. Juliette, 93, 200
Magnetometer Studies, 205
Malaria at Fort Jefferson, 32, 165, 211-212
March, J., 180
Marr, Patrick, 184
Marquette, Father 5
Martin, Charles, 186; Joseph, 28; Terrance, 127
Mason, George, 1
Mathews, Edward, 184
Mayfield (Liberty) Creek, 4, 6, 11, 29, 202; Black Slough, 10
Mayfield, Micajah, 179, 185; family, 179

McAuley, Mary, 179; Patrick, 179 (same as McCalley?)
McCalley, Patrick, 184
McCan, Moses, 190
McCarty's Company, 31, 181, 182, 187
McCarty, Richard, 35, 182, 194
McComb, Elizabeth, 10; Henry S., 10, Rebecca, 10
McCormack, John, 179, 190
McDaniel, James, 184
McDonald, David, 186
McGuire, John, 189
McKee, Samuel, 7, 8
McKensey, Mordiack, 187
McLaughlin, Charles, 188
McMeans, Andrew, 179, 190; Ann, 179; children (Anne, James [190], Jane, John, Isaac, Mary, Robert), 179
McMullen, J. 184
McMichael, John 185
Mead-Westvaco, 91
Meadows, Josiah, 191
Medicine at Fort Jefferson, 163-170; common ailments, 164; Jesuits Bark, 165, treatments, 165-167
Megarr, John, 184
Mercer, Fleet, 10
Meredith, Daniel, 179, 190; Luvana, 179; Lawrence or James, 179; widow, 179
Merewether (Meriweather), James, 7, 8, 185, 186; Lt., 195
Mershom, Nathanial, 186
Metivce, John, 188
Meyers (also Myers), Jacob, 7, 9; Treasury survey, 3, 12; map, 19
Michigan State University, 200
Michilimackinac, 200, 213
Miles, Mrs. Michael, 179, 180, 182; son, 179
Military land claims, 6; surveys, 26
Miller, Abraham, 184
Mississippi River, 4, 6, 29, 202
Mobile & Ohio Railroad, 11, 12, 202; map 11, 24
Molly Pitcher, 142
Moneral, Joseph, 185
Montogmery's Company, 199
Montgomery, John, 2, 31, 35-36, 191, 194, 211; evacuates Fort Jefferson, 126, 212; writes Clark 54-55, 67; writes Jefferson, 75-76; writes Nelson, 87-88
Montroy, Anthony, 188
Moore, John, 187
More, William, 184
Morgan, C., 184; Charles, 185
Morris, Graves, 189; J., 181; James, 185
Mouth of the Licking, 30

Mouth of the Ohio, 28
Mulboy (Mulby), William, 188
Munition Supplies, 118-125; gunpowder 120-121, 124; volleys, 121; armament, 122, 125; swords, 122; 125; rifles, 122, 125; musekets, 122, 125, canon, 121, 125.
Munsell, Luke, 6; map, 15
Murphy, John, 186
Murray, E., 182; Edward, 185; Matthew 179, 184; Thomas, 191
Music at Fort Jefferson, 171, 172, 176; fifer, 186; drummer, 187

NASA, 3, 204, 205
Nedinger, Nicholas, 190
Nelson, Enoch 187, John, 7, 8, 187; Moses, 187; Thomas, 126
New Orleans, 30, 32, 33
Nobel, Virgil, 127
North Caroina, 28
NWTA (Northwest Territory Alliance), 193

Oater, Samuel, 191
Ohio River, 6
Oiler (Mr./Mrs.?), 179; children, 179
O'Harrah, Mikel, 186
Old Northwest Territories, 213-214
O'Malley, Nancy, 127
O'Post, 30 (see Fort Patrick Henry)
Orser, Charles, 127
Ouneler, Charles, 185
Owens's (also Oins) Militia, 180; 189-190
Owens. Charity, 179; George, 179
Ozala, John, 191

Pagan, David, 186
Pancore (St. Louis), 212
Panther, Joseph, 188
Papin, J., 181
Parker, Edward, 189
Pepin (also Pipin), Peter (?), 188; John 188
Perrault, Michael (?), 187; Lt., 195
Phelps, Anthony, 190; Elizabeth, 179; George, 190; Josiah, 190; Thomas, 179; children, 179
Philaps, Henery, 189
Phister, John, 190
Picqua (old), 4
Piggott, Eleanor, 179; James, 30, 150; Levi, 179; Thomas, 179; William, 179
Piner, Jesse, 182, 188
Pines, Lewis, 191
Pittman, Buckner (boatmaster), 184

Pogue Library, 201
Pollack, Oliver, 33
Posey, William, 184
Postin (also Pastin), William, 184
Potter, James, 189; Bill, 94, 204
Prisoners, 32, 159-160, 192
Pritchet, James, 188
Pruitt, Isaac, 184
Pursley, (?), 188

Quartermaster Supply System-Western Department, 111-112, 191, 198
Quibes, Paul, 184
Quirk's Company, 199
Quirk, Thomas, 179, 191; family, 179

Racial slurs, 159
Ramsey, James, 184
Randall, J.G., 118
Raper (also Rahr), Baptist, 188
Ray (also Rey), 150, 192, 196; Dr. Andrew, 163 (surgeon)
Rectangular survey, 3
Reid, William, 190
Richmond, Virginia, 108, 201
Riion (also Ryan), Lazurus, 179
Roberts, Benjamin, 192; John, 191
Robeson (also Robson), William, 181
Robison, John 187
Roger's Company, 181, 185, 199
Rogers, John, 31, 150, 185; 194, writes Thomas Jefferson, 81-82; Patrick, 184
Ross, Betsy, 142; Joseph, 185
Rubido, F., 181; Francis, 185; Jake, 185
Rum, 211
Russill, David, 188

Saint Louis (Pancore), 29
Saint Patrick's Day, 2, 35, 211
Scott, Elizabeth, 127; H.L., 149
Senet (also Sinnat), Richard, 191
Sertain (also Certain), Page, 187
Shannon, William, 192, 198; writes Evan Baker, 51; writes Clark, 85
Shaver, David, 189
Shawnee villages, 4; expedition 30, 97, 210
Shepard, Peter, 189
Sherlock, James, 192, 197
Shilling, Jacob, 179, 190; Mary, 179; family, 179
Shoemaker, Leonard, 189

Sickness at Fort Jefferson, 211; sickly season, 32
Slaves, 180, 192, 199; Captain Smith's slaves, 192; Clark's slaves, 192; female, 181
Slaughter, L., 150, 182; Lawrence, 188, 196; writes Thomas Jefferson, 72, 73, 77-78
Smith, Captain, 181; Daniel, 28, 188; Dwight, 213; Edmund, 190, G., 181; George, 184, 188; Henry, 30, 179; Joseph, 189; Mary, 179; Mrs., 151; Sarah, 179, Sidy, 179
Smothers, John 184
Smyth, Samuel, 192, 196
Snellock (also Snarlock), Thomas, 185
Snow, George, 186
Snowden (also Swordin), J., 180, 181; Jonathon, 187
Spanish Territory, 1
Spies, 27
Spillman, Francis, 186; James, 186.
Springer, Enoch, 190
Stein, Julie, 204
Steward, Henry, 190
Stovall, B. Hardy, 11
Stovall Map, 11, 22, 202, 203
Sutherland, Lawrance, 187
Suverns, Ebenezer, 191
Swem, E.G., 201

Tailor, 192
Taylor's Company, 190
Taylor, Edward, 191; James, 192; Isaac, 190
Tennell, Richard, 191
Tennessee River, 6, 27
Terrill Map, 10, 202, 203
Tinklee, Michel, 184
Theel, Levi, 189
Thompson, J., 181; James, 188
Thomson, William, 189, 191
Thorington, J., 181; Josias (also Joseph), 187
Thornton, Joseph 152
Thurston, John 185
Thwaites, R. G., 213
Tibur, Christopher, 191
Todd Land Entry, 12
Todd Military Survey, 3
Todd, Robert, 7, 8, 29, 200; John 29; writes to Jefferson, 57-58
Todd Survey Map, 18
Tolley, Daniel, 191
Travis, Taylor, 184
Treaty of Paris, 214
Trent, Beverly, 179, 189; Sarah, 179
Tulfor (also Tulford), John 187

Turdorf, Judy 127
Turpin, Richard, 181, 185
Tuttle, Nicholas, 189, 191
Tyger, Daniel, 185, 191

Unnamed Soldier, 181
United States Geological Survey, 203

VanTyne, C.H., 213
Vaugh, John, 189
Venison, 211
Villier, F., 181; Francis, 188
Vincennes, 1, 27, 28, 211
Virginia, currency, 211; land claims, 1, 27; gentry, 1; government, 4, 30, 212; military warrant, 8, 9; military and treasury surveys, 3, 7
Virginia Military Surveys, map, 17
vonFrese, Ralph, 205

Wagner (also Waggoner), Peter, 181, 185
Waitt, Robert, 189
Walker, Dr. Thomas, 5
Wallis, David, 185
Washerwoman, 184 (Mary DeMore)
Washington, George, 35, 212
Washington University, 200
Watkins, Elizabeth, 160, 179; Samuel, 179, 191
Watts, Cato, 144
Wayne, Anthony, 91
Webb, William S., 203
Webb's Old Hotel, 202-203
Welch,m Dominick, 186
Western Commissioners, 168
Wesler, Kit 204
Westvaco Mill, 202
Wheat, Jacob, 185
Whitacre, D., 181
White, John, 187, 192; Randel, 189; William, 185
Whitehead, Robert, 189; William 31, 189
Wickliffe, 11, 91
Wicks, Mordicai, 191
Wigins, Barney, 186
Wiley, James, 190
Williams, Daniel, 181, 187; Jarret (also Jerrett), 150, 185, 196; John, 2, 150, 151, 187, 191, 194, writes Clark, 70; Zachariah, 187
Williamsburg, 29, 201
Willis, Jacob, 187

Wilson (also Willson), E., 181; Edward, 190; John 190, 191; Thomas, 192
Win, Thomas, 185
Witzel, Widow, 179
Wolf, Michael, 190
Worthington's Company, 34, 180, 186, 199

Yeates, Isaac, 187; John (drummer), 187; Rachel, 159
Young, Hugh, 189; James, 179, 190; John, 190; Margery, 179
Young, Poussin, Tuttle Map, 10

www.ingramcontent.com/pod-product-compliance
Lightning Source LLC
Chambersburg PA
CBHW050843230426
43667CB00012B/2131